To John & Martha Bryan

Two great libertarians!

THE
RIGHT
TO
EARN
A
LIVING

TIMOTHY SANDEFUR

THE
RIGHT
TO
EARN
A
LIVING

ECONOMIC FREEDOM AND THE LAW

CATO
INSTITUTE
WASHINGTON, D.C.

Library of Congress Cataloging-in-Publication Data

Sandefur, Timothy.
    The right to earn a living / Timothy Sandefur.
        p. cm.
    Includes bibliographical references and index.
    ISBN 978-1-935308-33-1 (hardback : alk. paper)
    1. Economic liberties (U.S. Constitution)   2. Constitutional law—Economic aspects—United States.
I. Title.

KF4753.S26 2010
342.7308'5—dc22   2010005484

Cover design by Jon Meyers.

Printed in the United States of America.

CATO INSTITUTE
1000 Massachusetts Ave., N.W.
Washington, D.C. 20001
www.cato.org

To the memory of

Stephen J. Field *and* Bernard H. Siegan

Two very different men, united by their love of freedom.

Contents

ACKNOWLEDGMENTS   ix

PREFACE   xi

1. "THE MOST PRECIOUS LIBERTY MAN POSSESSES"   1

2. "CORPORATIONS" AND "MONOPOLIES," PART I: 1602–1870   17

3. "CORPORATIONS" AND "MONOPOLIES," PART II: 1870
   TO THE PRESENT   39

4. THE CONTRACTS CLAUSE: VICTIM OF THE LIVING
   CONSTITUTION   67

5. THE ERA OF SUBSTANTIVE DUE PROCESS:
   SLAUGHTERHOUSE TO LOCHNER   83

6. THE RATIONAL BASIS TEST   123

7. PROTECTIONISM AND THE LAW   141

8. THE DORMANT COMMERCE CLAUSE   175

9. COMMERCIAL SPEECH   191

10. THE MANIPULATION OF CONTRACTS   213

11. THE ABUSE OF TORT LAW   239

12. REGULATORY TAKINGS   255

13. THE FUTURE OF ECONOMIC LIBERTY   279

NOTES   295

INDEX   361

Acknowledgments

I wish to thank the many people who helped me in so many ways in preparing this book. Two women in particular, my boss Deborah J. La Fetra and my secretary Barbara Siebert, are largely responsible for everything I manage to accomplish, and I thank them for their immeasurable contributions. Roger Pilon provided a meticulous and extremely helpful review of the entire project. Donna Matias and Christina Kohn read the whole manuscript and provided many helpful suggestions. Dominick T. Armentano, David E. Bernstein, Robert Hessen, and Stanley Martin also read portions of the manuscript and gave me important comments. Pagona A. Stratoudakis, Lauren A. Wiggins, and Kelly Thomas helped with research. Tom W. Bell and Meriem Hubbard helped by answering my questions and offering helpful sources. Any remaining errors are my own responsibility.

Many parts of this book are adapted from articles that originally appeared in the *Northern Illinois University Law Review*, the *Chapman Law Review*, *Law & Inequality*, *Environmental Law*, the *William & Mary Bill of Rights Journal*, and the *Journal of Law & Politics*, and I thank the staff of those periodicals for permission to revise and extend my remarks. Also, much of this book is based on briefs that I wrote or helped write for the Pacific Legal Foundation in the following cases: *Angelucci v. Century Supper Club*; *Craigmiles v. Giles*; *E.M.M.I. v. Zurich-American Insurance Corp.*; *Evans v. United States*; *Flamingo Industries v. United States Postal Service*; *Hernandez v. City of Hanford*; *Hojnowski v. Vans Skate Park*; *Illinois Motor Vehicle Review Board v. General Motors*; *In re. Lead Paint*; *Kelo v. New London*; *Kearney v. Salomon Smith Barney, Inc.*; *McDonald v. Chicago, Meadows v. Odom*; *Merrifield v. Lockyer*; *People of California ex rel. Lockyer v. General Motors*; *Philip Morris USA v. Williams*; *Powers v. Harris*; *Reeves v. Hanlon*; *Sagana v. Tenorio*; *RUI One Corp. v. City of Berkeley*; and *Weaver v. Harpster*. That work could not have been accomplished without the dedicated work of my colleagues, for which I will always be grateful.

Preface

My interest in the law of economic liberty was sparked in 2000, when as a law student, I was asked to investigate a lawsuit in Miami-Dade County, Florida, filed by prospective cab drivers against the government agency that regulated the taxi industry.[1] As I learned more about the laws regulating taxis, I was shocked to discover how government frustrates and burdens industrious, hardworking people who simply seek to earn an honest living for themselves and their families.

Driving a taxi in Miami is dangerous work. Some neighborhoods of Dade County—such as the inaptly named "Liberty City"—are so rough that most cab companies refuse to enter them.[2] Society Cab, the only black-owned and black-operated cab company in Dade County, is usually the only one that will serve Liberty City. "The other company takes them to Biscayne Boulevard," one driver told a reporter, "We take them from there." When one Hispanic driver tried to drive for Society Cab, he was robbed and locked in the trunk of his taxi during his first week on the job.

But it's also hard even to get into the taxi business in the first place. To operate a cab in Miami, as in every other major city in the United States, one must have a license.[3] Each license (or "medallion") allows a person to operate one car. These medallions are issued by Dade County's Consumer Services Department. By 2002, CSD had issued 1,856 such medallions, and the four largest cab companies controlled between 34 and 49 percent of the cab market.[4] For about 20 years, the county heavily restricted the market, but in 1998 a new ordinance created a lottery system to issue 25 new taxi licenses over the next five years.[5] Starting in June 2004, new licenses would be granted every year to keep a 1-to-1,000 taxicab-to-population ratio. But to enter the lottery required a $400, nonrefundable fee, and the winner was required to pay $15,000 for the license. Since taxi drivers can hardly afford such steep prices themselves, they lease their medallions at the rate of more than $500 per week from the handful of wealthy businesspeople who own licenses.[6] As one driver put it: "You'll spend up to Thursday making that money. Then you're forced to work the weekend if you want any money for yourself."

While $15,000 is a lot of money for a taxi medallion, it is nothing compared with the prices in New York City, where medallions cost as much as $600,000.[7] In July 2007, when an 80-year-old retired driver named Ray Kottner gave New Yorkers free rides in his old Checker cab, he found that passengers tipped so well that he ended up making more money that way than by charging a fare. Naturally, this bothered the taxi companies, who didn't like the competition. They complained, and the police quickly impounded his car. "This guy is nothing but a crook, and we are all glad he's finally off the streets," said one driver.[8]

Laws regulating taxicabs have an especially harsh effect on the poor and underprivileged. Taxi drivers, particularly in Miami, are not usually rich white men. In the early 1980s, economist Walter Williams explained that

> A free market in the taxicab industry will not produce a panacea for the disadvantaged. However, it is one small way to upward mobility for some, which has been cut off by government. As such, it demonstrates again one of the key differences between disadvantaged blacks and disadvantaged ethnic groups of the past. A poor illiterate Italian, for example, arriving in our cities in 1925 or 1930 could, if he had ambition and industry, go out and buy a car and write Taxi on it. Thus he could provide upward mobility for his family. Today a poor person of any race would find that industry and ambition are not enough, if he sought the same path to upward mobility. He would find the path barricaded by a license costing $20, $30, or $60 thousand—a considerable barrier.[9]

Taxi regulation also affects customers, who are often poor minorities themselves. For instance, Miami's requirement that all cars be less than five years old posed a real threat to Society Cab, since many of Society's cars are older than that, and its customers cannot afford to pay the higher prices that the company would need to charge to replace its cars more often. (The county eventually agreed to exempt Society from this requirement.[10])

While some taxi regulations exist to protect customers, many if not most exist for no reason except brazen protectionism. Take licensing restrictions, for example: taxi companies want to restrict the number of taxis on the roads in order to keep their prices up. Licensing laws—and particularly laws that limit the number of licenses available—are an extraordinarily effective way to accomplish this. Or price regulations: in Tampa, Florida, to name just one example, taxi companies persuaded regulators to require limousine companies to charge at least $40 per ride because they feared that limo driver Daniel Steiner was competing with them by offering cut-rate rides for sick people who needed transportation to their doctors.[11] Officials explained that the minimum price rule existed to "create a balance between the different transportation service 'markets'" so that taxis and limousines would "not directly compet[e] against each other. This way, both manage to survive in their respective market area and the 'balance' is maintained."[12] In other words, the rule prohibits fair competition by an entrepreneur who has a new and cheaper way of doing things, in order to enforce a market "balance" that government—not the consumer—prefers. Such protectionism isn't just a matter of dollars and cents. It's a matter of justice, freedom, and opportunity. For many people, owning a business is the very definition of the American dream.[13] But in today's America, such dreams are made increasingly difficult by laws and regulations that interfere with entrepreneurs and in many cases make it easier to get a welfare check than a paycheck.

As I learned more about the heavy regulation of the taxi industry, I was shocked to realize that these drivers had virtually no recourse before the law. Although earlier generations of lawyers and judges had declared that laws that protect some businesses against fair competition by others violate the Constitution's guarantees of due process and equal protection of the laws, modern-day precedents create an almost insurmountable barrier to entrepreneurs who try to challenge such laws. In fact, most lawsuits against even the most restrictive taxicab licensing regimes have failed because of the strong pro-government presumption first devised by the Progressives and finally written into American constitutional law by the New Deal Supreme Court.[14] That presumption is still largely unquestioned by both the bench and the legal academy today.

Equally absurd is the fact that this consensus view is generally characterized as "liberal," and that those who endorse it do so on the ground that it is more sensitive to the needs of the poor and underprivileged than is the earlier view that the Constitution protects economic freedom. In other words, serious judicial protection of economic freedoms, like that which existed before the Progressive Era, would benefit only wealthy elites—those "people at the top of the heap,"[15] as one legal scholar puts it—and would harm lower- and middle-class workers. But the reality is just the opposite: hardworking men and women, often the poor or members of under-represented minority groups, need judicial protection from government elites and established businesses who use the law to prevent competition and secure special favors for themselves. What taxi drivers in Miami needed, and what entrepreneurs nationwide need, is *more* protection for their economic liberty. These entrepreneurs are asking not for a handout but simply to be allowed to practice a gainful trade without unfair interference. They do not believe in abstract economic theories; they believe in the right to pursue happiness. They do not need more regulation, more control by bureaucrats, or more opportunities to "participate" in the regulatory "process." They certainly do not need a more "deferential" judiciary. They need the courts to take their economic freedom seriously.

Ironically, it was Roscoe Pound, one of the intellectuals who laid the groundwork for the evisceration of economic liberty in the 20th century, who claimed that judges defending freedom of contract were out of touch with the practical realities of everyday working life. A more "realistic" jurisprudence, Pound and his contemporaries claimed, would see that economic freedom was based largely on legal fictions and that workers actually needed government assistance to protect them from exploitation by employers. A century later, it is clear that the reverse is true: the Progressive consensus that prevails today is deaf to the real needs of entrepreneurs. Workers' right to earn a living is routinely violated by an intrusive regulatory state—a state that frequently acts in the service of wealthy, politically entrenched lobbyists rather than in the interest of all. Yet Pound's admirers, today calling themselves "realists," cling to the legal fiction that government agencies will conduct their business in a disinterested and fair manner and will seriously concern themselves with the constitutionality of their actions. Pound condemned the "formalism" of judges who defended the freedom of contract, but it is today's defenders of the regulatory state who adhere to the formalistic assumption that government actions should be presumed valid because they represent a "democratic" decision by a thoughtful representative body. Indeed, the "rational basis" test that courts now use to evaluate the constitutionality of economic regulations *requires* courts to presume that governments regulate in the public interest, even in the face of powerful evidence to the contrary.[16]

Moreover, today's consensus assumes that individuals who are burdened by government's decisions can just "vote the bums out," when in reality, individual entrepreneurs and property owners have almost no chance of prevailing under a political process dominated by their politically protected competitors. A taxi driver in Florida has no realistic ability to lobby the legislature to eliminate the protectionist schemes governing the taxi market, and even less chance of replacing the bureaucrats who staff the commissions that manipulate—and are regularly manipulated by—the industry. Nor should they be forced to try. Religious dissenters or people who want to print or speak controversial viewpoints are not required to ask permission from legislators, because the whole point of freedom of speech, press, or religion is that one does not have to ask permission to exercise one's rights. As the Supreme Court once put it, the reason the Founders wrote the Bill of Rights "was to withdraw certain subjects from the vicissitudes of political controversy, to place them beyond the reach of majorities and officials and to establish them as legal principles to be applied by the courts. One's right to life, liberty, and property, to free speech, a free press, freedom of worship and assembly, and other fundamental rights may not be submitted to vote; they depend on the outcome of no elections."[17] The same principle should hold true for the right to earn a living, which is an essential part of the "liberty" guaranteed by the Bill of Rights. If, as the Supreme Court has often declared, the judiciary has a "special role in safeguarding the interests of those groups that are 'relegated to such a position of political powerlessness as to command extraordinary protection from the majoritarian political process,'"[18] then judges certainly should provide protection for those whose right to earn a living is abridged by unreasonably restrictive licensing laws, economically senseless price controls, vague tort theories, and other legal limitations. But thanks to the dubious New Deal theories that still dominate the legal world, these hardworking men and women are barred from judicial protection and told that they must seek redress from the very political system that has harmed them.

Although I was unable to help Miami's taxi drivers, their experience inspired me not only to write this book but also to find ways to defend economic freedom in the courtroom. As the lead attorney in the economic liberty project at the Pacific Legal Foundation, I have had a unique opportunity to observe up close the unfair and often-ludicrous restrictions imposed on America's hardest-working citizens. Dozens of the cases described in this book are ones in which I participated either by representing entrepreneurs or by filing friend-of-the-court briefs in defense of important economic freedoms. The opportunity to work with America's wealth creators, by defending their moral and constitutional right to earn a living, has been among the great experiences of my life.

The pages that follow cover a variety of issues relating in different ways to the right to earn a living, proceeding in a roughly chronological fashion. Beginning with the common-law tradition of legal protections for economic liberty, we will see how 17th- and 18th-century judges came to recognize the individual right to earn a living as part of their attack on royal monopolies. Chapters 2 and 3 explain how terms like "monopoly" and "corporation" evolved over time in ways that, ironically, left the right to earn a living in a precarious position. Chapter 4 discusses the Constitution's contracts clause, once among the most important constitutional provisions protecting the right to earn a living, but today largely ignored. Chapter 5 describes the theory of "substantive due process" and the most famous—some would say infamous—case addressing economic liberty, *Lochner v. New York*,[19] while chapter 6 covers the "rational basis test," incorporated into the Constitution by the New Deal Supreme Court as it moved to dismantle the legacy of substantive due process. Today, that test stands as the single largest threat to the constitutional freedoms of entrepreneurs. The next chapters address some of today's most important controversies over the right to earn a living: Chapter 7 deals with some of the ways government abuses its powers to protect favored businesses against legitimate competition; chapter 8 discusses the "dormant commerce clause," which forbids states from engaging in economic discrimination; and chapter 9 deals with the free speech rights of business owners who want to advertise their products or services. Chapters 10 and 11 deal not with constitutional rights but with the ways in which today's entrepreneurs are hampered by vague tort theories like "public nuisance" and "interference with contract," as well as by courts that manipulate or nullify contracts to serve subjective notions of fairness. Chapter 12 discusses regulatory takings, an area of the law where economic freedom and private property rights strongly overlap. Finally, chapter 13 looks forward to what the future might hold for the right of Americans to pursue happiness by practicing a gainful trade.

1. "The Most Precious Liberty Man Possesses"

This book is intended as a general overview of the legal status of the right of individuals in the United States to engage in gainful trade, whether as entrepreneurs, investors, corporate directors, or otherwise. It is not intended as a thorough explanation or defense of that right in philosophical terms; that task has been undertaken by many others.[1] For our purposes, it suffices to say that the right to earn a living through trade or labor is as much a legitimate aspect of one's liberty as the freedom from bodily restraint, the right to marry, to study, to raise one's children, to travel, or to worship as one chooses; indeed, courts of an earlier generation frequently grouped these rights together when listing examples of constitutionally protected freedoms.[2] But a brief look at that right will help us understand its nature and why it is imperative to defend it in the nation's courts.

In 1848, a free black man named Willie Winfield appeared before the Tennessee Supreme Court. Winfield had been jailed under a Memphis ordinance that prohibited blacks from being out in public after 10 o'clock at night. Arrested as he walked home from work, Winfield was fined $10, but he appealed, arguing that the law he had been arrested under was unconstitutional and void.[3] Surprisingly for a slave state in the decades before the Civil War, the court agreed with him. In a decision by Justice William B. Turley,[4] the court observed that if such a law had been enforced "against a free white person, public indignation would have been aroused, and the [city] would not only have been sued to recover back the fine, but also for false imprisonment." And although free black people were "not, it is true . . . citizen[s] of full privileges in our state," it was still unjust to subject them to such laws:

> The lot of a free negro is hard enough at best, resulting from
> necessity arising out of the relation in which he stands to his

1

brethren who are in servitude, and it is both cruel and useless
to add to his troubles by unnecessary and painful restraints
in the use of such liberty as is allowed him. He must live,
and, in order to do so, he must work. Every one knows that
in cities, very often, the most profitable employment is to
be found in the night, loading and unloading steamboats
and other craft, waiting about hotels, theaters, places of
amusement, both public and private, wood-cutting, fire-
making, shoe and boot-cleaning, not to mention the various
handicraft employments, such as that of the barber, etc. All
these things are sources, in large cities, of much profit to the
free man of color, and you necessarily deprive him of them
entirely if you compel him, like a wild beast, to hide his head
in his den from ten o'clock till daylight, under the penalty of
being pursued by watchman and constables for the purpose
of being imprisoned and fined as if he had been committing
a crime against society.[5]

Justice Turley and his colleagues cited no cases in reaching their
conclusion. Instead, they stood on what they saw as the common-
sense proposition that a person has the right to earn an honest living
for himself and his family, and as long as he doesn't harm anybody
in doing so, no third party—and no government—should interfere
with that right. This conclusion was not based on any economic
theories but on simple moral philosophy and a long-standing tradition about what it means to be free—a tradition they evidently
considered so pervasive that providing citations and arguments to
support it would have been superfluous. In short, the justices recognized that the right to earn a living is a central component of the
liberty that makes a free person free. Just as liberty means the right
to speak one's opinions or to pray in accordance with one's religion,
so free people have the right to engage in productive enterprises to
support themselves.

Turley was right. As a legal matter, the right to earn an honest
living can be traced far back in the English common law. Almost
two and a half centuries before the *Winfield* decision, England's chief
justice, Sir Edward Coke, wrote that the Magna Carta and the common law protected the right of "any man to use any trade thereby
to maintain himself and his family."[6] A century later, that right,
which Coke saw as a traditional right of Englishmen, was among
those that America's Founders regarded as the natural rights of all

humanity. The right to "pursue and obtain happiness and safety," as Virginia patriot George Mason wrote in 1776—or the right "to pursue happiness," as his friend Thomas Jefferson would put it only months later—is fundamental to human life. Pursuing happiness, of course, means more than the right either to possess things or to engage in those pursuits that make us happy—such as educational or recreational projects or spending time with friends and family. It also means the right to take steps to provide a better life for oneself through work, trade, and commercial enterprise.

A contemporary of Willie Winfield put a very human face on this right in his memoirs. Born a slave, Frederick Douglass recalled how he escaped the home of his master Hugh Auld, reaching New York on the Underground Railroad in 1838. Walking the streets of Rochester, looking for a job, Douglass came across a house where a pile of coal had just been delivered. He had an idea that he might make some money, and he knocked at the door, offering to move the coal inside for the woman who answered. "I was not long in accomplishing the job," he wrote, "when the dear lady put into my hand *two silver half dollars*. To understand the emotion which swelled my heart as I clasped this money, realizing that I had no master who could take it from me—*that it was mine*—*that my hands were my own*, and could earn more of the precious coin—one must have been in some sense himself a slave. . . . I was not only a freeman but a free-working man, and no Master Hugh stood ready at the end of the week to seize my hard earnings."[7]

Like Justice Turley, Douglass understood the moral case for the individual's right to earn a living: All human beings face certain obstacles in their existence, including limited time and resources, and the need to obtain subsistence and shelter. Nature does not give these things to man; he must earn them through his own effort, or obtain them from others who have expended effort. Either way, his survival and that of his children depend on the creation of wealth, through the productive work of his mind and body. And if morality is to be a guide for human survival, it must place special emphasis on those productive virtues by which such wealth is created. When Master Hugh took away the fruits of Douglass's labor, he was asserting the power to control the essence of Douglass's humanity—his creative faculty—and thus treating him as a tool or as an inanimate object instead of as a fellow human deserving of freedom.

3

As Douglass's friend, the abolitionist and U.S. senator Charles Sumner explained, the "ever present motive power" of slavery was "simply to *compel the labor of fellow-men without wages*," by "excluding them from that property in their own earnings, which the law of nature allows, and civilization secures. . . . It is robbery and petty larceny under the garb of law," which presumed "that for his own good," the slave "must work for his master, and not for himself."[8]

The existence of slavery in America—an institution whose essential moral corruption Abraham Lincoln described as "the same old serpent that says you work and I eat, you toil and I will enjoy the fruits of it"[9]—was an intolerable contradiction from the nation's beginning. That contradiction manifested itself socially and economically in the difference between the industrious, enterprising North and the class-structured, static South. Another contemporary of Douglass, Alexis de Tocqueville, remarked on this difference in his *Democracy in America* when he noted that in the slave states "one might say that society has gone to sleep . . . man is idle," but in free states "a confused hum proclaims from afar that men are busily at work, . . . man appears rich and contented; he works. . . . On the left bank of the Ohio work is connected with the idea of slavery, but on the right with well-being and progress; on the one side it is degrading, but on the other honorable."[10] Thus, from an early age, the practical consequences of economic freedom were clear—but they were consequences of a *moral* challenge faced by all humans: whether to devote themselves to earning a living through productive enterprise, or to subsist off the compelled labor of others.

Although the legal institution of slavery was swept away with the Civil War, many of its political and cultural legacies remained. One important step toward fixing that problem came in 1868, when the Constitution was amended to protect the "privileges or immunities" of all Americans, including their common-law right to earn a living. Where southern states had enacted discriminatory laws to limit the economic opportunities of former slaves, Congress enacted the first national Civil Rights Act to ensure that all people "shall have the same right . . . to make and enforce contracts," and to "purchase" and "sell . . . real and personal property."[11] Only a few years later, Supreme Court Justice Stephen J. Field would explain that the right to go into business without being stopped by "disparaging and partial" laws is "the distinguishing privilege of citizens of the United States. To them, everywhere, all pursuits, all professions, all avocations are open without other restrictions than such as are imposed equally upon all others." This right, he concluded, "is the fundamental idea upon which our institutions rest."[12] Government may regulate businesses to protect the general public, of course, but Field contended that when laws served simply to protect one business against competition by another, or interfered with the right to earn a living without actually protecting the public welfare, such laws violated "the right of free labor, one of the most sacred and imprescriptible rights of man."[13]

Myths about Economic Liberty

But flash forward to 1992, a century and a half after the *Winfield* decision, and we find a prominent legal scholar writing the following:

> I do not count the Supreme Court decisions defending contract or property rights from state regulation as Bill of Rights decisions. None of these cases represents a defense of civil liberties. The Court merely used libertarian philosophy to protect the wealthy from progressive legislation. The Court eventually rejected these economic liberty decisions because they were not connected to the text of the Constitution or any philosophy with roots in the history and traditions of our nation and its democratic process.[14]

This statement is unfortunately typical of the attitude of the present-day legal academy toward the right to earn a living—a right that Justice William O. Douglas once called "the most precious liberty that man possesses."[15]

In fact, most modern legal academics who have discussed the history of American law have contended that judicial decisions upholding contract and property rights were in some way a betrayal of constitutional values. These academics have forged a consensus view that economic liberty was, in fact, concocted by ideologically biased 19th-century judges who acted as "a de facto arm of the capital-owning class," and who "invented, through a flash of revelation known only to them, the notion that due process of law . . . protected corporations against social legislation."[16] Nineteenth-century judges, claims one prominent legal historian, "recognized only the 'liberty' of powerful corporations and sweatshop owners."[17] Still another charges that Field and his colleagues were concerned only with rights such as "property and economic liberty," because these are the "freedoms that matter [ ] most to people at the top of the heap."[18] These tool-of-capitalist judges allegedly used "constitutional legerdemain" to incorporate the "root-hog-or-die theory of capitalist enterprise" into the Constitution, thus replacing the "originally humanistic doctrines of liberal democracy."[19] Only with the great judicial shift of the 1930s, when the courts dramatically turned away from protecting economic liberty, was "true" democracy restored to the American political system. In fact, this theory continues, economic *liberty* is not actually liberty at all. The right to engage in trade is simply a *privilege* that deserves little or no judicial protection. Legislatures and administrative agencies should be free to regulate economic matters in virtually any way they wish.

This book challenges that consensus and documents some of the legal and historical issues surrounding the right to earn a living.[20] Although I presume that free markets tend toward greater economic efficiency and more just outcomes than do centrally organized or government-controlled economies, and that free individuals make wiser economic decisions than do government bureaucrats,[21] this is not primarily a book on economics, and it is important to emphasize that point. A great many of the writers who have criticized the economic liberty decisions in American law—and particularly the decisions associated with the so-called *Lochner* era—have claimed that the judges in such cases were motivated by a commitment to certain "economic theories" and to the writings of Adam Smith, Herbert Spencer, and John Stuart Mill. The term "economic substantive due process" was coined to describe these decisions, as though the judges who wrote them were focusing on questions of supply and demand, or inflation, surplus, trade balances, and the like. A parallel accusation is that the judges in the "laissez-faire period" were "social Darwinists" who believed that the poor ought to be left alone to suffer and die off, thus ridding society of (in Ebenezer Scrooge's immortal words) "the surplus population."[22]

Doubtless there were some social Darwinists in the 19th century. But the judges who decided the economic liberty cases—whether they be Sir Edward Coke in the *Case of Monopolies* or Justice Turley in *Winfield*, or Justice Field in his many decisions, or Justice Rufus

Peckham[23] in *Lochner v. New York*—were not among them. Hardly a word of social Darwinism appears in their writings, and it seems likely that the only Supreme Court justice of his day who was familiar with the doctrine was Oliver Wendell Holmes Jr., who famously dissented in *Lochner*. Indeed, modern historians have questioned whether "social Darwinism" is even a meaningful term; the phrase was devised by leftist historian Richard Hofstadter, who used it as an epithet against free-market economists and sociologists he disliked, whether or not those thinkers actually had any affinity for Darwin, and it is often used to describe people who stood on different sides of ideological issues.[24] In fact, as Louis Menand explains, "What looks like Social Darwinism" during this era "was generally just a Protestant belief in the virtues of the work ethic combined with a Lockean belief in the sanctity of private property. It had nothing to do with evolution."[25]

Nor were the judges who supported economic liberty writing from an "economic" perspective. Although many of them were well versed in the economic literature of their day, these judges rarely relied on or cited such books. In fact, in the years before the New Deal, the Supreme Court cited Adam Smith in only four cases, one of which was merely as a historical note about a law to which Smith had referred.[26] More to the point, the decisions modern historians describe as "economic substantive due process cases" were not about economics but about legal, moral, and political philosophy. They involved questions about the definition of the word "liberty," about the meaning of justice and the limits of rights, and about whether government interference with economic choices was legitimate, given certain constitutional protections. So, too, this book is based on two propositions: (a) the freedom to make one's own economic decisions is not primarily rooted in economics but in political philosophy and (b) a free society is not a matter of efficiency but of justice.[27]

In his book *The Return of George Sutherland*, Hadley Arkes emphasizes this point in reference to the 1932 case of *Adkins v. Children's Hospital*.[28] When it was decided, *Adkins* became the focus of a battle over the Constitution's protections for economic liberty, and that case's reputation has sunk in the years since. Supreme Court Justice David Souter even claimed that *Adkins* bore "the echo of *Dred Scott*," the infamous case that precipitated the Civil War.[29] But no libel could ever be more misplaced.

Adkins was one of a pair of cases challenging a Washington, D.C., law that established minimum wages for women. The law did not apply to men, which naturally enough created an incentive for employers to discharge women and hire less-expensive male labor. When it was argued before the Supreme Court, the *Adkins* case was combined with the case of Willie Lyons, an elevator operator at Washington's Congress Hotel, where she was paid $35 per month, plus meals. Although Lyons was happy with this arrangement, the minimum-wage law forced the hotel to pay her $71.50 per month instead, making her services prohibitively expensive for her employer. As Arkes puts it, "[T]he law, in its liberal tenderness, in its concern to protect women, had brought about a situation in which women were being replaced, in their jobs, by men."[30]

This was not by accident. The minimum-wage movement had, in fact, focused on women primarily on the grounds that they were in need of special protections that men did not need. According to this argument, men were capable of bargaining with employers for satisfactory wages, but women were naturally more docile and less likely to demand higher pay. One of the leading proponents of this argument was Louis Brandeis, a Progressive lawyer and later Supreme Court justice, who spent his career as an attorney arguing in favor of minimum-wage laws and other regulations governing the employment of women. In *Muller v. Oregon*,[31] he had argued that government had to protect the weaker sex, to aid women in their natural roles as wives and mothers. The notion that "woman stands on the same plane with man" and had the same "inalienable right to enter into contracts," Brandeis argued, was "gilded sophistry."[32] Women were "unfitted" for most work, and considering "the duty she owes to the home and the family," any law that restricted the number of hours she could work was a legitimate exercise of government's power to protect "the safety, the morals, [and] the welfare of the public."[33]

These arguments played well to judges like Justice David Brewer, who, although otherwise a strong advocate of economic freedom, believed that women needed special protection from the rigors of the marketplace. Brewer wrote the decision for a unanimous Court in *Muller*, upholding an Oregon law that set the maximum number of hours that a woman could work. *Muller* came only three years after *Lochner v. New York*,[34] which had struck down a similar law applied to New York bakers; but for Brewer, the *Lochner* case was different because the present case involved "a widespread belief that woman's physical structure, and the functions she performs in consequence thereof, justify special legislation restricting or qualifying the conditions under which she should be permitted to toil."[35] Men were able to make their own economic decisions, so the bakers in *Lochner* did not need a paternalistic government to supervise their choices. But it was "obvious" that a woman "still looks to her brother and depends upon him." Given woman's inherent incapacity to make economic decisions, the state had the authority "to protect her from the greed as well as the passion of man."[36] Long hours of work inflict "injurious effects upon the body, and, as healthy mothers are essential to vigorous offspring, the physical well-being of woman becomes an object of public interest and care in order to preserve the strength and vigor of the race." In short, the maximum-hours law that Justice Brewer applauded in *Muller* and the minimum-wage law challenged in *Adkins* were rightly described by Ruth Bader Ginsburg, before she joined the Supreme Court, as laws "ostensibly [designed] to shield or favor the sex regarded as fairer but weaker," but in reality they were "premised on the notion that women could not cope with the world beyond hearth and home without a father, husband, or big brother to guide them."[37]

Justice George Sutherland rejected this notion in *Adkins*. As a "vigorous proponent of women's rights,"[38] Sutherland believed that women were as capable as men of making decisions for themselves. The differences between the sexes had diminished in the years following the *Muller* case. For one thing, women had now been granted the right to vote. "In view of the great—not to say revolutionary—changes which have taken place since [*Muller*], in the contractual, political, and civil status of women, culminating in the Nineteenth Amendment, it is not unreasonable to say that these differences have now come almost, if not quite, to the vanishing point."[39] Obviously women are different from men in some ways, and in "appropriate cases" those differences might be reflected in the law, but Sutherland could not accept "the doctrine that women of mature age . . . require or may be subjected to restrictions upon their liberty of contract which could not lawfully be imposed in the case of men under similar circumstances." A women ought to be emancipated "from the old doctrine that she must be given special protection or be sub-jected to special restraint in her contractual and civil relationships."[40] The challenged law did not implement safety standards or protect against fraud. It was merely "a price-fixing law, confined to adult women," which barred mature and competent adults from making contracts as they wished. And the consequence of the law would be to force some female employees "to surrender a desirable [job]," and to force employers "to dispense with the services of . . . desirable employee[s]."[41]

It should be clear by now how inaccurate it would be to describe the *Adkins* decision as based on an "economic" theory, let alone to claim that it had anything in common with the pro-slavery *Dred Scott* case. *Adkins* contained no economic theory or analysis and was not concerned with the interactions of supply and demand, except for Sutherland's passing mention that the law would put some women out of work. Instead, it was based on political philosophy: namely, the classical liberal, or Lockean, views articulated in the Declaration of Independence and reflected in the Constitution's references to "liberty." Sutherland and his colleagues viewed the minimum-wage law as a restriction on the freedom of Willie Lyons and other women to earn a living as they chose. This right—to formulate and agree to contracts—was not merely a privilege that the government granted and took away from people. Like the Founders, Sutherland and his colleagues held that it was part of the natural liberty to which all people are entitled by their very humanity.

The Declaration of Independence said that all men are endowed by their creator with inalienable rights, including liberty. Gradu-ally, American society had acknowledged that women were equally endowed with those rights. And since that liberty was a given—since all people were naturally free—the state bore the burden of proving the necessity of interfering with it. A century earlier, James Madison wrote: "In Europe, charters of liberty have been granted by power. America has set the example and France has followed it, of charters of power granted by liberty."[42] In other words, in the United States, people were presumed free to act as they chose—including agree-ing to economic transactions—unless government could give a good reason to prevent them from doing so (such as that the trade was fraudulent, or unreasonably dangerous). Firmly grounded in this natural rights tradition, Sutherland wrote in *Adkins* that, although government could regulate economic activities to protect the general public, "freedom of contract is, nevertheless, the general rule and restraint the exception, and the exercise of legislative authority to abridge it can be justified only by the existence of exceptional circumstances."[43] Where such circumstances did not exist, a law depriving a person of the right to earn a living violated the Constitution's protections for liberty.

The Progressive Assault on Economic Liberty

As we shall see in greater detail in chapters 5 and 6, the early 20th century witnessed the advent of a political movement called Progressivism, which, among other things, focused on increasing the degree of government control over what was viewed as the chaotic and disorganized nature of private life in the United States—a "disorder" simply reflecting individual freedom of choice. Progressives promoted an ambitious agenda of government expansion to remedy a host of perceived evils—everything from unsafe food and drugs to disparities of wealth and the availability of alcohol. The Progressives based their program on the belief that collective decisionmaking was more efficient and just than individual freedom; they rejected the idea that individual freedom was the natural state of mankind or that the burden of proof rested on those who would limit a person's freedom. In a 1924 commentary on the *Adkins* decision in the *Harvard Law Review*, for example, law professor Thomas Reed Powell attacked Sutherland's belief in the natural right to make contracts. "No such doctrine is stated in the Constitution," Powell wrote. "[R]egulation has long since become the rule, and freedom the exception. Whence, then, comes the rule that Mr. Justice Sutherland reveals? Needless to say, it comes from Mr. Justice Sutherland. It represents his personal views of desirable governmental policy."[44]

Such an attitude was common among Progressive legal theorists, who adhered instead to what Powell called "legislative freedom from judicial restraint."[45] In their view, decisions like *Adkins* got the Constitution's priorities backward. The Progressives emphasized government authority before individual freedom: to them, the majority's power to enact its preferences into laws was more essential than individual rights—indeed, it was the *source* of individual rights.[46] The Founders, by contrast, believed that individual rights had priority, while democracy was valuable only if it served the purpose of protecting those rights: the Constitution, after all, had explicitly declared liberty to be a "blessing," but had placed many stringent limits on the powers of democratic majorities.[47]

In addition, the Progressive critique of the right to earn a living— or "liberty of contract" as it was called—held that such freedom was really illusory because a worker could not realistically be said to bargain with an employer for acceptable terms in an employment agreement. Workers like Willie Lyons didn't really have a choice about accepting whatever deals were offered them, no matter how oppressive or unfair. A more "realistic" view of the marketplace would uphold the legislature's power to protect them from unfair bargains. Roscoe Pound, one of the leaders of the new "realist" school of legal thought, contended that the right of workers to enter into contracts as they saw fit was "utterly hollow."[48] The persistence of such a right in American law was due, Pound wrote, to "an individualist conception of justice, which exaggerates the importance of property and contract, exaggerates private right at the expense of public right, and is hostile to legislation."[49] He admitted that this individualism was "the theory of our bills of rights,"[50] but argued that modern scholars had unmasked this theory as senseless philosophical speculation. His contemporaries agreed: today's political philosophers, wrote Charles Edward Merriam in 1903, rejected "the idea that liberty is a natural right" and now viewed individual rights as having "their source not in nature, but in law."[52] "I do not wish to be understood as attaching any constitutional or moral sanction" to the right to earn a living, noted Justice Brandeis in a dissent written three years before *Adkins* was decided. "All rights are derived from the purposes of the society in which they exist; above all rights rises duty to the community."[53]

Having rejected the idea of natural rights, the Progressives held that the freedom to engage in a trade was really just a permission, which could be revoked when the government saw fit. In addition, the Progressives shared three other ideas that would fundamentally change the relationship of the individual to the government.[54] One was that the Constitution is a "living document," which changes to suit the exigencies of the moment. Another, closely allied with the first, was that courts should avoid interfering when legislatures enact laws restricting individual rights—the idea of "judicial restraint."

The third was the idea that government exists not to secure individual rights but to shape society into the form that the collective found most pleasing.

Thus, during the Progressive Era, regulation of the economy expanded beyond what previous generations could have conceived possible. Government's primary role was now viewed as *the shaping of society* rather than the protection of individual rights; it was to provide people with the necessities of comfortable living and to employ its coercive powers not merely to protect but to shape and even create individual personalities.[55] No longer a potential threat to freedom, autonomy, and dignity, the state was seen as the *originator* of these values, and because it created them, the government was also allowed to manipulate individual choices. For the Progressives, in fact, legal restrictions on liberty, or redistributions of property, were not really limits on freedom at all but expansions of a newly defined concept of freedom: the freedom to participate in collective decisions about how society should be governed and individual rights manipulated. Minimum wages, maximum-hours legislation, restrictions on prices and interest rates, occupational licensing requirements, and other economic controls were enacted alongside food and drug laws and workplace safety regulations. While some of the Progressives' innovations were reasonable and necessary protections against fraud and dangerous practices, many others were enacted out of a visionary zeal to do good—a zeal that often backfired. Many of their programs were enacted under the pretext of protecting society against harms inflicted by business concerns when in fact they only protected businesses against fair competition from outsiders. Historian Gabriel Kolko contends, "It is business control over politics . . . rather than political regulation of the economy that is the significant phenomenon of the Progressive Era."[56] Throughout the early 20th century, businesspeople frequently obtained monopoly protections under the guise of regulation—a phenomenon that has only become increasingly common in the decades since.

This outcome is not surprising. The Progressives failed, among other things, to recognize the full implications of the fact that there are two fundamentally different ways to decide how to use resources in society: the *economic* and the *political*. Choices about how to use raw materials, capital, or labor can be made either through individual decisions or through the commands of a government. If the former, the resources will be put to those uses that pay for themselves—that is, the uses that producers and consumers agree are most productive of their happiness or that best suit their needs. In the latter case, by contrast, such decisions will be based on political considerations—considerations that do not take into account the needs of consumers, or that prioritize other matters instead.[57]

The point can be clarified by a simple thought experiment. Imagine that there is a vacant lot in a neighborhood that can be used as the site for either a hardware store or a daycare center. If the lot's owner is left free to decide how to use the property, he may choose to build a store. Consumers who have no need for hardware, however, will not shop there, leading him to close down and convert the property into a more profitable daycare center. Consumers and the owner make the ultimate decision by freely choosing between themselves how to use the property in a way that optimally serves their different needs. But now suppose that the city council is to decide the ultimate use of the vacant property. In such a case, the property's use will be determined not by reference to consumer need but by political considerations: city council members will respond to influential interest groups, or to petitions and protests by vocal minorities. They may be influenced by personal or corrupt motives. And if the government decides to build a hardware store, the fact that it does not turn a profit will create no incentive for the government to convert it into a daycare center, because thanks to its taxing power, the government is not concerned with profit and loss; the costs of its economically wasteful choice to build a hardware store are borne by citizens, not by the politicians who made that decision. Consumers will therefore be stuck with a hardware store they do not want and will not get the daycare center they do want.

This same fundamental dichotomy—decisionmaking through the economic or the political process—runs through every economic decision, from the use of land to disputes about who should practice different trades, to choices about the prices that can be charged for goods or the wages that can be earned by workers like Willie Lyons. Decisions like these can be made either by individuals freely deciding for themselves or by politicians, who make their choices by reference

14

to lobbying and political influence, not the demands of the consumer, and who are insulated from the real costs of their determinations.

Many Progressives naively believed that shifting decisionmaking from the market to the political arena would be more scientific or objective, and that expert decisionmakers would pay greater attention to the true needs of the public. But the result was just the opposite: politically influential groups—big businesses, labor organizations, and politically powerful but economically unproductive lobbyists—quickly learned how to game the system, using the state's regulatory powers to benefit themselves at the expense of consumers. Powerful businesses were liberated from the discipline of the market and were instead subjected to the far more lenient, far less public realm of politics.[58]

At first, Progressive ideas were resisted by a judiciary that followed older traditions of free choice and limited government. Thus, the Progressive Supreme Court justices were generally in the minority, writing dissenting opinions as they did in *Adkins*. But in a series of cases beginning in 1934, the Supreme Court quickly reversed course, upholding some of the most sweeping economic controls ever enacted by government. Although the Court still protected economic freedom against some of these intrusions—most notably in the *Schechter Poultry* case of 1935, one of the last cases to hold an important New Deal program unconstitutional[59]—a new paradigm had taken hold by the close of the decade. Laws that restricted the freedom to engage in a lawful occupation, to trade for economic gain, or to hold and sell property were subject only to a loose, almost nonexistent level of judicial protection. In fact, the Court explicitly abandoned the presumption that motivated Sutherland's *Adkins* opinion: that individuals were endowed with natural liberty and that the government was required to justify its interference with that liberty. Instead, even where there was no evidence showing that there was good reason to limit economic freedom, courts would presume that the law was necessary and proper: "regulatory legislation affecting ordinary commercial transactions is not to be pronounced unconstitutional unless in the light of the facts made known or generally assumed it is of such a character as to preclude the assumption that it rests upon some rational basis within the knowledge and experience of the legislators."[60]

In other words, the burden was on the individual to prove that there could be no rational reason for the law. The right to earn a living was transformed into a privilege that could be revoked whenever politicians decided that doing so would be a good idea. And this remains the state of the law today. But although they may try hard to avoid it, judges will sooner or later have to face the fact that the right to earn a living free from unfair government meddling is an essential component of our cherished right to pursue happiness. That day must bring about a new birth of freedom.

2. "Corporations" and "Monopolies," Part I: 1602–1870

As with many of the rights that Americans take for granted today, the right to earn a living without unreasonable interference was won mostly as a result of conflict between English nobles and the Crown. Although the right was recognized on occasion long before,[1] it was really during the reign of Queen Elizabeth I and her successors that lawyers, judges, and intellectuals came to acknowledge that people have the right to work for their subsistence, to open their own businesses, and to compete against one another, without government's interceding to confer special benefits on political favorites. The law's recognition of this right originated in conflicts over the monarchy's power to grant unique trading privileges to groups of political insiders, thereby prohibiting open competition. Gradually, these monopolies became delegitimized, and the right to economic liberty became a staple of the English common law.

Throughout the 17th and 18th centuries, this right was widely acknowledged by courts, although it was often violated in practice. But beginning at the close of the 19th century, political and economic theory reversed course, and government power began to gain ascendancy over the individual's right to pursue happiness.[2] Today, an entrepreneur's right to go into business or to operate that business free from government meddling is widely ignored, and although some vestiges of the anti-monopoly tradition remain—for example, in the context of "noncompetition" agreements—modern government is at liberty to violate a citizen's right to earn a living almost at will. To trace the strange historical route of the right to earn a living, we must look at how the common law evolved, in particular at the way historical circumstances altered the meaning of two important terms: "monopoly" and "corporation."

The Common Law and Monopolies

In 1602, Thomas Allen made and sold a half-gross of playing cards in London for 16 shillings.[3] This was illegal, because Edward Darcy held a patent on the making and selling of cards, which Queen Elizabeth had granted to Ralph Bowes in 1576 and which Darcy later purchased. Allen was brought up on charges and was prosecuted by Attorney General Sir Edward Coke, who would go on to become one of the most influential legal scholars of all time. But the court refused to convict, concluding that the monopoly was an illegal violation of the Magna Carta. *Darcy v. Allen*,[4] also called *The Case of Monopolies*, became one of the most well-known precedents in the common-law canon, and for generations courts would rely on it to strike down monopolies in a variety of occupations. In 1615, after he had become Lord Chief Justice of England, Coke relied on that precedent when declaring, in *The Case of the Tailors of Ipswich*,[5] that

> at the common law, no man could be prohibited from work-
> ing in any lawful trade, for the law abhors idleness, the
> mother of all evil . . . especially in young men, who ought
> in their youth, (which is their seed time) to learn lawful sci-
> ences and trades, which are profitable to the commonwealth,
> and whereof they might reap the fruit in their old age, for
> idle in youth, poor in age; and therefore the common law
> abhors all monopolies, which prohibit any from working in
> any lawful trade.[6]

Cases like these were a focal point in the conflict between the Crown and the courts in the years after Queen Elizabeth's death. Her successor, James I, advanced an even more absolutist vision of royal authority. In James's view, the king ruled by divine right, with Parliament as merely an advisory council. Opposing him was a group of political leaders who argued that Parliament's role was more central and that it and the tradition of English law limited the king's power. This group came to be called Whigs, and one of their most articulate spokesmen was Sir Edward Coke. Although James appointed Coke as chief justice, the two distrusted each other, and Coke regarded James's willingness to imprison political enemies without proper trial and to issue commands without parliamentary backing as dangerous corruptions of the traditions of English law. The confrontation between the two men became intense at times.

In one incident—memorialized today in a sculpture on the bronze doors of the United States Supreme Court—Coke told the king that the Crown was subservient to the laws of the realm. No, James responded, "the king protecteth the common law." When Coke persisted, James flew into a rage. "A traitorous speech!" he shouted. "The King protecteth the law, and not the law the King! The King maketh judges and bishops. If the judges interpret the laws themselves, and suffer none else to interpret, they may easily make, of the laws, shipmen's hose!"[7]—meaning that the laws would develop so many exceptions and complications that they would soon resemble the shredded stockings worn by sailors. Coke immediately apologized, but after he issued more legal decisions challenging James's authority, the king removed him from the court.

Among the decisions that led to Coke's removal were several challenging the king's power to grant trade monopolies. These monopoly franchises, also called patents, allowed certain businessmen the exclusive right to engage in a particular trade and severely punished would-be competitors. More than a century later, Adam Smith described one of the more extreme examples of these monopolies: "the exporter of sheep, lambs, or rams, was for the first offence to forfeit all his goods for ever, to suffer a year's imprisonment, and then to have his left hand cut off in a market town upon a market day, to be there nailed up; and for the second offence to be adjudged a felon, and to suffer death accordingly."[8]

Monopolies offended the Whigs for three primary reasons. First, they were granted by the king without parliamentary backing, contrary to the Whig belief that royal power could be exercised only in conjunction with Parliament. Coke and others believed that England's monarch had only a limited prerogative and that royal authority depended on parliamentary support. Patents, including monopolies, expanded the king's independent power, giving him an opportunity to avoid the responsibility of bargaining with Parliament. He could instead bribe the opposition by granting them monopoly privileges. Second, monopolies prohibited workers from engaging in trades that would benefit both themselves and the economy of England. By limiting the right to compete, monopolies raised prices for consumers and deprived society of the skills that entrepreneurs had to offer.[9] As one court put it in 1727, rules restraining economic freedom are "not to be endured" if they "prevent the exercise

19

of [the trade] anywhere . . . because the public loses the benefit of the party's labor, and the party himself is rendered a useless member of the community."[10] Third, monopolies exploited government power for the private welfare of particular individuals rather than for the benefit of the society in general. The king was supposed to protect the whole realm rather than governing in his own self-interest or exploiting royal power to benefit his friends.

The Whig anti-monopoly tradition was only partly grounded on an inchoate theory of free-market economics. Rather, as William Letwin explained, the common law's recognition of the right to pursue an occupation without unreasonable interference was based on "the feeling that a man should not be denied the means to earn a living: he and his family ought not to starve, his neighbors ought not to be burdened by supporting him, and the Crown should not be deprived of his contribution to the nation's wealth and power."[11]

After being removed from the court, Coke was elected to Parliament, where he authored the Statute of Monopolies, a law prohibiting the Crown from granting exclusive trade privileges in most cases.[12] Enacted in 1623, it became a landmark of English law. Two centuries later, New York Chancellor James Kent would call it the "Magna Charta of British industry," because it "contained a noble principle, and secured to every subject unlimited freedom of action, provided he did no injury to others, nor violated statute law."[13]

But Coke's assault on monopolies did not end with the passage of his statute. In retirement, he wrote an important set of legal treatises called *The Institutes of the Laws of England* in which he excoriated the royal monopoly system: "all grants of monopolies are against the ancient and fundamental laws of this kingdom," he wrote. "[A] man's trade is accounted his life, because it maintaineth his life; and therefore the monopolist that taketh away a mans trade, taketh away his life."[14] But "no man ought to be put from his livelihood without answer."[15] Referring to *Darcy v. Allen*, he argued that economic freedom was guaranteed by the Magna Carta's "law of the land" clause:

> [I]f a grant be made to any man, to have the sole making of cards, or the sole dealing with any other trade, that grant is against the liberty and freedom of the subject, that before did, or lawfully might have used that trade, and consequently

> against this great charter [i.e., Magna Carta]. . . . Generally
> all monopolies are against this great charter, because they are
> against the liberty and freedom of the subject, and against
> the law of the land.[16]

Coke's challenges to royal authority placed him among the radical intelligentsia of his generation. Late in life, he helped write the Petition of Right, a demand for limits on royal authority, which was presented to King Charles I in the years leading up to the English civil war.[17] When Coke died, Charles had his papers searched to ensure that nothing seditious might later be published.[18] Yet Coke's reputation flourished, thanks to the *Institutes*, which became the standard textbook of law students in England and America and was studied closely by such lawyers as John Adams, John Marshall, James Wilson, and Thomas Jefferson. Jefferson in particular gagged on Coke's hard-to-read style[19] but credited his "uncouth but cunning learning" with raising a generation of revolutionary lawyers in America.[20]

Coke was not the only judge to resist royal monopolies in 17th-century England. In cases like the *Weaver of Newbury's Case*,[21] *The Case of the Bricklayers*,[22] and others,[23] courts struck down monopolies as violations of the right to earn a living. In *Colgate v. Bacheler*, for instance, the court held:

> [T]his condition is against law, to prohibit or restrain any
> to use a lawful trade at any time . . . for as well as he may
> restrain him for one time . . . he may restrain him for longer
> times . . . being freemen, it is free for them to exercise their
> trade in any place. . . . [A party] ought not to be abridged of
> his trade and living.[24]

Such cases developed into an anti-monopoly tradition that recognized the dangers inherent in allowing the practitioners of a trade to use law to exclude their rivals. When newcomers are not allowed to enter a marketplace, they are deprived of the opportunity to earn a living, and the general public is deprived of the competition that would decrease prices and increase the availability of goods and services. Of course, government and industry groups might protect consumers by regulating the quality of products and services, but they should not be able to pervert this power for their own benefit.[25]

The Whig anti-monopoly tradition prohibited not only royal "patent"-style monopolies created by government but also monopoly-like arrangements formed by private agreements. These were known as "agreements in restraint of trade": that is, contracts in which parties agreed not to do business with some other person or group. Boycotts and similar agreements to withhold goods and services caused some of the same problems as government-created monopolies: they inhibited competition and deprived society of useful goods and services. If all the merchants in an area agreed among themselves not to hire a man, for example, his ability to earn a living would be imperiled. One common type of contract in restraint of trade was imposed in apprenticeship agreements. These contracts—which today would be called "noncompetition clauses"—promised the master that in exchange for training, the apprentice would not set up shop next door to the master or otherwise go into competition with him once he learned the trade. Courts regarded these agreements with skepticism and often invoked the apprentice's right to earn a living as a reason for refusing to enforce them.

But prohibiting boycotts or similar agreements also posed some problems. Buyers, after all, could not be *forced* to shop at a particular store if they chose not to, and a business owner could not be *forced* to hire a particular employee. Truly consensual refusals to deal differ from government-created monopolies in that a person who is ostracized by a group of businesses or boycotted by customers has not had his rights violated, and in most cases he still retains the ability to do business in some form, perhaps by persuading consumers to return to him, by improving quality, or by moving to a new location. These options are not available to someone who is barred from the market by a government monopoly or is legally prohibited from entering a trade. Such a person's freedom of choice *has* been violated.

Courts therefore devised different rules for judging the validity of genuinely consensual agreements that restrained trade, as opposed to nonconsensual, government-imposed monopolies. Contracts in restraint of trade were permitted as long as they were "reasonable," and noncompetition agreements were valid if they were supported by consideration—meaning that each side received some genuine benefit in the transaction—and if they were geographically limited.[26] Government-imposed monopolies, on the other hand, which barred a person entirely from entering trade, were illegal in most cases.

Trade groups nevertheless often colluded to make it difficult for newcomers to enter a profession. Restricting entry into a profession kept up the rates that practitioners could charge clients. These practitioners often devised burdensome apprenticeship rules that made it harder for the new and unskilled to practice a trade. At a time when the economy of England was organized on mercantilist principles, the guild system prevailed as a sort of early labor union, controlling particular industries and setting the terms on which newcomers could enter a given trade. These guilds used their licensing power to create artificial scarcity in the market, thereby increasing the prices that they could charge. Following their earlier rulings against limiting competition, courts often declared these "bylaws" illegal as well. In one case, Lord Coke struck down a guild rule that required extensive training for any person seeking to go into the upholstery trade. The upholsterers argued that the training was required to protect the public from incompetent practitioners, but Coke rejected this proposition: "no skill there is in this, for he may well learn this in seven hours."[27] He concluded with a lucid explanation of the common law's balance between consumer protection and economic freedom:

> [B]y the very common law, it was lawful for any man to use any trade thereby to maintain himself and his family; this was both lawful, and also very commendable, but yet by the common law, if a man will take upon him to use any trade, in which he hath no skill; the law provides a punishment for such offenders, and such persons were to be punished in the court leet [i.e., by tort lawsuits].[28]

Coke cited the example of a blacksmith who injured a horse because he was not skilled in his trade—proper legal redress, he explained, was already available in the form of a suit for damages. "Unskilfulness is a sufficient punishment for him."[29] But the possibility that a practitioner might do a bad job was not a good excuse for restricting economic freedom, raising costs to consumers, and depriving entrepreneurs of economic opportunity.

The Right to Earn a Living as a Natural Right

The American Revolution brought an important change in the understanding of the right to earn a living. Where English courts had often protected this right out of a nationalistic concern for increasing the wealth of the realm, America's Founders saw the right to earn a living not as a matter of privilege or of public policy but instead as a matter of natural freedom. "Every one," wrote Thomas Jefferson, "has a natural right to choose for his pursuit such one of them as he thinks most likely to furnish him subsistence,"[30] and the "first principle of association" was "the guarantee to every one of a free exercise of his industry, and the fruits acquired by it."[31] Likewise, James Madison explained that the primary evil of monopolies was that they restricted an individual's natural right to earn a living through gainful trade: "That is not a just government, nor is property secure under it, where arbitrary restrictions, exemptions, and monopolies deny to part of its citizens that free use of their faculties, and free choice of their occupations, which not only constitute their property in the general sense of the word; but are the means of acquiring property strictly so called." In addition, monopoly laws or restrictive licensing schemes were often used to give economic favors to politically influential lobbyists, violating the principle of equality: "What must be the spirit of legislation where a manufacturer of linen cloth is forbidden to bury his own child in a linen shroud, in order to favor his neighbor who manufactures woolen cloth[?]; where the manufacturer and wearer of woolen cloth are again forbidden the economical use of buttons of that material, in favor of the manufacturer of buttons of other materials[?]!"[32]

In fact, the right to earn a living appears in the Declaration of Independence. Where John Locke had originally described fundamental rights as "life, liberty, and estate," Jefferson changed the wording to "life, liberty and the pursuit of happiness." Although some scholars continue to debate the significance of this change, it was most likely intended to refer, among other things, to the individual's right to pursue a trade and thereby improve his position in life.[33] The Founders believed that among the most important liberties was the individual's right to go into business and keep the fruits of his labor. Only a month before the Declaration of Independence was issued, Jefferson's friend George Mason had written the Virginia Declaration of Rights, declaring that "all men are by nature equally free and independent, and have certain inherent rights," including "the enjoyment of life and liberty, with the means of *acquiring* and possessing property, and *pursuing and obtaining* happiness and safety."[34] Property rights, in

24

fact, were viewed primarily as a function of the right to earn a living. "The personal right to acquire property, which is a natural right," said James Madison a half-century after the Revolution, "gives to property, when acquired, a right to protection, as a social right."[35] Professor Thomas West explains in his book *Vindicating the Founders* that Jefferson, Madison, and others saw liberty as including "the liberty to acquire property," and their defense of property rights rested not on notions of economic efficiency or class hierarchy but on the notion that "it is part of liberty."[36]

This reevaluation of economic choice as a natural or moral right instead of a merely national tradition coincided with a deeper understanding of the social and economic effects of such freedom. Adam Smith, a Scottish moral philosopher who believed that economic choice was "the most sacred and inviolable" of rights, argued that monopolies were a "manifest encroachment upon the just liberty both of the workman, and of those who might be disposed to employ him." Smith argued that as a moral matter, economic choices should be "trusted to the discretion" of workers and employers.[37] But Smith also pointed out the social and economic problems caused by monopolies, summing them up in a famous sentence: "Consumption is the sole end and purpose of all production; and the interest of the producer ought to be attended to, only so far as it may be necessary for promoting that of the consumer."[38] Government should not concern itself with protecting businesses against competition, Smith argued; instead, a wise economic policy sought to promote wealth in general, which meant *encouraging* competition and ensuring that consumers could obtain what they needed, even if it sometimes put less-competitive producers out of business. To subsidize unproductive or unsuccessful businesses, relieving them of the pressure to compete fairly for the consumer's money, ultimately harms the consumer, Smith argued. He excoriated the "absurd and oppressive monopolies" that "merchants and manufacturers had extorted from the legislature,"[39] which, by restraining the supply of needed goods and services, forced people to pay more for the things they needed. This, Smith wrote, both restricted the creation of wealth and violated principles of justice: "To hurt in any degree the interest of any one order of citizens, for no other purpose but to promote that of some other, is evidently contrary to that justice and equality of treatment which the sovereign owes to all the different orders of his subjects."[40]

25

Changes to the Definition of "Corporation"

In Smith's eyes, one leading culprit with regard to such unfair actions was the corporation. Corporations, Smith argued, were established by "prerogative of the crown" in an effort to "restrain[] that free competition" that would otherwise lead to a "reduction of price[s] and consequently of wages and profit."[41] But Smith's use of the word "corporation" can mislead today's readers because in the century after Smith wrote, the concept of a "corporation" underwent important changes. Coined in the medieval era, the word "corporation" originally referred to a very different type of organization than today's for-profit business association. As the 18th-century legal scholar William Blackstone explained in his *Commentaries on the Laws of England*, a corporation was any legally created entity designed to transfer rights and privileges indefinitely to a person and his successors. "The king, for instance, is made a corporation to prevent in general the possibility of an *interregnum* or vacancy of the throne."[42] This was still the case in Blackstone's day; in fact, never in his four-volume *Commentaries* does Blackstone describe the type of private, for-profit institution familiar to modern Americans. In 1771, the first edition of the *Encyclopedia Britannica* defined a corporation as "a body politic, or incorporate, so-called, because the persons or members are joined into one body, and are qualified to take and grant, &c." The *Encyclopedia* did not refer at all to private business corporations. Instead, corporations were

> either spiritual or temporal: spiritual, as bishops, deans, archdeacons, parsons, vicars, &c. Temporal, as mayor, commonalty, bailiff, burgesses, &c. And some corporations are of a mixed nature, composed of spiritual and temporal persons, such as heads of colleges and hospitals, &c. All corporations are said to be ecclesiastical or lay: ecclesiastical are either regular, as abbeys, priories, chapters, &c. or secular, as bishoprics, deanries, archdeaconries, &c. lay, as those of cities, towns, companies, or communities of commerce, &c.[43]

There is nothing in this definition to indicate what the word would come to signify within a century.

Today's corporations trace their roots to the English "joint-stock companies," organized in the 17th century to assemble capital and operate large-scale enterprises.[44] These joint-stock companies were granted royal charters—official permission to engage in a lucrative trade, which were monopolies by definition.[45] Any person engaging in projects such as establishing colonies, or transporting and selling tea or other commodities, without this royal approval ran the risk of severe penalties. When lawyers of the period looked for a name to describe these monopoly ventures they called them "corporations," borrowing the medieval word that referred to any group of people united in a common enterprise. Thus was born a notion that the word "corporation" was synonymous with monopoly. And thanks to Whig hostility to monopolies, early American political leaders regarded anything called a "corporation" with great suspicion. Thomas Jefferson, for example, warned about the "aristocracy of monied corporations" that "bid defiance to the laws of our country,"[46] but he was not speaking of modern business enterprises; rather, he was concerned with the dangers of government-created monopolies, and he even wrote to James Madison, urging him to add a prohibition on monopolies to the Bill of Rights.[47] Madison agreed that monopolies are "justly classed among the greatest nuisances in government,"[48] but he did not think it necessary to ban them in the Bill of Rights because the Constitution already "limited them to two cases, the authors of Books and of useful inventions."[49] At the Constitutional Convention, Madison did propose giving Congress the power to issue charters of incorporation to encourage the construction of canals, but George Mason objected to this on the grounds that he was "afraid of monopolies of every sort," and the proposal was defeated.[50]

In the early years of the 19th century, states granted monopolistic corporate charters for major public undertakings, such as building canals or railroads. But the democratic tide of the new nation resisted these special privileges, and ultimately this new way of thinking about economic opportunity changed the nature of American corporations. This change came about through general incorporation statutes that enabled corporate charters to be issued as a routine act (called a "ministerial" act) by state officers rather than one-by-one through legislative vote. These laws, writes historian Gordon Wood, "opened up the legal privileges to all who desired them."[51] Wood describes what he calls the radical transformation of corporations during this era: "Within a few years most of them became very different from their monarchical predecessors: they were no longer exclusive monopolies and they were no longer public. They became private property and what Samuel Blodget in 1806 called 'rivals for the common weal.' And they were created in astonishing numbers unduplicated anywhere else in the world."[52] By democratizing them and eliminating their privileged status, American states allowed corporations to proliferate. New York enacted its general corporation law in 1811, after demands for corporate charters forced the legislature to issue 222 in one decade.[53] Other states followed suit, and new states adopted constitutions expressly forbidding the legislature from creating corporations except through general incorporation laws. Thus, over the course of the 19th century, the corporation was shorn of its special monopolistic status and became instead what contemporaries called "self-created societies" whose existence was merely certified or recognized by the state's ministerial act.

During this period, as legal historian Lawrence Friedman notes, courts also "created a body of corporation law out of next to nothing. Old decisions and doctrines, from the time when most corporations were academies, churches, charities, and cities, had little to say about managers and directors that was germane to the world of business corporations."[54] In 1852, the Michigan Supreme Court commented on the rapid evolution of the corporation:

> [T]hree grand classes of corporations exist. 1st. Political or municipal corporations, such as counties, towns, cities and villages, which, from their nature, are subject to the unlimited control of the Legislature; 2d. Those associations which are created for *public benefit*, and to which the government delegates a portion of its sovereign power, to be exercised for public utility, such as turnpike, bridge, canal, and railroad companies; and 3d strictly private corporations, where the private interest of the corporators is the primary object of the associations, such as banking, insurance, manufacturing and trading companies; and in this class may also be included eleemosynary corporations, generally. . . . The object of *strictly private* corporations is to aggregate the capital, the talents, and the skill of individuals, to foster industry and encourage the arts. Private advantage is the ultimate, as well as the immediate object of their creation, and [the benefits] to the public [are] incidental, growing out of the general benefits acquired by the application of combined capital, skill, and talent to the pursuits of commerce and of trade, and the necessities and conveniences of the community.[55]

Today, thanks to general corporation laws, forming a corporation is a simple matter of paying a fee and filling out a form. They are given life not by government decree but by the contractual rights of the investors and directors who choose to open new businesses and use the corporate form.

Nevertheless, many writers today ignore this history and continue to describe corporations as "creatures of the state." Because states license or grant other official recognition to corporations, these writers claim, the state can heavily regulate them in exchange for those charters. Yet it is highly misleading to regard contemporary corporations, which bear little resemblance to the old-fashioned charter system, as creatures of the state. In fact, state laws do not "grant charters" to corporations at all. California law, for example, specifies that any person or group "may form a corporation . . . by executing and filing articles of incorporation," and that the corporations shall exist "automatically" once the proper documents are filed. No other government permission is required beyond compliance with the law.[56] The legal recognition of a corporation does not give it life or make it a government-created entity any more than a marriage license makes a marriage into a government institution.[57] Most people would indignantly reject the idea that the mere granting of a simple license entitles the government to regulate the activities of married couples, but corporations are in the same position: they are state-*recognized*, but privately *organized*, institutions.

Are "Corporations" Still "Monopolies"?

The 19th century saw another important change in the law of corporations, largely as a result of two important Supreme Court decisions: *Dartmouth College v. Woodward* in 1819[58] and *Charles River Bridge v. Warren Bridge* in 1837.[59] In *Dartmouth College*, the Supreme Court declared that a corporate charter was a contract between the state and the corporation's owners, and thus that any attempt by the state to alter that charter without the owners' consent would violate the contracts clause of the Constitution. This meant that corporations were no longer mere government privileges; they were private property that the government had to respect.

Once they were no longer quasi-government institutions, it was only a matter of time before corporations lost their inherently monopolistic status. The *Charles River Bridge* decision announced that corporate charters did not necessarily include the right to be protected against competition from other corporations. That case involved a charter granted by the Massachusetts legislature in 1785, authorizing a private company to construct a toll bridge between Boston and Charlestown. Forty-three years later, in 1828, the legislature issued a second corporate charter, authorizing another company to construct a new bridge close by. This new bridge, called the Warren Bridge, would be open to the public toll free, thus destroying the profits of the Charles River Bridge, whose owners sued, arguing that the destruction of their investment violated their constitutional rights. They claimed that, by granting the 1785 charter, the state had implied that it would not destroy the value of their bridge by later creating a competing (free) bridge. Their charter gave them an exclusive right to profit from transportation between the two cities, they argued.

The Supreme Court ruled against them. It would be a "singular spectacle," the Court declared, "if, while the courts in England are restraining, within the strictest limits, the spirit of monopoly, and exclusive privileges in nature of monopolies," the American courts "should be found enlarging these [monopoly] privileges."[60] On the contrary, "[t]here is no exclusive privilege given" to the owners of the first bridge,[61] and although it was true that "its income [was] destroyed by the Warren bridge,"[62] this could not give the Charles River Bridge's owners the right to block new competitors. After all, such monopoly privileges would bring progress to a standstill. If a business's corporate status entitled it to protection from competitors, "the old turnpike corporations" would soon demand that the courts "put down the improvements which have taken their place," and the nation would be "thrown back to the improvements of the last century, and obliged to stand still."[63] Established businesses would be empowered to restrict the innovations that improve the standard of living. *Charles River Bridge* set the important precedent that corporate charters would not be read as including a prohibition on competition unless the charter explicitly said so. Thus, as historian Stanley Kutler writes, the decision protected new enterprises "from the impeding, sometimes aggressive claims of obsolescent corporations that desperately tried to preserve exclusive earning opportunities."[64]

Shortly after *Charles River Bridge* was decided came a case that justified the Court's concern that outdated companies would demand monopoly protection against innovators. A Maryland company operating a toll road sued the state for granting a charter to construct a railroad along the same route, arguing that the railroad would impair its business and therefore deprive it of private property. In other words, they claimed to "own" the exclusive right to provide travel on that route. The Maryland Court of Appeals rejected this contention, and similar cases soon secured the principle that corporations could not rely on charters to guarantee them immunity from competition.[65] As Kutler concludes: "[T]he *Charles River Bridge* case opened the floodgates and courts now directly confronted and denied exaggerated implied claims of vested rights. The state court reports for the next two decades are replete with cases implementing the *Charles River Bridge* doctrine."[66]

The Archaic Vision of Corporations Continues

Despite this fundamental change in the nature of corporations, the idea that corporations are government-created privileges has never disappeared entirely. Indeed, although today's corporations are wholly private enterprises, "the aura of privilege remained,"[67] and vestiges of it can be seen today in three current controversies about them.

The first is found in court decisions regarding the power of eminent domain. In the notorious case of *Kelo v. New London*,[68] the Supreme Court upheld the power of government to condemn privately owned land and transfer it to private developers for use in ways that government officials believe will benefit the community. The theory behind the decision reaches back to 19th-century cases allowing privately owned railroads to use eminent domain to lay tracks. In those cases, courts allowed condemnation by private, for-profit railroads because they were considered quasi-public institutions, entrusted with the power to do a traditional government function: creating highways. And because railroads were "common carriers," required to serve the general public without discrimination and allowed only to charge prices that the government approved, they were viewed as similar to public utilities. Government could therefore give them the power of eminent domain, delegating to them its duty to construct

31

roads.[69] Whatever its inadequacies, this theory still cabined the power of eminent domain within predictable boundaries. But gradually the theory was expanded to justify the use of eminent domain by *other* private companies that were arguably "public," including telephone or electrical companies—even though they were privately owned and run for profit—and mining companies that needed to construct railheads at mines, even though the public could not use those tracks. These, the courts held, were still close enough to traditional public uses that the companies involved could use eminent domain.

During the Progressive Era, courts expanded this theory still further, allowing government to enlist private developers in reform-oriented efforts to eradicate slums and dilapidated neighborhoods. Eventually, courts expanded the doctrine further still, allowing private corporations to use eminent domain to eliminate "blight" and to "create jobs," even though they were not regulated public utilities, were not performing traditional government functions, and had all the rights of a private owner. Courts by this time had come to think of economic development as a semi-governmental enterprise, just as their predecessors had thought of railroads. And just as 19th-century courts viewed the economic advancement represented by the railroads as justifying the use of eminent domain, 20th-century courts considered private stores like Costco or Home Depot as "public uses" because of the economic benefits that would flow from completed projects, despite their fundamentally private status. The semipublic nature of premodern corporations thus left a legacy that lives to the present day.[70]

The second way in which the antiquated model of the corporation persists is in the oft-heard description of corporations as "creatures of the state." This description usually accompanies proposals for government control over corporations; in the 1970s, it even inspired Ralph Nader and colleagues to call for a federal corporations law that would take the regulation of corporate entities out of the hands of the states.[71] They argued that corporations were created by government permission and therefore owed a "responsibility" to the general public, which would take the form of government control over corporate decisionmaking. But as Robert Hessen wrote in his riposte to Nader and his coauthors, *In Defense of the Corporation*, to describe corporations as "creatures of the state" is to ignore centuries of legal evolution.[72] Today's corporations are not creatures of the state any more than they are medieval community enterprises. Instead, they are entities created by groups of individuals who have agreed by contract to invest their money toward a common goal, often—though not always—a profit-making goal. These corporations have little in common with their government-created ancestors, and although they have certain advantages that sole proprietorships or partnerships lack, such as limited liability, those advantages are not created by government fiat but by people joining in more complicated contractual agreements. Indeed, all the supposedly unique "privileges" of the corporate form are actually created by private contract: the corporate form simply bundles these various contractual arrangements into a single package. Private parties could agree by contract to limit their personal liability, to create business arrangements that "outlive" investors, to create a board of directors with power to make business decisions, and to do all the other things that corporations do. But making all these agreements by separate contracts would be cumbersome, so the corporate form takes all these separate contractual arrangements and groups them into a single, pre-made arrangement, like buying a ready-to-wear suit instead of one that is tailor-made. Corporate "privileges" are really just a collection of agreements that contracting parties have the capacity to create if they so choose.[73]

Even limited liability is not really a government-created privilege. Liability in the business world is often predicated on what lawyers call *respondeat superior*—the liability of a principal for the harms caused by his agent. This theory is based on the idea that the principal in some way controls the agent's action, or ought to. If a businessman sends a messenger out on an errand, the businessman is responsible for the injuries the messenger might cause because he ought to supervise the messenger and ensure that he is competent and does not act recklessly. But investors in a corporation, unlike corporate managers, do not supervise the actions of the corporation's employees. It seems unfair to hold them liable for an employee's wrongdoing when they could not take steps to prevent it. Nevertheless, current law does impose liability on shareholders, at least to the limit of their investment in the corporation: hence, "limited" liability. Far from being a government-created privilege, therefore, limited liability is a questionable imposition on shareholders.[74]

33

As Hessen observes, the supposed "privileges" of the corporate form are "created and sustained by freedom of association and contract." The "source of [that] freedom is not governmental permission, but individual rights."[75] The corporate form simply provides a more streamlined way of accomplishing ends that could be legitimately, but less efficiently, accomplished in other ways.[76]

A related complaint regarding corporations is that courts unfairly treat them as "persons" under the Fourteenth Amendment. Activists and academics often object that regarding corporations as persons has led to judicial decisions that benefit the wealthy at the expense of the poor. The Supreme Court first described a corporation as a person in the 1886 decision of *Santa Clara County v. Southern Pacific Railroad*,[77] and many legal commentators have objected that the amendment's authors never had any such intention.

But while it is somewhat odd to describe corporations as "persons," that term is just a useful shorthand for the fact that the persons who invest in and operate a corporation have rights that courts must respect. As Justice Stephen Field noted four years before the *Santa Clara County* case, state courts had been treating corporations as persons since the mid-19th century—when the modern business corporation was first coming into being—because "the property of a corporation is in fact the property of the corporators. To deprive the corporation of its property, or to burden it, is, in fact, to deprive the corporators of their property or to lessen its value." Anything that "affects the property of the corporation necessarily affects the commercial value of [the investors'] interests."[78] When government burdens a corporation, the rights of investors are burdened as well. This is why "the courts will look through the ideal entity and name of the corporation to the persons who compose it, and protect them, though the process be in [the corporation's] name."[79]

When a judge refers to a corporation's right to due process of law or to equal protection of the law by saying that the corporation is a "person," he is merely saying that the *investors* of the corporation are people who are entitled to these rights. "All the guaranties and safeguards of the constitution for the protection of property possessed by individuals may, therefore, be invoked for the protection of the property of corporations."[80] To hold otherwise would allow government to discriminate against investors who choose to use the corporate form and to treat their rights as less worthy of protection than the rights of people who choose to do business as individuals or in partnerships. Speaking of corporations as persons is therefore no more strange than speaking of a sports team as a single entity capable of acting—that is, "the Patriots won a game."[81] Just as a team only "does" things in the sense that individuals actually *do* those things, so a corporation is a voluntary association of people who have chosen to pool their resources. But both the team and the corporation are composed of people whose constitutional rights deserve respect and judicial protection.

Finally, the antiquated "aura" of corporate privilege has recently been revived as part of a theory that corporations ought to be run with the best interests of "stakeholders" in mind, not only of *share*holders. Stakeholders are noninvestors who are said to have some "stake" in the existence and operation of a business. According to the stakeholder theory, this interest entitles them to exercise some power over a corporation's decisions. This notion has gained increasing attention in recent decades as business ethicists contend that corporations ought to "give something back" to the communities where they do business. Corporate officers themselves often use this language, eager to appear as "responsible" corporate "citizens." Yet the stakeholder theory is a dangerously misleading way of understanding the corporation. As Milton Friedman put it in a famous 1970 article, the social responsibility of a business is to increase profits: A corporation's officers are agents serving the interests of the shareholders who elect them; when they spend the shareholders' money on projects they did not contemplate—projects which benefit the general public at their expense—the officials are exceeding their legitimate authority. An executive who devotes his energies to such projects "becomes in effect a public employee, a civil servant, even though he remains in name an employee of a private enterprise" and is not elected by the people.[82]

The "stakeholder" theory goes even further. Not only does it hold that private companies should divert the money of investors toward nonprofitable enterprises but it also would destroy the investors' ability to hold corporate employees accountable. At present, corporate directors are ultimately answerable to shareholders for their decisions, and their performance can be assessed simply by watching the company's bottom line. Dissatisfied investors can organize to replace executives, or they can sue the company for wasting their wealth. Under the stakeholder theory, by contrast, corporations would not exist primarily to maximize the return on investment, and corporate decisions would not be made with productivity as the primary goal. This would reduce accountability and make it harder for investors to ensure that their investments are being well managed. Moreover, it is impossible to determine what sort of "stake" is sufficient to entitle a person or group to participate in the corporate decisionmaking process. Are the neighbors who own land near the business, or whose own businesses depend on it, entitled to a say? What about *their* customers and neighbors? And how should the votes of people with different "stakes" be weighed? Without a clear dividing line as to what "interest" entitles a person to participate in controlling the corporation, the stakeholder theory is incoherent. Worse still, these stakeholders would be motivated not by the common purpose of seeing the corporation thrive but by a variety of often incompatible purposes. Allowing stakeholders to vote on corporate decisions would severely undermine a corporation's ability to succeed because it would be in the interest of any particular stakeholder to subvert the corporation's interest—that is, the interests of those who have invested in the company—for his or her own short-term gain. There would be little downside for the stakeholder who proposes to divert corporate assets for his or her own benefit.[83]

Corporations are among the great discoveries of humanity.[84] They allow people to pool their resources toward a common purpose without requiring people to take a role in managing the enterprise (which they may not be competent to do). Corporations enable people to cooperate—often without even realizing that they are cooperating—in enormous enterprises of productivity and wealth creation. These undertakings are largely responsible for the explosive progress of the past century—the rising standard of living and the increase in life expectancy. Despite the political rhetoric that often labels corporations as somehow inherently immoral, the corporate form helps bring together investors and talented workers to produce many of the products, services, and resources we take for granted. And many, if not most, Americans benefit directly from corporations by enjoying their products, by working for them, by investing in them, or by hiring them to manage investments for their retirement. No doubt there are corporations whose directors or managers do genuinely evil things. But corporations are not monsters, monopolies, or creatures of the state. They are an effective and vital way for individuals to exercise their right to earn a living.

Legal history has many ironies, but perhaps none is so strong as the ironic changes that have taken place in the redefinition of the words "corporation" and "monopoly." These two words were at one time virtually synonymous. But as the concept of a corporation changed over time to refer to a private entity based in contract rather than a public entity created by the government, so, too, the word "monopoly" was changing, with especially perverse results. We shall see how in the next chapter.

3. "Corporations" and "Monopolies," Part II: 1870 to the Present

With the end of the American Civil War and the country's ascendancy as a major industrial force, the increasing wealth and influence of corporations became the subject of political controversy, particularly among traditionalists who feared that the new companies were destroying the small-scale farming culture. New industrial giants, particularly railroad companies, were accused of exploiting small farmers, and in Illinois and other states, agrarian groups like the Grange began demanding legislation to control the prices charged by railroads and other businesses. This was the Populist Era, during which political leaders demanded that government assume greater power to oversee the decisions made by corporations.[1] But while politicians began searching for a rationale that would enable government to regulate these companies more strictly, the newly enacted Fourteenth Amendment was leading to some of the nation's most important legal decisions regarding economic freedom.

The Supreme Court Erases a Constitutional Protection against Monopolies

Thanks to the Whig anti-monopoly tradition, English and American law came to adopt the principle that government had no legitimate business interfering with a person's right to earn a living unless doing so was necessary to protect the public health and safety. Neither the king nor the elected legislature could deprive people of economic opportunity simply to provide higher income for other people whom the government preferred. This principle, though often violated in practice, was characteristic of the classical liberalism of America's Founders. They believed that the right to pursue happiness by working unhindered in a gainful trade was an inherent natural right, and a century later, as political controversies were spiraling toward civil war, this principle was widely preached by spokesmen for the abolitionist and "free labor" movements.[2] Abraham Lincoln explained the connection between anti-slavery principles and the right to earn a living when he said in his debates with Sen. Stephen Douglas that

> there is no reason in the world why the negro is not entitled to all the rights enumerated in the Declaration of Independence—the right of life, liberty, and the pursuit of happiness. I hold that he is as much entitled to these as the white man. I agree with Judge Douglas that he is not my equal in many respects, certainly not in color—perhaps not in intellectual and moral endowments; but in the right to eat the bread without the leave of any body else which his own hand earns, he is my equal and the equal of Judge Douglas, and the equal of every other man.[3]

At the end of the Civil War, Republican anti-slavery lawmakers saw an opportunity to vindicate this principle throughout the country. Southern states resisted Reconstruction by enacting laws that limited the former slaves' rights to earn a living or to own property. Republicans therefore drafted the Civil Rights Act of 1866, which declared that black people would have the same rights as white people to make and enforce contracts or to possess, use, buy, and sell property.[4] When the constitutionality of the act was called into question, the Republicans responded by preparing the Fourteenth Amendment, largely to secure a constitutional foundation for the act.

Section 1 of the amendment declared, first, that all persons born or naturalized in the United States were citizens of the United States, and of the state where they resided. Second, it announced that no state could make or enforce any law that would "abridge the privileges or immunities of citizens of the United States." This phrase, "privileges or immunities" was intended to protect, among other things, the traditional right to earn a living free from unreasonable interference. It was modeled on a similar phrase appearing in Article IV of the Constitution, which Supreme Court Justice Bushrod Washington famously explained in the 1823 case of *Corfield v. Coryell*.[5] The term "privileges and immunities," said Justice Washington, refers to those "fundamental" freedoms "which belong, of right, to the citizens of all free governments. . . . Protection by the government; the enjoyment of life and liberty, with the right to acquire and possess property of every kind, and to pursue and obtain happiness and safety; subject nevertheless to such restraints as the government may justly prescribe for the general good of the whole." The term also referred to the right "to pass through, or to reside in any other state, for purposes of trade, agriculture, professional pursuits, or otherwise," or "to take, hold and dispose of property, either real or personal; and an exemption from higher taxes or impositions than are paid by the other citizens of the state."[6]

The authors of the Fourteenth Amendment's privileges or immunities clause referred repeatedly to the *Corfield* case when crafting the amendment's language,[7] and several of them made particular mention of the right to earn a living without unreasonable government interference. Representative John Bingham, principal author of the clause, said that it included "the liberty . . . to work in an honest calling and contribute by your toil in some sort to the support of yourself, to the support of your fellowmen, and to be secure in the enjoyment of the fruits of your toil."[8] Another representative echoed this with a rhetorical question: "[H]as not every person a right, to carry on his own occupation, to secure the fruits of his own industry, and appropriate them as best suits himself, as long as it is a legitimate exercise of this right and not vicious in itself, or against public policy, or morally wrong, or against the natural rights of others?"[9] And Senator John Sherman explained that courts interpreting the privileges or immunities clause would "look first at the Constitution of the United States as the primary fountain of authority," but also to the Declaration of Independence, American and English history, and English common law, where "they will find the fountain and reservoir of the rights of American as well as English citizens,"[10] including, of course, the common-law cases protecting the right to earn a living free from government-created monopolies. In fact, as one federal court put it, 12 years after the amendment became law, "[I]t seems quite impossible that any definition of these terms [privileges and immunities] could be adopted, or even seriously proposed, so narrow as to exclude the right to labor for subsistence."[11]

Nevertheless, the Supreme Court essentially erased the privileges or immunities clause from the Constitution in an 1873 decision called the *Slaughterhouse Cases*.[12] *Slaughterhouse* was the first decision in which the Court interpreted the Fourteenth Amendment, and it radically undermined the powerful new protections that the amendment had promised to Americans. The case began in 1869 when the owners of the Crescent City Livestock Landing and Slaughtering Company bribed the Louisiana legislature into passing a law that required all butchers in the New Orleans area to do their butchering at a single slaughterhouse—one owned, of course, by the Crescent City Company.[13] The law meant ruin for dozens if not hundreds of small, private butcher shops, which would now be required to slaughter their livestock at the Crescent City abattoir. Those butchers filed lawsuits, arguing that the new requirement deprived them of their common-law right to earn a living—a right that was among the "privileges or immunities" of citizenship, which the state could not abridge. The state argued that the law was intended simply to protect the public health and safety, noting that many butcher shops were unsanitary affairs. Requiring that butchering be done at a single location would protect the public from the threat of disease. But this theory had one obvious flaw: if the law had been intended as a sanitary measure, why had it not regulated the conditions of those butcher shops? Instead, the law merely granted an exclusive economic privilege to a single private company.

The Supreme Court ruled in favor of the state in a sharply divided 5–4 decision written by Justice Samuel Miller. Although he recognized that the right to earn a living was, indeed, an important and long-recognized constitutional right, Miller held that it was not one of the rights the amendment protected. "The language," he pointed out, "is, 'No State shall make or enforce any law which shall abridge the privileges or immunities of citizens *of the United States.*'"[14] But the right to earn a living—while a genuine right recognized for centuries by the common law—was only protected by one's *state* citizenship, not by one's federal citizenship. It was therefore not a privilege or immunity covered by the amendment. Most of a person's privileges and immunities "lay within the constitutional and legislative power of the States," Miller wrote. "Was it the purpose of the fourteenth amendment . . . to transfer the security and protection of all the civil rights which we have mentioned, from the States to the Federal government?"[15] He thought not. The privileges or immunities of citizens of the United States included only the right to travel to the federal capital, the right to demand protection from the federal government when traveling at sea, the right to use the navigable waters of the United States, "[t]he right to peaceably assemble and petition for redress of grievances, the privilege of the writ of habeas corpus," and a handful of other rights explicitly listed in the Constitution.[16]

Justice Stephen J. Field strongly disagreed. The privileges or immunities clause could not refer only to those rights specified in the Constitution because those were already immune from state interference thanks to the supremacy clause. If that was all the new amendment meant to protect, then it "accomplished nothing, and most unnecessarily excited Congress and the people on its passage."[17] Citing *Darcy v. Allen* and many similar cases,[18] Field argued that the amendment was intended to incorporate, among other things, the common-law right to earn a living—what he called "the distinguishing privilege of citizens of the United States. To them, everywhere, all pursuits, all professions, all avocations are open without other restrictions than such as are imposed equally upon all others of the same age, sex, and condition."[19] States could enact protections for public health and safety, which might restrict some aspects of this freedom, "but when once prescribed, the pursuit or calling must be free to be followed by every citizen who is within the conditions designated, and will conform to the regulations. This is the fundamental idea upon which our institutions rest, and unless adhered to in the legislation of the country our government will be a republic only in name." The law restricting the butchering business, he argued, was not a legitimate public health measure, because rather than imposing certain legitimate safety standards, the law simply confined the slaughtering trade to a single private company.[20] The public health excuses offered by the state were a sham.

Given the decision in *Slaughterhouse*, it was no surprise that in the same year, attorney Myra Bradwell lost her case against the state of Illinois in which she alleged that a state law forbidding women from practicing law was a violation of her right to earn a living. Like the Louisiana butchers, Bradwell argued that this right was protected by the privileges or immunities clause. But "[t]he opinion just delivered" in *Slaughterhouse*, the Court concluded, "renders elaborate argument in the present case unnecessary," because "the right to control and regulate the granting of license to practice law" is "one of those powers which are not transferred for its protection to the Federal government."[21]

With one minor exception, the privileges or immunities clause would lie dormant and almost forgotten for more than a century after the *Slaughterhouse* decision.[22] The case effectively eliminated the clause as a meaningful constitutional protection and ensured that, except where other constitutional provisions applied, states would have the power to create monopolies and violate the economic freedom of entrepreneurs without being limited by federal courts.

Changing the Definition of "Monopoly"

Just as the meaning of the word "corporation" evolved during the 19th century, so too the concept of "monopoly" changed dramatically in post–Civil War America. Originally, the word "monopoly" referred to businesses that enjoyed legal immunity from competition. But today, the word is often applied simply to large, successful businesses that have no such privileges. During the latter half of the 19th century, as modern corporations began to proliferate, and mass production and industrialization changed America from an agriculture-based society to one dominated by manufacturing and large-scale industry, "people with the same Jacksonian and free-labor roots split over the meaning of liberty and the proper scope of government power."[23] The resulting division—between those who believed that the pursuit of happiness required the government to take an active role in apportioning economic opportunity and distributing wealth, and those who argued that such interference violated individual liberty and stifled prosperity—would etch itself permanently into American law.

Beginning in the late 1870s, the Populist movement evolved into the Progressive movement—a far more effective intellectual juggernaut that incorporated demands for increased government control over virtually every facet of private life, and especially over business relationships. The two are not easy to distinguish, but where the Populists had railed against corporate domination of small-scale agriculture, the Progressives brought a sophisticated, urban perspective to the movement for government expansion and centralized economic and social planning. Perhaps the most notable difference between the two was one of rhetorical emphasis: whereas the Populists emphasized the individualist values of self-reliance that they believed were threatened by industrial-age capitalism, the Progressives largely rejected the value of individualism, emphasizing instead unity and collectivism. As historian Michael McGerr writes, the Progressives

[d]eveloped a stunningly broad agenda that ranged well beyond the control of big business, the amelioration of poverty, and the purification of politics to embrace the transformation of gender relations, the regeneration of the home, the disciplining of leisure and pleasure, and the establishment of segregation. Progressives wanted not only to use the state to regulate the economy; strikingly, they intended nothing less than to transform other Americans, to remake the nation's feuding, polyglot population in their own middle-class image.[24]

During this transitional era between the Populist and Progressive ages, big businesses like Standard Oil were improving the standard of living for average Americans to an unprecedented degree through dramatic innovations in technology and efficiency.[25] Yet this very improvement was one reason that social activists complained of the growing influence and power of Standard Oil and other corporations. Traditional small-scale businesses, they argued, were being crushed in competition with large soulless corporations like Standard. Ignoring Adam Smith's lesson that government should not protect producers from competition because it increases costs to consumers and slows innovation, muckrakers often argued that government should curb the "lords of industry" so as to protect small businesses, regardless of the effects on consumers. Henry Demarest Lloyd, for example, whose attacks on Standard Oil and other companies received wide attention in the years leading up to the adoption of the Sherman Antitrust Act in 1890, complained that Standard ruthlessly "crush[ed] out the other refiners, who were its competitors"[26] and that "hundreds and thousands of men have been ruined by . . . Standard and the railroads."[27]

The Progressives accused big business of a wide variety of abusive and dangerous practices, including the allegedly unsanitary recklessness and corruption in the meat-packing industry, exposed in Upton Sinclair's *The Jungle*. But to many Progressives, such abuses were only manifestations of a deeper problem: America's obsolete infatuation with individualism. Attacks on the individualistic ethos and on economic self-interest were the major themes of Progressive writing.[28] The "'historical' or 'new' school economists frequently proclaimed that modern conditions rendered competition wholly or partially obsolete as a governing principle," writes one historian.

45

They "urged a new ethic of cooperation to replace older ideals of rivalry, at least in important sectors of the American economy."[29] Many Progressives were socialists; Edward Bellamy's 1888 communist utopian novel *Looking Backward*, which originated the phrase "from cradle to grave,"[30] was the most popular book of its day; it sold hundreds of thousands of copies and led to the formation of 150 socialistic "Bellamy Clubs" in communities across the country.[31] Likewise, Henry Demarest Lloyd argued that "[a] society cannot be made of competitive units,"[32] and that government should put an end to "the liberty of each to do as he will with his own."[33] "As [a] man is bent toward business or patriotism, he will negotiate combinations or agitate for laws to regulate them. The first is capitalistic, the second is social. The first, industrial; the second, moral."[34]

Other Progressives did not go quite so far, arguing instead that increased government oversight of important sectors of the economy could avert outright socialism. But both radicals like Bellamy and relative moderates like Theodore Roosevelt fundamentally agreed on the moral premise that each person should dedicate his or her life's pursuits to serving the needs of others. In his 1906 State of the Union message, Roosevelt called for "the steady endeavor to secure the needed reform by the joint action of the moderate men, the plain men who do not wish anything hysterical or dangerous, but who do intend to deal in resolute common-sense fashion with the real and great evils of the present system." The government, Roosevelt argued, "should not conduct the business of the nation," but "should exercise such supervision as will insure its being conducted in the interest of the nation." Businessmen should therefore aim their work not at providing for themselves and their families, but at serving the desires of others. "No country can develop its full strength so long as the parts which make up the whole each put a feeling of loyalty to the part above the feeling of loyalty to the whole. This is true of sections and it is just as true of classes. The industrial and agricultural classes must work together, capitalists and wage-workers must work together, if the best work of which the country is capable is to be done."[35] Thus, while they differed on some matters, the Progressives uniformly rejected the individual's legal or moral right to pursue his or her own happiness and held that government should restrict or coerce individual behavior so that it would serve "society's needs."

These ideas represented a major change in American political philosophy. Near the end of his career, the influential Progressive intellectual John Dewey explained that Progressivism was a "new liberalism"—one that, unlike the older, classical liberalism that gave birth to the American Constitution, did not hold that government should simply protect individual rights against interference by others. On the contrary, the government should actively "aid and support" the development of each citizen's personality. Progressivism, Dewey explained, is "as much interested in the positive construction of favorable institutions, legal, political and economic as it is in removing abuses and overt oppressions." It would accomplish this "construction" by forcibly redistributing wealth and by replacing the individual's freedom to make his own economic decisions with centralized planning by expert government agencies.[36]

The Progressive revolution was far-ranging indeed. Aside from the secret ballot, female suffrage, and food and drug laws, the Progressives gave the federal government control over the nation's money supply; passed the Sherman Act and established the Interstate Commerce Commission to control the behavior of business corporations; and required schoolchildren to recite the Pledge of Allegiance, helping to inculcate loyalty to the state.[37] They pursued the "science" of eugenics, creating government programs to force people to undergo sterilization programs, and racial segregation to purify and separate the races;[38] they enacted zoning laws to exclude racial minorities and immigrants from neighborhoods;[39] strengthened government's control over education to, in Woodrow Wilson's phrase, "make men as unlike their fathers as possible";[40] amended the Constitution to prohibit the sale of alcohol and to allow government to tax incomes and equalize the wealth of Americans;[41] and a host of other laws and regulatory agencies. Where the Founders held that government exists to protect the rights of individuals and leave them "otherwise free to regulate their own pursuits,"[42] Progressives believed government existed to improve society generally, and they sought to give it the power to dictate the terms on which people would live their lives. "Men are as clay," declared Woodrow Wilson, "in the hands of the consummate leader."[43]

Social scientists and historians of the late 19th century, sympathetic to Progressive theories, have tended to perpetuate two significant misconceptions about that era, which can often obscure our understanding of what the Progressives actually accomplished. First, contrary to a common opinion,[44] few of those who opposed the establishment of the regulatory welfare state were "social Darwinists" who believed economic policies should ignore or weed out the poor for the benefit of the rich upper classes. In fact, defenders of the free market, or "laissez faire," rarely if ever argued on the basis of Darwin or evolutionary theory. Although some writers like Herbert Spencer did use evolutionary theory to bolster their arguments, for the most part the free market's defenders relied not on biological science but on classical economic theory and the moral and political ideas of classical liberalism. In fact, the only Supreme Court justice who might plausibly be described as a Darwinist was Oliver Wendell Holmes Jr., who had no great fondness for the theory of laissez faire.[45] Holmes, for example, enthusiastically endorsed such social Darwinist measures as eugenics programs, but he did not believe in enforcing constitutional protections for the freedom of contract, which he considered a "shibboleth."[46] Although historian Eric Foner argues that Justice Field's dissenting opinion in the *Slaughterhouse Cases* "pioneer[ed]" the theory of social Darwinism,[47] neither Field nor his intellectual allies actually based their views on Darwin's writings or on a callous sink-or-swim philosophy. On the contrary, laissez faire was more often advocated because it offered the poor and underprivileged the best opportunity to advance socially and economically. Economic liberty, Field held, embodied the individual's natural right to "the pursuit of happiness."[48]

The second major misconception about the Gilded Age is that this period was, in fact, an era of laissez faire. In reality, the 19th century featured extensive government intervention in the economy, often in the service of business interests at the expense of their competitors or of workers. Many large corporate enterprises received government protections in the form of tariffs or subsidies.[49] Railroad companies, in particular, received government favors,[50] not only through direct cash subsidies but also by being authorized to use eminent domain to seize land they wanted or through grants of government-owned land. In some cases—as in the *Slaughterhouse Cases*—government gave outright monopolies to private corporations. Although businessmen of the era may have professed a belief in free markets, writes historian Vincent DeSantis, they actually "welcomed government intervention—high tariffs, land grants, and so on—when such interference benefited them."[51] This interference helps explain some of that century's most important criticisms of the "capitalist system." Often the wrongs that these critics saw as endemic to capitalism were, in reality, caused by government intervention on behalf of industry, at the expense of consumers and workers. From the perspective of the free market, such interventions were indeed abuses of government power, abuses that should not have been attributed to the market or used as justification for increased government control.

This confusion over the abuses of government and the free market was reflected in turn-of-the-century political debates as well. Although enemies of the free-market system, like Henry Demarest Lloyd, led the cry for reforms that would rein in the abuses of monopolies, other reformers saw themselves as defending the free-enterprise system, and they often appealed to concepts of fairness rooted in the Whig anti-monopoly tradition.[52] The efforts that led up to the creation of America's antitrust laws, therefore, were often undertaken in the name of the free market, rather than in opposition to it, thanks in part to "a popular association of publicly-chartered corporations with monopolies."[53] Perhaps most surprisingly, Senator John Sherman, the author of the Sherman Antitrust Act, argued that it would interfere only minimally with the operations of American companies but would simply give federal authorities the power to enforce the traditional common-law rules against restraints of trade. He argued that state courts lacked power to enforce long-standing rules against anti-competitive conduct in out-of-state markets and that his bill would simply give that power to federal courts. But it did "not announce a new principle of law."[54] It was only directed "at unlawful combinations. It does not in the least affect combinations in aid of production where there is free and fair competition. It is the right of every man to work, labor, and produce in any lawful vocation and to transport his production on equal terms and conditions and under like circumstances. This is industrial liberty, and lies at the foundation of the equality of all rights and privileges."[55] He believed that the act would not interfere with the opportunity to engage in business in the form of a corporation because "[c]orporate rights are open to all, are not in any sense a monopoly, but tend to promote free competition of all on the same conditions." Rather, "[i]t is the unlawful combination, tested by the rules of common law and human experience, that is aimed at by this bill, and not the lawful and useful combination."[56] The Sherman Act, in his view, would not apply indiscriminately to big businesses, only to those "combinations" that sought "to make competition impossible," that "allow[ed] no competitors," and that were "null and void and the just subject of restraint" under "the rule of both the common and the civil law."[57] Whatever the merits of his arguments, Sherman believed the act would enforce only traditional rules against a narrow class of contracts and that it would not allow control over the decisions of companies that simply gained large market share by hard work and low prices.[58] Sherman seemed to believe simply that the law would implement the principles of the Whig anti-monopoly tradition at the federal level.

The act was heavily amended before passage,[59] and the final result was a law prohibiting "[e]very contract, combination in the form of trust or otherwise, or conspiracy, in restraint of trade or commerce among the several States. . . ."[60] Critics soon charged that the act spelled the end of freedom of contract.[61] They made compelling arguments that the act exceeded its "avowed object" of "prevent[ing] only unlawful restraints of trade."[62] Unfortunately, whether Sherman intended the result or not, those prophesies would prove correct.

Persecuting Business

Today, the antitrust laws are a dangerous and unpredictable mess, threatening businesspeople with financial ruin and criminal prosecution for harmless and even salutary behavior and empowering private interests to exploit and persecute their competition almost at will.[63] The most prominent example of this is a famous 1945 decision finding the aluminum company ALCOA guilty of engaging in monopoly practices.[64] Although Judge Learned Hand acknowledged that ALCOA had not violated anyone's rights and that it had become the industry leader by "fair means," having employed "skill, energy and initiative" in its business,[65] he concluded that the antitrust laws were not restricted to dishonest behavior.[66] A business violated the act any time it triumphed over competitors in the free market by serving its customers well and charging low prices:

> It was not inevitable that [ALCOA] should always anticipate increases in the demand for ingot and be prepared to supply them. Nothing compelled it to keep doubling and redoubling its capacity before others entered the field. It insists that it

never excluded competitors; but we can think of no more effective exclusion than progressively to embrace each new opportunity as it opened, and to face every newcomer with new capacity already geared into a great organization, having the advantage of experience, trade connections and the elite of personnel. Only [if] we interpret "exclusion" as limited to maneuvers not honestly industrial, but actuated solely by a desire to prevent competition, can such a course, indefatigably pursued, be deemed not "exclusionary." So to limit it would in our judgment emasculate the Act; would permit just such consolidations as it was designed to prevent.[67]

In short, by anticipating and meeting the needs of customers, providing quality aluminum at the lowest possible cost, ALCOA had tried to "perpetuate its hold upon the ingot market" and violated the law.[68] This decision warranted Alan Greenspan's indignant comment years later that ALCOA was "condemned for being too successful, too efficient, and too good a competitor." The antitrust laws, he wrote, "have led to the condemnation of productive and efficient members of our society *because* they are productive and efficient."[69]

Federal courts eventually repudiated Hand's view that merely serving customers well can make a business into a monopoly,[70] deciding instead that antitrust laws "protect competition, *not* competitors."[71] Yet some prominent scholars have criticized this new approach[72]—and worse, some state courts have not followed the federal courts' lead. In 2005, for example, the Wisconsin Supreme Court allowed an antitrust case against Microsoft to go forward simply on the ground that Microsoft controlled "a 'dominant and persistent market share,'" which made it difficult for competitors to succeed.[73] As the court explained, the plaintiff in the case was complaining that Microsoft had "created a continuously increasing feedback loop: that is, because 'everyone uses Windows,' all new customers must buy Windows."[74] Among the plaintiffs' complaints was the following:

> Microsoft charged prices in Wisconsin . . . that were substantially above that which could be charged in a competitive market. Microsoft sold its products and distributed licenses to hundreds of thousands of consumers in Wisconsin and conducted extensive advertising and sales activities within Wisconsin. End-users . . . were the foreseeable victims of Microsoft's anticompetitive conduct and have paid artificially inflated prices for Microsoft's software licenses.[75]

Although the plaintiff never argued that Microsoft *forced* people to pay an allegedly high price, or that it had done anything to *forbid* competitors from offering alternatives in the marketplace, the court allowed the case to proceed. The mere fact that Microsoft's programs were successful and popular, leading people to want compatible software, was enough to subject Microsoft to antitrust lawsuits.

There are many other ways in which government uses the antitrust laws to persecute businesses that succeed in the marketplace, not by force or fraud but by providing the public with products and services they want at prices they are willing to pay. Consider, for example, laws that prohibit "loss leaders." Under many state laws, it is illegal to sell products for less than they cost.[76] The theory behind these laws is that large companies can afford to sell some products for below cost as a way of attracting customers, who then buy other products. The seller ends up with a profit, whereas smaller companies cannot afford to do away with their markups. Loss leaders are thus unfair to smaller businesses, and the law prohibits them even though they do no harm to consumers. These laws simply make it illegal to charge people low prices.

In 2005, the Midwest Oil Company was charged with violating Minnesota's prohibition on below-cost pricing when it sold gas for less than cost at its three gas stations in the greater Minneapolis area.[77] The state's Department of Commerce fined the company $140,000 for selling cheap gas after several other retailers complained that Midwest's stations were undercutting their business. Although it is hard to see how selling gas for low prices could harm the public, the Department of Commerce insisted that Midwest Oil should have been glad to escape a more severe penalty: "The record in this case indicates that Midwest Oil offered gasoline for sale below cost at its three stations for an aggregate of 293 days," declared Deputy Commissioner of Commerce Kevin M. Murphy. "The maximum possible fine could have been $2,950,000."[78]

The law Midwest Oil violated was the Minnesota Fair Business Practices Act, a New Deal–era regulation that prohibits any business from engaging in "predatory pricing." This theory holds that powerful businesses will adopt a strategy to undercut competition by selling their products for such a low price that competitors will be driven out of business. Once these competitors are eliminated, the large company will again raise its prices to above-market levels, thereby harming consumers. The problem with this theory is that, as long as new businesses are legally *allowed* to enter the marketplace, they will do so the moment the large "predator" raises its prices. Keeping the door closed to the new firms would require the predator to cut its prices once again, making the tactic so costly that it is unlikely a predator would find it worthwhile. This is why federal judge Frank Easterbrook has called predatory pricing "not a very good gamble, because it is quite unusual for a firm without a patent to hold a 100% market share *and* charge a monopoly price for very long."[79] Whenever new businesses are free to compete, a "predatory-pricing" scheme would at best be only temporarily successful, and consumers would benefit from the resulting "price war."

In fact, there is virtually no evidence that businesses actually engage in predatory-pricing strategies, or that they ever did.[80] Midwest Oil's three Minneapolis-area gas stations were never a threat to its gigantic competitors. And although Standard Oil is often accused of using predatory pricing, research has revealed that it "did not systematically, if ever, use local price cutting in retailing, or anywhere else, to reduce competition."[81] Similar research has debunked other alleged predatory-pricing cases.[82] This has led scholars to describe the predatory-pricing theory as a "myth,"[83] and to conclude that "[p]redatory pricing of the kind designed to eliminate a competitor" is "an infrequent occurrence of fairly insignificant competitive effects."[84]

In two important predatory-pricing cases, *Matsushita Electric Industries v. Zenith Radio*[85] and *Brooke Group v. Brown & Williamson Tobacco*,[86] the Supreme Court held that the federal Robinson-Patman Act—which prohibits predatory pricing, among other things—cannot be used to prosecute businesses that merely charge customers below-cost prices. Recognizing that "discouraging a price cut and forcing firms to maintain supracompetitive prices, thus depriving consumers of the benefits of lower prices in the interim, does not constitute sound antitrust policy,"[87] the Court held that a plaintiff must prove not only that a business charged less than cost but also that it did so with the intent to "harm competition" and that its activities presented a "dangerous likelihood" of creating a monopoly.[88] Given the weakness of the predatory-pricing theory, these decisions erected a significant barrier that protects businesses from most predatory-pricing lawsuits in federal court.[89] But some states, including Minnesota, still allow predatory-pricing lawsuits to go forward, even where there is no realistic possibility that the business accused of charging too little could ever become a monopoly.

Perhaps the biggest problem in antitrust law is vagueness. Antitrust law is so unpredictable that Edwin Rockefeller, former chair of the Antitrust Section of the American Bar Association, recently wrote, "[L]acking any coherent, ascertainable rules in the written antitrust statutes, judges and other government officials make arbitrary decisions using antitrust doctrines based on a faith not easily overcome by reason, logic, or empirical data."[90] Even where a business takes the utmost care to avoid violating the laws, clever lawyers can find ways to reinterpret them in order to accuse a business of breaking them.

One common trick is to change the scope of the relevant market so as to find a monopoly even where there is none. In 2003, when Nestlé sought to buy the Dreyer's ice cream company, federal antitrust lawyers claimed that this would create a monopoly of the "super-premium ice cream" market. Super-premium ice cream is no different from any other ice cream, except that it has a higher butterfat content and is marketed as gourmet ice cream. But the distinction between ice cream and the government-created category of "super-premium" ice cream was important to regulators because, while Nestlé's purchase of Dreyer's would certainly not create a monopoly of the *ice cream* market, federal regulators could declare it a monopoly of the *super-premium* ice cream market. This "monopoly" was thus only an artifact of the arbitrary characterization of a handful of companies as "super-premium" producers. In the end, Nestlé was allowed to purchase Dreyer's, but only after agreeing to sell off part of its business.[91]

More recently, Whole Foods Market's bid to purchase Wild Oats Supermarkets—both businesses specializing in organic and natural foods—was blocked by the Federal Trade Commission on the ground that it would create a monopoly. Of course, it would not have created a monopoly in the *grocery* business, since there are plenty of grocery stores. Nor would it have created a monopoly in the *organic* grocery business, since there are hundreds of thousands of such stores across America. So the FTC simply defined the relevant market as "premium natural and organic supermarkets" whose customers have chosen an "organic lifestyle," and voilá!—an antitrust violation.[92]

The same technique is used at the state level. Consider *Fisherman's Wharf Bay Cruise Corp. v. Superior Court*,[93] a case brought under California's Cartwright Act—a state antitrust law. San Francisco tourists have two choices when venturing out to visit Alcatraz: the Red & White ferry or the Blue & Gold ferry. Both sell tickets at walkup stands located on the city's famous Fisherman's Wharf, but Blue & Gold also marketed its service by wholesaling tickets to hotels, travel agencies, and others, who then resold the tickets to the general public. To turn a profit, Blue & Gold sold these wholesale tickets at a lower price than the "retail" tickets that it sold at the walkup window. Red & White therefore filed suit, arguing that Blue & Gold was offering a "loss leader."

The court acknowledged that "while some of Blue & Gold's wholesale tickets were sold below cost, all of Blue & Gold's walkup or retail tickets were sold substantially above cost."[94] The higher price for Blue & Gold's retail tickets balanced out the lower cost of its wholesale tickets. Thus, if the question were whether Blue & Gold was underpricing *tickets*, the answer was no; the average ticket was priced above cost. But by separating tickets into *wholesale* and *retail* tickets, instead of tickets in general, the court could find illegal price-cutting because Blue & Gold had charged too little for its *wholesale* tickets—even though there was no difference at all between the two kinds of tickets. "In so holding," the court added, "we are mindful of Blue & Gold's admonition that this conclusion sounds the death knell of the blue plate special, the Saturday matinee, and discounted events for the elderly and children." But this, the court said, was "hyperbole," because the law only prohibits loss leaders that are motivated by "an intent to injure competitors or to destroy competition, and not simply to increase sales."[95]

But what is the difference? If to succeed in the marketplace, a business lowers its prices, a competitor will naturally see this as an attempt to "injure" the competition. By the same reasoning, a Sunday matinee or blue-plate special that draws customers away from a competing theater or restaurant will "injure" that competitor. All price decreases, therefore, are subject to prosecution based on subjective characterizations of the company's motive. This is just one of many ways in which businesses that harm nobody, but merely provide goods to the public at low prices, can be persecuted under subjective and arbitrary legal standards. Regulators can define markets however they want in order to find a "monopoly" and then file a lawsuit. Meanwhile, the consumer pays higher prices to businesses that use the law to reduce competition.

Government's Freedom to Create Monopolies

While the antitrust laws pursue successful businesses in an often-pointless attempt to prevent the formation of "monopolies," the government allows itself to form genuine monopolies of its own. This may seem bizarre—especially since many of the Sherman Act's proponents thought it would simply enforce the traditional common-law rules that prohibited the government from setting up monopolies. Yet under the 1943 decision of *Parker v. Brown*,[96] government may monopolize an industry or give an entire sector of the economy to a preferred person or group without fear of obstruction by the antitrust laws.

The theory behind government immunity from the antitrust laws is that the government is inherently monopolistic, since it alone may use physical coercion to prevent or punish lawbreaking. In many cases, it would be silly to challenge legitimate regulatory programs as "restraints on trade," since that is precisely what regulation is for: to restrain trade considered harmful.[97] On the other hand, when government exploits its regulatory power simply to give economic preferences to preferred constituencies, it commits the same wrongs that the Sherman Act prohibits. As the Supreme Court has acknowledged: "It is not the form of the combination or the particular means used but the result to be achieved that the [Sherman Act] condemns. It is not of importance whether the means used to accomplish the unlawful objective are in themselves lawful or unlawful."[98] The same reasoning should apply with even greater force to cases where government acts not as a regulator but as a participant in the market—buying, selling, or providing services like any other business.[99] The Supreme Court admitted that "*with the possible market participant exception*, any action that qualifies as state action is . . . exempt from the operation of the antitrust laws."[100] Yet the Court has never clarified the market-participant exception, and lower court decisions allow government to engage in anti-competitive behavior when it merely runs a business.[101]

In *Sea-Land Service, Inc. v. Alaska Railroad*,[102] the Court of Appeals for the District of Columbia ignored the market-participant exception and held that immunity under the Sherman Act applies across the board to all federal government activities, including a government-run railroad in Alaska, which was sued by two private corporations for attempting to monopolize the railroad market. Acknowledging that it was "anomalous and unfair for a United States instrumentality to escape the regimen of antitrust laws the Government would compel its rivals in commerce to obey," the court nevertheless held that "redress for [this] alleged grievance entails a policy judgment" more properly addressed by the political branches.[103]

Unfortunately, the court did not discuss the distinction between government acting as a market participant and government acting as a regulator. By refusing to consider the history of the antitrust laws, *Alaska Railroad* managed to totally exempt government—the real originator of monopolies—from the Sherman Act, even though the Supreme Court had never gone that far. *Alaska Railroad* therefore "thwart[ed] the very purposes of the antitrust laws."[104] It is ironic that the Sherman Act, intended in part to break the railroad monopolies—and which was held to apply to government-run railroad corporations in the very first Supreme Court case to apply that law[105]—should be blocked a century later from reaching a monopolistic, government-run railroad.

Today, the results are perhaps even more perverse. Consider the case of *U.S. Postal Service v. Flamingo Industries.*[106] In 1970, Congress enacted the Postal Reorganization Act,[107] dissolving the U.S. Post Office and replacing it with the U.S. Postal Service, an ostensibly "independent establishment of the executive branch of the Government of the United States."[108] The act waived sovereign immunity for the USPS[109] and "launched" the Postal Service "into the commercial world," so that the Supreme Court "presume[s] that the Service's liability is the same as that of any other business."[110] In 1977, a House of Representatives report expressed hope that further development of the distinction between government's regulatory activities and government's market-participant activities might mean that antitrust laws would eventually apply to the USPS.[111] Today, the Postal Service acts as a private company, running television ads and selling everything from greeting cards and prepaid telephone cards to bicycling supplies.

The lawsuit began when the USPS breached a contract with Flamingo Industries, whom it had hired to make mail sacks. Flamingo filed suit both for breach of contract and for anti-competitive behavior in violation of the Sherman Act. The trial court dismissed the case, holding that the USPS was immune under *Parker*, but the Ninth Circuit Court of Appeals reversed, explaining that "the Postal

Service lost its sovereign status pursuant to the Postal Reorganization Act of 1970."[112] Thus, the USPS did not enjoy the "status-based" immunity of a government agency. Although it was still immune from antitrust laws for its mail-delivery operations because the Private Express Statutes grant it that privilege, it was not immune from suit as far as its *other* operations were concerned.[113] The Supreme Court, however, reversed that decision, holding that the USPS was immune because Congress had not declared an intention to open up the Postal Service to lawsuits for antitrust violations.

This decision is at odds with the law's clear declarations that the Postal Service has the "status of a private commercial enterprise."[114] Although the law also refers to the USPS as an "independent establishment of the executive branch,"[115] this description also applies to several other entities where antitrust immunity would be absurd, such as the Vietnam Education Foundation[116] or the Holocaust Memorial Museum.[117] Like these essentially private groups, the Postal Service is now "independent of ordinary legislative and executive control"[118] and has many of the characteristics of a private organization: for instance, it owns copyrights, which government agencies are not allowed to hold;[119] it claims a private character under securities trading laws;[120] and its Web address extension is .com rather than .gov.

What sense does it make to treat the Postal Service as a private company for some purposes and not for others? The Court gave several reasons: The Reorganization Act declared the USPS a part of the executive branch, not a public corporation;[121] the USPS has certain government powers, including eminent domain; it is charged with "nationwide, public responsibilities" concerning mail delivery;[122] and it cannot choose its own prices since its rates are set by the Postal Commission.[123] But the designation as an "independent agency" should not be enough, standing on its own, to make the USPS a government entity immune from the Sherman Act. The railroad company in *United States v. Trans-Missouri Freight Ass'n*[124] was also charged with public responsibilities and could exercise eminent domain, yet the Court found that it must obey the act. And the fact that the Postal Service is "isolat[ed] . . . from Presidential or congressional control over its program activities"[125] suggests that it should receive *greater* scrutiny under anti-monopoly laws. As Justice Stevens once noted, "the central concern of both the development of the common law of restraint of trade and our antitrust jurisprudence" has been "[t]he risk that private regulation of market entry, prices, or output may be designed to confer monopoly profits on members of an industry at the expense of the consuming public."[126]

The Court commented on the Postal Service's "nationwide responsibilities," suggesting that it saw protecting the USPS's mail-delivery operations as reason to exempt it from the Sherman Act. But those responsibilities were beside the point because the case did not involve the USPS's mail-delivery activities at all; indeed, subjecting the Postal Service to the Sherman Act would not have opened it to liability for mail delivery, because even private parties are immune from the act when acting on Congress's orders.[127] The real question in the case was whether the USPS was immune for its *other* business activities, where it openly competes with private firms at rates it sets for its own profit. But while the Court acknowledged that the USPS operates "nonpostal lines of business," it found this fact unimportant because "[t]he great majority of the organization's business . . . consists of postal services" and because "the Postal Service's predecessor, the Post Office Department, had nonpostal lines of business, such as money orders and postal savings accounts," but was still immune from the antitrust laws. "The new Postal Service's lines of business beyond the scope of its mail monopoly and universal service obligation do not show it is separate from the Government under the antitrust laws," the Court concluded.[128]

This was the entire analysis in the *Flamingo Industries* decision. The Court did not provide any legal citation or discussion of the intent of the Sherman Act's framers or the difference between government's sovereign acts and private, for-profit acts by the USPS. Instead, simply because the mail-delivery operations (which were irrelevant to the case) *outnumber* the Postal Service's private, admittedly anti-competitive actions, it was given immunity across the board. Under *Flamingo Industries*, the Postal Service may undertake an indefinite number of for-profit enterprises, engage in anti-competitive behavior, and even regulate its own competitors with impunity.[129]

Some critics, including former Chief Justice Warren Burger, have argued that government should not receive total immunity from the anti-monopoly laws. In Burger's view, it was absurd to suggest that the Sherman Act was written "to deal comprehensively and effectively with the evils resulting from contracts, combinations and conspiracies in restraint of trade," and yet "that any similar harms [government] might unleash upon competitors or the economy are absolutely beyond the purview of federal law." Government immunity from antitrust laws "inject[s] a wholly arbitrary variable into a 'fundamental national economic policy.'"[130] Burger was correct. If, as the Supreme Court claims, "the purpose, the subject matter, the context, the legislative history, and the executive interpretation" of the Sherman Act are relevant to determining the act's immunities, then the courts should focus on the *harms* the act aims to prevent, regardless of whether these harms are caused by the government or by private industry.[131]

Like states, local governments frequently use their power to monopolize trade. In no business is this more obvious than in the taxi and limousine business. The Public Transportation Commission of Hillsborough County, Florida, requires that all limousines charge at least $40 per ride, no matter how brief the ride might be. No such rule is required for taxis, which may charge as little as they wish. Asked to explain why the commission makes it illegal to charge low rates for limousine rides, city officials replied that the purpose of the $40-per-hour-minimum rule was to

> create a balance between the different transportation service "markets" . . . [and to] keep the two industries [taxis and limousines] separate and therefore not directly competing against each other. This way, both manage to survive in their respective market area and the "balance" is maintained. . . . The intent is to prevent a company from using a limousine to perform "taxicab" type service by transporting passengers at a rate comparable to that of a taxicab.[132]

In other words, the law is a price-fixing scheme designed to protect taxi companies from competition. If the limousine owners themselves were to adopt a $40-minimum price, they would be subject to criminal prosecution under the antitrust laws for price-fixing. Yet county officials can impose the same rule, having the same effects, for explicitly anti-competitive reasons, and courts will do nothing.

After the Supreme Court suggested in 1978 that cities could be sued for violating the antitrust laws,[133] the Federal Trade Commission filed cases against Minneapolis and New Orleans for monopolizing the taxicab industry. In another case, the Village of Grayslake in Illinois was found liable for $28.5 million for using its power to block a residential development.[134] Confronted with a potential flood of similar antitrust lawsuits, cities that abused their power to prohibit fair competition demanded that Congress give them immunity,[135] and in 1984 Congress complied, passing the Local Government Antitrust Act[136] to immunize local governments and the businesses that conspire with them from liability under the antitrust laws.

It is supremely ironic that the government is today exempt from a law that was modeled on the common-law prohibition against government-created monopolies, particularly given that government is far more capable of causing the kinds of injuries associated with monopolies than are private businesses. This irony reached its nadir in 1972 when a Supreme Court opinion described the Sherman Act as "the Magna Carta of free enterprise" in the United States.[137] When Chancellor Kent used this phrase to describe the English Statute of Monopolies,[138] he meant that the law protected every individual's right to earn a living without unreasonable interference from government. But today's antitrust laws allow government virtual carte blanche to interfere with the individual's right to earn a living.

Antitrust Immunity for Favored Private Groups

Not only is the government itself allowed to ignore the anti-monopoly laws, but private companies are also immune even when they lobby the government to give them monopoly status. In one of the earliest cases interpreting the Sherman Act, the Supreme Court held that it applied to a railroad company that had sought special government privileges against competition—the classic definition of a monopoly,[139] but today under the "the *Noerr-Pennington* doctrine,"[140] companies that urge lawmakers to give them such privileges cannot be charged under the antitrust laws. The theory behind this doctrine is that the Sherman Act "is a code that condemns trade restraints, not political activity,"[141] and that any attempt to control lobbying "would raise important constitutional questions" regarding freedom of speech.[142] But antitrust prosecutions that seek to bar businesses from conspiring with *each other* to set prices also restrict their freedom of expression, as do insider-trading laws that limit the disclosure or use of certain information about stocks. The Court also disingenuously asserted that there is "no basis whatever in the legislative history of [the Sherman] Act" for prohibiting businesses from colluding with government for economic favors.[143] In fact, state-sanctioned monopolies had long been forbidden by the common-law anti-monopoly rules on which the Sherman Act was based, and in the years immediately following the act's passage, some courts held that the term "to monopolize" *only* referred to attempts by firms to obtain special government favors, or attempts to draft contracts that violated the common law.[144] Finally, the Sherman Act's terms are broad, encompassing "anti-competitive behavior" in any form without distinction. As one critic writes:

> When a group of competitors or a single firm influence governmental process for the purpose of restraining trade or monopolizing the market, the statutory objectives of the Sherman Act are placed in serious jeopardy. The broad language of the antitrust statute ought to compel the federal courts to regulate this form of predatory "petitioning of government. . . ." To do otherwise might defeat the purpose of antitrust law. . . .[145]

Yet today, even if a private business's lobbying activity is "motivated by an anticompetitive purpose, has an anticompetitive effect, and injures competitors or competition," that business cannot be sued for conspiring to monopolize trade.[146] It is true, of course, that the First Amendment protects the right of businesses to lobby the government, which is the principle underlying the *Noerr-Pennington* doctrine. But the same principle should then also apply to protect the right of businesses to collude with each other. Prosecuting businesses on the one hand for conspiring to establish monopolies, while allowing them openly to obtain the establishment of even more stringent monopolies, is inconsistent and contrary to the purportedly pro-competitive intent of the antitrust laws.

Another group that receives immunity from the antitrust laws is organized labor. Just as manufacturers might form a cartel by agreeing among themselves to withhold products from the market except at an inflated price, workers can agree among themselves not to work except for an inflated wage. But the manufacturers would be prosecuted under the antitrust laws for price-fixing, whereas labor unions can do the same thing with impunity. Labor unions are price-fixing cartels, whose practices can be just as disruptive to the economy as price-fixing by other businesses, if not more so.[147]

At first, organized labor's anti-competitive conduct was prosecuted as violating the Sherman Act. In *Loewe v. Lawlor*,[148] for example—famous as the "Danbury Hatters' Case"—the Supreme Court held that labor unions that organized boycotts against businesses were liable under the act because the common law had long prohibited boycotts as "agreements in restraint of trade." Angry labor activists demanded that unions be exempted from the law,[149] and beginning with the 1913 Clayton Act, they were. Yet there is no principled justification for exempting the entire realm of labor relations from antitrust control. If government ought to police the marketplace to ensure "competitiveness," it makes no sense to give labor unions—which can be every bit as oppressive to workers and harmful to consumers as any other organized enterprise—a free pass. As Richard A. Epstein notes, exempting labor unions from the antimonopoly laws "shows all the indelible marks of special interest legislation."[150] Exempting unions from antitrust prosecution, Epstein concludes, "had one and only one function: to preserve and advance union monopoly power."[151]

As the law stands today, unions engage in practices far beyond what any other business entity would be entitled to do under the antitrust laws. Like the riverboat pilots in Mark Twain's day,[152] labor unions and similar trade organizations frequently control not only the terms of employment but also the terms on which newcomers may enter a trade. Consider, for example, the market for legal services. States require anyone who wants to practice law to first pass the state bar examination. But most states make it illegal to even take the examination without graduating from a law school accredited by the American Bar Association—a privately run professional organization, similar to a union, for lawyers. This gives the ABA a chokehold on new entries into the profession: a role that would clearly violate the Sherman Act's prohibition on cartels.[153] The bar exam itself is routinely used to protect insiders from fair economic competition. Florida, New York, and other states recently raised the score required to pass the bar because "too many" people were passing—something that makes no sense if the exam were intended to protect the general public from incompetent lawyers, but that makes perfect sense if the goal is to create an artificial scarcity of lawyers.[154] Yet the legal profession gets away with such conduct because it does so with government cooperation.[155]

The Strange Afterlife of Freedom of Trade

The Whig anti-monopoly tradition centered on a consensus on two major points: first, individuals ought to be free to earn a living without unfair government interference; and second, society suffers when either laws or private contracts restrict the availability of goods or services on the market. Early courts, therefore, routinely invalidated private agreements by which workers promised not to engage in a certain trade. Today, this principle survives in cases involving the enforceability of "noncompetition" clauses in employment contracts. Courts regard these contracts skeptically, enforcing them only where they are "reasonable" and generally requiring that the agreement apply only within a specific geographical area so that the parties may practice their trade outside a certain locale.[156] But courts also often invalidate such agreements, and many states outlaw them by statute. California, for example, forbids "every contract by which anyone is restrained from engaging in a lawful profession, trade, or business of any kind."[157] Yet there may be any number of legitimate reasons for entering into such contracts.[158] A skilled practitioner might be unwilling to take on an entry-level employee if he fears he might be training his own competition, for example. And businesses that deal with confidential information or trade secrets routinely require employees to sign noncompetition agreements in exchange for being allowed to learn a trade secret.

The remarkable result is that the Whig anti-monopoly tradition that began by proclaiming the right of each person to earn a living without unreasonable government interference has turned itself inside out. Businesses that do nothing worse than provide goods people want at prices they are willing to pay are prosecuted—while government-created monopolies that exclude innocent people from earning a living are shielded from the law. Companies like Standard Oil, ALCOA, and Microsoft, which revolutionized American life, saving countless hours of labor and countless millions of dollars, are treated like criminals—whereas labor unions that often terrorize "scab" workers (who seek nothing more than to earn a day's pay) are allowed to continue their practices virtually unmolested.[159] The very vocabulary of economic freedom has been perverted, so that the word "monopoly"—which once referred to the use of physical (i.e., government) coercion to prevent fair competition—now means the exact opposite: a business that has succeeded by treating customers well and cutting prices. Meanwhile, the antitrust laws prohibit businesses from lowering their prices, or from raising their prices, or from charging different prices to different people, or from charging the same price to different people! Laws that prevent people from earning an honest living are upheld as constitutional in almost every circumstance, whereas contracts in which people freely agree not to go into competition with their former employers are frequently invalidated. On all sides, the right to earn a living is under assault.

·

4. The Contracts Clause: Victim of the Living Constitution

The strange career of the Whig anti-monopoly tradition is echoed in some ways by the history of another of the Constitution's important protections for economic freedom: the contracts clause. Part of the original Constitution of 1787, this clause—which forbids states from making any law that "impair[s] the Obligation of Contracts"[1]—became a powerful restriction on state regulatory power during the 19th century, only to be eclipsed during the Great Depression and weakly revived in a barely recognizable form in recent decades. A century ago, the great legal historian Henry Maine called this clause the single most important provision in the Constitution;[2] in 1978, the Supreme Court could admit that it had "receded into comparative desuetude."[3]

Laws impairing the obligations of contracts have a long and gloomy history in Western politics. Ancient Greek cities were plagued by class conflicts between the wealthy few, who lent money, and the poor, who borrowed it, and who, in bad economic times, would sometimes rise up in bloody rebellion, demanding that their debts be "forgiven." In some cases, the heavy-handed actions of the lenders may have justified these rebellions,[4] but in general, laws abolishing debts harm societies by deterring lending. If creditors cannot be sure that they will be paid back, they will be far less likely to lend their less wealthy neighbors money to buy farmland, equipment, or other necessities. The consequences are economic stagnation and poverty.

America's Founders were deeply familiar with the classical examples of ancient Greece, but they were also familiar with a more recent example of anti-creditor agitation. In the 1780s, farmers burdened by heavy debts and inflation led what came to be called Shays's Rebellion, after its leader Daniel Shays.[5] This makeshift army of more than 1,000 men closed courts to prevent foreclosures and debt sales and stormed the state supreme court in Springfield, Massachusetts.

Although the rebellion was put down before much blood was shed, it and similar agitation in other states worried America's political leaders, who saw these scenes as all too reminiscent of the ancient troubles. Not all the resistance was violent; in an economically struggling America, state legislators eager for popularity with common voters often proposed laws restricting the contractual rights of those who had lent money. Such legislation was understandable, given the harsh circumstances of the day, but while it benefited debtors in the short run, it ultimately harmed them by drying up credit and making it harder to borrow money in the future. Moreover, such laws worked a positive injustice on financiers who invested their money in the mortgages on the condition that they could reclaim some of their investment, if necessary, through foreclosure.

Debt-relief laws replace the principles of justice with the mere power of political majorities. A person who lends money to another deserves to be repaid, but laws abolishing debts eliminate that right simply because there were fewer lenders than borrowers.[6] A law abolishing debts simply eliminates the rights of one person, the lender, for the benefit of another, the borrower—not in punishment for an actual crime but simply because the lenders lack the political power to see that their contractual rights are respected. Eliminating their rights in this way would be an injustice that the Founders believed the Constitution should ban majorities from committing. In *The Federalist*, James Madison described laws abolishing debts as "improper," "wicked," and "contrary to the first principles of the social compact, and to every principle of sound legislation,"[7] not merely because they damaged the economy but because they placed the rights of the minority (lenders) at the mercy of majority will.

Madison drew an instructive analogy between the laws that majorities enact and a lawsuit between two parties. "No man is allowed to be a judge in his own cause," he wrote, "because his interest would certainly bias his judgment, and, not improbably, corrupt his integrity."[8] But in a republican government, the majority not only makes the law but also indirectly judges the constitutionality of its own actions since it indirectly appoints judges. Suppose, therefore, that the legislature enacts a law abolishing debts. On this issue, "the creditors are parties on one side and the debtors on the other. Justice ought to hold the balance between them. Yet the parties are, and must be, themselves the judges" of whether such a law is legitimate, and "the most numerous party . . . [will] prevail." In such cases, there is an awful "temptation" for the "predominant party to trample on the rules of justice."[9] By prohibiting states from passing such laws, the Framers of the Constitution hoped to prevent legislative majorities from substituting might for right. The will of the majority would not, therefore, be the law— rather, the will of the majority would be constrained by law.[10] Thus, the contracts clause "prohibits all retrospective, redistributive legislation which violates vested contractual rights by transferring all or part of the benefit of a bargain from one contracting party to another."[11]

Public Contracts

The first important Supreme Court decision to explain the contracts clause was *Fletcher v. Peck,*[12] an 1810 case arising from a scandal in which almost every member of the Georgia legislature schemed to sell valuable lands at an enormous discount to four companies that had paid substantial bribes to the legislators. Angry voters threw the corrupt members out, and the new legislators quickly repealed the previous act, but not before some of the companies who had obtained land sold it to new buyers. Some of these new buyers were unaware of the fraud underlying the transaction, and when the original owners demanded that they return the land, they refused, leading to a lawsuit that reached the Supreme Court.

Fletcher is a classic work illustrating the genius of Chief Justice John Marshall. Only a little over 5,000 words long, it contains not a single case citation, but proceeds by irresistible logic from premises to conclusion. Every contract, Marshall held, is really made up of two agreements—first, the agreement to exchange one thing for another and second, "a contract not to reassert that right" to the thing that was exchanged. "A party is, therefore, always estopped by his own grant."[13] Thus, when Georgia sold the land, it agreed not only to exchange the land for money but also to respect that completed transaction and not to try to undo it later. Even if the first agreement was corrupt, therefore, the state could not violate the second component of its contract. To do so would impair the obligation of contract, in violation of the Constitution. "A law annulling conveyances between individuals, and declaring that the grantors should [possess] . . . their former estates, notwithstanding those grants, would be as repugnant to the constitution as a law discharging the vendors of property from

The Right to Earn a Living

the obligation of executing their contracts by conveyances."[14] The innocent purchasers of the land could not be forced to return it even though preceding sales were tainted by fraud.

The *Fletcher* doctrine became the basis for constitutional restrictions on state power to redistribute the fairly acquired wealth of private parties. It also limited state authority to change the terms of charters granted by the legislature. In *Dartmouth College v. Woodward*,[15] the Supreme Court held that under the *Fletcher* doctrine, states could not unilaterally alter corporate charters because it would deprive the corporation's owners of their settled rights, in the same way that Georgia had tried to deprive bona fide purchasers of land sold by the state. In 1769, the New Hampshire legislature issued Dartmouth College a charter to operate a college, specifying certain procedures for governing the school. In 1816, the legislature amended the charter, expanding the number of trustees and creating a new board of governors; the existing board of trustees refused to accept these alterations and a lawsuit ensued. Chief Justice Marshall ruled in favor of the college. "It can require no argument to prove, that the circumstances of this case constitute a contract," he wrote.[16] Dartmouth was not a government institution, but "a private corporation" that was "really endowed by private individuals, who have bestowed their funds for the propagation of the Christian religion among the Indians, and for the promotion of piety and learning generally."[17] The new law "re-organized" Dartmouth "in such a manner, as to convert a literary institution, moulded according to the will of its founders, and placed under the control of private literary men, into a machine entirely subservient to the will of government." Whether or not this was good policy, it was "not according to the will of the donors, and [was] subversive of that contract, on the faith of which their property was given."[18] Thus, the new law impaired the obligations of the existing charter, which was a contract protected by the Constitution. If states could unilaterally rewrite corporate charters granted to private investors, Marshall explained, "no man ever will be, the founder of a college," since he would know "that an act of incorporation constitutes no security for the institution . . . that it is immediately to be deemed a public institution, whose funds are to be governed and applied, not by the will of the donor, but by the will of the legislature."[19]

The *Dartmouth College* decision recognized corporate charters as private property and enforced strong limits on the state's power to manipulate the rights of the owners. But at the same time, the case had some troubling implications for the future of the free market. If the legislature could not manipulate a corporate charter once granted, such charters might become monopolies. If a state sought to open up a market it had previously reserved to a single group through a corporate charter, the holders of the charter could plausibly argue that allowing competitors would deprive them of their expectations and thus violate the contracts clause.

That was the issue confronting the Court in the case of *Charles River Bridge v. Warren Bridge*,[20] discussed in chapter 2. The owners of the Charles River Bridge contended that by granting a charter to the Warren Bridge Company, the state had essentially repealed the charter that it had earlier granted to the Charles River Bridge's owners, because the new, free bridge would destroy their corporation entirely. If the state could not unilaterally alter Dartmouth College's charter, how could it unilaterally destroy the value of the charter granted to their company? The opening of a free bridge next to their toll bridge not only violated the terms of their charter by depriving them of their alleged monopoly but also violated the contracts clause, just as New Hampshire violated the clause by tampering with Dartmouth College's charter.

Chief Justice Marshall heard arguments in the *Charles River Bridge* case but died before making a decision. He was replaced by Chief Justice Roger Taney, but the case was not decided until 1837, six years after the Court had first heard the attorneys argue. The decision shocked many of Marshall's admirers. The Court refused to read a monopoly privilege into the Charles River Bridge charter without explicit wording to that effect. And without a monopoly grant, there was nothing to stop the legislature from granting a competing charter to another company, even if doing so decreased the value of the existing charter. The purpose of government, Taney wrote, was "to promote the happiness and prosperity of the community," and if by granting a corporate charter to one group of investors the state thereby surrendered its power to grant other charters to others, then government could not accomplish this end.

> [W]hen a corporation alleges, that a state has surrendered . . .
> its power of improvement and public accommodation, in
> a great and important line of travel . . . the community have
> a right to insist . . . that its abandonment ought not to be

> presumed, in a case, in which the deliberate purpose of the
> state to abandon it does not appear. The continued existence
> of a government would be of no great value, if, by implica-
> tions and presumptions, it was disarmed of the powers neces-
> sary to accomplish the ends of its creation, and the functions
> it was designed to perform, transferred to the hands of priv-
> ileged corporations. . . . While the rights of private property
> are sacredly guarded, we must not forget, that the commu-
> nity also have rights, and that the happiness and well-being
> of every citizen depends on their faithful preservation.[21]

Taney's wording said nothing about the free market; his concern
was to protect the power of states to serve public needs by char-
tering new public works when old ones became obsolete. Corporations had not yet evolved into the purely private entities they are
today, so Taney naturally assumed that any public work would be
undertaken by a public "corporation" organized by government, in
which private parties would invest and on which they would expect
a return. But by holding that one corporate charter did not prevent
the legislature from granting a competing corporate charter later on,
Taney also inadvertently did a great service for the advent of market
competition among corporations.

Justice Joseph Story, a devout admirer of Marshall, argued in a bit-
ter dissent that the Court was abandoning the principles of *Fletcher*,
Dartmouth College, and other cases. First, he disagreed with the
Court's view that corporate charters should be strictly construed
to avoid inferring monopoly privileges. Throughout history, he
argued, contracts between the king and his subjects were "liberally
expounded, that the dignity and justice of the government may never
be jeoparded, by petty evasions and technical subtleties."[22] Thus, the
charter between Massachusetts and the owners of the Charles River
Bridge ought to be "construed favorably to the grantee[s], so as to
secure [them] in the enjoyment of what is actually granted."[23] Story
thought it was unfair to accuse the Charles River Bridge's owners
of seeking monopoly power. They were simply demanding a fair
return for their hard work: "If the government means to invite its
citizens to enlarge the public comforts and conveniences, to establish bridges, or turnpikes, or canals, or railroads, there must be some
pledge, that the property will be safe; that the enjoyment will be
co-extensive with the grant; and that success will not be the signal

of a general combination to overthrow its rights and to take away its profits."[24] The owners of the first bridge had undertaken all the risk and difficulty of building the bridge, uncertain that their doing so would be financially worthwhile. Indeed, it is hard to argue with Story's observation that if the Warren Bridge's charter had been granted only one year after the Charles River Bridge's instead of 40 years, the unfairness would have been obvious and the legislature would have been universally condemned.[25]

A half century later, in 1884, the Supreme Court reiterated that the contracts clause did not forbid legislatures from revoking monopoly privileges after granting them. In *Butcher's Union Slaughter-House & Live-Stock Landing Co. v. Crescent City Live-Stock Landing and Slaughter-House Company*,[26] the Court held that the state of Louisiana could eliminate the same butcher monopoly that it had created a decade earlier, giving rise to the *Slaughterhouse Cases*. The state had adopted a new constitution that explicitly banned monopolies in the slaughtering trade. The Crescent City Company, which had received a monopoly a decade earlier, lost its monopoly and the value of its stock collapsed. The company sued, arguing that revoking this grant violated the contracts clause. The Court rejected this argument. "'No legislature can bargain away the public health or the public morals,'" it explained. "'Government is organized with a view to their preservation, and cannot divest itself of the power to provide for them. For this purpose the legislative discretion is allowed, and the discretion cannot be parted with any more than the power itself.'"[27] Likewise, in *Stone v. Mississippi*,[28] the Court held that when the legislature authorized a group to conduct a lottery, and then later revoked that permission, the investors organizing the lottery could not sue under the contracts clause. The legislature was incapable, the Court said, of making a binding promise not to exercise in the future its authority to protect public health, safety, and morality, even when such authority deprived a person or a company of its expected income.

Reserved Power to Regulate

These cases indicate some of the intriguing tensions in the jurisprudence of the contracts clause. First, states were obligated to respect the terms of the charters that they granted to private companies, but those charters would not usually be construed as creating monopolies, in violation of other basic values of American constitutional law. Second, although contracts were protected from state interference in most cases, the state still retained some power to act in protection of the general public, even if doing so would interfere with the value of a charter. This latter tension developed into the doctrine of *Stone* and *Butcher's Union*, under which all contracts were interpreted as including a reserved power on behalf of the state to intervene in some cases.

The Supreme Court first addressed this theory in an 1827 case[29] but elaborated on it in the 1848 decision of *West River Bridge Company v. Dix*,[30] when the justices concluded that all contracts, regardless of their terms, incorporate certain "conditions" that "are superinduced by the preexisting and higher authority of the laws of nature, of nations, or of the community to which the parties belong." Since "[e]very contract is made in subordination" to the state's power to impose such conditions, contracts "must yield to their control, as conditions inherent and paramount, wherever a necessity for their execution shall occur."[31] The *Stone* Court also took this approach. Since legislative powers were incorporated into each contract, it did not impair a contract for the government to exercise these powers. In other words, contracts with the government included certain unwritten provisions allowing government to alter the agreements as necessary to protect the general public.

But *Stone* revealed problems with this theory. That decision meant that government could alter agreements to advance a loosely defined class of public policies regardless of the effects those policies might have on people or businesses that thought their contractual rights were clear and secure. For example, the government could "protect" the public from lotteries—the Court considered gambling "wrong in [its] influences"[32]—despite its clear promise to allow them. That promise had induced investors to devote their time and money to the enterprise. But the state's actions destroyed those investments and injured the company's directors, proving the wisdom of Chief Justice Marshall's warning that if states always retained power to alter contractual terms, they would be free to do as they pleased, overriding the contractual or property rights of citizens and businesses. A state could pass a law "declaring that all contracts should be subject to legislative control, and should be discharged as the legislature might prescribe," for example, and under the *Dix* theory, such a provision "would become a component part of every contract, and be one of its conditions." Contracts would then be rendered without meaningful protection, and the contracts clause "would lie prostrate . . . construed into an inanimate, inoperative, unmeaning clause."[33] *Stone* took a long step in this direction, and later cases went even further, holding that the "superinduced" powers of government also controlled contracts between private parties. The state therefore reserved authority to alter any and all contracts to accomplish whatever goals legislatures believed to be in the public interest.[34]

At first, a broad national consensus about the appropriate limits of government power kept in check this threat to the freedom of economic choice. The same year that *Dix* was decided, Alexis de Tocqueville commented: "[T]ill now no one in the United States has dared to profess the maxim that everything is allowed [to government] in the interests of society, an impious maxim apparently invented in an age of freedom in order to legitimize every future tyrant. Thus, while the law allows the American people to do everything, there are things which religion prevents them from imagining and forbids them to dare."[35] Society's mores thus restrained the tyranny of the majority that might otherwise override the Constitution's protections for individual freedom. With the coming of the 20th century, however, the police powers were increasingly stretched by Populist and Progressive activists.[36]

The Modern Contracts Clause

At the end of World War I, several East Coast cities faced serious housing shortages. Rents were rising, and many residents faced foreclosure and eviction. New York, Washington, and other cities responded by passing rent-control measures prohibiting landlords from evicting tenants who paid a "reasonable" rent. The landlords challenged these laws as violations of the contracts clause because they impaired their lease contracts. But the Supreme Court upheld the laws, explaining that "contracts are made subject to [the] exercise of the power of the state"[37] and that the emergency justified the government's actions.

A decade later, an even greater emergency struck: the Great Depression. In Minnesota, the Depression was particularly hard on farmers who were unable to make payments on their mortgages and faced foreclosure. About half the land in the state was mortgaged, and the foreclosures were so numerous that the foreclosure sales drove down land values, meaning that even after debtors had their land sold from under them they were still often unable to discharge their debts.[38] The situation became so bad that mobs disrupted mortgage sales and marched menacingly on the state capitol. The state's socialist governor, Floyd Olson, warned that "if the legislature—the Senate in particular—does not make ample provision for the sufferers in this state," he would "declare martial law" and "[a] lot of people who are now fighting the [proposed debtor-relief] measures because they happen to possess considerable wealth will be brought in by provost guards."[39]

The legislature caved in to these threats on April 18, 1933, unanimously approving a law modeled on the New York rent-control law. The Minnesota act extended the period during which a resident could reclaim mortgaged property after the bank had foreclosed and sold it. That period had been one year, but the new law allowed judges to extend it to two years. The law also sought to avoid constitutional conflict by declaring that no such extension would be granted if it would "substantially diminish or impair the value of the contract . . . without reasonable allowance to justify the exercise of the police power."[40] The law also allowed courts to reject a foreclosure sale and to require a new sale if the sale price was judged to be "inadequate."[41]

The problem with this law is that the Constitution's ban on laws impairing contractual obligations contains no "emergency" exception. On the contrary, one of the primary reasons for adopting the contracts clause was to prevent disruptions such as Shays's Rebellion, in which farmers had mobbed foreclosure sales and closed courts just like their Minnesota descendants a century and a half later. Indeed, more than one state enacted so-called debtor stay laws, similar to the Minnesota act, at the time of Shays's Rebellion, which was one reason the contracts clause was written. Law professor William Prosser, who had consulted with the legislature on drafting the Minnesota law, confessed a year later that the contracts clause "was inserted in the Constitution for the purpose of preventing precisely the type of legislation which was contemplated in Minnesota in 1933."[42]

Although the law was aimed primarily at relieving farmers, the Blaisdells were not farmers but owners of a large house in Minneapolis, 11 rooms of which they rented out to boarders. They defaulted on their mortgage and the bank foreclosed, purchasing the property for $3,700, whereupon the Blaisdells applied for an extension of the redemption period. The trial court rejected the application on the ground that the law violated the contracts clause, and the Blaisdells appealed. The Minnesota Supreme Court reversed this decision, holding that the economic emergency justified the legislation. The United States Supreme Court agreed: "[T]he reservation of the reasonable exercise of the protective power of the State is read into all contracts."[43] And to "protect" the public, the state could act by altering the terms of the Blaisdells' lease.

Perhaps more than any other Supreme Court decision, *Blaisdell* demonstrates the dangers of the "living Constitution" theory, under which the meaning of constitutional provisions can change to meet changing circumstances.[44] Chief Justice Charles Evans Hughes, who wrote the opinion, admitted that the contracts clause was adopted to prevent the sort of legislation at issue in the *Blaisdell* case, but he held that the Constitution must be interpreted broadly to allow broader legislative discretion than the Founders had allowed: "It is no answer to say that this public need was not apprehended a century ago, or to insist that what the provision of the Constitution meant to the vision of that day it must mean to the vision of our time." But he provided no explanation of why the Constitution's terms should be interpreted differently at different times. Instead, he simply shrugged off the question: "If by the statement that what the Constitution meant at the time of its adoption it means today, it is intended to say that the great clauses of the Constitution must be confined to the interpretation which the framers, with the conditions and outlook of their time, would have placed upon them, the statement carries its own refutation."[45]

But that is fallacious—the statement does not carry its own refutation, and Hughes's claim does not qualify as an argument at all. It certainly did not adequately answer Justice George Sutherland's observation in dissent that "[i]f the contract impairment clause, when framed and adopted, meant that the terms of a contract for the payment of money could not be altered *in invitum* by a state statute enacted for the relief of hardly pressed debtors to the end and with the effect of postponing payment or enforcement during and because of an economic or financial emergency, it is but to state the obvious to say that it means the same now."[46] For Hughes to claim that this statement "carries its own refutation" was merely to dodge the need for serious explanation and to assert that the Constitution's terms would simply no longer be enforced. As one commentator has written, Hughes's declaration that the constitutional ban on laws abridging contracts would only bar *unreasonable* abridgments was reminiscent "of the scene from *Animal Farm* in which reexamination of a provision that '[n]o animal shall drink alcohol' reveals it to outlaw drinking '*to excess.*'"[47]

Nevertheless, the *Blaisdell* decision would cripple enforcement of the contracts clause for the rest of the century. Although in theory the decision applied only to emergency circumstances, it was a mere six years later that the Court allowed legislatures to alter contracts even in nonemergency situations. "The emergency of the depression may have caused the [legislation at issue in *Blaisdell*]," the Court noted, "but the weakness in the financial system brought to light by that emergency remains. If the legislature could enact the legislation . . . in that emergency," then there was "no reason" why similar legislation could not be enacted in less urgent circumstances.[48] The English poet John Milton once warned that "necessity" is "the tyrant's plea,"[49] and *Blaisdell* proved that what is permitted for the sake of temporary emergencies often becomes routine conduct in later years.[50] From that point on, legislatures were free to disturb contracts whenever their actions were "reasonable," which meant that legislatures could do whatever they thought was good for the public. The theory of the "living Constitution" had killed off one of that document's most vital provisions.

In the 1970s, the contracts clause experienced a brief and strange revival in a short series of cases involving government's breaching contracts with private parties. In *United States Trust Co. v. New Jersey*[51] and *Allied Structural Steel v. Spannaus*,[52] the Supreme Court considered the constitutionality of state laws repealing charter rights held by private parties. In *United States Trust*, the legislatures of New York and New Jersey repealed certain promises made to the Port Authority, promises that had protected Port Authority funds from being siphoned off to uses that the Port Authority's shareholders did not approve. The Port Authority contended that the repeal violated the contracts clause, and the Supreme Court agreed. It acknowledged that *Blaisdell* and later cases gave states "wide discretion" to "protect the . . . general welfare" by manipulating contractual relationships and that states were limited only by the requirement that the legislation "must be upon reasonable conditions and of a character appropriate to the public purpose." These requirements were extremely lax because "courts properly defer to legislative judgment as to the necessity and reasonableness of a particular measure."[53] Yet the Court announced that such deference should not apply"[w]hen a State impairs the obligation of its own contract."[54] In such cases, "the State's self-interest is at stake," meaning that *Blaisdell*-style deference might blind the Court to unfair self-dealing by legislatures.[55]

In *Spannaus*, the Court's attention returned once more to Minnesota, which passed a law requiring businesses to maintain existing pension plans; if a company shut down its pension plan or closed a Minnesota branch office, it would be fined unless it provided full pensions for all employees who had served for 10 years or more. The steel company's pension plan covered only employees who had not quit or been fired before reaching the age of 65. Thus, when the company closed its Minnesota office and laid off several workers, most of them did not qualify for a pension under the company's plan; but because they had worked for the company for more than 10 years, they were entitled to a pension under the new law. When the company was fined, it filed a lawsuit arguing that the law impaired the contract established in the company's pension plan.[56] The Supreme Court agreed. Unlike *United States Trust*, the *Spannaus* case did not involve a contract between the government and a private party; nevertheless, the Court found that the law violated the contracts clause because it had "nullifie[d] express terms of the company's contractual obligations and impose[d] a completely unexpected liability" on it.[57] Yet this decision's sweeping language never translated into a serious revival of the contracts clause; in 1987, the Court returned to its deferential attitude, refusing to "read literally" the Constitution's prohibition on laws impairing the obligations of contract.[58] Today, the clause appears to forbid only completely irrational laws—already forbidden by the due process clause—or to restrict the government's ability to alter its own contractual obligations as in *United States Trust*.

In a way, this is an ironic reversal of the contract clause's original purpose; it was aimed at protecting *private* contracts, not contracts with the government. Although *Fletcher*, *Dartmouth College*, and *Charles River Bridge* all involved contracts with the government, there is "no evidence that the framers intended the contracts clause to apply to any contracts to which the state was a party," and many Framers expressly denied such a possibility.[59] For one thing, laws altering government's obligations are probably less prone to abuse than laws altering contracts between private parties, because a public contract is likely to have a politically influential constituency able to resist legislative attempts to alter it, whereas the private parties to an everyday contract—like the mortgage contract in *Blaisdell*—are less likely to have the political power to defend their contractual rights. It is also far more likely that the alteration of a public contract will be genuinely in the public interest: normally, the state's "self-interest" is the same as the "public interest," at least when it comes to conserving taxpayer money.[60]

Today, government is almost completely free to alter contractual arrangements between private parties, and only slightly less free to alter contracts between individuals and the government. Politicians have almost unreviewable power to change the terms of bargained-for agreements retroactively, which deters investment, harms innovation, and prevents the creation of new jobs.

One typical example of government manipulation of private contract rights occurred in Berkeley, California, in 2000.[61] Well known for their leftist views, Berkeley officials were quick to embrace the idea of "living wage" laws—laws that require a business that has some special relationship with the government to pay its employees no less than a specified amount.[62] Although there is strong reason to doubt that living wages actually help the poor,[63] they have been adopted by cities across the country in hopes that they will raise the incomes of day laborers. Berkeley's law required any business that "received some form of financial benefit from the city"[64] to pay its workers $9.75 per hour plus medical benefits, or if medical benefits were not included, $11.37 per hour. Whether or not this policy was wise, it was almost certainly constitutional—government has long had the power to impose such requirements on businesses that have unique relationships with the government.[65]

But three months later, the city amended the law so that it would apply to any business operating on property leased from the city, employing more than six people, and receiving a gross income of more than $350,000 per year. The ordinance also included an exception allowing an employer to pay below the living wage if the employer had a collective-bargaining agreement with a union. That meant that the law would apply to only one business in the entire city: a restaurant called Skates by the Bay, owned by a corporation called RUI One and located on land leased from the city under a 1967 contract.[66] In other words, the Berkeley ordinance essentially rewrote the agreement between the city and this one restaurant, requiring as a condition of its lease that Skates by the Bay pay its employees the specified rate. Unlike a minimum wage law—which is a generally applicable rule that all businesses must obey—the Berkeley living wage was applied to the restaurant by adding a new demand to the agreement that the city and the restaurant signed almost four decades earlier.

The company filed a lawsuit arguing that, among other things, the living wage law impaired its 1967 contract. But the Ninth Circuit Court of Appeals rejected this argument. The fact that the lease agreement did not require a specific wage, the court found, meant that there was no arrangement between the company and the city in the first place—and therefore the law did not impair such an agreement.[67] But, the court continued, even if the lease had included a provision specifying the wages that RUI would have to pay its employees, the city would still have been free to alter it because "the lease agreement contains a provision mandating that RUI 'comply with all applicable laws, ordinance[s] and regulations of the City. . . .' California courts have consistently interpreted such provisions to mean that a party to a contract will 'comply with existing as well as future law.'" This meant that the lease would be interpreted as requiring the company to comply with "regulation that may change with time."[68] In other words, the city could write a contract with RUI One, sign it, and then change that contract in any way it wanted by passing an ordinance months or even years later and the company would have no recourse. Thus, RUI's contractual rights depended entirely on the will of the city government—precisely the situation the contracts clause was written to prevent. Yet the Supreme Court refused to take RUI's case, and city officials celebrated their victory by telling the press that the decision allowed them to "target a particular industry, a business that operates in a particular way or in a certain zone of the city."[69] The contracts clause—once among the most powerful constitutional devices for protecting economic freedom and property rights—had been rendered void.

5. The Era of Substantive Due Process: *Slaughterhouse* to *Lochner*

The decline of the contracts clause as a significant protection for the right to earn a living coincided more or less with the rise of what is today called the theory of "economic substantive due process." Unfortunately, this theory is difficult to understand on its own terms because it has become the focus of so much partisan debate. Today, it is hard to get around the rhetoric and see the true nature of the concept, let alone to assess its validity. Even the very name is misleading: to its leading articulators, such as Supreme Court Justice Stephen J. Field, that phrase, which was invented in the 1940s,[1] would have been meaningless. To them it was simply "due process of law," a long-established legal tradition with roots in the Magna Carta and the English common law. The "economic" substantive due process cases were not in fact based on economic theory; nor did they use economic terms or methodology the way that modern "law and economics" theory does. Instead, what came to be known as "economic substantive due process" was grounded in classical liberal principles of political philosophy, principles that also lie at the heart of the Constitution. Although the cases on occasion quoted from economists such as Adam Smith, they did so only to support arguments based in moral and political theory, not to support economic arguments.[2]

The fact that the theory of substantive due process seems to have originated during the so-called Gilded Age of the 19th century has led some historians to characterize it as an intellectually dishonest rationalization for a legal structure that benefited the wealthy elite at the expense of abused industrial workers. Historian Robert McCloskey, for example, claimed that Field and his colleagues "reshaped" the Constitution in the service of "procapitalist prejudice."[3] But this interpretation fits the facts even less than the storied "Switch in Time" of 1937—the supposedly sudden abandonment of the theory during the New Deal—and it does no justice to a sophisticated jurisprudence that prevailed, rightly or wrongly, for a long time among thoughtful judges for reasons other than cynical self-interest. The true story of "economic substantive due process" is far more interesting.

Sovereignty and Its Limits

In the years leading up to the Civil War, thinkers allied with the Whig, Free-Soil, and Republican Parties espoused a political theory rooted in Lockean classical liberalism. This ideology held that political society is a contract among individuals who are born naturally free and equal, with inalienable rights that government is instituted to protect—rights that include private property, personal liberty, and the right to pursue happiness by, among other things, working for a living. To support this view, these thinkers pointed to the Declaration of Independence.

In addition to their belief that natural rights limited government's sovereign powers, these early Republicans—beginning with John Quincy Adams, his protégé Charles Sumner, and later Abraham Lincoln—added two other important ideas: First, many of them subscribed to an idea that Professor Akhil Reed Amar recently labeled "*Barron* contrarianism,"[4] which held that the Bill of Rights applied to the states as well as to the federal government. The Supreme Court had rejected this view in its famous decision in *Barron v. Baltimore*,[5] but those who believed either that *Barron* was wrongly decided in the first place, or that the Constitution should be amended to overturn it, eventually became important players in the writing and ratification of the Fourteenth Amendment.

Second, and more fundamentally, many of them held that the Declaration of Independence did more than enunciate the philosophical basis of the Union; it also *created the Union itself* as a political body. That is, the Union was not formed by the states' ratifying in the Constitution of 1787, but by their declaring independence collectively in 1776.[6]

This classical liberalism was hotly disputed by many important legal theorists, who took their guidance from the writings of William Blackstone and other non-Lockeans.[7] They argued that rights were created by society, not by nature, and that the state or the legislature that spoke for it held the ultimate sovereign power to determine what rights would or would not be politically recognized. In addition, they believed that the Constitution created only a treaty between these sovereign states, whose legislatures could extend or revoke rights enjoyed by the people with virtually no interference from the federal government.

Thus, there emerged in the run up to the Civil War two perspectives on the authority of government and the rights of individuals. The first, associated with the classical liberal tradition, held that the Declaration of Independence enunciated a revolutionary principle that no government could rightfully exceed certain inherent boundaries—in essence, that certain rights were off limits to government. In James Madison's words, "the sovereignty of the society as vested in & exercisable by the majority, may do anything that could be *rightfully* done by the unanimous concurrence of the members; the reserved rights of individuals (of conscience for example) in becoming parties to the original compact being beyond the legitimate reach of sovereignty, whenever vested or however viewed."[8] Some who took this view of the limits of sovereignty also held that, notwithstanding the Supreme Court's decision in *Barron*, the federal Constitution protected these rights against the states because state sovereignty was secondary to the sovereignty of the American people as a whole. This national sovereignty, formulated by the Declaration of Independence, was in their view the source of the common-law rights that citizens enjoyed.[9]

According to the second perspective, the Declaration, whatever aspirations it expressed, imposed no enforceable limit on state governments. Nor could it, since on declaring independence each colony became its own independent sovereignty, only later forming the Union through the Articles of Confederation. Along with the sovereignty that each state enjoyed came the power to determine the common-law rights of citizens, since it was through their *state* citizenship that they enjoyed such rights. The federal government could not restrain the states in this regard. On the contrary, except where they were explicitly limited by their own constitutions, states had absolute authority.

At a time when slavery and states' rights were matters of intense debate, the differences between these two theories had very real implications. And we can see the two perspectives being worked out by comparing two particularly interesting state court decisions issued during the 1850s. In 1853, Pennsylvania Supreme Court Justice Jeremiah Black—who later became attorney general and secretary of state under President James Buchanan and an adviser to President Andrew Johnson—wrote a decision called *Sharpless v. Mayor of Philadelphia*[10] in which he took a strong states' rights position. When the United States declared its independence in 1776, Black wrote, Parliament's sovereignty over the colonies was assumed by each state respectively, not by the American Union. And since Parliament's sovereignty was, in Blackstone's theory, "supreme," "irresistible," and "absolute," the people of each state obtained complete, unlimited authority. "The transcendant powers of Parliament," wrote Black, "devolved on them by the revolution. Antecedent to the adoption of the federal constitution, the power of the states was supreme and unlimited. If the people of Pennsylvania had given all the authority which they themselves possessed, to a single person, they would have created a despotism as absolute in its control over life, liberty, and property, as that of the Russian autocrat."[11] The only boundaries to state power were those explicitly specified in the state constitution, and even these could be repealed by the majority. Thus, Black recognized no limit in principle on the majority's power. Had the people so chosen, he wrote, they could have "given to the Assembly an unlimited power to make all such laws as they might think proper. They would have had the whole omnipotence of the British parliament." This meant that, although state governments were restricted by some explicit and revocable constitutional provisions, they retained "full and uncontrolled possession" over "a vast field of power," and "[t]heir use of it can be limited only by their own discretion."[12]

Sharpless contrasts tellingly with a California Supreme Court decision issued only four years later, called *Billings v. Hall*.[13] In that case, the court invalidated a law that confiscated land owned by absentee landowners and transferred it to trespassers. In explaining its ruling, the court rejected the theory advanced in the *Sharpless* decision:

> It has been erroneously supposed, by many, that the Legislature of a State might do any Act, except what was expressly prohibited by the Constitution. Whether there is any restriction upon legislative power, irrespective of the Constitution, is a question upon which ethical and political writers have

differed. Many of the ancient writers have based this claim of omnipotence upon the doctrine of the absolute and sacred character of sovereignty, assuming that princes bear rule by divine right, and not by virtue of the expressed or tacit consent of the governed. Some contend that the very existence of government depends upon the supreme power being lodged in some branch of the Government, from which there is no appeal, and, if laws are passed which are immoral, or violate the principles of natural justice, the subject is bound to obey them. Others contend that there are boundaries set to the exercise of the supreme sovereign power of the State, that it is limited in its exercise by the great and fundamental principles of the social compact, which is founded in consent, express or implied; that it shall be called into existence for the great ends which that compact was designed to secure, and, hence, it cannot be converted into such an unlimited power, as to defeat the end which mankind had in view, when they entered into the social compact . . . .[14]

After quoting at length from Locke and other writers who opposed the principle that the legislature has limitless authority, the court concluded that "[w]hatever doubt may have formerly existed on this subject, the question has been settled, by an overwhelming weight of authority, in this country, that the spirit of free institutions is at war with such a principle."[15] Given that the "security of life, liberty, and property lies at the very foundation of the social compact," it could not be assumed that the legislature had the authority "to attack private property," since that would be "equivalent to saying that the people have delegated to their servants the power of defeating one of the great ends for which governments were established."[16]

The conflict between these two different views of the limits on, and the location of, sovereign power formed the intellectual background for the Civil War. The classical liberal theory was embraced by the Republican Party, which insisted that certain natural rights were beyond the reach of any government, whereas the absolutist theory of states' rights was embraced by the intellectual leaders of the Confederacy. It was not surprising, then, that when the war ended, Republicans saw a unique opportunity to ensure that these essential elements of their constitutional theory—that American sovereignty rested primarily in the nation, rather than states; that the rights of citizenship derived primarily from a person's national citizenship; and that legislative enactments beyond the state's moral limits were legally invalid—would be made a permanent part of the American constitutional order. They hoped to use the Fourteenth Amendment to cement into the Constitution political principles they had always considered constitutionally sound. Since they believed in the classical liberal proposition that government exists to protect equally each person's rights, they reflected this belief in the amendment's opening paragraph: *equality* in the equal protection clause, *protection* in the due process clause, and *rights* in the privileges or immunities clause.

The amendment began by defining citizenship and making federal citizenship primary: from now on, people would be "citizens of the United States" first, and only derivatively "of the State wherein they reside." Their traditional common-law rights thus sprung from their national, not their state, citizenship, and those rights would now be protected from the interference of state governments: "No State shall make or enforce any law which shall abridge the privileges or immunities of citizens of the United States." These are abstruse concepts, but they became immensely important in 1873 when the Supreme Court decided the *Slaughterhouse Cases*, the first decision ever to interpret the Fourteenth Amendment. The result was a disaster—the decision mangled the amendment badly, permanently handicapping its ability to protect minorities from injustice.

As we saw in chapter 3, *Slaughterhouse* involved a state law that established a monopoly in the slaughtering trade, shuttering the businesses of hundreds of Louisiana butchers. They argued that the law deprived them of their right to earn a living, which they claimed was one of the "privileges or immunities of citizens of the United States." But the Supreme Court ruled against them, declaring in direct contrast to the views of the amendment's authors, that a citizen's common-law rights, including the right to earn a living, derived from his *state*, not *federal*, citizenship. And because the Fourteenth Amendment protects only the "privileges or immunities of citizens *of the United States*," meaning their *federal* rights, this made all the difference. The slaughterhouse monopoly had not deprived the butchers of a right pertaining to *national* citizenship and therefore did not violate the Fourteenth Amendment. Justice Miller, writing for the five-member majority, held that the amendment protected only those rights "which own [*sic*] their existence to the Federal government, its National character, its Constitution, or its laws,"[17] but that the right to earn a living, like other common-law rights, sprang from state citizenship. In reaching this conclusion, Miller essentially adopted the understanding of sovereignty that the Fourteenth Amendment's authors had intended to overthrow. The *Slaughterhouse* majority simply ignored the most fundamental reason for passing that amendment: "Was it the purpose of the fourteenth amendment," Miller rhetorically asked, "to transfer the security and protection of all the civil rights which we have mentioned, from the States to the Federal government?"[18] The answer to that question was an unambiguous *yes*, and Miller's failure to cite any of the records documenting the amendment's history only underscored this fact. Miller was right, of course, that the amendment guarantees only federal constitutional rights. But its enactment was intended to constitutionalize the Republican theory that no just government may violate the natural rights that all persons have (including the right to economic freedom) and that the common-law protections for those rights are enjoyed by virtue of national citizenship, not state citizenship. By denying that the Fourteenth Amendment had "radically change[d] the whole theory of the relations of the State and Federal governments to each other and of both these governments to the people,"[19] the Supreme Court nullified what the amendment's authors had specifically sought to do. Instead, it harkened back to the theory of absolute state sovereignty that Jeremiah Black had expressed in his *Sharpless* opinion, and fittingly so, since in *Slaughterhouse*, Black served as one of the attorneys arguing the case in defense of the butcher monopoly.

The result of *Slaughterhouse* was to render the privileges or immunities clause—in the words of dissenting Justice Field—a "vain and idle enactment."[20] After all, if the amendment had not changed the nature of the state-federal relationship, then it was simply a redundancy: the supremacy clause already barred states from interfering with federal authority.

Field's prediction was right: *Slaughterhouse* marked the demise of the privileges or immunities clause; that clause has almost remained a dead letter ever since. In the ensuing years, American courts focused their attention instead on the due process clause as a protection of individual rights against state interference.

What *Is* "Substantive Due Process," Really?

Although some historians have argued that the Court retreated from *Slaughterhouse* by commandeering the due process clause to do the work of the now moribund privileges or immunities clause, this is not quite accurate. In fact, the Fourteenth Amendment's Framers knew even before the *Slaughterhouse* catastrophe that the due process clause would impose limits on state power.

The theory that is now known as "substantive due process" is somewhat obscured by the language used to discuss it. For one thing, the phrase "substantive due process" was devised only later as a pejorative by those who rejected the theory; at the time when substantive due process was widely accepted, it was simply referred to as "due process of law." Also, lawyers today typically refer to the "due process clause" but leave out the most important words of that clause: due process *of law*. This phrase derived from language in the Magna Carta—the *legem terrae* clause—which barred the king from taking away a person's property or subjecting him to criminal punishment except by "the law of the land." In his *Institutes of the Laws of England*, published posthumously in 1642, the English lawyer Sir Edward Coke noted that the terms "law of the land" and "due process of law" were interchangeable.[21] The important word in both of these formulations is "law." Because government may deprive a person of life, liberty, or property only through *law*, the question in a particular case is whether the government's actions qualify as law. If not, then the action would obviously deprive a person of life, liberty, or property without due process "of law."

So, what is "law"? Although aspects of that question have been debated at length by philosophers,[22] it is at least clear that law has both formal and substantive components; in other words, whether an enactment qualifies as a law depends on both the method of its enactment and its contents. An enactment that falls short in either of these ways will not qualify as law, as James Wilson, a signer of the Constitution, acknowledged: "[I]t is possible that the legislature, when acting in that capacity, may transgress the bounds assigned to it, and an act may pass, in the usual *mode*, notwithstanding that transgression."[23] Law does not just mean "whatever is emitted by a legislature"; it means the use of government's coercive power in the service of some general justifying principle. The opposite of law is arbitrariness: the use of force to serve whim, prejudice, mere

90

self-interest, or unaccountable desire.[24] Moreover, law does not mean a direct command to a particular person to do a particular thing—it is a rule that requires all people under certain circumstances to act in specified ways.[25] Law sets a *general* rule of conduct to be followed by all who fall within its ambit. "Law," wrote Wilson shortly after the Constitution was ratified, "is called a rule in order to distinguish it from a sudden, a transient, or a particular order: uniformity, permanency, stability, characterize a law."[26] Obviously, each case is different, and a legislature must differentiate between cases, so the generality requirement does allow lawmakers a broad range of choices. But it does set boundaries that prohibit government from treating each case as sui generis, or from acting on the basis of private self-interest. To put it another way, law is to mere force as reason is to mere will, and a society in which the government acts on the basis of mere will, with each case being treated as entirely unique, or in which government's coercive power is exercised to serve the arbitrary desire of a temporary ruling junta instead of the "permanent and aggregate interests of the community,"[27] is not governed by a rule of law. It is instead a "state of nature, where the weaker individual is not secured against the violence of the stronger."[28] Citizens in such a society would be subjected to the ruler's mere whim, unable to predict whether what they do today will incur punishment tomorrow. Their freedom would depend entirely on the mood of the person or group holding ruling authority. *Law*, by contrast, does not treat similarly situated people differently for no good reason; it is not arbitrary or self-interested.

The point is that when a citizen's rights to life, liberty, or property are made revocable at the whim of the ruler, the individual is no longer free but is unfree—is, in some sense, a slave. Aristotle recognized this fact more than 2,000 years ago, when he wrote that "governments which have a regard to the common interest are constituted in accordance with strict principles of justice, and are therefore true forms; but those which regard only the interest of the rulers are all defective and perverted forms, for they are despotic, whereas a state is a community of freemen."[29] But this is also true if the ruler whose whims can trump individual rights is a group, or even a majority. For Aristotle, a democracy in which the majority could override legal restrictions could not even be described properly as a democracy. A society where "not the law, but the multitude, have the supreme power, and supersede the law by their decrees" is actually a type of monarchy and "not a constitution at all; for where the laws have no authority, there is no constitution. . . . [T]he sort of system in which all things are regulated by decrees is clearly not even a democracy in the true sense of the word, for decrees relate only to particulars."[30] James Madison made a similar point when he observed that the economic or personal interests of the majority cannot be the "political standard of right and wrong" because it would be "in the interest of the majority in every community to despoil and enslave the minority of individuals." This would be "re-establishing, under another name and a more specious form, force as a means of right."[31]

Thus, to say that the will of the majority automatically qualifies as law would be to substitute power for justice. If the majority could override individual rights, "anarchy may as truly be said to reign as in a state of nature, where the weaker individual is not secured against the violence of the stronger."[32] Such a world would not be a rule of law but of arbitrary rule. In short, when its power is used for the private interest of the rulers—whether the rulers be a self-interested majority or a single ruler who governs by whim—a government lacks legitimacy, and its actions do not qualify as *law*, just as a bank guard's actions would lack legitimacy if he were to use his gun to rob the bank instead of protecting it. Such an act would exceed the legitimate powers of a bank guard—or of a government. The constitutional requirement that government act in a lawful rather than an arbitrary manner means that individual rights are protected against private-interest groups and majorities who, in Madison's words, might pursue their own "passion or interest" instead of "the permanent and aggregate interests of the community."[33]

Judges play their part in protecting constitutional freedom by testing the legislature's actions by what the American legal scholar Thomas Cooley called "those principles of civil liberty and constitutional defence which have become established in our system of law, and not by any rules that pertain to forms of procedure only." Writing shortly before the enactment of the Fourteenth Amendment, Cooley explained that due process of law meant "such an exertion of the powers of government as the settled maxims of the law sanction, and under such safeguards for the protection of individual rights as those maxims prescribe."[34] This theory was already well known to lawyers more than a century before Cooley wrote.[35] But probably the most influential explanation of "substantive due process" came in Daniel Webster's 1819 argument before the Supreme Court in the *Dartmouth College* case.[36] The phrase "law of the land," said Webster,

> most clearly intended, the general law; a law, which hears before it condemns; which proceeds upon inquiry, and renders judgment only after trial. The meaning is, that every citizen shall hold his life, liberty, property and immunities, under the protection of the general rules which govern society. Everything which may pass under the form of an enactment, is not, therefore, to be considered the law of the land. If this were so, acts of attainder, bills of pains and penalties, acts of confiscation, acts reversing judgments, and acts directly transferring one man's estate to another, legislative judgments, decrees and forfeitures, in all possible forms, would be the law of the land.

Without these ingredients, a legislative enactment could not be considered law, even if it satisfied the *formal* requirements of lawfulness. Otherwise—if anything a legislature enacted was ipso facto law—"constitutional provisions, of the highest importance," would be rendered "completely inoperative and void." And the Constitution's guarantees of justice would then "be an empty form, an idle ceremony. Judges would sit to execute legislative judgments and decrees; not to declare the law, or to administer the justice of the country."[37]

Due process of law therefore means that government must use its coercive powers in the service of the general welfare, for public reasons, and not for the benefit of private groups (even large and powerful majorities). Only a distinct category of acts by the ruling majority—those that satisfy the procedures required before a bill can become a law, and that substantively serve the "permanent and aggregate interests of the community"[38]—can qualify as law. Otherwise, government would be exercising arbitrary, unpredictable, lawless power over individual freedom—just the sort of situation that government exists to prevent.[39]

This understanding of due process helps explain the protection of "unenumerated" rights—rights not specified in a written constitution—in the legal theory of due process. American law originated in the common law of England, which has and (except for one brief experiment in the 17th century) always had, an unwritten constitution. All individual rights in English law are therefore "unenumerated" rights,[40] and when English courts protect those rights under the "law of the land" principle, they are enforcing unenumerated rights. Written bills of rights were a relatively new invention in the days of America's Founding; the Constitution's Framers would have thought it absurd that they were "creating" the individual rights they wrote down, or that courts would lack power to protect rights left unenumerated. They knew, as English common lawyers had always known, that courts would take unwritten legal norms of tradition and reason into account when deciding whether a government enactment qualified substantively as "law." If an enactment violated these principles, it lacked legitimacy and failed to serve the genuine good of society; it was therefore not law. This was how the "law of the land" clause of the Magna Carta, or the "due process of law" provisions in American constitutions, imposed substantive limits on state action. The lawfulness requirement means that not only must the form of legislative enactments meet the Constitution's rulemaking requirements, the substance must also serve the public good and respect the written and traditional guarantees of individual rights and fairness.

The argument is easy enough to understand when put in terms of the federal government's enumerated powers: Article I, section 8, of the Constitution lists the federal government's limited authority. If Congress acts in a way not authorized by those enumerations, then it has exceeded its legitimate scope, and its enactments cannot qualify as "law." The First Amendment bars Congress from making a law respecting an establishment of religion. If Congress were to pass a bill, and the President to sign it, declaring the United States to be a Christian nation, such an enactment would exceed Congress's authority and would therefore not qualify as "law." If federal officers acting pursuant to that declaration were to imprison a religious dissenter, such an act would deprive that person of liberty without due process *of law*. This theory is not limited to the specific prohibitions in the Bill of Rights. Any government action not authorized by the grant of power in the Constitution is *ultra vires*—a Latin phrase meaning "beyond the power"—and is therefore not a "law" as required by the "due process of law" limitation. For example, laws exceeding Congress's power under the commerce clause may not violate a specific right, but they still do not qualify as law because they lack any constitutional authorization.

The argument becomes more complex when we move away from the federal government's enumerated powers, but it remains fundamentally the same: legislative acts do not qualify as law when they are flawed in either their form or their substance in such a way that they exceed the lawmaking authority. We can divide these constitutional flaws into three broad categories.[41] First, as we have seen, the Constitution's requirement that government limit liberty only through *law* imposes a requirement of "generality" on government's actions. Government acts directed against particular groups, or serving only the self-interest of political leaders rather than the "permanent and aggregate interests of the community," are not law but acts of arbitrary power.

Second, the Constitution's lawfulness requirement means that government must abide by certain long-standing substantive guarantees when it deals with a citizen. Edward Coke wrote that the Crown must follow the long-standing procedure of common-law writs in criminal cases and give the accused an opportunity to "heare the interrogatories, and take a reasonable time to answer the same with deliberation."[42] Rules such as the jury requirement help ensure that criminal proceedings are fair, so that even though they cannot be logically deduced from the lawfulness requirement, they are recognized rights that cannot be eliminated without radically departing from legal procedure. The same is true of rights of property or commerce. If, as the Founders believed, individual rights are something more than permissions that the legislature gives to the people by grace, then the legislature cannot have absolute power to abolish those rights by fiat. If a person has a *right* to a thing, rather than a mere government license, then the government may not confiscate that thing simply by declaring it contraband; to do so deprives a person of property without his having committed a wrong or having any opportunity to be heard and judged—that is, without any process at all. Thus, the elimination of rights by legislative decree violates the principle of due process of law. In 1843, the Pennsylvania Supreme Court struck down a statute that deprived a man of his inheritance and gave it to someone else. The Constitution, explained the court, forbids the state from depriving a person of property "unless by the judgment of his peers or the law of the land. What law? Undoubtedly, a pre-existent rule of conduct, declarative of a penalty for a prohibited act; not an *ex post facto* rescript or decree made for the occasion." The Constitution was written "to exclude arbitrary power from every branch of the government," but that purpose would be evaded "if such rescripts or decrees were allowed to take effect in the form of a statute."[43] New York's highest court relied on the same argument in 1856 when it invalidated a law that banned the sale of liquor. "Where rights of property are admitted to exist, the legislature cannot say they shall exist no longer; nor will it make any difference although a process and a tribunal are appointed to execute the sentence. If this is the 'law of the land,' and 'due process of law,' within the meaning of the constitution, then the legislature is omnipotent."[44] And again in 1856, the United States Supreme Court declared that the principles of due process put "a restraint on the legislative as well as on the executive and judicial powers of the government and cannot be so construed as to leave congress free to make any process 'due process of law' by its mere will."[45]

As these cases indicate, the "procedural" aspects of due process of law necessarily overlap with its "substantive" aspects. This explains the third category of flaws that render government action a violation of the due process clause. Because government is forbidden to act arbitrarily, it must act through procedures that are fair—through regular, unbiased legal proceedings pursuant to clear rules that are known beforehand and not subject to unforeseen change. This requirement is today called *procedural* due process because it focuses on the procedures, or means, rather than on the substantive goal of a particular case (the end). But this terminology is misleading, because procedural due process is a *subset* of substantive due process: the reason for fair procedures is that the government's proper role is to serve individual rights by using coercive power in the service of the general public good. This broader principle encompasses both the "substantive" prohibition on arbitrary, corrupt, or self-interested rulemaking *and* the "procedural" proscription on unfair, rigged procedures. Procedural due process is one of the many ways in which the Constitution requires government to abide by the basic elements of "lawfulness" instead of acting by mere force.

Today, many writers contend that the due process clause protects *only* procedural fairness, not substantive commitments or philosophically chosen political goals.[46] But this argument begs the question;

it sees due process as a means without an end—as a journey without destination. Protecting fair government processes would be pointless unless a society is committed to certain organizing principles—principles derived from political philosophy. In *The Federalist*, Madison wrote: "Justice is the end of government. It is the end of civil society." Because justice is the purpose of government, it "ever will be pursued until it be obtained, or until liberty be lost in the pursuit."[47] Fair procedures are necessary to ensure that government does not obliterate justice instead. If such procedures did not exist, then people would be as much at risk from their government as they were from other citizens. The "risk" they would run would be that their rights might be eliminated by arbitrary fiat, which is precisely the same risk whether characterized as substantive or procedural. People exposed to that risk do not live under a rule of law but under a rule of men. Thus, the substantive commitment to justice is the rationale for implementing fair procedures. One role of the independent judiciary is to rein in the factions that might use government power to serve their "impulse[s] of passion or of interest"[48] under the formal appearance of law; by looking to both the substance and the form of legislative enactments—to ensure that they are "laws" and not arbitrary pronouncements—courts help ensure that the legislature serves the genuine public good and does not simply eliminate by decree the preexisting rights of innocent people.

These basic themes of lawfulness—that legislation must serve general public goals and not the specific self-interest of rulers or favored constituents, or even of the majority; that legislation must be consistent with the constitutional authority; that it must not simply eradicate existing rights by fiat; that it must be procedurally as well as substantively fair—were brought together in the Supreme Court's early substantive due process cases.[49] Only a year after the *Slaughterhouse* decision, the Court explained in *Loan Association v. Topeka*[50] that "the essential nature of all free governments" imposes certain basic, if sometimes unarticulated, limitations on government power: "No court, for instance, would hesitate to declare void a statute which enacted that A. and B. who were husband and wife to each other should be so no longer, but that A. should thereafter be the husband of C., and B. the wife of D. Or which should enact that the homestead now owned by A. should no longer be his, but should henceforth be the property of B."[51] As Madison had written almost a century earlier, any such society would be as hazardous to individual rights as a society without government at all; it would therefore not be a rule of law but one in which the ruling authority acted however it wanted without reference to the actual public good—even if its acts were disguised under the forms of law. As the *Loan Association* Court concluded:

> To lay with one hand the power of the government on the property of the citizen, and with the other to bestow it upon favored individuals to aid private enterprises and build up private fortunes, is none the less a robbery because it is done under the forms of law and is called taxation. *This is not legislation. It is a decree under legislative forms.*[52]

Not everything that the legislature enacts qualifies as a law.[53] Government actions that serve only an impulsive desire to injure one group or benefit another are merely acts of arbitrary force. They cannot qualify as a *law* because they are not justified by general principles and do not advance the genuine public good. They therefore deprive people of life, liberty, or property, without due process *of law*.[54]

The justices reiterated these points in the 1884 case of *Hurtado v. California*.[55] Legislative power is not "absolute and despotic," the Court noted; otherwise, the Fourteenth Amendment would be meaningless, and even the most arbitrary legislative enactments would be constitutional, meaning that individual rights would be put at the mercy of legislative whim. "Law is something more than mere will exerted as an act of power. It must be not a special rule for a particular person or a particular case, but, in the language of Mr. Webster, in his familiar definition, 'the general law . . . .'"[56] If the government adopted "special, partial, and arbitrary exertions of power under the forms of legislation," these enactments would nevertheless violate the Constitution: "Arbitrary power, enforcing its edicts to the injury of the persons and property of its subjects, is not law, whether manifested as the decree of a personal monarch or of an impersonal multitude." It is the judiciary's role under the Fourteenth Amendment to protect individual rights whether threatened by individual rulers or by legislative majorities that "transcend[] the limits of lawful authority . . . in the name and wielding the force of the government."[57]

Almost 25 years later, the Court confirmed this view in *Twining v. State of New Jersey*[58] when it observed that the term "due process of law" incorporates "certain general principles" that protect individuals against arbitrary government action. While these principles can be understood first by examining "those settled usages and modes of proceedings existing in the common and statute law of England"[59] before American independence, mere tradition did not conclusively determine what "due process of law" meant; rather, traditional legal practices must be viewed in light of those "fundamental principles, to be ascertained from time to time by judicial action, which have relation to process of law, and protect the citizen in his private right, and guard him against the arbitrary action of government."[60]

More recently, Professor Cass Sunstein captured the essence of substantive due process when discussing the Constitution's prohibition against what he calls "naked preferences." These are benefits extended to particular interest groups "solely on the ground that those favored have exercised the raw political power to obtain what they want." Such preferences are prohibited by the due process, equal protection, and takings clauses. They and other constitutional provisions require that all government actions must result "from a legitimate effort to promote the public good rather than from a factional takeover."[61]

This is the theory of "substantive due process," whether in its early "economic" manifestation or in those areas of the law in which substantive due process is still applied today. In short, certain principles, or substantive commitments, are incorporated into a constitution even if they are not spelled out in so many words. The Lockean political philosophy of the Framers is thus incorporated into the Constitution through, among other things, its reference to "law."[62] That term reflects the Framers' belief that government exists to protect individual rights and that it cannot legitimately use its coercive powers to violate those rights without good reason; such an act would not be "law." If a government adopted a law designed to protect the interests of a particular interest group, at the cost of another, for no general public reason, it was the role of the courts to declare such a law void, as a violation of the plaintiff's right to earn a living, or freedom of religion, or whatever the relevant right might be in a particular case. Yet at about the same time that the Fourteenth Amendment was enacted, economic regulations were becoming increasingly common—for example, in the area of occupational licensing.[63] Cases involving occupational licensing, beginning with

Dent v. West Virginia[64] in 1889, sometimes used substantive due process principles to conclude that licensing laws protecting the general public safety and welfare were constitutional; at other times, courts concluded that such laws bore no serious relation to the public welfare but merely protected one economic interest group from competition from another, in violation of the due process clause.

The Granger Cases

There are four major mileposts in the history of "economic substantive due process": *Munn v. Illinois*[65] in 1876, which created the "affected with a public interest" standard; *Lochner v. New York*[66] in 1905, which became the most notorious example of substantive due process in American law; the 1934 case of *Nebbia v. New York*,[67] which abandoned the *Munn* standard and replaced it with the "rational basis" test; and *United States v. Carolene Products*[68] in 1938, which slightly restricted the rational basis rule—but not in the area of economic freedom.

Munn, one of the so-called Granger Cases, involved an Illinois law that limited the prices that owners of grain silos could charge farmers who wished to store grain. The silos were located in Chicago, one of the most important stops on the trade route by which farmers sent their products to markets throughout the country. After farmers complained that silo owners charged exorbitant rates, agrarian activists associated with the Grange movement persuaded the state legislature to enact a price limitation. The owners of the silos brought suit, arguing that this regulation violated the due process clause because it benefited farmers' interests at their expense, not for the public welfare but simply because the farmers had greater political influence. The owners argued that a business agreement between two contracting parties was nobody else's business and that voters or politicians had no authority to interfere; if A and B agreed to the terms of a grain storage contract, it did not violate C's rights; thus, C had no grounds on which to complain. Government's attempts to regulate in these areas were therefore unauthorized uses of coercion and not *laws*. Depriving the owners of the rights of ownership therefore took their property without due process of law.

Before *Munn*, certain categories of businesses had always been held to be basically public affairs, including railroads and other common carriers, as well as businesses enjoying special privileges from the government (such as the authority to use eminent domain). Moreover, government could regulate businesses that polluted streams, burned down crops, or otherwise harmed nonconsenting individuals or the public at large. Finally, government could regulate businesses that qualified as "natural monopolies": those situated in such a way that consumers had no genuine choice and could easily be exploited.

Although the grain silos in *Munn* did not qualify under any of those categories, the Supreme Court upheld the laws. Government, it held, could regulate private businesses if they were "affected with a public interest"[69]—that is, if the property in question was "used in a manner to make it of public consequence, and affect the community at large."[70] When an owner uses his property in a way that the public obtains such an interest in it, the Court declared, "he, in effect, grants to the public an interest in that use, and must submit to be controlled by the public for the common good, to the extent of the interest he has thus created."[71] After *Munn*, any company with an unusually important connection to the general welfare could be regulated by the government.

Justice Field dissented in *Munn*, as he had in *Slaughterhouse*, arguing vehemently that the due process clause prohibited business regulations that simply promoted the economic interests of politically successful groups at the expense of others. The grain silos were private property, and "[t]he receipt and storage of grain in a building erected by private means for that purpose does not constitute the building a public warehouse."[72] If a business were rendered public—and thus subject to government control—whenever the public had an "interest" in it, Field warned, there could be "no protection . . . against [the] invasion of private rights," and "all property and all business in the State [would be] held at the mercy of a majority of its legislature."[73] Since the legislature's enactment regulating the prices of grain silos was merely a naked preference benefiting the farmers at the expense of silo owners—a "pretence of providing for the public good"[74]—it did not qualify as a *law* and thus violated the due process clause.

Field acknowledged that "legislation which secures to all protection of their rights" could justly deprive people of life, liberty, and property under the Fourteenth Amendment: "Indeed, there is no end of regulations with respect to the use of property which may not be legitimately prescribed, having for their object the peace, good order, safety, and health of the community."[75] But the grain silos "are not nuisances," and they "infringe[d] upon no rights of others."[76] The price regulation was not designed to protect people who were being injured but simply to give farmers a benefit at the expense of the property owner; it was "nothing less than a bold assertion of absolute power by the State to control at its discretion the property and business of the citizen, and fix the compensation he shall receive."[77]

Munn was a watershed for the Populist movement, which sought to impose severe new regulations on a postwar economy that was booming with unprecedented growth. After the decision in that case, states began declaring a wide variety of businesses to be "affected with a public interest" so that the legislature could regulate them. Courts were frequently called on to determine whether these declarations were justified or were mere pretenses. The eventual result was a complex, confusing, and inconsistent series of cases deciding whether or not certain businesses were affected with a public interest. But drawing a distinction between those that were or were not affected with such an interest meant trying to draw clear boundaries between conduct subject to government oversight and conduct that was simply not the government's concern.[78] At the end of Field's career, the Court acknowledged that the word "liberty" in the Fourteenth Amendment included not only freedoms of speech or religion but also a person's right "to earn his livelihood by any lawful calling; to pursue any livelihood or avocation; and for that purpose to enter into all contracts which may be proper, necessary, and essential to his carrying out to a successful conclusion the purposes above mentioned."[79] In some cases, it struck down laws that too severely imposed on the right of business owners to charge what they wanted for their services.[80] But it did not repudiate its decision that businesses affected with a public interest could be controlled by the state and that the government could dictate their prices or their practices.

Lochner

The most famous of the "economic substantive due process" cases came in the 1905 case of *Lochner v. New York*,[81] which declared a section of New York's "Bakeshop Act" unconstitutional. Joseph Lochner owned a small bakery, a common trade for immigrants and lower-class workers. Many of these bakeries operated in cramped quarters, where a handful of employees would work in long shifts, with cots nearby so that they could sleep during their off-hours. The work was strenuous, and many employees had little time to spend with their families. Nevertheless, they chose to work under such difficult conditions, believing that it would benefit them more than unemployment, and in fact there is little evidence that the work was particularly hazardous compared with other trades available at the time. Bakers did not face the threat of injury and death that factory or farm workers faced, and given the state of medical knowledge in that era, the illnesses they sometimes attributed to the inhalation of flour dust may more often have been caused by viruses or bacteria.

Although some parts of the Bakeshop Act established health and safety standards—forbidding the presence of animals near food-stuffs, for example—these provisions were not at issue in the *Lochner* case. Instead, the case focused on a provision of the law that limited the number of hours that bakers could work. Labor activists at the time were demanding that government prohibit employees from working long shifts so as to guarantee workers more leisure time and to alleviate poverty by forcing employers to hire more labor.

Both these rationales for the law, however, were based on dubious public policy arguments. While forbidding an employee from working more than 10 hours per day might have compelled employers to hire more workers, they would do so only if it were cost-effective, which would mean a general decrease in the wages paid to each worker hired. Moreover, the cost of hiring new workers and other administrative costs (let alone new legislation forbidding pay cuts) would mean higher prices for consumers. The fallacy in the economic arguments of the Bakeshop Act's proponents becomes clear if we consider an extreme case: it would be quite easy to create "more jobs" in the bakery industry by simply legislating a five-minute workday for each worker, but the results would be a disastrous increase in the cost of production, leading to a collapse in the supply of baked goods and a radically inefficient economy. Likewise, it would be easy to provide people with leisure time by prohibiting them from working on Fridays, or only allowing them to work one day per week. But these options would ignore the economic tradeoffs that each person faces. Instead of pursuing leisure activities, some people prefer to work to provide for their families or their futures. For the proponents of the Bakeshop Act to take that choice away from bakery workers—and with it the economic opportunity that workers might have prioritized above leisure time—was not a humanitarian act.

Nevertheless, certain New York activists, led by *Baker's Journal* editor Henry Weismann, began agitating for a maximum-hours law. In the pages of the *Journal* and at meetings of the baker's union, for which Weismann served as general secretary, reform of the working hours in the city's bakeshops became a common theme. In 1894, Weismann led a drive to present petitions and resolutions on behalf of the city's bakers urging a maximum-hours law. Insisting that the law would increase employment, Weismann convinced allied unions to support the proposal as well, and in 1895 the state legislature unanimously approved a law forbidding the owner of a bakery to "require[], permit[] or suffer[]" an employee to work more than 60 hours per week or 10 hours per day. Weismann soon became an assistant to the state's chief factory inspector, charged with enforcing the Bakeshop Act.

Joseph Lochner broke the law by allowing, requiring, or suffering an employee named Aman Schmitter to work more than 60 hours during a week in April 1901. There is no evidence to suggest that Lochner employed any sort of coercion against Schmitter; rather, it seems likely that Schmitter worked overtime for the same reason that people work overtime today: for the money. But to Progressive theorists like Roscoe Pound, this fact was beside the point since Schmitter was one of the "weak and necessitous"[82] who, unable to make mature decisions regarding his employment conditions, needed protection from the government. Of course, the legislation that prohibited Schmitter from working overtime so as to preserve his leisure time was not accompanied by compensation for his diminished income.

Lochner was convicted of violating the Bakeshop Act, a misdemeanor. His conviction was affirmed on appeal, and affirmed again by New York's highest court. Lochner then appealed to the United States Supreme Court where, strangely, he was defended by the very Henry Weismann who had led the campaign to pass the law but who had now switched sides. Weismann won: the Court reversed Lochner's conviction by a 5–4 ruling, holding that the law deprived Lochner of his liberty without due process of law.

The majority opinion, written by Justice Rufus Peckham, was quite straightforward. Beginning with the rule that a person has a right to earn a living without unreasonable government interference, Peckham acknowledged that the government could protect "the safety, health, morals, and general welfare of the public" through laws that limited how a person might earn a living:[83] "Both property and liberty are held on such reasonable conditions as may be imposed by the governing power of the state in the exercise of those powers, and with such conditions the 14th Amendment was not designed to interfere."[84] But a restriction on the number of hours a baker could work must have some connection to the health and safety of the baker or of the public, and there was "no reasonable ground for interfering with the liberty of person or the right of free contract, by determining the hours of labor, in the occupation of a baker. There is no contention that bakers as a class are not equal in intelligence and capacity to men in other trades . . . or that they are not able to assert their rights and care for themselves without the protecting arm of the state."[85] If the law was designed simply to limit the number of hours a baker worked, and not to protect a baker's health, then "the public is not in the slightest degree affected by such an act," and such a law was really a mere exercise of arbitrary force, in violation of the due process clause.[86]

The Bakeshop Act, therefore, could be constitutional only if it "pertain[ed] to the health of the individual engaged in the occupation of a baker."[87] Yet there was no such connection: "the trade of a baker has never been regarded as an unhealthy one,"[88] and there was no evidence that the law protected bakers from unhealthful working conditions. Nor was there evidence of any "connection between the number of hours a baker may work in the bakery and the healthful quality of the bread made by the workman."[89] As such, the law was "an unreasonable, unnecessary, and arbitrary interference with the right of the individual to his personal liberty, or to enter into those contracts in relation to labor which may seem to him appropriate or necessary for the support of himself and his family."[90] In short, Aman Schmitter's and Joseph Lochner's rights to earn a living as they chose could only be limited if the restriction served the public good, but there was no evidence that this restriction did so. It was therefore an arbitrary legislative decree interfering with their constitutional rights. "*Lochner*," writes political scientist Edward Keynes, "did not preclude the states from justifying regulatory policies that burden economic and personal liberties," but it "did require the government to show a direct relationship between such regulations and public health and safety."[91]

Justices Harlan, White, and Day dissented. They agreed that the state "may not unduly interfere with the right of the citizen to enter into contracts that may be necessary and essential in the enjoyment of the inherent rights belonging to everyone, among which rights is the right . . . 'to earn his livelihood by any lawful calling, to pursue any livelihood or avocation.'"[92] But in their view, it was "plain that this statute was enacted in order to protect the physical well-being of those who work in bakery and confectionery establishments."[93] It was at least plausible, and in such a case, they contended, the legislature's judgment ought to prevail.

But it was the separate dissent by Justice Oliver Wendell Holmes that was the most extraordinary opinion in *Lochner*. The question of whether or not the law was a health and safety measure was more or less irrelevant, he contended. Several laws "regulate life in many ways which we as legislators might think [of] as injudicious or if you like as tyrannical," but the Constitution did not forbid such laws.[94] Holmes adopted a powerful presumption in favor of government, concluding that "the word 'liberty,' in the 14th Amendment, is perverted when it is held to prevent the natural outcome of a dominant opinion, unless it can be said that a rational and fair man necessarily would admit that the statute proposed would infringe fundamental principles as they have been understood by the traditions of our people and our law."[95] Such was not the case here, because all sorts of laws interfered with liberty and were generally accepted, and this wasn't as bad as many others. Most importantly, Holmes rejected the very foundations of substantive due process. "[A] constitution," he wrote, "is not intended to embody a particular economic theory, whether of paternalism and the organic relation of the citizen to the state or of laissez faire. It is made for people of *fundamentally differing views*."[96]

The italicized phrase may be the most bewildering statement in Supreme Court history. It would be little exaggeration, in fact, to say that Holmes's claim—that a constitution is written for people who differ on fundamental principles—is a rejection of the entire corpus of Western political philosophy up to that point. Previous generations believed that constitutions were written for people of fundamentally *shared* views, who differ only as to particulars. The Declaration of Independence begins with the "truths" that the Founding Fathers agreed lay at the heart of American society, and the Constitution also asserts at the very outset that liberty is a "blessing." The 1776 Virginia Declaration of Rights asserted that "no free government, or the blessings of liberty, can be preserved to any people, but by . . . frequent recurrence to fundamental principles."[97] Holmes's contention that the Constitution is neutral between fundamentally different conceptions of government—fundamentally differing views of the proper relationship between the individual and the state—threw the Founders' legacy overboard. They believed that there were certain truths about human beings, certain universal principles of justice, and a genuine public good, on which a constitution could be based; no just government could ignore these principles. But Holmes's innovation allowed the door to swing two ways: either government could "create" freedom and "allow" individuals to enjoy it, or it could employ unlimited power whereby the governing authorities could "embody their opinions in law."[98] Holmes was spurning the notion that people are born free and that restrictions on their freedom must be justified in some way. This he referred to disdainfully as a "shibboleth."[99] Instead, Holmes held that government chooses when to make individuals free, based on a cost-benefit analysis. Having rejected the idea of moral limits on the state, as well as any distinction between law and mere force, Holmes found himself prepared to accept as legitimate whatever order claimed the support of a legislative majority.

The Attack on *Lochner*

During the *"Lochner* era," running until the mid 1930s, the Court actually sustained economic regulations more often than not. Still, the case became the target of criticism by the rising tide of Progressives who saw their entire program threatened by the decision. In particular, Roscoe Pound attacked the decision in a famous law review article on the ground that the Court was focusing on legal fictions and formalities and not on the "actual industrial conditions" that bakers faced.[100] Bakers, he contended, had no real bargaining power vis-à-vis their bosses; they needed the state to protect them.

The fact that a worker had less money than an employer "impair[ed] his freedom of contract [and] put him at the mercy of his employers" and justified government intervention.[101]

The problem with this argument is that contracting parties are never in a state of perfect equality, and parties have other ways of organizing to demand better conditions, including strikes or boycotts, which are noncoercive and consistent with the rights of employers as well as employees. Nor is there any suggestion that baker Aman Schmitter—or Willie Lyons, for that matter, in the *Adkins* case discussed earlier—suffered in any way from his position relative to his employer. In fact, Pound's critique of the Court's "formalism" is itself formalistic, falling far short of the mark: the Court actually *did* look at the statistical evidence regarding the health of bakery workers—statistics provided in Joseph Lochner's brief to the Court.[102] Indeed, the justices' examination of these statistics may be one reason why in a similar case three years later, attorney Louis Brandeis filed a brief full of statistics about the nature of the industry at issue and the effect of the law challenged in that case.[103] The Court once again relied on statistical evidence in that case. Pound's charge that the Court was blind to the realities of industrial life is simply not supported by the facts.

Moreover, his normative argument also ignored the fact that legislative "solutions" to the alleged problem of unequal bargaining power tend to create far greater imbalances of power. Even if Aman Schmitter had been "at the mercy" of Joseph Lochner, today's Aman Schmitters are far more at the mercy of bureaucracies and regulatory agencies whose rules restrict lower-class and blue-collar workers from getting a start in an occupation.[104] The extensive bureaucratic state made possible by Pound's paternalistic theory frequently ends up stifling the economic opportunities of the working class. There are many workers who, like Aman Schmitter, might actually want to work overtime. Barring their economic opportunity is both harmful and unjust. If the legislature had simply forced bakers to give up a portion of their potential income, for no reason other than that a legislative majority had chosen to pass a law for that purpose, that requirement would clearly deprive bakers of their liberty without due process of law and would be unconstitutional. Yet that is precisely what the Court found the New York legislature had done by simply forbidding bakers from working long hours, without any justification rooted in the government's role as a protector of the public health and safety.

Yet the principles underlying the *Lochner* decision were already weakening significantly when that decision was made; by 1905, the acid of Progressivism had already corroded much of the philosophical foundation on which rested the Constitution's protections for individual rights. By then, and increasingly over the next 30 years, intellectual leaders turned away from the classical liberalism of the Constitution. Individual rights, they held, were just superstitions, which might have some social utility but were not attached to morality or to the prepolitical nature of human beings. They saw rights as social devices; privileges granted to individuals by the state, which could revoke or alter those rights to solve social ills.[105] In the words of historian Louis Menand, the Progressives came to see individual rights as "socially engineered spaces" that are "created not for the good of individuals, but for the good of society. Individual freedoms are manufactured to achieve group ends."[106] This abandonment of the natural rights foundation of the Constitution had important ramifications for the courts, since it led to another of the Progressives' intellectual innovations: the notion of judicial restraint. Judges, writes legal historian G. Edward White, came to see the job of "policing the boundary between the public and private spheres" as "a less vital task," and to view "legislation conferring particular benefits on one class in society" as "less threatening to other classes" than earlier generations had believed. "[T]he increased encroachment of government on private activities through paternalistic legislation was not a cause for concern because those drafting the legislation were engaged in the purposive betterment of their fellow citizens along the lines of modern science and democratic theory."[107] The Progressives argued that courts should not intercede when the legislature violates individual rights—which they viewed as mere permissions, anyway. "If my fellow citizens want to go to Hell, I will help them," remarked Oliver Wendell Holmes. "It's my job."[108] According to the Framers of the Constitution, the job of the judiciary was not to aid the people in "going to Hell," but to protect individual rights against the inevitable tendency of legislatures to overstep their constitutional limits. Holmes and his Progressive allies, however, believed the judiciary should abet these efforts in the service of social improvement and "the right of a majority to embody their opinions in law."[109]

Progressivism transformed government from an institution for protecting rights into a tool for improving the living conditions of citizens; from a "necessary evil," as the Founders saw it,[110] into a positive good. And it shifted the focus of American constitutional law from liberty to democracy. From then to the present day, the primary concern of political leaders would be ensuring that legislative majorities could enforce their preferences rather than protecting the freedom and safety of individuals. For many people, this actually became the very definition of freedom: majority power, rather than the right to pursue happiness, came to be seen as the meaning of liberty.[111] This explains Holmes's otherwise perplexing statement in his *Lochner* dissent that protecting the rights of individuals was a "perversion" of the word "liberty."[112]

Modern criticism of *Lochner* is based on the same appeal to majoritarianism that animated Holmes's dissent. Most of today's critics share the Progressive assumption that government has an inherent right to control people's choices and that individual freedom is merely a privilege granted by the state for its own purposes; thus, they view the decision as judicial interference with the legislature's rightful power to restrict freedom in the purported interests of society. As James W. Ely has concluded, these critics attack the concept of substantive due process because of their "disagreement with particular applications of the doctrine," and in the process they often ignore or misrepresent the long and respectable tradition of substantive due process theory.[113]

Robert Bork

One of the chief critics of *Lochner* and its legacy is Robert Bork, who has developed an elaborate argument that substantive due process lies at the root of most of America's constitutional ills.[114] Bork contends that substantive due process made its first appearance in *Dred Scott v. Sandford*,[115] the infamous case in which the Supreme Court declared that Congress could not forbid the spread of slavery into the western territories and that blacks could never be citizens of the United States. A constitutional right to "slave ownership," Bork contends, "is nowhere to be found in the Constitution," but Chief Justice Roger Taney "was passionately convinced that it must be a constitutional right." Therefore, he "transform[ed] . . . the due process clause from a procedural to a substantive requirement" so as to protect slavery. This "was the first appearance in American constitutional law of the concept of 'substantive due process.'"[116]

According to Bork, substantive due process has ever since wreaked havoc on American society by allowing judges to read their own political preferences into the Constitution, thereby subverting democracy and implementing the visions of a liberal elite whose moral views are not shared by most Americans. The underlying theme of *Dred Scott*, *Lochner*, and later controversies like *Roe v. Wade*[117] is that they represent undemocratic obstacles to the will of the majority.

Almost none of this is true. To begin with, his characterization of *Dred Scott* is erroneous. Several passages of the original Constitution recognized the existence of slave property, although the text itself avoids the word "slave."[118] The content of the "property" protected by the Fifth Amendment was set, then as now, by the "background principles" of state law, which meant that slave property was undeniably included in that amendment's property clauses. For a court, therefore, to hold that a slave owner could not be deprived of slave property without due process of law was perfectly valid.

Moreover, the question in *Dred Scott*, as Taney framed it, was "simply this: Can a negro . . . become a member of the political community formed and brought into existence by the Constitution of the United States[?]"[119] Taney held that the Declaration of Independence and the Constitution did not make slaves into citizens; it was at this point that he made his awful statement about blacks having no rights that whites are bound to respect and referred to "the negro race" being "a separate class of persons" who "were not regarded as a portion of the people or citizens" under the Constitution.[120] After a very long explanation, Taney concluded that blacks were not citizens of the United States, but rather that

> [t]he only two provisions [of the federal Constitution] which point to them and include them, treat them as property, and make it the duty of the Government to protect it; *no other power, in relation to this race, is to be found in the Constitution*; and as it is a Government of special, delegated, powers, no authority beyond these two provisions can be constitutionally exercised. The Government of the United States had no right to interfere for any other purpose but that of protecting the rights of the owner. . . .[121]

The italicized portion is important because it is the central error in *Dred Scott*:[122] Taney's declaration that Congress lacked authority to ban slavery in federal territories was blatantly false, given that Article IV, section 3, gave Congress plenary power to legislate there. But if it *had been* true, then his conclusion—that depriving a slave owner of property through an *ultra vires* law would violate of the Fifth Amendment—would be valid.[123] Any attempt by Congress to exercise a power it lacked would result not in a valid law but in a nullity, and to deprive a person of property under anything less than a valid law would be a violation of the due process of law requirement. Taney's reference to due process took up only a single, unremarkable sentence in *Dred Scott*: "[A]n act of Congress which deprives a citizen of the United States of his liberty or property, merely because he came himself or brought his property into a particular Territory of the United States, and who had committed no offence against the laws, could hardly be dignified with the name of due process of law."[124]

As far as due process is concerned, this conclusion was valid: assuming humans could be legitimately classified as property (an assumption the original Constitution did appear to make), and that Congress lacked authority to ban slavery in the territories (which it did not), then depriving a slave owner of his property merely because he traveled from one place to another would, indeed, have violated the due process clause. Bork's characterization is highly misleading: Taney did *not* claim that the due process clause *itself* forbids Congress from enacting anti-slavery legislation. Instead, he argued that Congress was acting beyond the scope of its constitutional authority and therefore that its acts lacked the force of law; as a consequence, depriving an owner of slaves through such an invalid action violated the due process requirement. This interpretation of the clause was so widely accepted at the time that neither of the dissenting justices challenged it; nor did Taney feel obligated to defend it. As Mark Graber writes, by the time *Dred Scott* was decided, "property owners could cite a substantial body of state constitutional law decisions as providing precedential support for claims that due process . . . forbade legislatures from confiscating property."[125]

Bork thus mischaracterizes this enormously complicated case as a simple instance of "legislating from the bench," which contributes nothing to a reader's understanding of the most important Supreme

Court decision of all time. He takes that decision radically out of context and ignores its most essential elements; if one read only his description of it, one would be at a loss to understand Abraham Lincoln's and Frederick Douglass's arguments against it. Bork's broader attempt to slander the reputation of substantive due process theory by attaching it to *Dred Scott* must therefore fail: the case was *not* the first use of substantive due process—we have seen how that theory was widely discussed at least 50 years earlier, including in Daniel Webster's *Dartmouth College* argument—and the one minor reference to due process in that decision was logically valid and was not challenged by the dissenting justices.

If anything, Bork's description of *Lochner* is even more misleading. Labeling it the "quintessence of judicial usurpation of power," he simply caricatures the case as "giv[ing] judges free rein to decide what were and were not proper legislative purposes."[126] He fails to note that the *Lochner*-era Court upheld many regulations on businesses; nor does he recognize the centuries-long rule that government could restrict economic liberty only if doing so actually protected the public. More remarkably, Bork's belief in the virtually unlimited power of the majority reaches such an extreme that he even criticizes Oliver Wendell Holmes for not being majoritarian *enough*. In his view, whatever a majority decides to outlaw (or to permit) may be outlawed (or permitted) with no apparent limits whatsoever: "Moral outrage is a sufficient ground for prohibitory legislation."[127] The foundation for his belief in the primacy of government over the individual is his "view of morality" according to which no person may "act on the principle that 'a person belongs to himself and not to others.'"[128] In other words, individuals exist for the sake of society, and while society may accord them certain privileges, they have no inherent rights that are valid against collective "moral outrage." In another book, he accuses "Enlightenment liberals" like Jefferson of making a "mistake" about human nature when they declared that individuals could responsibly manage their own lives in freedom; instead, he sees the real "consequences of liberalism, liberty, and the pursuit of happiness" as "'rot and decadence.'"[129]

Incredibly, Bork tries to attribute his own positivist and collectivist views to the Founding Fathers: he writes that in a "Madisonian system . . . in wide areas of life majorities are entitled to rule, if they wish, simply because they are majorities."[130] It would be difficult to come up with a phrase that more precisely contradicts the actual views of James Madison, who, as we have seen, believed that government may only do things "that could be *rightfully* done by the unanimous concurrence of the members" of society, and that "the reserved rights of individuals" always remain "beyond the legitimate reach of sovereignty."[131] In other words, Madison believed that majorities are *never* "entitled" to rule but are instead *authorized* to rule, and that legitimate government has no authority to infringe on individual rights. Bork, by contrast, rejects the notion that the majority's power is limited by prepolitical rules of justice. He believes that government authority is *inherently* legitimate, whereas individual freedom is to be regarded with suspicion.

James Madison believed that individual freedom is the rule and state-imposed limits on that freedom are the exception; he noted that in monarchies, "charters of liberty have been granted by power," while in America, "charters of power [were] granted by liberty."[132] His fellow Founders declared that freedom is primary—that "all men are created equal," endowed with certain rights—and that government is secondary, created as an instrument "to secure these rights" and subject to being altered or abolished if it became destructive to such rights. They held that individual rights are the source and the limit of government's authority. But for Bork, government power is the source and limit of individual rights. In his view, "[t]he fundamental freedom recognized in democracies is the right of the people to govern themselves. Specified constitutional rights are meant to be exceptions, not a rule."[133]

It is hardly surprising, therefore, that Bork rejects *Lochner* and goes to such untenable lengths to smear that decision with the reputation of *Dred Scott*. *Lochner* stands for the proposition that individuals have basic human rights with which the majority may not arbitrarily interfere. In the end, Bork's objection to *Lochner* springs from his more basic rejection of these principles of individual liberty and the judicial power that protects them against the majority.

Souter, Tribe, and Sunstein

More sophisticated than Bork's interpretation of *Lochner* is that of Supreme Court Justice David Souter, who wrote about the case in his dissent in *Seminole Tribe of Florida v. Florida*.[134] Relying in large part on the works of law professors Laurence Tribe and Cass Sunstein, Souter holds that the "characteristic vice" of *Lochner* was that the Court assumed that freedom provided a natural baseline from which to judge the constitutional legitimacy of legislative actions: "the Court treated the common-law background (in those days, common-law property rights and contractual autonomy) as paramount, while regarding congressional legislation to abrogate the common law on these economic matters as constitutionally suspect."[135] Souter, like Bork, embraces the Progressivist notion that rights are created by government fiat and that freedom of contract is nothing more than one of the many political theories society may adopt. All these theories—freedom or tyranny or anything in between—are equally legitimate. The *Lochner* Court was therefore wrong to see the question as whether the government may restrict the *freedom* of a baker and his boss. Such a question is meaningless since "governmental rules lie behind the exercise of rights of property, contract, and tort,"[136] and a regime of private property and economic freedom is therefore itself just a different kind of regulation. Thus, the question involved nothing more than a cost-benefit analysis of one regulatory regime against another[137]—not *whether* the government may regulate, but *how*. To advocate restrictions on economic freedom is not to "plea[d] for government intervention where none existed before" but simply to argue "for a new regulatory system."[138]

Laurence Tribe, who shares this view, illustrates this approach with an elegant analogy drawn from modern physics. Just as gravity "curves" space, so law is said to permeate and "curve" human life; one cannot speak of society outside of the influence of government. "Newton's conception of space as empty, unstructured background parallels the legal paradigm in which state power, including judicial power, stands apart from the neutral, 'natural' order of things," writes Tribe. But we must learn to reject the idea that there can be such a "neutral, 'natural' order of things."[139] Instead,

> just as space cannot extricate itself from the unfolding story of physical reality, so also the law cannot extract itself from social structures; it cannot "step back," establish an "Archimedean" reference point of detached neutrality, and selectively reach in, as though from the outside, to make fine-tuned adjustments to highly particularized conflicts. Each legal decision restructures the law itself, as well as the social setting in

115

> which law operates, because, like all human activity, the law is inevitably embroiled in the dialectical process whereby society is constantly recreating itself.[140]

Tribe concludes that there is really no such thing as an absence of regulation—that is, no such thing as freedom. "The legal 'freedom' of contract and property came [in the 1930s] to be seen as an illusion, subject as it was to impersonal economic forces. . . . [C]ommon law doctrines and decisions [are] expressions of positive governmental intervention to achieve identifiable, though not always laudable, human purposes. . . ."[141] Were the government to do nothing with regard to a particular issue, that in itself is a political decision creating a political-economic framework (X) that is no different from framework Y (a state of heavy regulation) in terms of legitimacy. Sure, in framework X, John might have more of a particular good and Betty have less of it, whereas in framework Y the opposite might be the case. But this difference does not affect the legitimacy of X over Y. There is no normative difference between a regulated and unregulated states of affairs; for Tribe "[t]here was no 'natural' economic order to upset or restore" through government intervention. In short, Tribe, Sunstein, and Souter argue that one cannot evaluate a proposed law by comparing it with a baseline of freedom because there is no such baseline: all possible states of affairs are created by government action. Just as Lewis Carroll's Red Queen tells Alice that she can't have lost her way because all ways here are *the Queen's ways*, so Tribe and Sunstein argue that there is no such thing as an unregulated state, because all ways are *the government's ways*.[142]

Professor David E. Bernstein has attacked this thesis by pointing out that the *Lochner*-era Court was quite willing to accept the constitutionality of a wide array of legislation limiting the common-law rights of property and contract.[143] But on a deeper level, Sunstein, Tribe, and Souter see to the real heart of the matter. *Lochner* became a controversial case because it occurred at a time when legal theorists were beginning to abandon the notion that individuals have a natural, prepolitical right to freedom, or that laws limiting this natural freedom must be justified in some way. Progressives were replacing this notion with the premise that individual freedom is a privilege granted to individuals by government for social reasons, revocable when it suits society's interests. If, in fact, freedom is merely

116

a government-created privilege, then Tribe and the others are right: the choice to restrain that freedom is simply a prudential matter of cost-benefit analysis by the collective, not a morally problematic initiation of force against innocent individuals otherwise entitled to respect.

The idea that man is born free cannot be defended at length here. But it is worth pointing out—as many others have done[144]—that the notion of individual liberty logically antecedent to political society is a well-supported philosophical argument and one that remains alive in today's civil liberties decisions.[145] On their premises, Souter, Tribe, and Sunstein are, like the Progressives, unable to articulate any meaningful limit on government power. If the state creates property rights and freedom of contract and may revoke them for whatever social ends it deems desirable, it follows that freedom of speech, freedom of religion, the right of bodily integrity, and other freedoms are likewise social constructs that may be revoked whenever society deems it expedient. In fact, Sunstein argued for just this, calling for a "New Deal" for freedom of speech whereby government would regulate expression in essentially the same way it currently regulates the economy.[146]

Paul Kens

Paul Kens's 1998 book, *Lochner v. New York: Economic Regulation on Trial*,[147] appears to be the only single-volume work ever published on the case. Although it provides many interesting historical details, the book is deeply flawed in ways typical of most *Lochner* scholarship.

Kens makes no apparent attempt to understand, let alone explain, the reasons behind the decision in *Lochner*. His loaded language and conspiracy-theory approach to the "Gilded Age" caricatures the era's jurisprudence. Like Bork, he argues that courts should be even more deferential to majority power than Justice Holmes advocated in his dissent. Kens portrays the *Lochner* majority as captivated by "substantive due process" theory, without ever explaining what that phrase means. He repeatedly describes the decision as an instance of "laissez-faire social Darwinism," even thought not a word about Darwin or Darwinism is to be found in the opinion or in other writings of the era's judges.[148] His repeated claims that the *Lochner* majority (and Justice Field earlier) invented the notion of liberty of contract out of thin air—indeed, that the right to earn a living "had absolutely no basis in the law"[149]—ignores the long history of that right, a history that reaches back in a long line to 17th-century decisions by English courts and the writings of Sir Edward Coke. It also ignores the long and respectable tradition of substantive due process theory, found in such early American cases as *Trevett v. Weeden* (1786),[150] *Butler v. Craig* (1787),[151] *Ham v. McClaws* (1791),[152] *Anonymous* (1794),[153] *Hoke v. Henderson* (1833),[154] or in Daniel Webster's argument in the *Dartmouth College* case. Instead, he contends that due process, as originally conceived, "had nothing to do with the content of legislation" and that substantive due process was invented by the 19th-century legal scholar Thomas Cooley.[155] This cannot be an oversight, for Justice Field—about whom Kens has published a biography[156]—cited much of this history in his *Slaughterhouse* dissent, more than 30 years before *Lochner*. When Kens says that "[t]here was no basis for liberty of contract in common law, much less in constitutional law,"[157] he ignores the overwhelming evidence to the contrary, such as Blackstone's pronouncement that "[a]t common law every man might use what trade he pleased"[158]; or Coke's statements that "by the very common law, it was lawful for any man to use any trade thereby to maintain himself and his family; this was both lawful, and also very commendable"[159]; that "at the common law, no man could be prohibited from working in any lawful trade, for the law abhors idleness,"[160] and that "the common law abhors all monopolies, which prohibit any from working in any lawful trade."[161] Nor does Kens discuss the views of the Constitution's Framers. He refers to such obscure writers as Arthur Latham Perry, a professor at the College of William and Mary and author of the 1865 book *Political Economy*, but he never refers to John Locke, or to James Madison's observation that the "protection" of the citizens' "faculties of acquiring property" is the "first object of government."[162] Kens ridicules "vague principles . . . [such as] 'the liberty of citizens to acquire property and pursue happiness,'"[163] as though Field or the *Lochner* Court invented these terms—yet he fails to mention such documents as the Virginia Declaration of Rights of 1776, which declared that "all men . . . have certain inherent rights . . . [including] the enjoyment of life and liberty, *with the means of acquiring* and possessing property, *and pursuing* and obtaining *happiness* and safety."[164] Kens quotes Roscoe Pound's statement that opposition to *Lochner* "was in part a movement for the adjustment of legal doctrines to human conditions they are to govern *and away from first principles*,"[165] but he does not seem to understand Pound's point: that the decision rested on a solid legal and philosophical foundation but that Progressive critics of *Lochner* were in the process of rejecting that foundation.

Because Kens refuses to acknowledge that the right to earn a living had at least three centuries of legal history behind it by the time *Lochner* was decided, his only alternative is to endorse a sort of conspiracy theory in which the early 20th-century legal profession colluded to perpetuate this right as a sort of urban legend. Kens is astonished by what he perceives as strange ironies and sinister silences on the part of judges he critiques, but these are in fact indications that his theory fails to account for details that would fit very well into a more robust understanding of that case.

On top of his silence about the pedigree of the right to earn a living, Kens seems ignorant as to the meaning of substantive due process. For instance, he describes one case this way:

> Judge Werner . . . conceded that the state had the authority to abolish employer defenses. But substituting a system of workmen's compensation was to him another matter entirely. "One of the inalienable rights of every citizen is to hold and enjoy property until it is taken from him by due process of law," he reasoned. "When our constitutions were adopted it was the law of the land that no man who was without fault or negligence could be held liable for injuries sustained by another." Judge Werner concluded that having done just this, the workmen's compensation law violated both federal and state due process guarantees. This was an ingenious line of reasoning. Though based upon procedural arguments, it sought to create a new fundamental right against which judges could test the substance of state legislation.[166]

But substantive due process theory had *always* been based on a connection between procedure and substance: procedural fairness is only a subset of the substantive commitments embodied in the constitutional requirement that the legislature act only through "law" rather than by arbitrary pronouncement. And the proposition that the legislature may not by fiat abolish a substantive legal right without violating the due process clause was at least 60 years old by the time Judge Werner wrote his decision.[167] Kens may disagree with this theory; he may hold that whatever the majority decides to do is automatically law, and therefore that the "due process" requires only a majority vote. But failing to explain what substantive due process really is, and simply labeling the *Lochner* majority as "social Darwinists," sets up a straw man.

Kens frequently contradicts himself. For instance, he argues that liberty of contract is simply not protected by the Constitution, yet he later says that "[i]f what proponents of a double standard are seeking is something in the 'spirit' of the Constitution that justifies treating economic and noneconomic liberties differently, the history of ideas of which *Lochner* is a part demonstrates that *the distinction is not there*."[168] This sentence undoes Kens's interpretation of the *Lochner* era and its aftermath. If there is no distinction in the Constitution or in "the history of ideas" between economic and noneconomic liberty, and if the Constitution protects "liberty" (which it explicitly does), then Kens cannot deny that the Constitution protects economic liberty, including Joseph Lochner's and Aman Schmitter's freedom of contract.

Kens contradicts himself in other ways. He admits several times that there was no evidence that overwork in bakeries was actually a health threat to bakers, and he admits that the New York attorney general essentially conceded this point when arguing the case,[169] yet he condemns the Court for not caring about the bakers' health. Also, he writes that in 1937 the Court "suddenly reversed" itself and endorsed "an unabashed expression of a reformer's view of fairness" by "[drawing] a new boundary for the police power"[170]—but he says this after attacking the *Lochner* Court for supposedly "inventing" new theories and imposing them on the law. It is contradictory to applaud the Court for inventing new theories in the 1930s while condemning it for (allegedly) inventing new theories in 1905.

Although there are many other problems with Kens's book,[171] consider one last example. Kens repeatedly claims that the *Lochner*-era Court essentially created by fiat the judicial authority to look into the substance of state laws, and he argues that the Court should "abdicate[] its right to review them."[172] But this is an argument against judicial review itself, a position of such extreme majoritarianism that not even Holmes endorsed it. Kens's argument is really with *Marbury v. Madison*,[173] not with *Lochner*.

120

In itself, *Lochner* was an unremarkable case. The Supreme Court found that a restriction on a person's liberty to work for a living was valid if the restriction had some genuine connection to public health and safety. But it found that no such connection existed in the case and thus that the maximum-hours law was an unconstitutional deprivation of liberty without due process of law. *Lochner* was therefore consistent with a long and rich tradition of legal history and scholarship based solidly on the principles of the American Founding. But it came during a period of profound changes in American political philosophy. When the new theories of Progressivism finally prevailed and the Court abandoned the right to earn a living in the 1930s, it adopted a version of majoritarianism advanced in Justice Holmes's dissent—a dissent that marked a radical break with the political philosophy of the Founders.[174] Collective decisionmaking, whether by democratic majorities or by "expert" administrative agencies, came to be viewed as self-justifying: rather than being limited by (and devised to protect) the rights of individuals, democracy now *defined and created* individual rights, meaning that the majority could revoke or alter those rights by fiat. The legal community came to believe, as Justice Louis Brandeis did, that the legislature could "remold" the "liberty of the individual" in order to meet "the changing needs of society."[175]

Although the Court has at times acted in the *Lochner* tradition to enforce some limits on democracy and to protect certain individual rights, the legitimacy of doing so has been severely weakened by the modern Court's refusal to take substantive due process principles seriously. Meanwhile, many of today's legal scholars misinterpret or misrepresent *Lochner*, perpetuating the myth that lies at the center of the modern judiciary's hostility to economic freedom.

6. The Rational Basis Test

By 1934, attacks on the traditional concepts of economic liberty were a common feature of legal discourse. For years before *Lochner* was decided, Populists and Progressives had argued that economic freedom must be curtailed to serve the interests of society and that both economic freedom and property rights were actually privileges created by the state, to be altered whenever the interests of society required it.

Philosopher John Dewey, a leading Progressive intellectual, described the Progressive movement as a new kind of liberalism that abandoned the classical liberal focus on "individuality and liberty."[1] While 18th- and 19th-century liberals believed that "[g]overnmental intervention in industry and exchange" was "a violation not only of inherent individual liberty but also of natural laws" and that government's business was to protect a person's freedom to act without unreasonable interference by others, Progressives like Dewey had discovered "that an individual is nothing fixed, given ready-made," and that each individual's personality is "something achieved" through various "economic, legal and political institutions as well as science and art." Progressives sought, therefore, to manipulate the social institutions by which individuals were formed. Government "is as much interested in the positive construction of favorable institutions, legal, political and economic as it is in removing abuses and overt oppressions," and it should therefore assume control over every aspect of society relevant to the shaping of citizens' moral, spiritual, social, and economic development. Where the Bible had declared that people would "live, move, and have their being" in God, Dewey declared that man would now "live, move, and ha[ve] his being" in "social conditions" manipulated by the state.[2] The state would control society's resources to give meaning to people's lives. Although Dewey, like other Progressives, denied that their theories lead inexorably toward totalitarianism, it is difficult to find any clear dividing line that would prevent such theories from collapsing into an all-controlling dictatorship.[3]

Progressives like Dewey argued that social ills could be cured by expert government planners who would be insulated from politics and would therefore make the "correct" decisions about how people ought to live. This extended not only to government control over economic choices but also over private property, sexual freedom, freedom of speech, and a variety of other areas.[4] As Supreme Court Justice Louis Brandeis concluded, "[I]n the interest of the public and in order to preserve the liberty and the property of the great majority of the citizens of a State, rights of property and the liberty of the individual must be *remoulded*, from time to time, to meet the changing needs of society."[5] "Remoulded," of course, was a helpful euphemism for "violated." Individual rights that stood in the way of the central planner's vision would simply be obliterated.

Progressive Supreme Court justices like Holmes and Brandeis originally found themselves in the minority, writing dissenting opinions in cases like *Lochner*. But their admirers applauded what they considered the wave of the future. One contemporary of Justice Holmes named Dorsey Richardson observed in 1924 that he "came to the bench . . . when the transition from individualism to collectivism in England was in progress" and, being "too learned in the history of the law to be blind to the . . . socialistic trend in American political thought," he was prepared to "acquiesce" in such legislation despite clear constitutional rules that blocked it. Although Holmes perceived "the necessity for the establishment of a benevolent attitude towards social reform," actually amending the Constitution was a difficult task, so he and his supporters developed a new constitutional interpretation instead: "Next to amendment of the Constitution, the most feasible means of giving validity to new principles was to change the interpretation of [its] provisions," wrote Richardson. "'Liberty of contract' and the broad powers of review assumed by the courts under the 5th and 14th Amendments were the elements that barred the way to reform, and it is against these interpretations that Justice Holmes' most significant attacks have been directed."[6]

In the decade following these words, the upheaval of the Great Depression brought profound legal changes via a series of decisions that climaxed in the abandonment of meaningful constitutional protection for economic liberty. Among these decisions, the landmark 1934 case, *Nebbia v. New York*,[7] abandoned the framework established in *Munn v. Illinois* and opened the way for a vast expansion of government power. Under *Munn*, government could control private economic choices only if they were "affected with a public interest," meaning that the business in question was similar to a public entity—natural monopolies, for example, or common carriers. Although that standard was regrettably vague, it nevertheless provided a more or less clear line, ensuring that government could regulate only private economic activities that had some arguably direct effect on unconsenting third parties. *Lochner* itself was decided within this framework: the Court found that baking was not a business affected with a public interest and that the bakers and the general public were not threatened by long working hours. Thus, the maximum-hours law was an unjustified interference with bakers' right to labor as they chose.

Nebbia abolished the *Munn* model, declaring that government could regulate businesses of any sort so long as the regulation was "rationally related to a legitimate government interest."[8] That is, so long as elected officials might have believed the law had some connection to some goal the legislature had the authority to pursue, the law would be upheld as constitutional. Virtually no law could fail this new, extremely deferential standard. The Court backed away only slightly four years later, in *United States v. Carolene Products*, when it declared in a footnote that some cases—such as those involving burdens on "discrete and insular minorities" or restrictions on voting rights or free speech—would call for more serious judicial skepticism.[9]

This footnote was the birth of the legal notion of "tiers of scrutiny," which ever since the New Deal era has governed how courts evaluate the constitutionality of laws. In cases in which government intrudes on certain favored kinds of individual rights, such as speech or the right to travel, courts will examine the law at issue more closely to ensure that it is not a disguised attempt to accomplish illegitimate goals, such as censorship or political favoritism. But in cases in which government action intrudes on disfavored rights, including private property and economic freedom, courts use the lenient "rational basis" standard instead, which only requires that government actions be "rationally related to a legitimate state interest." This standard is so lenient that it effectively allows the legislature power to act as it pleases, on the theory that the rights at issue do not need serious protection by courts.

Nebbia involved a New York law that prohibited the sale of milk for less than 9 cents per quart. It is strange to think that during the Great Depression, government officials would make it illegal to sell milk for *low* prices, but the theory behind the law was quite popular with intellectuals at the time. In a free market, the interactions of supply and demand move the economy toward greater efficiency because producers will cut costs and improve quality in order to attract consumers. This helps drive innovation, as producers find faster and better ways to provide consumers with the goods and services that they want. It also encourages economic efficiency by removing from the marketplace those producers who are unable or unwilling to compete against more efficient firms. They can choose to go into another business instead or to find a niche market wherein they can specialize. This is admittedly disruptive to the entrepreneurs and workers who work for the less efficient firms and who, when those firms fail, find themselves temporarily unemployed and must obtain new jobs or new skills. This is the process that economist Joseph Schumpeter famously called "creative destruction." Although these economic readjustments may be difficult for workers, the result will be greater economic efficiency and more wealth for everyone, including those who were formerly unemployed.[10]

In the 1930s, the creative nature of this dynamism was not widely respected, and intellectuals professing a doctrine of "rational" economic planning by government assailed the basic concepts of supply and demand, claiming that government control over the economy would eliminate the alleged inefficiencies of capitalism, equalize income among citizens, and organize economic activity with precision.[11] This planning was generally characterized as "reform" and as a way to protect small-scale producers and family farmers from unfair competition by powerful industries, but the reality was quite different: the new economic planning systems stifled entrepreneurship and innovation and worsened the Great Depression. In fact, many of the production codes implemented in this period were designed by politically influential industrialists to secure monopoly privileges for themselves.[12] Big business was in a far better position to manipulate regulatory agencies to act in ways that benefited them and to comply with price-fixing rules that blocked the small producer's ability to compete.

In 1933, declaring that the milk industry was related to "the well being of our citizens" and "the strength and vigor of the race" and was therefore "affected with a public interest,"[13] the New York legislature created a three-member commission to set the price of milk. This Milk Control Board declared it a crime to sell milk for less than 9 cents per quart. When Leo Nebbia sold two quarts of milk and a loaf of bread for 18 cents, he was charged and convicted of violating this law. He appealed, arguing that selling milk at low prices was not the sort of thing that harmed the general public, meaning that the government had no business prohibiting low milk prices. The New York Court of Appeals upheld the law, and the United States Supreme Court agreed. In a 5–4 decision, the justices abandoned the entire scheme of "affectation with a public interest." After listing the wide variety of moral and economic matters that government was already allowed to control, the Court declared that

> a state is free to adopt whatever economic policy may reasonably be deemed to promote public welfare, and to enforce that policy by legislation adapted to its purpose. The courts are without authority either to declare such policy, or, when it is declared by the legislature, to override it. If the laws passed are seen to have a reasonable relation to a proper legislative purpose, and are neither arbitrary nor discriminatory, the requirements of due process are satisfied. . . .[14]

This was the birth of "rational basis" scrutiny: the rule that so long as a law has a "rational relationship" to a "legitimate state interest," it satisfies the due process clause. The rational relationship, or rational basis, test has remained the controlling rule with regard to economic regulations ever since.

The Problems with Rational Basis

The phrase "rational basis" can be misleading. Considering whether a challenged law has a rational basis does not mean that the court decides whether the law is actually *rational* in an economic, scientific, or logical sense. As Justice McReynolds pointed out in his dissenting opinion in *Nebbia*, there was nothing rational about prohibiting low-cost milk during a national Depression.[15] The rational basis test does not require that the law actually make sense—but simply asks whether a legislator *might have thought* that the law was good for the public. As the Court has noted more recently, "[W]e never require a legislature to articulate its reasons for enacting a statute."[16] Even where the facts demonstrate that a law *cannot* accomplish its alleged purpose, courts will not find it unconstitutionally irrational.[17] Economists are in almost universal agreement, for example, that minimum-wage laws increase unemployment and raise prices, particularly on those goods and services purchased by the poor.[18] Yet no amount of expert testimony by economists could persuade a court to find the minimum wage unconstitutional under this test. Indeed, the legislature is not even required to have any actual evidence that a proposed law would work. The reasonableness of an economic regulation is "not subject to courtroom fact-finding and may be based on rational speculation unsupported by evidence or empirical data."[19] Instead, a judge using the rational basis test asks whether there is *any* conceivable reason to uphold the law—and it is "entirely irrelevant for constitutional purposes" whether the justification that the judge finds to be sufficient is actually the same reason that the legislature had in mind.[20] In other words, even if lawmakers actually meant to do something unconstitutional, or even if they had no particular goal in mind at all, courts will uphold the law if they can think of some *other*, legitimate purpose that might also be advanced by the law.

It should be clear why virtually no law is ever held unconstitutional under the rational basis standard. Put simply, it holds that as long as a judge can imagine that a politician could have thought the law would be a good idea—even if no actual politician did so, or had any reason for doing so—the judge will find the law constitutional. But thanks to the New Deal legacy, this is the standard applied when a plaintiff challenges the constitutionality of a law that restricts economic freedom or property rights.

As we shall see, there are at least four flaws in this test that make it meaningless and therefore futile for plaintiffs to challenge a law subject to rational basis review. First, the test assigns the burden of proof in a way that violates basic principles of logic and makes it almost impossible for a litigant to win in an actual lawsuit, no matter how serious the abuse of which he complains. Second, rational basis inquiry allows courts to devise wholly speculative justifications for a challenged statute, with no requirement that the legislature actually considered those justifications. This means, essentially, that courts may make up the law as they go along. Third, rational basis scrutiny invites and excuses the sort of sloppy government actions and unprincipled legal thinking that courts have struggled to eliminate elsewhere. Fourth, and worst of all, although the rational basis test has been the law of the land for 70 years, courts have yet to articulate what, precisely, *is* a legitimate state interest. There is therefore no logical sense in discussing whether a law is rationally related to such an interest.

One basic rule of logic—and one of the oldest rules of the law—is that the party asserting a claim bears the burden of proving it.[21] The person who denies the assertion does not bear the burden of disproving it. More colloquially, "you can't prove a negative." This is not mere convention, but an inescapable part of the way people think. It is impossible, for example, to prove that Congress has *not* been taken over by Martians whose perfect disguises allow them to masquerade as members of Congress. One might argue that they look like humans—but, of course, the Martians are just well disguised. One might take blood samples of the members, but this, too, would be unavailing since of course the Martians thought of that and made sure to implant facsimile blood to fool the test. One might argue that there is no proof that anyone lives on Mars—but, of course, the Martians are just hiding from us. Disproving an arbitrary claim is a hopeless task because an arbitrary assertion can simply be reinforced by other arbitrary assertions, each of which, untethered to any evidence, has equal standing in logic (that is, no standing at all).

To presume in favor of the truth of arbitrary assertions, therefore, is to expose oneself to exploitation at the hands of those who can simply make things up. If we are required to respect every person's assertions, even when they are backed by no evidence, rational discourse is at an end. The logical fallacy involved is called *argumentum ad ignorantium*, or "the argument from ignorance." One manifestation of this fallacy is the argument that, because something has not been proved to be false, it must be true. The problem with such arguments is that the mere fact that something has not been disproved does not say anything one way or the other about whether it is true: it might just be that the evidence has merely not been discovered yet. Shifting the burden of proof from the person who asserts the claim to the person who denies the claim is fallacious because it presumes the truth of things for which there is no evidence.

129

The dangerous real-world consequences of this fallacy are especially clear in the realm of criminal law. If the state presumed a person guilty of a crime whenever an allegation was made—and required that person to prove his innocence—defendants would be unable to exonerate themselves, and many innocent people would end up in jail. The presumption of innocence in criminal law is a manifestation of this timeless logical rule. In addition, that presumption works to prevent wrongful convictions because of the risk involved in case of error. It is better to presume innocence than guilt because the severity of error operates more harshly on the wrongly accused innocent than on the wrongly acquitted guilty person; hence, the legal tradition that it is less bad for a guilty person to go free than for an innocent person to be convicted.

Just as the presumption of innocence protects innocent people from wrongful convictions, the presumption in favor of freedom protects innocent people's liberty to act. As philosopher Anthony de Jasay explains, for any action that person A might consider undertaking, there are a potentially infinite number of reasons for person B to object to that action. Requiring A to disprove these reasons before acting would paralyze him, because he would be required "[t]o falsify the hypothesis that the act is objectionable," or to prove a negative. This "is a needle-in-the-haystack type of task, very difficult and costly if the set of potential objections is large, and logically impossible if the set is not finite."[22]

The "rational basis" test shifts the burden of proof in just such an illogical manner. Under that test, a person who argues that an economic regulation is unconstitutional is legally required "to negative every conceivable basis" that might support the regulation, even if the government does not explain what the basis for the regulation is.[23] The plaintiff must therefore imagine every possible rationale supporting the law and prove that each is unfounded. Moreover, the government need not prove that the assumptions that led the lawmakers to enact the regulation are actually true. It is not enough, for example, to argue that an occupational licensing law or a zoning restriction or a taxicab medallion requirement is unnecessary because there is no real risk to the public from the business in question; as long as the legislature *might* have thought that there *could* be some risk *someday*—even without evidence to support that concern—the government will win the case.

This would be bad enough if the courts considering the constitutionality of such laws limited themselves to the actual justifications advanced by the legislators who voted for the challenged law, but the rational basis test allows judges to devise their own, entirely speculative rationalizations for a challenged law, even reasons not offered in the legislature or in court, and even if the court received no briefing and heard no evidence about such a justification.

If a businessman argues that an economic regulation is not reasonable, he is not only required to look through the history of the regulation to find out why it was actually adopted, and then to disprove that reason, he must also simultaneously be on the lookout for any rationale that government attorneys might dream up during the course of the lawsuit, even if those justifications have nothing to do with—or are even the direct opposite of—those the legislature actually had in mind. And if he does manage to disprove these, the judge may still devise his or her *own* justification for the law when writing the decision. The rational basis test, as one federal judge has observed, "can hardly be termed scrutiny at all. Rather, it is a standard which invites us to cup our hands over our eyes and then imagine if there could be anything right with the statute."[24] With the deck so heavily stacked against litigants, it is little wonder that virtually no law is ever found to violate the rational basis test.

The irrational rational basis test allows government officials so much leeway that they are often negligent, or simply dishonest, when dealing with people's economic freedom. Attorney Clark Neily points out the problem by imagining what a criminal trial would look like if it operated under the same test:

> "Objection—lacks foundation; hearsay; assumes facts not in evidence."
> "Counsel?"
> "The witness is speculating, your honor."
> "Is it rational speculation?"
> "Why, yes your honor, it is."
> "Overruled!"[25]

This is a standard that, as Neily writes, "most litigators can only fantasize about."[26] Yet under the rational basis test, it is literally how lawsuits play out. Government officials, called on to state under oath the justifications for the law, are allowed to invent their own reasons—even outlandish ones—to support the law, even if there is no proof that those justifications actually animated the law, or that those justifications make any sense. And judges are invited to invent their own reasons as well.

The rational basis test has an even more fundamental flaw. Although it requires laws to be rationally related to a "legitimate government interest," the Supreme Court has never defined what that phrase means. On the contrary, the Court has admitted that it has "not elaborated on the standards for determining what constitutes a 'legitimate state interest.'"[27] This is an astonishing confession for the nation's highest court to make: although the rational basis test requires laws to have some relationship to an acceptable purpose, the nation's chief judges do not know what purposes are or are not acceptable, or even how to approach that question. The reason for this failure is obvious: to draw such lines would require the justices to state forthrightly that some things are simply off limits to the legislature. Yet the entire purpose of the rational basis test is to ratify the exponential growth of legislative power over the last century. For the Court to hold that certain things are not legitimate state interests would be to tempt the wrath of the legislative leviathan whose growth the Court has abetted. In fact, in those few cases in which the Court has staked out some subjects as beyond the legitimate reach of the legislature, the political branches have reacted with incandescent fury. In *Lawrence v. Texas*,[28] for example, the Court declared that the private sexual activities of consenting adults were none of the government's business—a comparatively minor matter, considering that few states had such laws and fewer still ever enforced them. Even one of the dissenters acknowledged that such laws are "uncommonly silly."[29] Nevertheless, the decision enraged commentators and pundits unaccustomed to the idea that legislative power is limited by the Constitution. They were unused to that idea precisely because of Supreme Court precedents that abdicated the duty to keep legislatures within their bounds. This role, which legal historian G. Edward White calls "guardian review,"[30] conforms to the Framers' vision, but thanks to the Progressives and their New Deal heirs, it has been almost entirely replaced by a deferential attitude toward the elected branches, a deference adopted to enable the expansion of the regulatory welfare state. The generations of lawyers who received their training after this deference became the norm do not react well to the relatively rare cases when the judiciary intervenes to block legislation.

But assuming the Supreme Court must eventually explain what a legitimate state interest is—and it is hard to see how that can be avoided forever—how should the justices analyze the issue? Here, too, the modern judiciary is stymied by the New Deal legacy. In some cases, the Court has suggested that the "legitimacy" of a government interest can be judged simply by the amount of legislative support the interest has.[31] This is why Professor Richard A. Epstein writes that the phrase "legitimate state interest" is only "a convenient label for serious inquiry."[32] The phrase itself suggests that judges should consult the philosophical charters of American constitutionalism—particularly the Declaration of Independence, with its classical liberal theory of individual freedom.[33] But doing so would be deeply controversial, since it would challenge the Progressive legacy that has largely succeeded in transforming constitutional law from a means of securing the blessings of liberty to the advancing of "democratic" decisionmaking by unelected, expert bureaucracies.[34]

Whether one supports or opposes the Court's abandonment of guardian review, one thing is unavoidably clear: no reasonable mind can make sense of the requirement that laws relate to a legitimate state interest unless one has some idea of what state interests *are or are not legitimate*. With that matter unsettled, one cannot sensibly discuss whether a law does or does not advance such an interest. A means cannot be judged without understanding the desired end, just as a traveler cannot know whether he is taking a "rational" route if he has no idea what his destination is.[35] In Justice Stevens's words, the rational basis "formulation sweeps too broadly, for it is difficult to imagine a legislative classification that could *not* be supported by a 'reasonably conceivable state of facts.' Judicial review under the 'conceivable set of facts' test is tantamount to no review at all."[36]

Litigating under the Rational Basis Test

Given the inadequacies of the rational basis test, one can easily imagine how hard it is for citizens to prevail in cases reviewed under this lenient degree of scrutiny. This was demonstrated in a recent case challenging a Louisiana law that imposes an occupational licensing requirement on florists. The law requires applicants to pass a one-hour written examination and a three-hour performance examination, the latter testing people on such subjective criteria as the "harmony" and "effectiveness" of their flower arrangements. Obviously, the licensing regime makes it very difficult for would-be florists to obtain licenses; in the years since 2000, fewer than 50 percent of applicants have passed the test.

The notion that such a licensing scheme protects the public health and safety is nothing short of preposterous. The Michigan Supreme Court struck down a similar law in 1939, noting that there was no evidence "of any evil in connection with the sale of flowers and potted plants"[37] and that the law was "not [designed] to protect the citizens of Detroit in their public health, safety, morals or general welfare, but was for the financial benefit of a few" because it restricted the liberty of entering the florist trade.[38] Yet in the Louisiana case, the trial court upheld the law. Rejecting the plaintiffs' argument that "'people handle millions of unlicensed floral arrangements around the world every year without being harmed,'" the court found that the evidence "does reveal and support Louisiana's concern for the safety and protection of the general public." The court quoted one witness:

> I believe that the retail florist does protect people from injury. . . . We're very diligent about not having an exposed pick, not having a broken wire, not hav[ing] a flower that has some type of infection, like, dirt that remained on it when it's inserted into something they're going to handle, and I think that because of this training, that prevents the public from having any injury. . . .

The court concluded that the legislature's decision to "license those engaged in the industry by administering a floral licensing examination is rationally related to the state's desire that floral arrangements will be assembled properly in a manner least likely to cause injury to a consumer, and will be prepared in a proper, cost efficient manner." The law therefore was "rationally related to the government interest of public welfare and safety."[39] In other words, the licensing scheme was a legitimate way of protecting the people of Louisiana from *scratching their fingers on the wires that florists use to hold their floral arrangements together.* This conclusion, although insufficient to pass the laugh test, did pass the rational basis test.

Higher Scrutiny

In 1938, four years after *Nebbia*, the Supreme Court reiterated that the existence of valid reasons for restricting economic freedom "is to be presumed," and that "regulatory legislation affecting ordinary commercial transactions" is immune from judicial scrutiny whenever it "rests upon some rational basis."[40] But it added a footnote to say that some other types of laws would be subjected to a more stringent test: laws affecting "discrete and insular minorities" or interfering with the political processes or affecting those individual rights specifically described in the Bill of Rights might be viewed more skeptically by the Court.

This was the famous "footnote four" of *United States v. Carolene Products*, and with it was born the theory of "varying standards of scrutiny." In the decades to follow, certain rights that judges considered important received serious judicial protection, whereas laws regulating private property and economic liberty received virtually none.[41] This led to a gradual revival of substantive due process with a new focus (or, rather, with one eye closed): sexual privacy, abortion, and freedom of expression would be given increased judicial attention from the 1950s on, while disfavored freedoms, including the freedom of contract, would be largely ignored. But where the older version of substantive due process focused on the abuse of political systems by politically powerful groups against their rivals, this new version of substantive due process focused on the importance of the specific action that a citizen claimed as a protected right. The former substantive due process analysis was concerned with whether a challenged law actually protected the general public from harm, or whether that was merely a pretext for serving the private interests of political favorites. The new version of substantive due process protected specific types of action based on whether they were socially important (such as freedom of speech) or whether the judges thought them important to personal life (such as sexual privacy or abortion). The importance of these activities was often assessed by the judges' own subjective standards, thus seriously undermining the legitimacy of substantive due process theory and exposing it to the charge that it was simply a way to "legislate from the bench." Yet while this charge has some merit when levied against the renovated, activity-based variety of substantive due process, it is less appropriate when applied to the older, class-legislation theory of *Lochner* and similar cases.[42]

More importantly, the Court's decision to apply more demanding levels of scrutiny to certain "preferred" rights over other kinds of rights—what lawyers call the constitutional "double standard"—makes little philosophical sense. Can we really say that the rights the Court considers "fundamental" (including the freedom to vote or to travel to Washington, D.C.) are really "more important" or deserve more protection than the right to earn a living without government intrusion or the right to own property? Regular citizens seem equally concerned—perhaps more concerned—with these latter rights. The average person certainly engages in commercial transactions more often than he or she votes or participates in a political protest, and many people would place a higher value on their freedom to make a living for themselves and their families than on their right to travel to Washington for a chance to lobby a member of Congress. As Laurence Tribe acknowledges, failing to protect economic rights "overlooks the importance of property and contract in protecting the dispossessed no less than the established; it forgets the political impotence of the isolated job-seeker who has been fenced out of an occupation; and in no event could it justify more than a modest difference in degree between the judicial roles in the two areas."[43]

Why, then, have courts treated economic freedom like "a poor relation"?[44] In part, it may be that lawyers and judges—intellectuals who make their living from words rather than manual labor—tend to place a higher value on expression and related rights than on labor.[45] Be that as it may, it is also because the Progressive political theory that the Court adopted during the New Deal era held that the Constitution's primary purpose was to foster government decision-making rather than to protect individual freedom against intrusions by the state. For the Progressives, "democracy" took precedence over liberty as a constitutional value. Thus, speech and voting rights continued to receive protection because of their role in the "democratic process," while property and economic rights were seen as expendable, or as matters that government ought to restrict for the "common good." But whatever the reason for the modern double standard of constitutional law, it is at least clear, as Justice Scalia has observed, that "[t]he picking and choosing among various rights to be accorded 'substantive due process' protection" as well as "the categorical and inexplicable exclusion of so-called 'economic rights' (even though the Due Process Clause explicitly applies to 'property') unquestionably involves policymaking rather than neutral legal analysis."[46]

The double standard becomes especially cumbersome in cases that overlap the unwieldy categories of "fundamental" and "not-so-fundamental" rights. Take, for example, a group of recent lawsuits challenging laws in Alabama and other states that restrict the sale of adult novelties or sex toys on moral grounds.[47] These laws obviously have an adverse effect on sexual privacy (a "fundamental" personal right), but they are aimed solely at commercial activity (a "nonfundamental" economic right). Because the "rational basis" test is biased so severely in favor of the constitutionality of economic regulations, plaintiffs in these cases have used privacy theories or sought protection on other fundamental rights grounds. Alas, courts have not been fooled into seeing these cases as privacy cases. They have upheld the laws under rational basis scrutiny, concluding, as the Eleventh Circuit did, that all commercial transactions are "inherently public" and subject to government oversight.[48] The result is that private consensual sexual activity cannot be intrusively regulated by the state[49]—but the purchase of the objects used in the bedroom can be.

This overlap between "economic" and "noneconomic" rights is to be expected. Economic freedom, after all, is not in principle different from other types of freedom. Freedom of the press, to use one common example, would mean little if private individuals and groups could not own presses, or if their right to buy or sell newspapers were controlled by the government. Economic freedom is often essential to the exercise of other types of rights—as when a person leases a billboard (an economic right) to advertise a political message (a speech right). The interrelationship of economic and personal rights is nowhere more obvious than in the case of homeownership. When, in the notorious *Kelo* case, the Supreme Court held that government can condemn homes via eminent domain and give the property to private developers for their own use and profit, Justice Clarence Thomas pointed out the basic absurdity of the post–New Deal bias against economic and property rights: "Something has gone seriously awry with this Court's interpretation of the Constitution. Though citizens are safe from the government in their homes, the homes themselves are not."[50]

Given the untenable nature of the rational basis test, it is no surprise that courts have applied it in inconsistent and confusing ways.

In some rational basis decisions, they have struck down laws that would seem likely to withstand the usual "rubber stamp" rational basis theory. For example, in 1985 the Supreme Court invalidated a local government's decision to bar the creation of a group home for the mentally retarded in the city of Cleburne, Texas.[51] The justices found that the only reason the city had denied the permit was prejudice against the mentally handicapped, and to placate this unreasonable fear was not a proper government purpose. Thus, even though the city's decision involved only property rights and did not qualify for anything more than the deferential rational basis test, the Court still found it unconstitutional. Again, in the 1996 case of *Romer v. Evans*,[52] the Supreme Court struck down a Colorado ballot initiative that prohibited the state from extending benefits to homosexuals. The Court held that the law violated the rational basis test because it, too, was enacted out of irrational prejudice. Justice Kennedy explained that the rational basis test did not mean government could do anything it wanted:

> [E]ven in the ordinary equal protection case calling for the most deferential of standards, we insist on knowing the relation between the classification adopted and the object to be attained. . . . [There must be a] link between classification and objective . . . [and] . . . some relation between the classification and the purpose it served. By requiring that the classification bear a rational relationship to an independent and legitimate legislative end, we ensure that classifications are not drawn for the purpose of disadvantaging the group burdened by the law.[53]

It is so rare for courts to declare laws unconstitutional under the rational basis test that some commentators refer to these cases as "rational basis with bite" and suggest that judges are actually applying something other than the rational basis test. But the justices have rejected this suggestion, insisting that rational basis analysis is consistent with a serious analysis of the law, regardless of what previous rational basis cases suggested. This claim is plausible, given that what the Court did in *Romer* and *Cleburne* was to inquire whether the challenged government actions were actually *rational*.[54] If, as the Court claims, *Romer* and *Cleburne* did represent a step in the evolution of a more serious rational basis test, that step should be welcomed. If rationality is the very minimum requirement of constitutionality, then it should require at the very least that laws advance the common good and not a mere desire to exclude political outsiders. Many of the economic restrictions adopted by legislatures today would fail even this minimal degree of scrutiny.

In fact, the rationale usually given for treating some rights as "more fundamental" than others should itself suggest the need for greater judicial protection from certain kinds of economic regulation, even aside from the dubious nature of the double standard. According to the "footnote four" theory, courts apply higher scrutiny whenever there are special circumstances that handicap "discrete and insular minorities" in the political arena, making them more vulnerable to exploitation. The justices have explained that courts have a "special role in safeguarding the interests of those groups that are 'relegated to such a position of political powerlessness as to command extraordinary protection from the majoritarian political process.'"[55] But certain economic groups often face precisely these disadvantages. When a legislature is swayed by powerful lobbyists to adopt a regulation that prohibits entrepreneurs from entering the market, those entrepreneurs are just as much victims of the political process as are other kinds of minority groups. As Professor Robert McCloskey wrote,

> [T]he scattered individuals who are denied access to an occupation by State-enforced barriers are about as impotent a minority as can be imagined. The would-be barmaids of Michigan or the would-be plumbers of Illinois have no more chance against the entrenched influence of the established bartenders and master plumbers than the Jehovah's Witnesses had against the prejudices of the Minersville School District.[56]

To say that these would-be entrepreneurs must resort to the political process rather than the judiciary is, McCloskey concluded, "to sacrifice their civil rights in the name of an amiable fiction."[57] Disfavored minorities, whether they be the mentally handicapped, homosexuals, or entrepreneurs, have no realistic opportunity to persuade legislatures to respect their rights. They must receive protection from the courts or not at all. Yet even with *Romer* and *Cleburne* in place, the rational basis test usually blinds judges to the very real obstacles that prevent small businesses from receiving just treatment from the legislature.

139

The argument that businesses must resort to the political arena rather than the judiciary for protection is particularly hollow, given that economic regulations are generally not enacted by legislatures at all but by administrative agencies not answerable to voters. These agencies are not staffed by elected representatives; they are staffed by appointed or hired bureaucrats who cannot be removed from their posts without long and complicated delays. These bureaucrats adopt and enforce an enormous variety of rules, often with no review by elected officials. Moreover, legislative rules that protect elected incumbents—including gerrymandering and campaign finance restrictions—even make it difficult for voters to remove sitting legislators who in theory supervise the bureaucracy. Once again, the idea that businesspeople who are harmed by a regulation can just "vote the bums out," rather than seek judicial redress, is extremely unrealistic.

The double standard, therefore, fails even to serve the "democratic" values most frequently advanced to justify it. If a legislature were to adopt a law placing even a relatively small burden on a racial minority, courts would no doubt scrupulously enforce the Constitution's promise of equal treatment. But if the legislature passes a law that imposes a serious burden on an economic minority—perhaps even destroying their businesses entirely—courts will simply look the other way as long as the government offers some barely plausible explanation. It seems ironic, indeed, that so many defenders of the "rational basis" rule would be quick to criticize older court decisions for so-called formalism. The rational basis test—by simply assuming the legitimacy of virtually anything the legislature claims as its goal—enshrines formalism *à outrance*.

Until more sense is made of the rational basis test, or until the Court devises a new mechanism for constitutional analysis, people seeking protection for the right to earn an honest living face one of the most uneven playing fields American law has ever devised. Judges explicitly presume against them from the outset, allowing defendants to make up far-fetched excuses not grounded in evidence; they invent excuses on behalf of defendants, and then they make rulings without reference to the most important question involved in every stage of the analysis: *is this a proper thing for government to be doing?* Ordinary American citizens hoping for protection of their economic freedom can only hope that judges can someday inject some rationality into the rational basis test.

7. Protectionism and the Law

One recurring theme in the law of economic liberty is the issue of protectionism. The government's power to regulate products and services can also be used to insulate one business from competition by others. Because such protection can bring a lot of money to the protected company, businesses are willing to invest a great deal of time and money in efforts to influence that power in their favor. In a free market, a company that wants to succeed and grow must increase the quality of its products, decrease its prices, or find some other way to appeal to consumer needs. But businesses that cannot or do not want to compete in this way will often try to exploit government authority for their own advantage by illegalizing their competition or by making competition inordinately expensive through the creation of what economists call "barriers to entry": rules that bar new companies from entering the marketplace.

The classic example of a barrier to entry is a tariff: a tax on imports that makes them more expensive than domestic products. Tariffs make it difficult for foreign companies to compete against domestic producers, needlessly increasing costs to consumers and allowing domestic manufacturers to produce lower-quality merchandise, safe from higher-quality imports. Domestic manufacturers, therefore, often favor tariffs but rarely admit that their support is a matter of their own private gain. Instead, a domestic steel company or car manufacturer will argue that less expensive imports are somehow "unfair," perhaps because other countries have less restrictive labor or environmental laws that enable foreign companies to produce goods more cheaply. Or domestic companies may encourage irrational prejudices, claiming that it is unpatriotic to buy foreign products, for example, or that imports are substandard because foreigners are racially or ethnically inferior. Political leaders often impose such restrictions in the name of patriotism or "protecting jobs." In reality, such laws amount to taxes levied on consumers, "taxes" that do not fund government programs but instead transfer wealth to private businesses in the form of higher prices and decreased competition. This is why, in 1621, Sir Edward Coke likened those who promote tariffs to a man in a rowboat: they "look one way and row another; they pretend public benefit; intend private."[1]

Three centuries later, in 1932, the United States Supreme Court decided the case of *New State Ice Co. v. Liebmann*.[2] *Liebmann* challenged the constitutionality of an Oklahoma law limiting the number of businesses that could deliver ice to customers. The law set up a government agency to grant or withhold permission to entrepreneurs who wanted to enter the ice trade. An applicant who desired to start a new business was required to prove to the board's satisfaction that a new ice company was necessary; if the board was not convinced, permission would be denied. The board was staffed by representatives of companies that were already in the ice delivery business and who were naturally reluctant to allow new competitors into the marketplace. Justice George Sutherland, writing for a 7–2 Supreme Court, found the law unconstitutional under the Fourteenth Amendment's due process clause because it served the private interests of politically influential businesses rather than the genuine public good. The board's obvious conflict of interest meant that the scheme could not possibly be fair. "Stated succinctly, a private corporation here seeks to prevent a competitor from entering the business of making and selling ice," he noted. "There is no question now before us of any regulation by the state to protect the consuming public. . . . The control here asserted does not protect against monopoly, but tends to foster it. The aim is not to encourage competition, but to prevent it; not to regulate the business, but to preclude persons from engaging in it."[3] Most importantly, the law interfered with the basic right of all Americans "to engage in a lawful private business," without interference by the government.[4]

In dissent, Justice Louis Brandeis, an outspoken Progressive who enthusiastically endorsed government regulation of the marketplace, defended the law. States, he argued, should be free to experiment with legislation. "It is one of the happy incidents of the federal system that a single courageous state may, if its citizens choose, serve as a laboratory; and try novel social and economic experiments without risk to the rest of the country."[5] But while this statement has become an icon of federalism, Justice Sutherland's response to it is less often quoted. The Constitution, Sutherland answered, does not allow states to "experiment" in ways that deprive citizens of their liberty. "It is not necessary to challenge the authority of the states to indulge in experimental legislation; but it would be strange and unwarranted doctrine to hold that they may do so by enactments which transcend the limitations imposed upon them by the Federal Constitution. . . . [T]here are certain essentials of liberty with which the state is not entitled to dispense in the interest of experiments."[6] For example, states were not allowed to "experiment" with censorship, or to "experiment" by depriving people of their religious freedom. The right "to apply one's labor and skill in an ordinary occupation with proper regard for all reasonable regulations is no less entitled to protection."[7]

This basic conflict between the constitutional limits on government designed to preserve individual liberty and the power of legislatures to enact laws that limit liberty was and remains a recurring theme in American law, particularly the law of economic freedom. Moreover, the question of whether regulatory agencies serve the public welfare or the private interest of insiders is inescapable. If government controls an industry in ways that protect some groups from competition by others, businesses will invest resources in trying to convince the agency to act in ways that will benefit them—all under the pretext of advancing the public welfare.

Although the regulatory scheme struck down in *Liebmann* may seem bizarre by present standards—how could "too many" ice businesses possibly endanger the public?—it is today the model by which most major metropolitan areas regulate taxis and other forms of transportation. Most cities require taxis to obtain government licenses, called "medallions," before operating, and getting such a license requires an entrepreneur first to obtain a "certificate of necessity"— he or she must prove to the government's satisfaction that a new taxi company is "necessary." This is usually extremely difficult, especially if the regulatory agency is staffed by people with close ties to the existing companies that want to forestall competition. But constitutional challenges to this regulatory scheme have failed, thanks to the rational basis test courts use when evaluating such laws. In 1992, for example, when Leroy Jones and a group of friends asked the city of Denver, Colorado, for a certificate allowing them to operate a taxi company, more than 10 existing cab companies showed up at a public hearing to argue against their application, and the government turned Jones down. Jones filed a lawsuit, pointing out that the city had refused every such application since 1947 and arguing that its refusal to grant new permits arbitrarily created a monopoly at the expense of consumers and honest entrepreneurs. Nevertheless, the trial judge threw Jones's case out of court.[8]

Even where licensing boards are not staffed by owners of competing businesses with an obvious conflict of interest or by bureaucrats with friends or family members in the business, laws like these present problems for entrepreneurs trying to earn a living. The general public is usually unaware of the Byzantine rules companies are required to follow, while the companies seeking protection are very familiar with them. Thus, although regulatory agencies often open their hearings to the public, members of the public rarely attend and are usually not organized. The agencies hear forceful arguments from representatives of existing companies but rarely from consumers, and they are consequently biased. Even ignoring such biases, "certificate of necessity" schemes impose a nearly impossible burden on newcomers. Proving that a new business is "necessary" is virtually impossible, even with extensive polling data and research. Existing companies can always argue that a newcomer is not "necessary" because the existing businesses could handle any increased consumer demand by increasing their prices, adding another office, or getting a government subsidy. What's more, many businesses that consumers enjoy patronizing are not strictly "necessary" but only *convenient*. Are cell phones really *necessary*? What about decorative covers for cell phones, or amusing ringtones? The term "necessary" is itself hard to define, and the notion that a government bureaucracy can decide what businesses are or are not necessary for consumers is a fantasy, and a dangerous one because it plays directly to the self-interest of established businesses that seek protection against competition.[9] The only group capable of deciding whether a business is really necessary for a community, and the only group that can be trusted with the power to make such a decision on behalf of consumers, is consumers themselves.

Although there are any number of ways for interested businesses to use the law to exclude competition, four methods are of particular interest: occupational licensing laws, zoning regulations, "agricultural adjustment," and franchise acts.

Licensing

The justification for modern occupational licensing, as it was developed in the 19th century, was that such laws would protect the public from dangerous or incompetent practitioners. By requiring doctors to prove that they knew how to perform operations safely and effectively, for example, the government could ensure that consumers did not fall victim to quacks and con artists. In 1889, in *Dent v. West Virginia*,[10] the first Supreme Court decision to address occupational licensing, Justice Field held that such laws were a legitimate way to protect "the general welfare of [the] people" and "secure them against the consequences of ignorance and incapacity, as well as of deception and fraud."[11] But if the licensing requirements had "no relation to such calling or profession," or if licenses were "unattainable by . . . reasonable study and application," such laws would "operate to deprive one of his right to pursue a lawful vocation" and thus violate the Constitution.[12] More than half a century later, the Court reaffirmed this conclusion when it held that the state may not bar a person from a profession on the basis of irrelevant factors, such as his political opinions.[13] Unfortunately, despite claims that it would protect the general public, licensing is often used as a tool to prevent competition from disfavored groups.

Abuses started early.[14] In 1878, California called its second constitutional convention at the behest of a powerful political organization called the Workingmen's Party. The party advocated new restrictions on corporations, particularly railroads, as well as an end to what it called the "Chinese Menace": the enormous influx of immigrant labor from China, which increased the supply of available labor and thereby drove down the costs not only of labor but of the goods and services that labor produced. Although the lower prices were good news for consumers, the decrease in the price of labor—that is, wages—made it harder for natives and European immigrants to demand high pay for their work. Whites were explicit about their outrage over this state of affairs. As one delegate to the convention put it, a Chinese worker was "a creature, whose muscles are as iron, whose sinews are like thongs, whose nerves are like steel wires, with a stomach case lined with brass; a creature who can toil sixteen hours of the twenty-four. . . . The white man cannot compete in the field of labor with such a being as that. . . . If the white man is to compete with the Chinaman he must adopt a cheaper style of dress, must inure himself to the cold, he must labor in the night; sleep shall not come to his pillow until the midnight bell . . . [and he must] arise at the first gray streaks of dawn."[15] In other words, while racists sometimes accuse racial minorities of being lazy, those who attacked the Chinese accused them of being intelligent and hard working. As one railroad laborer later recalled, the Chinese were hated "not for their vices but for their virtues . . . because [they] are so much more honest, industrious, steady, sober, and painstaking."[16]

Hostility to Chinese competition manifested itself in many ways in California: Whites imposed harsh restrictions on the economic freedom of Chinese workers, including special taxes and laws that barred them from carrying laundry on poles or from delivering laundry except on horseback or from fishing in local waters.[17] Often, these restrictions were cleverly designed to impose burdens that white lawmakers knew would be especially difficult for the Chinese, even though the laws did not explicitly identify the Chinese as targets.

The delegates at the constitutional convention proposed many ideas for excluding the Chinese from California, including prohibiting them from owning any property in the state and prohibiting any California corporation from employing a Chinese person. One delegate spoke for many when he explained that he was "willing to go as far as any gentleman on this floor by way of police, sanitary, criminal, or vagrant regulations, or refusing to license this class of aliens to carry on any trade or business whatever, if we can in any way, by statute or otherwise, prevent the same." His goal was "to hamper them in every way that human ingenuity could invent."[18] As this hateful proposal suggests, occupational licensing laws have often been used as a tool for excluding racial minorities from trade, thereby keeping up the income of politically powerful racial groups.

California's abuse of the Chinese led in 1886 to one of the most important early Supreme Court cases regarding economic liberty: *Yick Wo v. Hopkins*.[19] San Francisco had enacted a municipal law requiring laundry businesses to be housed in buildings made of brick. Any laundry in a building made of wood had to be licensed by a city official, who was given complete discretion to grant or to deny such permits. The city claimed the law was intended as a fire-safety measure, but the Supreme Court disagreed. It was plainly meant to persecute the Chinese, who ran most of the city's laundry businesses.

By allowing city officials carte blanche to grant or deny permits, the law made business owners into "tenants at will . . . of their means of living"[20]—meaning that they could in a sense be "evicted" from their jobs at any time. The law put no limits on what officials could do when granting or withholding permits; it gave them unbridled discretion. That was intolerable because "the very idea that one man may be compelled to hold his life, or the means of living, or any material right essential to the enjoyment of life, at the mere will of another" was "the essence of slavery itself."[21] The justices did not buy the argument that the law was intended to prevent the spread of fire; even a law appearing equal on its face could "amount to a practical denial by the state of [the] equal protection of the laws" if the government enforced it "with an evil eye and an unequal hand, so as practically to make unjust and illegal discriminations between persons in similar circumstances, material to their rights."[22] The right to earn a living was one of the rights "secured by those maxims of constitutional law which are the monuments showing the victorious progress of the [human] race in securing to men the blessings of civilization under the reign of just and equal laws."[23]

Yick Wo was, and remains, a milestone in the protection of racial minorities. But while the Chinese business owners were successful in that case, similar abuses continued,[24] not only against the Chinese but against many other minorities. Professor David E. Bernstein has documented the ways that licensing laws were used to bar blacks from earning a living legally during the Jim Crow era.[25] On rare occasions, courageous judges would hold these licensing laws to be unconstitutional. For example, in 1924, the Arkansas Supreme Court invalidated a licensing law for plumbers on the ground that it did not actually protect the public from dangerous or shoddy practices but was instead "passed from other motives."[26] The licensing examination tested obscure knowledge and unusually difficult tasks, which gave the bureaucrats in charge of the licensing scheme "arbitrary and oppressive power" to "deprive one who is thoroughly qualified to do the practical work of plumbing of his constitutional right to pursue his avocation, and perhaps his only livelihood, because, forsooth, he was unable to answer some technical or theoretical question, not in any sense germane to the real and practical trade of a plumber, and not having even the remotest connection with the actual conservation of the public health."[27] But in general, successful challenges to occupational licensing laws were rare. As Bernstein observes, "The results of judicial acquiescence in the licensing system," along with other factors such as union violence against black workers, "were disastrous for African Americans who sought work as plumbers" or as practitioners of other licensed trades.[28] In fact, racial exclusion played such an important role in economic regulation in the late 19th and early 20th centuries that civil rights leader Frederick Douglass railed against labor unions and similar groups for scheming to bar blacks from earning a living for themselves and their families. And in 1951, Thurgood Marshall, a lawyer for the National Association for the Advancement of Colored People and a future Supreme Court justice, complained that the rational basis test was so deferential toward government that courts were failing to protect the rights of blacks, including the right to earn a living.[29]

Of course, even in the absence of explicit racist intent, many occupational licensing schemes have significant racial biases. JoAnne Cornwell discovered this in the 1990s when she opened her San Diego business called Sisterlocks, devoted to performing a unique hair-braiding method called "locking," similar to traditional African methods of hair care. Like African hair braiding, Cornwell's locking method did not involve chemically treating or cutting the hair. But when California regulators heard about her business, they demanded that Cornwell and all natural hair care stylists get a license from the Board of Barbering and Cosmetology. Obtaining a cosmetology license required applicants to spend 1,600 hours at a state-approved cosmetology school, at a cost of more than $5,000, before even taking the test. And the hairstyling techniques taught in the school had no relation to Cornwell's business since, as a federal court later pointed out, "African hair styling is uniquely performed on hair that is physically different—alternatively described as tightly textured or coily hair—and that this physical difference is genetically determined to be in close correlation with race."[30] The curriculum Cornwell would be required to take, moreover, involved learning hairstyles that had not been popular for decades and that could only be performed on the hair of white customers. Worse, they required the use of chemicals that Cornwell and her fellow hairstylists did not believe in using.

Cornwell and others filed suit in federal district court, arguing that her business was not "barbering" or "cosmetology" and that it was irrational for the state to force her to obtain a barbering or cosmetology license. They claimed that the requirements violated the equal protection and due process clauses of the Constitution by restricting their liberty without any sensible connection to public health and safety. The court ruled in their favor. Forcing Cornwell to "spend nine months attending a cosmetology school, at a cost of $5,000–$7,000, learning skills, 96% of which [she] will never use" violated the rational basis requirement.[31]

Cornwell's victory was unusual. As we have seen, under the "rational basis test," entrepreneurs who challenge the constitutionality of absurd and abusive occupational licensing laws rarely succeed.[32] The Louisiana florist case discussed in the last chapter typifies everything wrong with occupational licensing laws: they represent a thin pretext of public benefit stretched over blatant anticompetitive practices. In 2004, after the Louisiana House of Representatives voted overwhelmingly in favor of a bill to eliminate the florist licensing requirement, the bill nevertheless died in the Senate's Agriculture Committee after intense lobbying by licensed florists. Even the state commissioner of agriculture lobbied against the bill, after interviewing several licensees—but not speaking to any unlicensed, would-be florists—because (as he later testified) "I have committed to the florists when I ran [for office] in 1980 that I would support their desires of either having or get[ting] rid of the law."[33] The Louisiana florist law exemplifies what the "public choice" school of economics calls "legislative capture": the exploitation of government's coercive powers for the benefit of private-interest groups. In this, it is only one of the many examples of the legalized protection racket known as occupational licensing.

Even when licensing is advanced by responsible public-minded groups, the government agencies in charge of licensing are routinely captured by businesses that stand to gain from controlling competition. This is why Milton Friedman contended that licensing "almost inevitably becomes a tool in the hands of a special producer group to maintain a monopoly position at the expense of the rest of the public. There is no way to avoid this result."[34] Economists and lawyers have assembled a mountain of evidence supporting Friedman's

149

conclusions: licensing raises costs to consumers, with little observable improvement in the quality of many licensed services.[35] Moreover, such laws appear to benefit highly paid practitioners more than those who are paid less, because "more highly educated and influential occupations may be more powerful in state or local jurisdictions and may be able to control supply more effectively."[36]

Some abuses of occupational licensing are remarkably brazen. In 2007, psychics in Salem, Massachusetts, urged the city to create a licensing requirement, allegedly to protect consumers from incompetent psychics, despite the fact that it is literally impossible to be a *competent* psychic.[37] But they sought a licensing scheme both to provide them with sham legitimacy and to shut out competition in what is otherwise an entry-level business with low start-up costs.

Strangely enough, two of the three most important economic freedom cases decided after the New Deal involved occupational licensing for people selling coffins.[38] These cases raised the question of whether the Constitution allows the government to create licensing laws solely for the *explicit* purpose of granting benefits to one business or group of businesses over another or whether licensing laws must be related in even the most abstract way to protecting the public health, safety, and welfare.

The funeral industry was an early convert to occupational licensing.[39] But licensing was only one of the ways the industry sought to raise prices. In 1881, American coffin makers founded the National Burial Case Association, which set prices for the whole industry. Two years later, the National Funeral Directors Association fixed the price of an adult coffin at $15, a large sum in the 19th century. Today, the national casket market is dominated by two corporations, York and Batesville, who together account for two-thirds of American coffin sales. Nationally, the funeral industry takes in about $25 billion per year.[40] This industry benefits tremendously from the fact that many customers are grieving the loss of a loved one when they purchase coffins or funeral services. But the industry benefits even more from excluding competition through occupational licensing.

Beginning in 1984, in response to new Federal Trade Commission regulations, entrepreneurs began selling caskets to the public directly at wholesale prices. By specializing and cutting out the middleman, these businesses could offer caskets to consumers at greatly reduced rates. The FTC prohibited funeral homes from refusing to accept caskets from outside retailers,[41] and competition began to decrease prices and increase choice.

But this new economic freedom ran up against significant barriers. For many decades, the funeral industry had benefited from special legal privileges. Several states, for example, passed laws prohibiting the sale of caskets by anyone except a licensed funeral director. Under a 1972 Tennessee law, the practice of funeral directing was defined to include "the selling of funeral merchandise."[42] To sell a casket, therefore, one must first hold a funeral director's license. Becoming a funeral director was a major undertaking: an applicant was required either to attend Gupton College's 12- to 16-month training program for funeral directors (at a cost of more than $10,000), as well as serving a year in an apprenticeship, or to serve a 2-year apprenticeship and assist in 25 funerals. Only after these requirements were met could the applicant pay another $200 for the opportunity to take the Funeral Board examination.[43]

Nathaniel Craigmiles, a pastor who became frustrated at seeing his parishioners exploited by funeral homes, decided to open his own business selling caskets at discount prices. But Craigmiles was not a licensed funeral director, so the state soon began enforcement proceedings against him. He filed a lawsuit alleging that the licensing requirement limited his liberty to earn a living but had no sensible connection to public safety. Thus, it violated his constitutional rights as guaranteed by the privileges or immunities, due process, and equal protection clauses of the Fourteenth Amendment.

Although the district court acknowledged that because the Tennessee statute was an economic regulation it was subject only to low-yield "rational basis" review, it nevertheless held a full-scale trial to determine whether the law was actually rationally connected to public health and safety. Concluding that it lacked such connections, the court struck it down.[44] A coffin is simply a wooden box, wrote Judge R. Allan Edgar, and requiring retailers to go through such extensive training for licensure was absurd. Neither Craigmiles nor his partners were officiating at the funerals or constructing caskets. Although public health concerns about pollution of the ground due to faulty caskets might justify regulating their manufacture, no such concern was served by requiring *retailers* to be licensed. In fact, Tennessee law did not actually require that people be buried in caskets at all, further undermining the allegation that the law protected public health. As the court concluded:

> [T]he purpose of promoting public health and safety is not served by requiring two years of training to sell a box. . . . [N]one of the training received by licensed funeral directors regarding caskets has anything to do with public health or safety. The training and the exam questions regarding caskets relate only to product information and merchandising. These topics have no relationship to health and safety, but might be helpful to one who sells any product. In sum, a casket does not differ from any other product in the marketplace. No health and safety reason rationally relates to requiring an individual to undergo two years of training, pay a fee, and pass a test in order to sell a casket.[45]

On appeal, the state argued that the district court had engaged in "*Lochner*ism" by substituting its own judgment for that of the legislature, but the court of appeals upheld the decision.[46] After reviewing the facts demonstrating that the Tennessee statute had little to do with protecting consumers, the court concluded that the state's proffered explanations for the law came close to "striking us with 'the force of a five-week-old, unrefrigerated dead fish.'"[47] It was simply absurd to see the law as anything other than "an attempt to prevent economic competition."[48] And this was not a proper goal: "Courts have repeatedly recognized that protecting a discrete interest group from economic competition is not a legitimate governmental purpose."[49] For the first time in almost 70 years, a federal court struck down a state economic regulation using the rational basis test.

But only six days after *Craigmiles* was decided, a federal trial court in Oklahoma issued a directly contrary ruling in an almost identical case. *Powers v. Harris*[50] involved an Internet-based retail casket company called Memorial Concepts Online, Inc., started by entrepreneurs Kim Powers and Dennis Bridges. Like Tennessee, Oklahoma law defines any person selling funeral merchandise as a funeral director and requires such a person to obtain a funeral director's license.[51] Getting a license in Oklahoma is nearly as onerous and expensive as it is in Tennessee: an applicant must complete at least 60 hours of study in an accredited college, graduate from an approved mortuary science program, and serve a year as a registered apprentice.[52]

Unlike the *Craigmiles* court, the trial court in *Powers* found this requirement rational.[53] Using the rational basis standard, the court said that judges must allow "any reasonably conceivable purpose [that the challenged] laws might serve," and not "evaluat[e] the effectiveness of a legislative measure" or "its economic benefits and detriments."[54] The court criticized the *Craigmiles* decision for using *Lochner*-style analysis and then upheld the Oklahoma licensing scheme, even though it was "not persuaded that the provisions in question advance the cause of consumer protection. Maybe they do and maybe they don't."[55] That question was unimportant, the court concluded, because even absent any evidence showing that the law could or did serve the public health, safety, and welfare, it was "readily conceivable that the licensing provisions challenged by the plaintiffs could have been thought by the legislature to promote the goal of consumer protection."[56] And that was all the rational basis test required.

The Tenth Circuit Court of Appeals upheld this decision, but went much further.[57] After a long recitation of the deference accorded to the government under the rational basis test, the court declared that it was "obliged to consider every plausible legitimate state interest that might support [the licensing requirement]—not just the consumer-protection interest forwarded by the parties."[58] The restriction would be upheld not only if it advanced consumer safety but also if "protecting the intrastate funeral home industry . . . constitutes a legitimate state interest."[59] This, the court held, was a proper government function: "intrastate economic protectionism constitutes a legitimate state interest."[60] Thus, the law was constitutional even though it had *nothing* to do with protecting the public: the legislature could also enact the restriction merely to grant economic favors to politically influential economic constituencies.

The *Powers* court based this extraordinary conclusion on three primary considerations. First, it noted that the *Craigmiles* decision had relied on three cases when declaring that mere protectionism was not a constitutional government purpose under the Fourteenth Amendment: *City of Philadelphia v. New Jersey*,[61] *H.P. Hood & Sons, Inc. v. Du Mond*,[62] and *Energy Reserves Group, Inc. v. Kansas Power & Light*.[63] But none of these was a Fourteenth Amendment case. Accusing the *Craigmiles* court of "selective quotation," the Tenth Circuit noted that *Du Mond* and *Philadelphia* involved the dormant commerce clause, and *Energy Reserves Group* involved the contracts clause.[64] The dormant commerce clause has long been held to forbid states from discriminating against businesses located in other states but has not been read as having any relation to protectionist legislation *within* states. Within state boundaries, laws are subject only to the Fourteenth Amendment, and since the advent of rational basis review, the court noted, judges have frequently upheld laws that protect one industry against another *inside* a state.

But while this is true, the *Powers* court was ignoring the bigger picture illustrated by the cases that the *Craigmiles* court relied on: the ultimate purpose of the commerce clause, the contracts clause, and the Fourteenth Amendment's equal protection clause is to protect individual liberty. As Professor Sunstein has put it, these clauses are "united by a common theme and focused on a single underlying evil: the distribution of resources or opportunities to one group rather than another solely on the ground that those favored have exercised the raw political power to obtain what they want."[65] Although the federalist system does protect state sovereignty, it does so not as an end in itself, but as a means of securing individual freedom.[66]

Second, the *Powers* court held that applying a skeptical analysis of protectionist laws would threaten the validity of the post–New Deal regime: "adopting a rule against the legitimacy of intrastate economic protectionism and applying it in a principled manner" would require invalidating countless laws already on the books that perform no legitimate public function but merely protect one interest group from another.[67] Indeed, the court noted that economic protectionism is so common in state legislatures that "while baseball may be the national pastime of the citizenry, dishing out special economic benefits to certain in-state industries remains the favored pastime of state and local governments."[68] In short, because legislatures pass such measures so often, and have done so for so long, they must be constitutional. But this argument is a non sequitur. The mere fact that states frequently act in unconstitutional ways is hardly enough to make those acts constitutional: certainly segregation was a common state policy when it was finally held unconstitutional in the 1950s.

Because the *Powers* decision declares that providing economic favors for preferred groups is itself a legitimate state interest regardless of the effect that such laws may have on the public welfare, it is not too much to say that the case was the most disastrous economic liberty decision since the New Deal. In previous cases upholding the constitutionality of economic restrictions, courts based their rulings on the theory that the law protected the public in *some* way, even if the connection was tenuous in the extreme. In many cases, such as the Louisiana florist case, the idea that the restriction protected the public was barely plausible, but in the end those cases still declared that economic liberty could be restricted only as a means of protecting the general public from some perceived harm. *Powers* was the first case in which a court held that the government could enact an economic regulation without *any* such connection at all, and *solely* to secure an economic benefit for those businesses the government prefers. If the legislature chooses to grant legal favors to one group over another *just because it wants to*, the law will nevertheless be upheld under *Powers*. The case was, in a sense, the mirror image of the substantive due process cases from a century before: anything the government chooses to do—even if it explicitly serves private interests rather than the general public good—is a legitimate law *simply because the government chose to do it*. In the eyes of the *Powers* court, law is not the use of government force in the service of some independent standard of public good but is instead the use of force in the service of arbitrary legislative will. What one writer has said when describing a different legal issue is equally applicable here: such a theory leads to "the legal enforcement of private bias, casting lawmaking as a kind of Nietzschean struggle of will, with various . . . interest groups trying to gain legal enforcement of their [desires] without having to give reasons."[69]

Obviously, the conclusion that protectionism is a legitimate state interest invites abuses in the service of irrational prejudice or favoritism. If a city chooses to grant a preference to, say, Target by outlawing Wal-Mart for no other reason than that the members of the city council prefer Target, then it can do so. Just as granting protection to licensed funeral directors was somehow a public goal because the legislature chose to adopt it, so protecting Target becomes a public goal simply because the city considers it worthy of protection. Of course, government officials will rarely if ever admit to acting in the interest of a private party; they will virtually always claim their acts are for the public welfare.[70] And whenever a private-interest group demands special favors from lawmakers, it always claims that the public will ultimately benefit from subsidies to the interest group. If a business wants government to exclude its rivals, it will tell lawmakers that its rival is somehow a threat to the public welfare, or that the public will prosper if a monopoly is given to the private company. For example, the racists who agitated for laws restricting Chinese labor in 19th-century California claimed that white supremacy was good for society and that the Chinese were a "menace" to the public. Such self-serving disguises often dissolve in the light of common sense, but under the *Powers* decision, courts are not expected to apply common sense. If the legislature chooses to confer monopoly power to a lobbyist, that lobbyist's private interest becomes, ipso facto, the public interest.

Pest Control—or Economic Control?

A third illustrative occupational licensing case in the post–New Deal era challenged a requirement that applied to wildlife control workers, and the story of its litigation is an example of how difficult it is for businesses to defend themselves against protectionist schemes that powerful interest groups get translated into law.

Wildlife control workers trap the vertebrate pests that infest buildings, such as pigeons, rats, skunks, or raccoons, or they use spikes or screens to keep birds and squirrels away from buildings. They do not use pesticides, however, which they consider ineffective and dangerous. Alan Merrifield is a widely respected leader in the wildlife control trade. But when he sought a state contract to install anti-bird netting on a state office building in Oakland, California, he learned that under the state's Structural Pest Control Act, no person may install such nets without a "Branch 2 Structural Pest Control Operator" license. That license is only granted to people who pass the state's 200-question licensing examination, and to take the test, an applicant must first show proof that he or she has been employed for two years by a person with a license. More surprisingly, the exam has little to do with an applicant's knowledge of nonpesticide techniques of pest control. In fact, although a person must take and pass this test before putting spikes on a building to keep pigeons away, the examination does not contain a single question about pigeons, or about spikes. Instead, the exam is overwhelmingly devoted to testing an applicant's knowledge of the proper ways of handling, using, and storing *pesticides*—pesticides Alan Merrifield and his fellow wildlife control workers do not use—and about how to deal with insects, spiders, and moths, which they do not treat.

Perhaps recognizing the perversity of forcing people who do not use pesticides to become experts on the use of pesticides, one state legislator sought to amend the law in 1995 to eliminate the licensing requirement for people who do not use pesticides. But when this proposal was announced, pest control workers who already had licenses feared that they might lose control over the industry, and they opposed the bill. One organization in particular, the Pest Control Operators of California, lobbied heavily against the bill. Its vice president later testified that industry lobbyists finally resolved the controversy by dividing up the pest control market. The expensive and time-consuming licensing requirement would be imposed on anyone dealing with pigeons, rats, and mice, since they make up the most lucrative part of the pest control trade; people like Merrifield would then be allowed to deal with only the less common pests like raccoons and squirrels.[71] This effort to cartelize the market for pest control services succeeded: the legislature altered the 1995 bill so that it allowed pest control workers who chose not to use pesticides to do their business without undergoing unnecessary and expensive training in pesticide use—unless their work involved pigeons, rats, and/or mice! In other words, if Merrifield installed a screen on a building to keep a raccoon out, he did not need a license, but if he installed the *same* screen on the *same* building to keep a *rat* out, he needed to spend two years learning to use pesticides and take a difficult and time-consuming test about the lifespan of insects and the dangers of chemical poisons.

Asked for an explanation of this bizarre scheme, the state's expert witness testified under oath that the law was "a political piece of legislation in order to make a particular constituency happy, *but it harms the consumer* because the consumer ends up with somebody coming in and doing what has traditionally been a behavior that requires a professional license."[72] He acknowledged that it made no sense to require a license for trapping or excluding pigeons, rats, and mice, but not for trapping or excluding any other kind of pest:

> Q: Does it protect the public health and safety to require a person who does pigeon exclusion work without pesticides in structures to have a . . . license?

Mr. Paulsen: Absolutely.

Q: Does it protect the public health and safety not to require the same license for seagull exclusion work?

Mr. Paulsen: No, it does not.

Q: Would you call this irrational?

Mr. Paulsen: Yes, I would.[73]

Asked a third time to explain the licensing scheme, he reiterated, "[F]rom a public perspective, it might be irrational."[74]

Nevertheless, despite the plain absurdity of the law's requirements and regardless of the fact that the state's own expert witness testified repeatedly that the licensing scheme was positively irrational, the trial court still upheld the law.[75] Requiring a license for excluding pigeons but not seagulls was rational, wrote Judge William Schwarzer, because the legislature might have concluded "that rats, mice, and pigeons are overwhelmingly the most common vertebrate pests infesting structures."[76] Yet if this were the purpose of the restriction, it made no sense that the test included no questions at all about pigeons and next to none about rats or mice. Still, Schwarzer continued, the legislature might have thought that "requiring that pest control operators be knowledgeable about alternative methods of control, about the public health hazards posed by pests, and about ways of protecting themselves and the public from pesticides previously applied by others" would protect the public and advance the public interest.[77] But this rationale was inconsistent with the fact that practitioners dealing with other kinds of animals were not required to have such training—so that a professional might show up at a person's house to treat a bat infestation, knowing nothing whatsoever about the pesticides previously applied to that structure by others.

The *Merrifield* decision shows the lengths to which courts can go and the contortions in logic courts perform under the rational basis test. The undisputed evidence established that the bizarre pest control licensing scheme was designed simply to protect licensed practitioners against competition from outsiders, not to protect the public health and safety. The state's expert witness testified that the licensing scheme was positively irrational. Yet the rational basis test allowed the court to ignore all the evidence and manufacture its own, self-contradictory justification for the law.

Fortunately for Merrifield, and entrepreneurs in general, the Ninth Circuit Court of Appeals reversed this decision. In a 2–1 opinion, Judge Diarmuid F. O'Scannlain concluded that "just as in *Craigmiles*, the licensing scheme in this case . . . was designed to favor economically certain constituents at the expense of others similarly situated, such as Merrifield."[78] The justifications that the state offered for the licensing requirements were "so weak that [they] undercut[] the principle of non-contradiction"[79] and revealed that the real purpose of the law was to divide up the trade in a way that benefited political insiders. And this the court explicitly declared unconstitutional:

> [M]ere economic protectionism for the sake of economic protectionism is irrational with respect to determining if a classification survives rational basis review. In doing so, we agree with the Sixth Circuit in *Craigmiles* and reject the Tenth Circuit's reasoning in *Powers v. Harris*. . . . We do not disagree that there might be instances when economic protectionism might be related to a legitimate governmental interest and survive rational basis review. However, economic protectionism for its own sake, regardless of its relation to the common good, cannot be said to be in furtherance of a legitimate governmental interest.[80]

Now that the courts of appeal are in conflict over this issue, with the Tenth Circuit upholding protectionism as a legitimate purpose for occupational licensing and the Sixth and Ninth Circuits disagreeing, the stage is set for the Supreme Court to resolve the issue definitively in some future case.

Zoning

Wal-Mart is one of the great American success stories. Not only does it demonstrate how a new idea can prevail against the common assumptions of the business world, but it also shows how a business can grow by providing customers with the products they need at prices they can afford. Today, it is the largest company in the world, and it employs more people than any other employer in the United States (except the government, of course). Wal-Mart makes more than $77 billion per year,[81] and it does this not by forcing people to hand over their money but by inviting the public to choose for themselves whether or not to shop there. To picture Wal-Mart as a cruel bully, as many activists do, is to imagine the exact opposite of the truth.[82] Wal-Mart's business tactics make it hard to compete, no doubt, but that is simply because the company's managers are good at what they do. Indeed, that is what they are paid to do.

While Wal-Mart, like any other major success story, inspires a good deal of criticism, much of it seems to stem from simple envy. For example, many owners of small businesses complain that Wal-Mart disrupts communities, drives out competitors, exploits workers, and destroys the local charm of small towns. Yet despite these complaints, customers in these communities continue to shop there of their own free will, and employees continue to work there when they are free to go elsewhere. Naturally, this has led many critics to ask the government to intercede and stop both customers and Wal-Mart itself from making their own economic choices.

One of the handiest tools for restricting economic freedom in this way is land-use regulation, including zoning laws. The use of these restrictions for protectionist purposes is as old as zoning itself. In fact, one of the original purposes of zoning was to exclude racial minorities from white neighborhoods.[83] Today, it is often used to bar a different type of unpopular minority: economic groups that lack political influence in a community.[84] When given the choice, most consumers prefer convenient stores with low prices to stores with higher prices and smaller selection, regardless of whether they provide a "small town atmosphere"; this is evident from the fact that Wal-Mart succeeds without forcing anyone to shop there. But politically active businesses are often able to persuade the government to enact laws that essentially ban low-priced businesses in order to increase the wealth of those with better connections to the government. By establishing zones where new companies cannot enter, existing business owners not only can restrict competition and keep prices high but also can ensure that the real estate values of their business locations will remain constant over time. City officials, in turn, benefit by portraying themselves to voters as effective leaders who have helped "save" jobs or preserve the traditional small-town atmosphere. The burden falls on families with low incomes who must pay higher prices or go without new job opportunities because they lack the wherewithal to lobby government to allow a lower-priced store to be built. For example, an ordinance designed to prevent a Wal-Mart Supercenter from opening in Los Angeles was recently estimated to cost neighborhood families an average of $482 per year because the cheaper groceries that the store would have provided were kept out of the market.[85]

Unfortunately, two recent cases from California illustrate the way courts turn a blind eye on laws that injure consumers for the benefit of private industries. In 2004, the city of Turlock adopted an ordinance relegating "big-box" stores like Wal-Mart to a specified area of the city and prohibiting them anywhere else. City officials were quite explicit in their protectionist motive: the ordinance declared that a Wal-Mart would "negatively impact the vitality and economic viability of the city's neighborhood commercial centers by drawing sales away from traditional supermarkets located in these centers"[86]—in other words, it would be cheaper than "traditional" supermarkets, and customers would want to shop there. The city's staff went even further: "While any large-scale retail store can draw customers with low prices and a wide selection of goods," they wrote, "the big box grocers present a unique threat because of the inclusion of discount retail and full-service grocery under a single roof."[87] Customers would call this "threat" by another name: "convenience." But the owners of "traditional" supermarkets, who did not want to, or could not, compete fairly certainly saw it as a threat, and they persuaded the city to block construction of the Wal-Mart. The company challenged the ban as unconstitutional, but the state's appellate court upheld it, declaring that the city's purpose was really to protect the general public from the "decay" that would result from the possible failure of competing stores.[88] According to the court, bureaucrats, not consumers, should have the power to "control and organize development," and thereby ensure that certain commercial areas remained insulated from competition; this served the "public welfare."[89]

Shortly after this decision, the California Supreme Court agreed, upholding a similar ordinance in another community that relegated the sale of furniture to a specific portion of the city—although this ordinance contained an exception allowing a Wal-Mart and a then-unbuilt Target to sell furniture outside of the designated area. The "Planned Commercial (PC) Zone" essentially created an oligopoly of large department stores that kept the supply of furniture artificially low, thus forcing up the prices of available goods. The purpose of this distinction was to serve the interests of established furniture retailers who told the city council that allowing furniture sales elsewhere in the city "would be detrimental to downtown" because it would "[c]ause severe economic damage to those small businesses" that already existed there.[90] In other words, if consumers were free to decide for themselves, they would have chosen to shop somewhere other than downtown.

When small-business owner Adrian Hernandez found a loophole allowing her to sell furniture outside the PC Zone, other furniture stores lobbied the city council to find some way of closing down her shop. "Allowing furniture sales outside the downtown," they told the city council, "would be detrimental to the existing furniture stores in the downtown."[91] The local Thomasville Home Furnishings, in particular, repeatedly lobbied the city, arguing that allowing competition in furniture sales would do "measurable harm [*sic*] . . . to our beloved Downtown that so many of your constituents identify with," and would have "a potential life-threatening effect" to other furniture retailers.[92] Although the Hernandezes only wanted a chance to engage in free competition selling furniture to the public, city officials decided to exclude them because bureaucrats, not consumers, should decide what businesses flourish in an economy. "[Z]oning," the mayor said, "is what allows you to shape your city."[93]

The California Supreme Court upheld the city's decision. Because the city claimed that giving favors to a particular economic interest group would benefit the general public, it could do as it pleased with the zoning power. If officials want to "protect or preserve the economic viability of [a] downtown business district or neighborhood shopping areas," they may adopt ordinances that "control[] competition."[94]

Sensing that their decision would give bureaucrats almost unlimited power to grant economic favors to particular businesses, the justices tried to distance themselves from the special-interest lawmaking allowed in cases like *Powers v. Harris*. Government, they wrote, could limit competition, raise costs to consumers, and prevent job creation

> so long as the primary purpose of the ordinance or action—
> that is, its principal and ultimate objective—is not the
> impermissible *private* anticompetitive goal of protecting or

> disadvantaging a particular favored or disfavored business
> or individual, but instead is the advancement of a legitimate
> *public* purpose—such as the preservation of a municipality's
> downtown business district for the benefit of the municipal-
> ity as a whole . . . .[95]

But this distinction offers little real hope for protecting against government abuses. Every politically influential private interest is going
to insist—and often quite plausibly—that its own private welfare is
really good for the public in some sense. All businesses provide jobs
and spur commercial activity. But if that were enough to justify the
implementation of policies that simply profit those businesses, the
distinction between the public good and the private welfare of interest groups would dissolve. If a buggy-whip manufacturer asks the
government to prohibit the sale of automobiles, for example, his motivation is entirely self-regarding. But he could rightly claim that many
people in the community are employed making buggy whips, and if
consumers were free to choose automobiles instead, existing buggy-
whip factories would lose jobs, leading to economic deterioration in
the neighborhood. These could be called "public" concerns—yet they
are really no different from the private interests of buggy-whip makers. Certainly they do not represent the interests of consumers who
would rather buy automobiles, let alone the interests of car retailers.
Protecting existing businesses from competition is a private benefit
to those businesses, not a genuine public interest. The real interests
of the public can only be discovered by allowing the public to choose
for themselves whether to buy buggies or cars—not by taking that
choice away from them and giving it to political leaders.

Moreover, even the most corrupt government official is unlikely to
admit in public that his intentions are to benefit a particular private-
interest group. Bureaucrats will always declare that their intention is
to help the general public in some way or other. And because courts
apply the "rational basis" standard of review to economic regulations, they will rarely if ever look behind the government's asserted
justifications. As long as the government couches its actions in the
language of protecting the general public ("excluding automobiles
will protect the jobs of buggy-whip makers"), judges will take its
claims at face value and uphold laws that benefit private interests at
the expense of innovative companies and consumer welfare.[96]

Agricultural Adjustment

"Agricultural adjustment" refers to a collection of New Deal–era federal programs that regulate the production and sale of fruits, vegetables, or other foodstuffs for the explicit purpose of raising the price of food. The euphemism used for this process is "stabilization," but the goal is to force people to pay more for the food they need, so as to benefit farmers who would otherwise have to compete by lowering prices. The architects of agricultural adjustment in the 1930s believed that competition drove down prices, leading to the economic "chaos."[97] After all, they observed, one symptom of the Great Depression was that farmers were impoverished; what better way to cure this than to raise their income? And what better way to do that than to compel farmers to throw away a certain portion of their crop, or prohibit them from growing more than a certain amount to begin with, thus making the remaining product scarcer and more expensive? More expensive goods meant the farmers' income would go up: problem solved.

But this argument rests on a mirage.[98] Throwing away food means destroying wealth. Since there is less food to be consumed, the cost of food in terms of other available goods increases, which means that although farmers may get a higher price for each bushel of raisins or bag of peanuts, they will sell fewer raisins and peanuts *in total*. Society in general will also be less well off, having fewer raisins or peanuts to enjoy. The farmer's higher income is really just a tax imposed on consumers and transferred to the farmer. Worse, agricultural adjustment disrupts the market mechanisms that allow farmers to know how much of their crop is actually needed by the public and distracts them from producing the goods that the public really wants. A farmer who lets a field lie fallow because of a government edict cannot grow the plums or peaches for which consumers are actually willing to pay. There may be few hard-and-fast rules in economics, but surely this is one of them: it is never wise to discourage the production of needed food.

Despite these profound flaws, agricultural adjustment has remained government policy for more than 70 years, and in 2004, California raisin grower Marvin Horne learned just how strict these laws can be when he was fined more than a quarter of a million dollars for selling his entire raisin crop.[99] Every year, thanks to the federal Agricultural Marketing Agreement Act,[100] an agency called

164

the Raisin Administrative Committee announces an annual percentage of raisins that growers must turn over to the government, which then sells them under its own brand name to public schools and other buyers. The proceeds from these sales are then used to subsidize American companies that sell raisins overseas, and whatever money is left over is at last given to the growers who had their raisins confiscated. Under this program, the government confiscates up to a quarter or even half of the entire California raisin crop. Horne complained that this policy was wasteful and that he had the right not to participate if he chose. "This is America," he told reporters. "I don't owe anybody any portion of my crop. The government cannot confiscate any of my produced raisins for the benefit of their program."[101] But the Department of Agriculture fined Horne more than $1,000 per day for each violation of its orders, and when Horne and his wife were found guilty, they were penalized $275,000 for selling their raisin crop as they chose.

There is virtually no empirical or theoretical justification for the "price stabilization" rationale behind agricultural adjustment laws.[102] In fact, research shows that such schemes have "conveyed few long-term benefits to the industry" and "reduced . . . long-run grower returns" on investment.[103] Consumers pay the price, but even the alleged beneficiaries—family farms—do not really benefit much. Most of the benefits go to large agribusiness concerns.[104] Even aside from the fact that these programs take from the poor and give to the rich, small farmers also suffer because they are blocked from implementing new, innovative ways to compete with large conglomerates. A company responsible for a million peach trees, for example, can afford to throw away a quarter of its crop, particularly when it draws subsidies from a friendly Congress. But a small farmer needs every peach he grows and can't count on favors from politicians who have never heard of him.

The perversity of agricultural adjustment is particularly acute with regard to milk prices.[105] The American dairy industry is heavily regulated under "marketing order" systems similar to that used for the control of raisins; and, as with raisins, the purpose of this maze of rules and regulations is (as the Senate acknowledged when creating the program in the 1930s) "to raise producer prices."[106] First, the country is divided into 11 regions, with a minimum price for milk established in each region. Businesses that buy raw milk from farmers and process it into cheese, butter, or milk for consumers must pay the price set by the government within that region. This price is calculated each month based on the end products for which the milk is destined, and since it is often higher than the prices for imported substitutes, federal tariffs are used to increase the price of foreign raw milk. The middlemen pay the difference between this artificial price and the actual market price for the milk to a "pool," which is then distributed to farmers on the basis of a "weighted average" calculated by the government based on how much milk was produced. As a result, the middlemen pay for milk based on how they use it, but farmers receive the "weighted average" price regardless of how the milk was actually used. This means that farmers whose milk was used for a high-demand product and who might have received a higher price if allowed to ask for it are instead paid the same government-imposed average price as farmers whose milk was used for a low-demand purpose.

These abstruse policies force families to pay higher food bills. Economists estimate that the milk-marketing scheme costs families $1 billion per year.[107] In one year, consumers in Boston were forced to pay 30.5 cents more per gallon and consumers in Hartford, Connecticut, 31.4 cents more per gallon due to the agricultural adjustment schemes.[108] But many farmers, too, are harmed by the program. Since farmers receive their pay based on the average in their geographical area, they cannot ship their milk to other regions where demand—and prices—might be much higher. And the "weighted average" sometimes fails to reflect the actual market demand for their products. Since under the government's scheme milk in a carton brings a higher profit than does cheese, a weighted average based on a heavy use of milk for cheese production will be skewed downward from what farmers would have received on a free market.[109] And it means that farmers who want to sell milk for less than the government-determined price are forbidden to do so.

The federal government allows some states to operate their own price-regulation schemes for milk. California, which produces more milk than any other state, not only sets minimum prices for milk but also sets certain quality-control requirements that effectively bar importation from other states, even though other states' milk is healthy enough. California's state milk regulations have been estimated to cost consumers $600 million per year.[110] In 2000, Dutch immigrant Hein Hettinga discovered a loophole in the layers of state and federal milk price regulation. Because Hettinga not only milked his cows but also bottled and distributed his own milk, his Arizona-based Sarah Farms was not subject to the price-setting rules enforced by California, Arizona, or the federal government. He began selling his milk to Costco and other retailers, and because he was able to charge 20 cents less per gallon, his company grew and consumers paid less for milk.[111] The dairy industry immediately responded by calling on Congress. Rep. Devin Nunes of California and Sen. Jon Kyl of Arizona, both Republicans receiving large campaign contributions from established dairy companies, immediately introduced what they called the Milk Regulatory Equity Act[112] to shut Hettinga down. Their complaint was not with the complicated regulations that increase the price of milk for American families; their concern was with the alleged unfairness of allowing Hettinga to charge less than his competitors charged. "The hard working dairy farmers in Arizona have witnessed a steady decline in their pool since unregulated handlers began to flourish," complained Nunes. "Regulated processors in Arizona are no less efficient or innovative than their unregulated competitors. They are simply unable to compete with businesses that do not have to play by the rules. This situation is wrong and must be resolved by Congress." In a classic example of doublespeak, Nunes urged Congress to "restore free market principles and fair regulation to the dairy industry" by prohibiting Hettinga from selling his milk as he chose.[113] The new law, signed by President George W. Bush only four months after it was introduced in the Senate, and without any congressional hearings, required Hettinga to pay into the "pool" established by federal law, with the result that he would be subsidizing his own competitors.

Agricultural adjustment laws often include a spurious element of "democratic" decisionmaking that gives the illusion of voluntariness to a coercive government program. The law that prohibits raisin farmers from selling their crops, for instance, allows any raisin producer to petition the U.S. Department of Agriculture to adopt a "marketing order" that will apply to all producers, whether or not those others agree with the proposal.[114] Once the proposal to establish a cartel is accepted by the USDA, the law provides for a referendum where growers may debate it, but agricultural cooperatives are allowed to bloc-vote on behalf of all their members. This has an important effect because one cooperative typically dominates production of a particular agricultural product—such as Sunkist's dominating the orange trade—and that cooperative can cast the votes necessary to adopt or reject a proposal, regardless of the actual desires of constituent farmers, not to mention independent producers who want to go their own way.[115] In one case in 1993, citrus growers who did not agree with a proposed cartel agreement were forced to abide by it when Sunkist bloc-voted in favor of the agreement.[116] The dissenters sued, arguing that this violated their constitutional right to vote, but although the right to vote is usually given powerful protection by federal courts, the court of appeals upheld the bloc-voting scheme by applying the rational basis test to dissenters' voting rights. Those rights, the court declared, were "not 'a bedrock of our political system' like voting in an election for . . . legislative representatives."[117] Thus, individual growers, whether or not they belong to agricultural cooperatives, have no real voice in the process.

Similarly, the marketing order system for milk requires two-thirds of the farmers within the region to vote in favor of the marketing order before it applies. But although the processors who are forced to pay the inflated price are entitled to a vote, their vote can be overridden by the secretary of agriculture.[118] And consumers get no vote at all. In 1980, a group of consumers challenged the constitutionality of the milk programs designed to raise their costs.[119] "[C]onsumer participation," the Supreme Court held, "is not provided for or desired under the complex scheme enacted by Congress."[120]

Farmers also have little real chance of having their rights protected in court. In 2004, the same year that Marvin Horne was punished for selling his entire raisin crop, a group of Fresno raisin growers filed a lawsuit demanding that the government compensate them for the raisins it confiscated each year. The Fifth Amendment, after all, says that when the government takes private property for public use, it must pay the owner just compensation. But the Court of Federal Claims—which hears all just-compensation cases brought against the federal government—turned them away. The farmers knew about the confiscation scheme when they entered the business, the court explained, and the forced confiscation was simply "an admissions fee or a toll—admittedly a steep one—for marketing raisins." The government "does not force plaintiffs to grow raisins or to market the raisins"; instead, it merely requires that "if they grow and market raisins, then passing title to their 'reserve tonnage' raisins to the [government] is their admission ticket."[121] An appellate court upheld this decision without writing an opinion, and the Supreme Court refused to take the case.[122]

The Court of Federal Claims ignored a long-standing principle of Anglo-American law: the producer of a product has a natural or inherent right to sell the product of his labor. That right is not a government privilege for which the farmer can be required to pay a "toll"; it is a natural right, part of the very fact of ownership, and when government takes that right away, it must compensate the owner under the Fifth Amendment.[123] The right to sell the product of one's labor, in fact, is a critical aspect of freedom. As Sir William Blackstone noted in the 1760s, "Where the vendor hath in himself the property of the goods sold, he hath the liberty of disposing of them to whomever he pleases, at any time, and in any manner."[124] Indeed, the very term "fruits of one's labor" indicates that among individual rights, the farmer's right to sell his produce was one of the first to be recognized.

For the court to declare that the farmers could have avoided the taking of their raisins by choosing not to sell them begs the question. Obviously, a person can avoid the penalties incurred by an unjust law by obeying it—but that does not change the injustice of the law. Reverdy Johnson, a famous 19th-century attorney, put this point succinctly in a case challenging the constitutionality of a law imposing a loyalty oath requirement on people seeking jobs: the citizen "is gravely told, 'You are not obliged to take [the oath],'" Johnson explained. "Certainly, he is not obliged to take it. No man is obliged to follow his occupation; but unless he takes it he must starve, except he have other means of living."[125] Worse still, given the Supreme Court's expansive readings of the commerce clause since the 1930s, it is practically impossible for a person selling raisins or any other commodity to *avoid* entering the interstate market.[126] Under federal law, raisin producers cannot even sell raisins from a roadside stand to pedestrians on the sidewalk without entering the "interstate" market and subjecting themselves to the raisin-confiscation rules.[127]

In the end, adjustment schemes such as marketing orders protect entrenched businesses against competition by outsiders who want to offer their products to the general public at lower prices. As one commentator concludes, "True to the fundamental insight of modern public choice theory, agricultural legislation routinely delivers benefits to concentrated, well-organized groups within the farm sector at the expense of food and fiber consumers, who are too broadly dispersed to offer effective political resistance."[128] Farmers who wish to remain independent are essentially forced into federally created cartels because they are subjected to regulations any time they sell products in "interstate commerce"—meaning any commerce at all—and because the regulations apply to them whenever their competitors convince the Department of Agriculture to impose such regulations. But when they seek just compensation for the property the government takes from them, they are told that the system is essentially voluntary, that they chose to participate in it, and that they can be required to pay a "toll" for the privilege of selling their product. American consumers, meanwhile, pay higher food bills, many of them unaware of their government's vigilant efforts to keep the cost of living from going down.

Franchise Acts

Franchises are among the most popular forms of business in the United States. Companies like McDonald's and Subway offer extraordinary opportunities for entrepreneurs to start and run their own businesses without the difficulty of establishing a new brand name in a highly competitive market. The franchise allows a business owner to work for himself or herself while also becoming part of a company whose name consumers will recognize. But there is a natural conflict of interest between the person running the franchise (the franchisee) and the company that owns the brand name (the franchisor). A franchisor wants to ensure that there are as many franchises as possible in a given area—the more Subway shops, the better. But the franchisee wants to be the only such business in his or her area. If another Subway opens up next door, the franchisee faces competition that makes business harder.

The concept of franchising took off after the end of World War II when Americans turned to the highways for recreation: the 1950s was the age of motels and fast food. It was not long before franchisees began complaining that franchisors were unfairly creating franchises next to one another. Some simply added provisions to their contracts barring franchisors from doing this, but others demanded that government become involved. Most states adopted relatively mundane regulations, imposing requirements of "good faith" or other basic "fairness" rules. But some states, such as Illinois, went further. That state's Motor Vehicle Franchise Act[129] declares that franchises for new automobile sales must be approved by a government Motor Vehicle Review Board. Whenever a franchisor considers establishing a new dealership, the existing dealers are allowed to file a protest with the board, which then has the authority to veto the proposed franchise contract.

The Illinois law gives the board 11 factors to consider before deciding whether to allow a new franchise to open. Unsurprisingly, some of these factors are vague enough to allow the board to bar a new franchise whenever existing businesses lobby hard enough. Moreover, some factors explicitly *require* the government to protect established businesses from new competition. Factor 10, for example, requires the board to consider "the effect of an additional franchise . . . upon the existing motor vehicle dealers [selling] the same [types of cars] in the relevant market area." Factor 2 requires the board to consider "the retail sales and service business transacted by the objecting motor vehicle dealer or dealers . . . during the 5 year period immediately preceding." Factors 3 and 4, respectively, require the board to consider "the investment necessarily made and obligations incurred by the objecting motor vehicle dealer" and "the permanency of the investment of the objecting motor vehicle dealer."[130] Factor 7 explicitly declares that "good cause" for the board to allow a new business *"shall not* be shown solely by a desire for further market penetration."[131] In other words, the desire of a manufacturer to succeed economically—by providing the best-quality goods and services to customers at the lowest possible prices—is not a good enough reason to allow it the "privilege" of competing by executing a new franchise agreement.

These rules go far beyond what is necessary to protect franchisees against unfair acts by franchisors. A franchise operator who fears that the franchisor might open up a second franchise right next door can provide against that contingency in the language of the contract, and if further legal protections are needed, laws imposing good-faith obligations would suffice. A state might even impose objective distance requirements or time limitations on the issuing of new franchises. But the factors in the Illinois statute allow bureaucrats to veto new competition based on the desire of existing franchisees to keep their prices high. If the "investment made" by an existing business is a legitimate reason to bar competition from new businesses, economic innovation will be stifled and the right of entrepreneurs to earn a living will be curtailed, all to serve the private interests of companies that have been in business longer. Business owners usually invest a lot of time and money in their businesses, but that does not give them a right to use the law to prevent competition by others who could provide better or cheaper products. One English court recognized this more than five centuries ago when it declared: "[D]amage alone is not a cause of action. Thus, [where] an innkeeper or other victualler comes and dwells next to another [innkeeper] and thereby more of the customers resort to him than to the other, it is a damage to the other but no wrong, for he cannot compel men to buy victuals from him rather than from the other."[132] Protecting people who establish franchises against breach of contract or other abuses certainly is a legitimate function of government, but it can hardly justify giving bureaucrats the power to bar new competition merely because it might force established companies to lower their prices and work harder to meet consumers' demands. No business is entitled to a legally enforced permanent market share.

Protectionist franchise acts like this one increase the costs of products and decrease their availability to the public. In 1982, economist Richard L. Smith conducted a thorough analysis of the effect of automobile franchise regulations between 1954 and 1972, finding a 15.3 percent reduction in the number of new-car dealerships in states that had enacted such laws.[133] Cars in those states cost 13.7 percent more than cars in other states.[134] This price difference means that consumers are forced to pay more for cars without getting any increased value; the extra money is merely transferred into the pockets of politically influential car dealers. In 1972 alone, franchise acts transferred $6.7 billion from consumers to dealers.[135] Smith concluded that laws like Illinois's Motor Vehicle Franchise Act protect existing dealerships "from the entry of new dealerships, from discipline by the manufacturer, and from involuntary termination [of the franchise]. The net effect is fewer dealerships and increased market power resulting in higher prices."[136] This conclusion was supported by attorney Stewart Macaulay who, after closely observing automobile franchise legislation, published an encyclopedic article on the origins of automobile franchise acts.[137] Macaulay pointed out that in 1955, the year after federal legislation was enacted to protect auto dealer franchises, car prices increased an average of $117 (in 1955 dollars). In 1956, the price increased another $186, and another $176 the next year.[138]

These laws, Macaulay reported, were enacted at the behest of existing businesses that lobbied the government with emotional rhetoric about "villain[ous] . . . giant corporation[s] with wealth and power."[139] Although cloaked in the language of public benefit, such laws are really private-interest legislation designed to allow the government to choose each company's "fair share" of the trade.[140] But the only valid way of determining what share of the trade is "fair" for any business is its success with consumers who are free to choose.[141] If bureaucrats, rather than consumers, decide what amount of economic success is "fair," businesses will devote their time not to providing quality products at affordable prices but to wooing government officials to give them special favors. This only makes it harder for new entrepreneurs with good business ideas but no political connections to start new companies and spur innovation. In fact, franchise act protectionism has already led major companies, including Yamaha and Harley-Davidson, to give up opening new franchises in Virginia and possibly elsewhere.[142] Consumers, again, are victims of anti-competitive laws of which most of them are not even aware.[143]

Unfortunately, although the Illinois law was challenged in a 2007 lawsuit, the state supreme court upheld it.[144] Although one justice pointed out that "notwithstanding its seemingly lofty purpose of protecting 'the public interest and welfare' and 'consumers generally,' this Act is clearly nothing more than a protectionist measure favoring existing motor vehicle dealerships, and it should be acknowledged as such,"[145] the rest of the justices upheld the law under the lenient rational basis test.[146]

In his 1980 book *Economic Liberties and the Constitution*, Bernard Siegan observed that "[i]n earlier times in our history, the success of a business was dependent upon its acceptability in the marketplace," but that in modern times, "this economic competition is increasingly replaced by political competition. Losers in the economic arena seek relief from legislators who have the power to make them winners."[147] This tendency is largely attributable to the erosion of constitutional protections for economic freedom over the course of the 20th century. Occupational licensing laws, zoning, agricultural adjustment, franchise acts, and a host of other restrictions deprive people of their right to economic freedom or treat economic groups differently for no legitimate reason. Thanks to the lenient rational basis standard that courts apply when reviewing the constitutionality of economic regulations, these laws remain on the books, stifling fair competition, raising the cost of living, and frequently obliterating the economic opportunities of the poor and underrepresented.

8. The Dormant Commerce Clause

The Constitution grants Congress the power to "regulate commerce with foreign nations, and among the several states, and with the Indian tribes." The Supreme Court has broadened the interpretation of this provision to the point that Congress can now control virtually any economic activity it chooses to regulate[1]—certainly much more than the Founders ever intended.[2] But there is another way in which this clause has spurred controversy. Since the nation's earliest days, courts have been asked to decide whether the commerce clause gives Congress the *exclusive* power to regulate commercial matters that take place across state lines, or whether states retain some authority to regulate interstate commerce. The principle that federal control in this area is exclusive is called the "dormant commerce clause," but it is really just a theory of preemption: because Congress has the power to regulate in this area, states may not interfere and may not act even in cases in which Congress has deliberately refrained from exercising its power.

In a 1949 case, the Supreme Court made clear why the Framers gave Congress exclusive power over national economic matters:

> Our system, fostered by the Commerce Clause, is that every farmer and every craftsman shall be encouraged to produce by the certainty that he will have free access to every market in the Nation, that no home embargoes will withhold his exports, and no [other] state will by customs duties or regulations exclude them. Likewise, every consumer may look to the free competition from every producing area in the Nation to protect him from exploitation by any.[3]

The commerce clause therefore creates a "national free trade area," forbidding states from erecting protectionist trade barriers.[4]

Interstate protectionism was a subject with which the Framers were all too familiar. When the Constitution was written, states regulated trade in different and often conflicting ways. They printed their own currencies, taxed products differently at state borders, and imposed tariffs to benefit in-state producers. Motivated by "radically democratic" ideologies, some state legislatures enacted "disastrous commercial policies," including "debtor relief laws, which enabled borrowers to avoid their contractual obligations and authorized the emission of worthless paper money."[5] Others prohibited the export of rare goods and many sought to restrict trade with England, leading to conflict with sister states with more liberal trade policies. When some merchants chose to bring in items through ports that did not tax foreign trade and then to transport them by land into neighboring states, legislatures closed this loophole by taxing products that crossed state lines or that came from states without import duties. These laws, of course, raised the cost of living for all Americans and obstructed economic opportunities for citizens of other states.

As legal scholar Brannon Denning concluded after reviewing many of the discriminatory regulations that states enacted before the Constitution took effect, "[I]nterstate discrimination (along with the general lack of mechanism to effect a uniform national trade policy) was hindering the development of the United States and was, by 1787, causing friction among its constituent members."[6] Sensitive not only to the economic and social problems caused by these policies but also to the potential damage if these trends worsened, the Founders took steps to prevent the spread of conflicting state regulations. The authors of *The Federalist* repeatedly warned that "competitions of commerce" could be a "fruitful source of contention" between the states,[7] which might lead to "serious interruptions of the public tranquility."[8] The commerce clause, they explained, would help fix this problem by giving the federal government a "superintending authority over the reciprocal trade of [the] confederated states."[9] Moreover, as James Madison told his fellow Constitutional Convention delegates, giving this power to Congress would "seem to exclude this power to the states."[10]

The first Supreme Court decision to interpret the commerce clause raised the question of whether and to what degree this "superintending authority" barred states from passing laws that affected interstate commerce. The case of *Gibbons v. Ogden*[11] arose when Aaron Ogden, who operated steamships between New York City and Elizabethtown, New Jersey, asked a court to enjoin the business of his competitor, Thomas Gibbons, who also ran boats between the same points.

Ogden held an exclusive license from the state of New York that gave him a 10-year monopoly on steamship navigation between the two cities, but Thomas Gibbons, a former business partner of Ogden's, had obtained a federal license allowing him to run a ferry in the same waters. Ogden won his case, but on appeal the Supreme Court ruled in favor of Gibbons, holding that the federal government's power to regulate commerce between the states trumped state actions governing such commerce. If nothing else, the word "commerce" at least included "navigation" between states and allowed the federal government to pass laws regulating river transportation on interstate waterways. True, states retained some authority to regulate navigation, just as both state and federal governments had the power to tax. But "when a State proceeds to regulate commerce with foreign nations, or among the several States, it is exercising the very power that is granted to Congress, and is doing the very thing which Congress is authorized to do."[12] Since the Constitution and federal laws consistent with it are the supreme law of the land, state laws contrary to federal regulations of commerce "must yield to the law of Congress."[13]

Interfering with State Autonomy

Of course, the dividing line between state laws regarding internal matters that might incidentally affect interstate commerce and laws aimed at interstate trade that directly contradict congressional authority has often been unclear. Most state regulations of commerce *within* a state would have *some* effect on the commerce between states: regulating a New York corporation, for example, would necessarily affect shareholders who live in other states. And critics have long worried that Supreme Court decisions enforcing the preemptive effect of the commerce clause have gone too far—to the point where they interfere with legitimate state power to regulate intrastate affairs.[14] These critics have a reasonable complaint; in many cases, state powers have been wrongly obstructed on the grounds of a relatively minor effect on interstate commerce.

Consider, for example, the case of *Camps Newfound/Owatonna, Inc. v. Town of Harrison*,[15] involving a summer camp run in Harrison, Maine, for children of the Christian Science faith. Most of the children were not Maine residents, which was a serious detriment to the unprofitable camp because a Maine law gave charitable institutions certain tax breaks if they primarily served state residents. Organizations like Camps Newfound received only a much smaller deduction. The camp sued, arguing that this discrimination violated the dormant commerce clause, and the Supreme Court ruled in its favor. The camp, wrote Justice Stevens, was like a hotel in that it was designed to attract visitors from all states, and it provided services that substantially affected interstate commerce. And although states certainly have the power to set their own real estate taxes, those taxes must not "burden" such commerce. For example, states may not "impos[e] a special real estate tax on property used to store, process, or sell imported goods. By gearing the increased tax to the value of the imported goods at issue, the State [might] create the functional equivalent of an import tariff."[16] A tax exemption that differentiated between companies on the basis of whether they served in-state or out-of-state residents therefore violated the dormant commerce clause's nondiscrimination requirement. It "functionally serve[d] as an export tariff" because it levied different tax burdens on businesses that served primarily out-of-state customers. "[T]his sort of discrimination is at the very core of activities forbidden by the Dormant Commerce Clause."[17]

But while it is true that the clause was intended to prevent states from creating protectionist schemes that might disrupt the interstate market, it seems hard to believe that the Framers meant to bar states from granting the kind of tax exemption provided by the Maine law. For one thing, a tax exemption for charities is probably not what the Founding generation considered a regulation of commerce. Charitable organizations are often exempted from taxation, not to set the terms on which commerce takes place but to encourage charitable activities where profit incentives are lacking. Although the incentives created by such exemptions might encourage people to invest in one state over another, that fact alone cannot be enough to intrude on Congress's exclusive power to regulate commerce. And given that the Supreme Court has declared that the dormant commerce clause "does not prohibit all state action designed to give its residents an advantage in the marketplace, but only action of that description *in connection with the State's regulation of interstate commerce*,"[18] it seems unreasonable to interfere with the taxing prerogatives of states—which are not regulations of interstate commerce—simply to ensure that individuals see no distinction between states when choosing where to spend their money. State tax incentives benefiting in-state charities cannot reasonably be said to interfere with Congress's exclusive authority to regulate commerce between states. It certainly seems implausible to regard the Maine tax exemption as a protectionist device to exclude trade from out-of-state businesses. As Justice Scalia noted in his dissenting opinion, Maine's "distinction between charity 'bestowed within her borders and for her people' and charity bestowed elsewhere or for others did not implicate commerce at all, except to the indirect and permissible extent that innumerable state laws do."[19]

Admittedly, states might use their taxing powers to grant tax exemptions to corporations that locate within state boundaries and thereby encourage businesses to relocate from other states. But that cannot be enough to violate the dormant commerce cause; it does not forbid all differential treatment by states but only regulations of interstate commerce that interfere with Congress's exclusive power to set national trade policy or regulations that set up protectionist barriers against businesses from other states. Nor is there reason to fear that such tax breaks would harm society. Instead, they provide a beneficial economic stimulus. If, in a variation on the "predatory-pricing" scheme, a state were to drop its taxes to encourage companies to move into the state and then raise those taxes to confiscatory levels, the strategy would fail for the same reason that "predatory-pricing" schemes fail: the companies would be free to leave the state once the taxes increased.

This very issue was brought before the Supreme Court in 2006 in *DaimlerChrysler Corp. v. Cuno*.[20] The plaintiffs were a group of Ohio taxpayers who objected to their home state's using tax breaks to lure companies to locate there. These objectors were represented by Peter D. Enrich, a law professor who developed a theory that such tax incentives violated the dormant commerce clause.[21] Enrich's argument was based on the notion that tax incentives are bad for society because they "incur a very substantial loss of tax revenues"[22] and because they are not effective tools for encouraging businesses to locate within a state.[23] Why, then, do governments offer such incentives? Enrich argued that they are simply the product of political manipulation and ignorance: politicians want to be perceived as "doing something," and businesses then contribute to politicians or otherwise manipulate the political process to obtain further tax breaks.[24]

Some economists do dispute the effectiveness of tax incentives, which often work only in the short term and frequently come with so many strings that companies consider them not worth the trouble.[25] But others argue that tax competition between states encourages economic efficiency and leads to more restrained government policies since officials worry about losing productive constituents to more business-friendly neighbors.[26] It is at least clear that when taxes rise too high, businesses move elsewhere. As a *Wall Street Journal* editorial put it: "Tax competition between states is a good thing. The power of individuals and companies to vote with their feet is one of the most potent weapons against overweening government. Any attempt to deprive them of places to run must surely be considered an attack on freedom and a threat to prosperity."[27] But whether or not tax incentives work, the legal question is whether the Constitution forbids them. The answer is no: the Constitution only forbids states interfering with congressional authority over interstate commerce. If a state were to impose significant taxes on businesses located in other states, such a trade barrier might indeed intrude on the federal government's powers, but nothing in the Constitution prohibits normal tax competition between states.

Enrich argued that interstate competition for the attention of businesses "engender[s] intense and often hostile rivalries between the states," but there is little evidence of interstate "hostility" arising from economic development incentives.[28] Trade wars are generally fought by each side's *increasing* trade barriers, not lowering them. Eliminating trade restrictions is good for consumers because it encourages investment and innovation and allows people to keep more of what they earn. The only evidence Enrich found of the interstate "hostility" allegedly caused by tax incentives was the "martial metaphors" that state politicians used when debating attempts to make states more attractive to business.[29] But the fact that legislators and lawyers sometimes employ rhetorical flourishes like "first-strike attack" and "war between the states" is hardly the sort of genuine interstate conflict that the Constitution's Framers had in mind when giving Congress the exclusive power to regulate interstate commerce. There is no reason to believe that tax incentives are a threat to peace or that they harm citizens. Most astonishingly, Enrich objected

180

that tax incentives are implemented by "decision makers [who] are accountable to voters"![30] Economic policies, he argued, should be set instead by "rational" decisionmakers who are not subject to "a wide range of political considerations."[31] But the Framers believed that government ought to be accountable to the people.

The commerce clause encourages a national system of exchange and competition in which states may operate (within limits) as "laboratories" for the development and implementation of innovative policies. As the Supreme Court explained in a 1988 case: "The Commerce Clause does not prohibit all state action designed to give its residents an advantage in the marketplace, but only action of that description in connection with the State's regulation of interstate commerce. Direct subsidization of domestic industry does not ordinarily run afoul of that prohibition; discriminatory taxation of out-of-state manufacturers does."[32] Only laws that obstruct interstate commerce for self-interested reasons violate the Constitution, not laws that simply encourage trade and development.

Despite the flaws in Enrich's theory, the Sixth Circuit Court of Appeals struck down the Ohio tax incentive because it led to the "diversion of interstate commerce from the most economically efficient channels."[33] This conclusion has troubling implications for the federalist system. If the commerce clause prohibits states from "diverting" trade from other states, the natural conclusion is that all states must adopt a uniform level of taxation and regulation. After all, under the current system of "competitive federalism,"[34] states can set up widely different business environments. Oregon and Montana have no sales tax, for instance, and Nevada allows gambling and prostitution. These variations cause significant "diversions" of interstate commerce. In fact, the court's "diversion" theory would not just override the states' discretion to set tax policies, it could also threaten state power in noneconomic matters, such as laws regarding homosexual marriage. After all, gay couples might be more likely to choose to reside—and do business—in states that allow such marriages than in states that do not. Under Enrich's theory, this too would unfairly "tilt" the "playing field" by pressuring noncomplying states to legalize such marriages.[35]

Concerns about a "race to the bottom,"[36] wherein states would cut taxes and decrease regulations to attract businesses, are overblown. States face a natural disincentive to enact reckless tax policies: such policies cost them revenue. This counteracts pressures to lower taxes in ways that harm the general public. In fact, forbidding states to "divert" interstate commerce would create the opposite of a race to the bottom, namely, a "ratchet" effect under which states would be free to raise, but not to lower, taxes; to increase, but not to decrease, their regulatory burdens. States would not be allowed to implement policies that might draw businesses or citizens away from neighboring states. It would mean the end of the "laboratory" theory of competitive federalism.

Although the Supreme Court agreed to hear the *Cuno* case, it ended up dismissing it on the ground that the plaintiffs lacked the legally required standing to challenge the tax incentives.[37] This annulled the Sixth Circuit's decision, but other courts are free to adopt the same theory in future cases. As things stand now, this dormant commerce clause theory remains a serious threat to the states' ability to encourage economic development through tax incentives.

The Dormant Commerce Clause Protects Freedom: The Wine Shipment Cases

The concern that the dormant commerce clause might interfere with legitimate state actions has led some law professors, and Supreme Court Justices Clarence Thomas and Antonin Scalia, to declare that there is simply no such thing as a dormant commerce clause. But while some commerce clause cases have indeed gone too far, it is at least clear that the Founders did intend to bar states from discriminating, directly or in disguise, against their sister states.[38]

Although protectionist schemes harm the general public by raising the prices for products, stifling entrepreneurialism, and making the economy less efficient, legislatures are often persuaded to enact them by powerful lobbyists that stand to profit from them. These groups generally claim that they are acting in the service of public health and safety rather than admitting outright that they stand to gain from the restrictions. But in some cases, the effort is so strained as to be downright absurd.

Consider, for example, New York's and Michigan's laws against the importation of wine from other states. New York required that any out-of-state company seeking to ship wine to consumers must do so either through an in-state distributor or by operating a business physically situated within the state. The cost of setting up physical sales locations instead of running Internet or catalog sales was burdensome enough that no out-of-state wine seller even tried to comply with the New York law.[39] Instead, they simply didn't sell wine directly to New York consumers. Michigan's laws made the in-state bias explicit. In-state wineries could sell wine directly to Michigan consumers who ordered it over the Internet or through a catalog; out-of-state wineries could not. If a wine lover wanted a special bottle of imported wine, the law required him to go to a licensed merchant who would order it for him at an extra charge.

These laws had particularly severe effects on small-scale wineries that depended on their mail-order business to survive and that could not afford to lobby the legislatures of New York and Michigan to change their laws. When Virginia winemaker Juanita Swedenburg tried to sell her wine directly to Michigan or New York consumers through the mail or over the Internet, she found that she could not; state law created a barrier that set aside that market exclusively for companies located in New York and Michigan. But Swedenburg was not a citizen of these states and could hardly expect to convince the legislatures to respect her right to earn a living. Like others with little political influence, she had only the Constitution to rely on.

The constitutional law regarding wine importation is complicated by the legacy of Prohibition. In the early 20th century, when activists began demanding the prohibition of alcohol, courts held that Congress lacked the authority to prohibit the purchase or transportation of alcohol *within* states because the Constitution allows the federal government to regulate only *interstate* commerce. This meant that the Constitution first had to be amended before federal authorities could control alcohol within state borders.[40] But when the Twenty-First Amendment repealing Prohibition was ratified in 1933, it gave states the power to retain statewide prohibition if they so chose. The amendment declared that "[t]he transportation or importation into any State, Territory, or possession of the United States for delivery or use therein of intoxicating liquors, *in violation of the laws thereof*, is hereby prohibited."[41]

This language gave rise to an interesting problem. Could states now ban the importation of alcohol for *any* reason at all? Or did they only retain the power to ban alcohol for the "moral" purposes for which national Prohibition had been enacted? Before Prohibition, it was clear that states were not allowed to prohibit the importation of alcohol for merely protectionist purposes. Did the Twenty-First Amendment reverse this rule?[42] By 2005, all varieties of alcohol were legal in New York, so the state could not claim that its law was a sobriety measure. Instead, it claimed that the law was designed to protect the public from the possibility of minors ordering wine over the Internet or through catalogs. However, it was not very plausible that juvenile delinquents were trying to get their hands on alcohol by ordering gourmet wine through the mail. The bare fact was that these laws were designed to protect New York wine producers from out-of-state competitors.

Swedenburg and others sued and eventually won in the United States Supreme Court. While the Twenty-First Amendment allowed states to control or even prohibit alcohol for "sobriety" reasons, it did not allow them to pick and choose what alcohol to allow or to ban merely to protect domestic industries against fair competition.[43] "The mere fact of nonresidence should not foreclose a producer in one State from access to markets in other States," the Court declared. "States may not enact laws that burden out-of-state producers or shippers simply to give a competitive advantage to in-state businesses. This mandate 'reflect[s] a central concern of the Framers that was an immediate reason for calling the Constitutional Convention: the conviction that in order to succeed, the new Union would have to avoid the tendencies toward economic Balkanization that had plagued relations among the Colonies and later among the States under the Articles of Confederation.'"[44]

On the whole, cases involving the dormant commerce clause have adhered to the principle that the Constitution forbids states from enacting discriminatory laws against out-of-state competitors. Even Justice Stevens—no admirer of economic liberty—has conceded that the reason for the commerce clause was to create a nationwide free-trade zone. Unfortunately, he and most other judges do not recognize that preventing conflict and ensuring peace among differing interests require economic liberty not only between states but also between individuals. While protectionist trade barriers between states are considered per se invalid in dormant commerce clause cases, similar barriers granting preferences to particular companies or trade groups *within* states are usually upheld in cases involving the Fourteenth Amendment. We have seen, for example, that in *Powers v. Harris*, the Tenth Circuit Court of Appeals declared that although interstate protectionism is unconstitutional, "*intrastate* economic protectionism constitutes a legitimate state interest."[45]

But in one case, the Supreme Court held that protectionism, albeit between different states, also violated the Fourteenth Amendment. In *Metropolitan Life Insurance v. Ward*,[46] the Court invalidated an Alabama law imposing higher taxes on out-of-state insurance companies. Congress had explicitly waived its exclusive regulatory power in such matters, meaning that states were free to act in ways the commerce clause would normally prohibit. But the Court still found that the discriminatory tax violated the equal protection clause. "In the equal protection context," the Court declared, "if the State's purpose is found to be legitimate, the state law stands as long as the burden it imposes is found to be rationally related to that purpose."[47] But the purpose of this law was to protect domestic insurance companies against competition from out-of-state companies, not to protect consumers or provide any other genuine public good. This goal was "purely and completely discriminatory," and "the very sort of parochial discrimination that the Equal Protection Clause was intended to prevent."[48] It is "legitimate and often admirable" for states to try to attract new businesses, but laws that seek to "benefit domestic industry within the State only by grossly discriminating against foreign competitors" violate the state's constitutional obligation to treat people equally.[49] The "promotion of domestic business by discriminating against nonresident competitors is not a legitimate state purpose."[50]

The *Ward* Court rejected Alabama's argument that the law was not an attempt to harm outsiders but only to benefit insiders. This was a "distinction without a difference," the Court observed, citing a 1984 dormant commerce clause case called *Bacchus Imports v. Dias*[51] that annulled a protectionist law against interstate wine shipments. In *Bacchus Imports*, the Court had observed: "Virtually every discriminatory statute can be viewed as conferring a benefit on one party and a detriment on the other. . . . [I]t could always be said that there was no intent to impose a burden on one party, but rather the intent was to confer a benefit on the other."[52] Such an excuse could not shield a discriminatory law from judicial review. Thus, under either the dormant commerce clause or the equal protection clause, the government's mere desire to protect preferred merchants from competition by others is illegitimate. If the Constitution requires states to treat in-state and out-of-state businesses equally, it even more clearly requires them to extend equal treatment to their own citizens. If the equal protection clause forbids "parochial discrimination" across state lines, it should also forbid the same type of discrimination within a state.

The Dormant Commerce Clause and Local Communities

In recent years, the dormant commerce clause has become more important due to political agitation against nationwide franchises and "big-box" retailers such as Wal-Mart. As noted in chapter 7, established businesses often seek to bar the opening of such low-cost retailers in order to protect themselves from competition.[53] Labor unions, too, often campaign to prohibit the opening of stores that have chosen not to make contracts with the union.[54]

Some towns have bowed to these pressures by adopting "formula retail" ordinances forbidding the opening of "chain" stores. In Islamorada, Florida, for example, village officials passed a law imposing special permitting requirements on any business that featured a "standardized array of services or merchandise, trademark, logo, service mark, symbol, décor, architecture, layout, uniform, or similar standardized feature."[55] Any such business was limited to 50 linear feet of street frontage and 2,000 square feet of total floor area. The regulations prohibited businesses like McDonald's, Dairy Queen, K-Mart, or Best Buy, although certain other businesses, including banks, real estate brokerages, and accountants, were given special exemptions.

Islamorada residents Glenn and Virginia Saiger owned a small store on Highway 1. Not long after the ordinance went into effect, they agreed to sell their store to a company that planned to transform it into a Walgreen's pharmacy. But when city officials learned of the deal, they informed the Saigers that Walgreen's was a formula business and that their plans would violate the city code. The $2.6 million deal collapsed. Meanwhile, another nearby business, an Eckerd drugstore that was also a formula retailer, was purchased by CVS, which began operating a pharmacy there with its usual trademark, designs, and uniforms and even erected a large advertising billboard. Village officials declared that this was acceptable under the ordinance and took no action.

The Saigers sued, arguing not only that they were deprived of their rights under the privileges or immunities, due process, and equal protection clauses but also that the formula retail ordinance discriminated against out-of-state companies in violation of the commerce clause because Walgreen's is a national chain and the city's decision to protect local businesses by excluding it and other nationwide chains intentionally interfered with interstate commerce.[56]

At trial, members of the village's governing board testified about the purpose of the ordinance. "[Y]ou want to talk about legislative intent, what did we have in mind," testified the village's vice-mayor.

> We didn't want none of them darn chain stores coming to town. That's what it was all about, in plain words. My words anyway. So the thought was how do we stop that. We wanted to do something to prevent that. And we wrote it the way we thought and we tried to provide for some exceptions. We tried to make the law fair. And we put a provision in there that spoke about professional services. And I think we were referring to like chain real estate companies, you know, Century, whatever, you know, ReMax or whatever . . . that have multiple offices around the state or country.[57]

Perhaps more revealing was the fact that two of the five members of the village council owned businesses in the village—one a restaurant and another a grocery store—which the ordinance would protect against competition.[58]

Although the village claimed that it was trying to preserve the historical atmosphere of Islamorada, the court found that it actually had no historic atmosphere. There was no historic district or historic buildings. In fact, Islamorada itself featured only a single structure of historical significance: a 65-foot-long stone monument dedicated to the memory of hurricane victims. In reality, the court concluded, the ordinance was designed solely to protect businesses that were already operating in Islamorada against competition from "them darn chain stores." And this, the court declared, violated the dormant commerce clause. "The purpose of this ordinance and its practical application is economic protectionism," wrote Judge James Lawrence King.

"This kind of local protectionism is 'the very sort of protectionism against out of state competition that the Commerce Clause was designed to prohibit.'"[59] The ordinance was explicitly "tailored to serve local business interests by preventing competition from national chains."[60] Even if it had been designed to preserve the small-town atmosphere, the law did not actually accomplish this task because already-established formula retailers, or formula stores with little floor space, were allowed to continue operating despite the fact that they "would presumably affect the Village's small town character as well."[61] Most importantly, the ordinance barred only chain stores but allowed "other types of large, artificial, or noisy buildings, besides chain stores and restaurants" even though they could "still interfere with the Village atmosphere."[62] Whatever the case might be, the ordinance's purported goal of preserving the community's local character was a sham.[63] The real goal of the law was the "illegitimate advantage[] of economic protectionism for local business interests."[64]

Yet the court did not go on to discuss the Saigers' arguments that the ordinance violated their rights under the Fourteenth Amendment. Had it done so, the rational basis standard would have applied, and although some courts have found protectionism unconstitutional under this standard, most have not.[65] In short, the village's protectionist motive was unconstitutional under the dormant commerce clause but would probably have been upheld under the Fourteenth Amendment.[66] As noted in chapter 7, the Tenth Circuit decision upholding Oklahoma's discriminatory licensing requirement for coffin sellers did conclude that while the dormant commerce clause bars interstate protectionism, the equal protection clause does not forbid *intra*state protectionism.[67] But the Fourteenth Amendment is not silent on protectionist legislation. Not only does it forbid states from denying to "any person within its jurisdiction" the "equal protection of the laws," but it also includes a clause forbidding states from depriving citizens of their "privileges or immunities." This provision echoed the older privileges and immunities clause in the original Constitution, which had long been understood as requiring roughly equal treatment for out-of-state merchants who enter a state to do business. By creating a second privileges or immunities clause directly applicable to states, in addition to an equal protection clause, the Framers of the Fourteenth Amendment demonstrated an unmistakable concern that the evils of discriminatory treatment and interference with individual rights—including the right to earn a living—be barred by federal authority, even if they occur within, and not between, states. The amendment's authors sought "to protect fundamental national rights that the state could not abridge."[68]

One reason courts treat intrastate protectionism and interstate protectionism differently is their legitimate concern for protecting state autonomy in the federalist system. But this concern must be balanced by an understanding of the ways in which the amendment fundamentally altered the federalist system to protect legal equality and the security of individual rights. And it makes no sense in light of decisions like *Ward*,[69] where the Court openly acknowledged that the same concerns for unequal treatment and protectionism that animate the commerce clause are also applicable under the equal protection clause. More commonly, and more disturbingly, the double standard of treatment for economic discrimination under the dormant commerce clause and the Fourteenth Amendment reflects the unjustifiable deterioration of judicial respect for the Fourteenth Amendment's protections for economic freedom. In many other ways, this deterioration often compels plaintiffs to make strained arguments when challenging laws that restrict economic rights. In campaign finance cases, for example, candidates or contributors are forced to argue that legal restrictions on their use of money violate their First Amendment expressive rights, when they are more clearly restrictions on their property rights. Similarly, in cases challenging laws that ban the sale of sexual devices, plaintiffs are often forced to argue that the laws violate their privacy rights because the courts are unsympathetic to the more obvious argument that such laws violate the freedom of economic choice. So, too, business owners whose freedom of trade is restricted by discriminatory laws must argue that (often trivial) effects on interstate commerce require the courts to nullify laws that would be better seen as violations of the due process, equal protection, and privileges or immunities clauses of the Fourteenth Amendment. As is often the case in the law, an error in the past—the abandonment of serious judicial protection for economic liberty—leads not to repentance but to greater confusion and increasingly strained arguments in the present day.

9. Commercial Speech

The First Amendment, among other things, prohibits government from abridging the freedom of speech or of the press. Yet in 1942, the Supreme Court declared in *Valentine v. Chrestensen*[1] that this guarantee did not apply to "purely commercial advertising." In fact, whether to prohibit businesses from advertising their products to the public was entirely a matter "for legislative judgment" that simply did not involve First Amendment considerations at all.

The *Valentine* case was decided at a historic low point for economic liberty in the United States, less than a decade after the adoption of the rational basis test and in the midst of the New Deal, which implemented Progressive theories limiting economic freedom. For America's Founders, freedom of speech was one of the prepolitical rights that government may not justly violate; because a person owned himself, he also owned his beliefs and could therefore express them as he chose. In James Madison's words, each person "has a property in his opinions and the free communication in them."[2] But the Progressives and their New Deal heirs rejected the Founders' conception of freedom, arguing instead that individual rights were created by society. Freedom of speech, therefore, was really a privilege created for society's own purposes. "Persecution for the expression of opinions," wrote Justice Holmes in an opinion joined by Justice Brandeis, "seems to me perfectly logical."[3] But because "the ultimate good desired is better reached by free trade in ideas," government extended to individuals the privilege of expressing themselves.[4] Holmes and Brandeis believed that the Constitution's principal role was not to protect individual liberty but to facilitate collective decisionmaking. One consequence of this view was that while political expression would receive strong protection, expression regarding other matters, namely commercial enterprise, was of far less concern.[5] Throughout the 1930s and 1940s, Progressive intellectuals therefore tried to establish a historical claim that the Founders had no intention of protecting commercial expression when they wrote the First Amendment. Freedom of speech did not cover expression relating to commercial transactions, they held, but only "expression on political, sociological, religious, and economic subjects," and restricting government's authority to regulate commercial speech would "set at naught the efforts of towns and cities . . . to bring some degree of quiet, dignity, decency, and orderliness back to urban life."[6] To this day, their argument that the Founders did not mean the amendment to protect advertising remains influential.[7]

Yet this claim lacks historical support, primarily because the Founders simply did not view expression as being divided into commercial and noncommercial varieties. They believed that, except where barred by traditional legal doctrines regarding libel, slander, fraud, or public decency, individuals had the right to express themselves without government interference on any matter. In their day as in ours, public expression was frequently intertwined with commercial enterprise.[8] Opposition to the Stamp Act centered in large part on the economic effect the British tax would have on the newspapers that Americans relied on to express themselves on political or social affairs. Benjamin Franklin's career as a commercial publisher preceded and made possible his position as a leading Founder. Then as now, censorship often took the form of restricting the commercial transactions on which the spread of forbidden ideas depends. A generation before the Founding, John Milton wrote his famous *Areopagitica* in opposition to a law requiring that books be officially cleared for sale to the public. The authors of the First Amendment were mindful of this and of their experience under the Stamp Act, in which newspapers and other publications were singled out for special taxes that could limit the spread of information. In 1814, informed that a Philadelphia book dealer had been investigated for ordering copies of a skeptical religious book, Thomas Jefferson wrote that he was "really mortified to be told that in *the United States of America*, a fact like this can become a subject of inquiry, and of criminal inquiry too . . . that a question about the sale of a book can be carried before the civil magistrate."[9] The idea of dividing expression into commercial and noncommercial would have struck the Founding generation as odd.

But more important, the actual text of the Constitution expressly protects the freedom of "the press" and makes no distinction between expression connected to commerce and expression that is not. In fact, "the press" is a commercial industry—the only one mentioned by name in the Bill of Rights. The right to transact business and the right to express oneself are simply inextricable in the Constitution, and the *Valentine* decision provided no citations to history or law to justify distinguishing between these categories of expression. In fact, as Alex Kozinski, chief judge of the Ninth Circuit Court of Appeals, noted in an article written with law professor Stuart Banner, the Court does not even appear to have viewed the case as one involving expression at all but rather as one involving the mere regulation of a business. There is no reference in the case to Mr. Chrestensen's expressive rights; rather, the Court focused on his right to "promote or pursue a gainful occupation in the streets,"[10] and the decision's language might have been identical, they note, "had Mr. Chrestensen claimed only a right to open a store in the middle of Park Avenue."[11] Thus, the case fit very easily with "the then-recently-adopted deferential economic substantive due process jurisprudence."[12]

In fact, Kozinski and Banner point out that the *Valentine* case echoes a 1915 decision in which the Supreme Court unanimously upheld an Ohio law establishing a board of censorship for motion pictures. Where the *Valentine* Court simply ignored the possibility of expressive rights, the earlier decision explicitly rejected the idea that movies could be regarded as a form of speech. "[T]he exhibition of moving pictures is a business pure and simple," that Court declared, "originated and conducted for profit, like other spectacles, not to be regarded . . . as part of the press . . . or as organs of public opinion."[13] That attitude toward films obviously has not survived; movies today are a form of constitutionally protected expression. The *Valentine* Court's attitude toward advertising should also be rejected.

In the decades since *Valentine* was decided, the Supreme Court has come to recognize that advertisement is a form of expression that deserves at least some protection. In 1976, the Court acknowledged that the First Amendment *does* limit the degree to which government can interfere with expression by businesses. In *Virginia State Bd. of Pharmacy v. Virginia Citizens Consumer Council, Inc.,*[14] a group of citizens successfully challenged a state law prohibiting pharmacists from advertising the prices of prescription drugs. "[W]e may assume that the advertiser's interest is a purely economic one," the Court held, but that "hardly disqualifies him from protection under the First Amendment." The free speech guarantee applies even where a speaker's interests "are primarily economic."[15] Moreover, stifling the expressive rights of businesses hurts consumers, who need commercial information to make wise decisions just as they need political information to make wise choices of candidates or policies.[16] While advertising may be tasteless or demeaning, it still serves an important role in disseminating information. "So long as we preserve a predominantly free enterprise economy, the allocation of our resources in large measure will be made through numerous private economic decisions. It is a matter of public interest that those decisions, in the aggregate, be intelligent and well informed. To this end, the free flow of commercial information is indispensable."[17]

One central reason for the Court's shift toward greater protection for commercial speech was the virtual impossibility of drawing a categorical difference between commercial and noncommercial forms of expression. There is no clear line between "political" speech and "commercial speech": companies often advertise their products and services by referring to political issues or controversies, and newspapers that publish important political information survive on the basis of advertising. What's more, commercial enterprise and types of expression are often impossible to separate. Courts have found that the First Amendment protects the rights of businesses that operate newspaper stands,[18] highway billboards,[19] movie theaters,[20] and bookstores.[21] In the years since *Virginia Board of Pharmacy*, the connections between commerce and speech have only become stronger. As Pacific Legal Foundation attorney Deborah J. La Fetra points out, modern marketing tactics include music videos, product placement in movies and television, and sponsorships of public events, such as sporting events, all of which make it increasingly difficult to separate commercial from noncommercial speech.[22]

In 2001, country music singer John Michael Montgomery added recorded images of his father Harold, as well as his father's voice, to the video of his song "I Miss You a Little," which was recorded as a tribute to Harold. But Harold's widow Barbara sued, arguing that this violated the rights of Harold's estate. Montgomery contended that his video was a form of speech and therefore that the lawsuit was barred by the First Amendment. The Kentucky Supreme Court agreed.[23] Barbara contended that the First Amendment did not apply because a music video is merely a commercial advertisement for the

recording, but the court pointed out: "Most creative works are produced for sale and profit. This, of course, includes the songs that
underlie music videos. While music videos are not produced primarily for the sale of the video but, rather, the underlying song, this
does not strip them of their First Amendment protection." Likening
videos to "mini-movies," the court noted that they "often require the
same level of artistic and creative input . . . as . . . motion pictures,"
and such creative expression is protected by the Constitution.[24]

Separating commercial and noncommercial elements from speech
not only presents a practically impossible task in many cases, it also
inevitably leads courts into evaluating the *content* of speech. Yet one
of the cardinal rules of the First Amendment is that the content of
an expression should not determine the degree of protection that
it receives. Judges in commercial speech cases routinely "do precisely what the First Amendment forbids any government official
from doing: judging the social worth of the speaker's underlying
message" when deciding whether the speech receives constitutional
protection.[25]

Yet while *Virginia Board of Pharmacy* promised much in the way of
protecting the expressive rights of businesses, the Court distanced
itself from it only four years later in *Central Hudson Gas & Electric
Corp. v. Public Service Commission of New York*.[26] There, the Court
declared that the Constitution gives commercial speech "lesser
protection" than other kinds of speech and that the strength of the
constitutional guarantee "turns on the nature both of the expression
and of the governmental interests served by its regulation."[27] The
government may prohibit untrue commercial messages or commercial messages that are "related to illegal activity." But it may also
interfere with other kinds of commercial speech. To determine when
a restriction is constitutional, the Court set forth what has come to be
called the "*Central Hudson* test":

> If the communication is neither misleading nor related to
> unlawful activity . . . [t]he State must assert a substantial
> interest to be achieved by restrictions on commercial speech.
> Moreover, the regulatory technique must be in propor-
> tion to that interest. The limitation on expression must be
> designed carefully to achieve the State's goal. Compliance
> with this requirement may be measured by two criteria.
> First, the restriction must directly advance the state interest

> involved; the regulation may not be sustained if it provides only ineffective or remote support for the government's purpose. Second, if the governmental interest could be served as well by a more limited restriction on commercial speech, the excessive restrictions cannot survive.[28]

Terms like "designed carefully" and "substantial interest" are too vague to provide serious protection for most forms of expression associated with commercial transactions, let alone the speech that is related to both commercial and noncommercial affairs. Many courts, including the Supreme Court, have acknowledged the *Central Hudson* test's crippling ambiguity and the fact that this ambiguity allows government to silence expression that ought to be constitutionally protected.[29]

The *Central Hudson* test fails to provide either clear rules for determining which speech is commercial and which is not or sensible guidelines for what sorts of restrictions are permissible and impermissible. This is problematic because the messages expressed by businesses do not always invite commercial transactions. As Justice Stevens has observed, "[T]he Government should not be able to suppress . . . truthful speech merely because it happens to appear on the label of a product for sale."[30] In addition, when an expressive message is found *not* to be commercial speech, a court will often relegate it to the category of *nonprotected conduct* rather than finding that it is some other type of constitutionally protected speech. This allows the government to shut down such "conduct" entirely.

Silencing Businesses

No case illustrates the faults of commercial speech doctrine more clearly than *Nike v. Kasky*,[31] a 2002 California Supreme Court decision that allowed a brazen act of censorship to go forward under the commercial speech doctrine. That case began when the Nike Corporation defended itself against charges brought by various activist groups claiming Nike manufactured its products in third-world "sweatshops" where workers were mistreated. In response, Nike hired former United Nations ambassador Andrew Young to investigate the allegations and draft a report. Nike then publicized the report, which exonerated the company, by issuing press releases and letters to opinion makers. Such conduct is typical of the give-and-take of any public political dispute.

But Mark Kasky, a San Francisco–based political activist, sued Nike under California's extraordinarily broad Unfair Competition Law (see chapter 11), alleging that Nike's dissemination of these statements was "unfair" and "misleading." The trial court dismissed the case, holding that the First Amendment protected Nike's actions, and the court of appeal agreed. "The press releases and letters at issue here cross the boundary between political and private decision-making," the court noted. People might rely on statements by Nike or by Kasky when choosing whether or not to buy Nike's products or whether to protest the company. "In either case, 'the First Amendment protects the public's interest in receiving information.'"[32]

The California Supreme Court, however, reversed the court of appeal. It found that Nike's comments were less-protected commercial speech "[b]ecause in the statements at issue here Nike was acting as a commercial speaker, because its intended audience was primarily the buyers of its products, and because the statements consisted of factual representations about its own business operations."[33] Thus, the fact that Nike's expression concerned a matter of public debate did not entitle it to full constitutional protection, and Mark Kasky could sue Nike for making "deceptive" public statements. Although the United States Supreme Court agreed to review the case, Nike settled with Kasky before a decision was rendered. The justices dismissed the case, meaning that the California Supreme Court's decision remains on the books.[34]

The *Nike* case dramatically expanded the traditional definition of commercial speech, from "speech that does no more than propose a commercial transaction"[35] to speech by which a business seeks to influence public opinion by the dissemination of factual statements. But as attorney Thomas Goldstein, who represented Nike in the case, points out, "[V]irtually everything a business says or does is intended to increase its sales in some ultimate sense."[36] The California Supreme Court's conclusion that the comments were not immune from prosecution threatens to turn almost every comment made by a business into "commercial speech."

The classification of Nike's statements as commercial speech meant that the state could restrict them in ways that it could not restrict other types of expression. In *New York Times v. Sullivan*,[37] the Supreme Court held that government may *not* punish people for making false statements of fact in most discussions of public matters. But classifying a statement in a public debate as "commercial" means that the government may punish it as false or misleading advertising. The rationale for treating these two categories of expression differently is in part that commercial speech is allegedly more "hardy" than other types of speech. In the case of political speech, prosecuting people for making false statements might scare innocent third parties, deterring them from expressing themselves and creating a kind of censorship through intimidation. But those engaged in commercial speech are supposed to be less susceptible to intimidation because the profit motive will ensure that they will continue to express themselves.[38] Thus, subjecting businesses to potential liability for making false statements will in theory not deter them from participating in public controversies. In addition, the California Supreme Court held, businesses are better able to verify the accuracy of their statements than are private citizens, so subjecting them to greater liability is fairer.

But it is not true that commercial speech is easier to verify than noncommercial speech: competing businesses, or businesses and consumers, frequently differ over the quality or effects of their products, and it is difficult or impossible to test the objective truth of the claims on either side. On the other hand, outside the commercial context, the Constitution protects the expression of statements about public figures that turn out to be untrue, even when their veracity might easily have been checked. The assumption that commercial speech is more "hardy" than noncommercial speech is also dubious. Punishing companies for making false statements can frighten businesses away from merely controversial but true, or opinionated, statements that ought to be heard. That may be the case more often in the commercial arena than in the realm of noncommercial speech, in fact, because businesses are often more concerned with the bottom line than is the political idealist who is willing to risk punishment to make a political statement. Moreover, as Professor Daniel Farber notes, a chilling effect "depends as much on the potential penalty as on the motivation for the speech. A five dollar fine in a political speech case is probably less of a deterrent than a jail sentence—or disbarment—in a commercial speech case."[39] The greater liability in commercial speech cases may therefore chill much more speech than today's judges realize.

Some businesses may have already begun censoring themselves because of the *Kasky* decision: when activists ramped up their claims that fast-food companies like McDonald's were responsible for the increasing obesity of American youths, the National Restaurant Association implemented a "Rapid Response Program" to defend restaurants in the media. But in 2003, a *Fortune* magazine article expressed fear that such campaigns might lead to liability under California's unfair competition law.[40] About the same time, a leading trade magazine for attorneys recommended that when advising a business client, lawyers "should alert the client that the safest choice is silence. While this is the textbook example of a chilling effect, a business client runs a substantial risk in California if it makes a statement that is mistakenly false, or true but misleading."[41] Many businesses continue to participate in public controversies, but they often craft their statements to include as few factual assertions as possible, to avoid potential lawsuits.[42]

The most common reason for distinguishing commercial from noncommercial speech is that government ought to protect consumers against deceptive and false advertising. Of course this is true, but it no more justifies limiting the political expression of people operating businesses than the possibility of libel allows the government to limit a newspaper's right to publish editorials. Recognizing full constitutional protection for freedom of speech would not require government to repeal laws against fraud, defamation, or misrepresentation, laws that have always been held to be consistent with the First Amendment. But it would remedy the unfair distinction that allows government to restrict expressive rights. As attorney Jonathan Emord has observed, protecting commercial speech "will not cause crimes, torts, and contract violations to go unremedied. It will merely remove government from the paternalistic business of policing speech content and imposing on the innocent and the wrongdoers alike a speech orthodoxy."[43] Private citizens or social clubs that issue public statements can be sued if they deceive a customer or defame a private citizen. But they can also express their views on political matters free from fear of punishment—even views based on misrepresentations or misunderstandings of the facts—whereas the directors of a business cannot. The same rules ought to apply to businesses. In fact, every justification for curtailing Nike's speech would also justify restricting speech by private parties on matters of public concern. Under the *New York Times* case, however, the latter type receives the strongest possible protection, even if it includes false statements of fact, while speech by business groups in public debates do not receive such protection.

The different treatment accorded to these two kinds of speech leads to an especially perverse effect: people like Mark Kasky are constitutionally free to make inaccurate or even knowingly false statements against the Nike Corporation when speaking on matters of public debate, yet Nike can be sued if it responds in kind in the same debate.[44] Perhaps most disturbingly, Kasky's lawsuit was *explicitly aimed* at silencing Nike in a public dispute over politics. His complaint was not that Nike had made misleading statements about the quality of its products but that the company expressed itself in an allegedly misleading way in a political controversy. Kasky targeted Nike precisely because of the content of Nike's speech and its likely persuasiveness. Goldstein concludes that this fact alone "shows why Nike's statements belong at the very core of the First Amendment's protections."[45]

Businesses, whether large corporations or mom-and-pop stores, compose an important part of every community. They have a legitimate and important role to play in the debates in a democracy. "Who has a greater interest," ask Professors Martin Redish and Howard Wasserman, "in what actions the government takes with regard to the economy than corporations, whose very survival may well turn on the success or failure of those actions?"[46] Often, corporations make public statements about policies they believe will be good or bad for the economy or job creation or the environment. Many believe in being "good corporate citizens" by participating in social and political disputes. Others are forced to defend themselves against proposals that would harm their investors and customers.[47] In 2000, two years before *Kasky* was decided, the California legislature considered a bill, AB 84, which would have prohibited the construction of Wal-Mart Supercenter grocery stores. Not surprisingly, since Wal-Mart employees are not unionized, the United Food and Commercial Workers, a labor union, backed the bill.[48] Wal-Mart, Costco, and other companies opposed it by issuing public statements, newspaper advertisements, and leaflets urging the public to call elected officials and demand that the governor veto the bill.[49] Had the *Kasky* decision been the law at that time, the bill's proponents could easily have silenced the bill's opposition by filing lawsuits.

Given the significant role that commercial speech plays in democratic deliberation, why have courts and legal intellectuals so often treated business's expressive rights with such contempt? One reason may be a simple desire to censor business executives who, as Redish and Wasserman note, are "likely to advocate an anti-regulatory, free market philosophy that is widely unpopular among many academics today."[50] Those who argue for greater restrictions on economic freedom are less likely to zealously defend the businesses that oppose such restrictions. By characterizing a business's expressive activity as a mere transaction that deserves little constitutional protection, lawyers advocating greater regulation can bolster their claims that society "really" wants such regulation and that it is opposed only by selfish, corrupt private interests whose views are not worth hearing.

Commercial Speech as Individual Self-Expression

When lawyers, judges, and law professors discuss the subject of commercial speech, they often assume that such speech is generally undertaken by enormous enterprises like Wal-Mart or Microsoft. In fact, most commercial speech is small-scale, just as most businesses in America are small businesses. Restrictions on commercial speech usually affect individuals who run small businesses or are proposing only a single economic transaction.

In 2007, the Sixth Circuit Court of Appeals ruled on a case from the village of Glendale, Ohio, in which a man named Christopher Pagan tried to sell his 1970 Mercury Cougar by parking it on the street with a For Sale sign in the window.[51] This was prohibited by the town's traffic code, so officials ordered Pagan to remove the sign from his car or face a fine. Represented by lawyers from the Institute for Justice, Pagan sued, arguing that the law violated the First Amendment. The city claimed that the regulation merely prohibited conduct: namely, parking a car on the street with a For Sale sign that, according to the city's police chief, would lead to traffic obstructions as people stopped to look at the car. The court easily found that the law restricted Pagan's commercial speech rights and rejected the city's rationalizations.

The only evidence the city offered to justify restricting Pagan's speech was an affidavit by the chief of police, which cited no supporting proof. Although this seemed like a weak basis for the city's actions, the city argued that no such evidence was required in the first place. "Instead of actual evidence," the judges noted, the city "ask[s] us to adopt a standard of 'obviousness' or 'common sense,' under which we uphold a speech regulation in the absence of evidence of concrete harm so long as common sense clearly indicates that a particular speech regulation will directly advance the government's asserted interest." But this was not enough. The First Amendment "requires *some* evidence to establish that a speech regulation addresses actual harms with some basis in fact."[52] The city argued that demonstrating the need for, or the effectiveness of, its commercial speech ban would be expensive and time-consuming; and that it should be free to restrict public expression *without needing to prove that there was reason to do so.* Of course, given the extreme deference applied by courts in most cases involving economic freedom, the city's argument was understandable. As we have seen, courts using rational basis scrutiny often simply presume that there is a factual basis for the law, even if none is presented. But because the rational basis approach is not used in First Amendment cases, the court rejected the city's argument: the Constitution does not allow government to restrict speech in "the absence of any evidence of the need for regulation."[53] Those who care about freedom should be deeply disturbed by the city's attitude toward its own authority—that it had no obligation to explain its exercise of power—an approach all too common when it comes to the rights of small businesses, which generally succeeds when courts employ the rational basis test.

In a similar case in 1997, the city of Redmond, Washington, adopted an ordinance prohibiting the use of portable advertising signs. That law provided exemptions for real estate signs, banners on a nearby railway overpass, construction signs, celebration displays, political signs, and other types of expression. But when businessman Dennis Ballen, owner of Blazing Bagels, hired someone to stand on the sidewalk with a sign advertising his company, the city threatened to prosecute him.

Ballen, also represented by the Institute for Justice, filed a lawsuit arguing that the law violated his free speech rights. Because it was clear that the speech at issue was commercial speech, the court applied the *Central Hudson* test to determine whether the law was too broad and whether it actually achieved the city's asserted goals of "promoting vehicular and pedestrian safety and preserving community aesthetics."[54] The law was riddled with so many exceptions that the city's defense of the ordinance appeared quite weak. The court found that there was no sense in exempting "ubiquitous real estate signs," for example, which are a "greater threat to vehicular and pedestrian safety and community aesthetics than the presence of a single employee holding an innocuous sign that reads: 'Fresh Bagels—Now Open.'"[55] And while billboards and other large signs might disrupt the look of a town, portable signs like those Ballen was using "can be removed at the close of business and standing advertisers can take a seat when their feet are tired."[56] The court concluded that the city did not have a good enough reason to restrict Ballen's free speech rights.

Logos and Branding

The Supreme Court has yet to address whether and to what degree the First Amendment protects branding or the use of logos or common insignia by businesses. Branding is often subject to intrusive government regulations by state and local governments. In 2005, for example, Florida's highest court declared that the state could prohibit lawyers from using a logo depicting a pit bull, which the lawyers had chosen, along with the phone number 1-800-PIT-BULL, because it conveyed the image that they were especially fierce litigators, ready and eager to protect their clients' interests. The state bar complained that this was unprofessional conduct. Although the lawyers replied that their freedom of speech included the right to depict themselves as "pit bulls," the state's highest court ruled against them. Because it was merely "commercial" speech, the brand style could be strictly regulated. In other cases, the court explained, advertising images have received protection if they are an "accurate representation" that is unlikely to "deceive, mislead, or confuse the reader." But the use of the pit bull symbol "contains no indication that they specialize in either dog bite cases generally or in litigation arising from attacks by pit bulls specifically." Thus, it did not "convey objectively relevant information about the attorneys' practice," instead "connot[ing] combativeness and viciousness." This fell "outside the protections of the First Amendment."[57]

But "precision" is not required with regard to other kinds of speech. Sculptures or paintings, for example, often convey broad aesthetic impressions rather than precise issue-oriented messages. In a case in which the Supreme Court found that the First Amendment protects the right to march in a parade, the justices declared that the Constitution protects even imprecise forms of expression, including "such acts as saluting a flag (and refusing to do so), wearing an armband to protest a war, displaying a red flag, and even '[m]arching, walking or parading' in uniforms displaying the swastika." Thus, a message need not be "narrow" or "succinctly articulable" to be covered by the First Amendment.[58] There is simply no "precision" requirement in the First Amendment: even imprecise, impressionistic expression is protected by the Constitution.

If constitutional protections for free speech are meant to protect a person's right to express himself or herself and to ensure that ideas travel freely in society, then surely logos and commercial symbols deserve the same security. Not only does the Constitution protect general aesthetic impressions, but courts have already found that it protects the use of a business's name, which conveys information about price and quality,[59] as well as symbolic expression such as the display of religious symbols,[60] or erotic dancing,[61] or wearing long hair,[62] distinctive clothing,[63] or black armbands.[64] Even the acts of standing or sitting are constitutionally protected.[65] Courts have also held that *noncommercial* logos are protected speech. For example, the state of Virginia allowed private organizations to arrange for symbols to be added to license plates for a fee but refused to allow the Sons of Confederate Veterans to participate because their symbol included the Confederate battle flag, which some people find offensive. The Fourth Circuit Court of Appeals found that this refusal violated the group's First Amendment rights.[66]

In some cases, courts have even held that symbolic depictions for commercial purposes are protected expression. In 1998, the Second Circuit struck down a law that prohibited the Bad Frog beer company from using a label on its bottles depicting a frog raising a middle finger.[67] The state of New York claimed that this was a business practice that could be regulated; the beer company argued that it was speech. Admitting that commercial speech cases had left the legal community with "doctrinal uncertainties,"[68] the court nevertheless concluded that the beer label "attempts to function, like a trademark, to identify the source of the product . . . [and] to propose a commercial transaction." So while the label only communicated the source of the beer, "that minimal information, conveyed in the context of a proposal of a commercial transaction, suffices to invoke the protections for commercial speech."[69] Applying the *Central Hudson* test, it held that the state's restrictions were too broad and failed to advance the state's goals.

In 1979, the Supreme Court tried to rationalize the difference in treatment that logos receive vis-à-vis other types of protected speech, both commercial and noncommercial. In *Friedman v. Rogers*,[70] an optometrist who wanted to use a special trade name for his business challenged a Texas law restricting the use of such names. The Court upheld the regulation, claiming that a person "who uses a trade name 'does not wish to editorialize on any subject . . . [or] to report any particularly newsworthy fact, or to make generalized observations even about commercial matters.' His purpose is strictly business."[71] But this conclusion is troubling; courts reviewing free speech claims are not ordinarily supposed to examine the content of a message to determine whether it is constitutionally protected. Nor should the motive of the speaker be a consideration, except in cases where the communication falls into the categories of "fighting words" or incitement to break the law. Fraud, of course, does involve speech, but that expression is only part of a nonexpressive activity and therefore does not fall within the scope of protected speech in the first place. If the nonfraudulent use of a trade name is protected speech, it generally should not matter why a person wishes to use the name. Certainly, the Court should not refuse to defend speech simply because it considers the speaker's goals vulgar or unbecoming.

Even worse was the court's conclusion that logos deserve less protection because they have "no intrinsic meaning." A business's name "conveys no information about the price and nature of the services," the Court held; "it acquires meaning over a period of time by associations formed in the minds of the public."[72] But *no* expression has "intrinsic" meaning—all messages have meaning only "by associations formed in the minds" of the readers or viewers. Ballet dancing, for example, or a poem by Tennyson or T. S. Eliot, have no meaning *at all* until a viewer or a reader associates the dancing or the words with other thoughts or feelings. The *Friedman* Court found that the lack of "intrinsic meaning" meant that a trade name might confuse or deceive the public. But the same rationale could justify intrusive restrictions on other forms of speech as well: some religious denominations would probably contend that for other denominations to use certain religious symbols is misleading, since those others do not represent the "true faith." This would hardly allow the government to regulate the use of such symbols. The reasons advanced in *Friedman* simply do not justify censoring speech by businesses that choose to adopt a symbol or a trade name.

The Court's failure to develop a First Amendment doctrine with regard to logos and trade names makes even less sense when viewed from a consumer's perspective. Expression by businesses plays an important part in the expressive rights of buyers as well as in their ability to make wise buying choices. Customers who pay more for a popular label are paying for the convenience of not having to shop around; they can tell from the brand name whether the product or service is of the quality and value they want. Second, and perhaps equally important, branding has become a medium of communication by and among consumers themselves. As marketers have long understood, a strong brand image "taps into consumer needs and leads to a relationship that drives purchasing decisions." The strongest brand styles blend "the functional, emotional and self-expressive benefits delivered by a brand."[73] Customers receive these messages and understand them not only as indicators of quality but as part of a collective expressive enterprise in which they participate to express themselves as well. Consumers, writes Virginia Postrel, buy into aesthetic statements like logos and symbols by displaying them on their clothing or jewelry because symbols allow consumers to "define [them]selves aesthetically. . . . *I like this* becomes *I'm like this*."[74] A person wearing a T-shirt with a logo on it is often expressing more than mere brand loyalty because, as another scholar puts it, "ideograms that once functioned solely as signals denoting the source, origin, and quality of goods have become . . . valued as indicators of the status, preferences, and aspirations of those who use them."[75] Although in previous decades advertisements more directly explained a product or service, plainly declaring the price and availability, today's advertising focuses on lifestyles—creating images and feelings rather than simply proposing a transaction. Lifestyle advertising has become a common, perhaps the most common, advertising tool.

One good example would be Ben & Jerry's ice cream company, which has worked hard to establish a reputation for social and political activism, usually for causes associated with the political left, such as environmentalism or "social conscience."[76] A consumer who wears a tie-dyed Ben & Jerry's T-shirt is choosing to express his or her association with that image and those causes. Once one realizes "that modern advertising is multidimensional, the task of designing coherent First Amendment policies for such advertising becomes problematic."[77] The First Amendment certainly protects the right of individuals to express their identification with others who share their values through the display of religious or political symbols, clothing, or hairstyles.[78] Shouldn't the same protection apply to the display of logos and business symbols as well?

Yet courts have failed to guarantee the expressive freedom of businesses using common branding images. A Rhode Island law, for example, prohibits stores from using common insignia to identify themselves as chain stores. When one retailer challenged this law, arguing that it violated the First Amendment, the First Circuit Court of Appeals found that the use of common insignia was not communication but simply a business activity that could be regulated. The law against common insignia, the court declared, "does not target speech" because it "merely proscribes conduct—the launching of advertisements resulting from pre-agreed commercial strategies."[79] But expressing oneself in conjunction with others according to a pre-considered plan is still expression, which should be protected as such rather than regarded as merely unprotected "conduct." The Constitution protects the display of a symbol, the conveyance of product information, conduct intended to express solidarity with a group, conduct that conveys only a feeling or impression rather than a particularized message and, to at least some degree, expression that proposes a commercial transaction. Yet in Rhode Island, at least, advertising through the use of common insignia, which combines all these features, is *not* protected because it is only conduct and not expression. This profound confusion permeates today's commercial speech jurisprudence.

Compelled Speech

A third intersection of free speech and business rights arises in the context of *compelled* speech: government often forces business owners to subsidize the promulgation of messages with which they disagree, in violation of their rights. But the past decade has witnessed a series of conflicting Supreme Court rulings on this issue, resulting in confusion and contradiction.

Some federal and state agriculture regulations establish "check-off" programs that require businesses to contribute money toward collectively advertising the commodity the businesses sell, without mentioning individual brand names. The theory is that the product is generic and does not differ between producers, so cooperative advertising is more efficient than competing advertising schemes run by each business. The most famous of these publicity campaigns is the Got Milk? campaign, which is paid for by money "contributed" by the nation's dairy farmers. These programs are often described as voluntary, but they are actually compulsory; and some farmers do not want to contribute to them because they think their products *are* superior to those of their competitors.[80]

Check-off programs raise important free speech issues because the freedom to speak includes the right *not* to speak. In one famous case, the Supreme Court held that the state of New Hampshire could not prosecute a man who covered up the state motto on his license plate (Live Free or Die) with tape.[81] Freedom of speech, the Court noted, "includes both the right to speak freely and the right to refrain from speaking at all."[82] The government may not force a person to salute the flag,[83] force newspapers to publish responses to editorials,[84] or force veterans to allow homosexuals to march in the veterans' parade.[85]

In *Glickman v. Wileman Brothers & Elliott, Inc.*,[86] a group of California fruit farmers asked the Supreme Court to invalidate a government program requiring them to pay for generic advertisements of nectarines and peaches. The farmers wanted to advertise under separate brand names instead. The Supreme Court rejected their argument that the law violated their expressive rights, declaring that the law did not bar growers from communicating any message, nor were they actually forced to speak or to "endorse or to finance any political or ideological views." Instead, the law merely required growers to pay for speech made in their names by others, and the Court declared that "since all of the respondents are engaged in the business of marketing California nectarines, plums, and peaches, it is fair to presume that they agree with the central message of the speech that is generated by the generic program."[87]

But these conclusions are either irrelevant or false. It is absurd to say that the fruit growers, who spent a great deal of time and money to get their case to the Supreme Court, actually "agreed" with the messages to which they objected. If that were true, they would hardly have pursued the litigation. They may have believed that peaches and plums are good things to buy, but generic advertising tells the public to choose *any* peaches and plums, and the litigants instead wanted the public to choose *their* peaches and plums. More importantly, the three factors the Court used to distinguish the lawsuit from other types of compelled speech were not really relevant. While it is true that the law did not compel endorsement of a *political* message, the First Amendment's protections have never been thought of as limited to political messages; a person can no more be compelled to endorse a nonpolitical message than a political one. And while it is true that the farmers were not *themselves* compelled to speak, they were still forced to fund others who spoke on their behalf, something that is not tolerated in the realm of, for example, religion, where the government is forbidden from subsidizing religious speakers with money taken from nonbelievers. The Court has also frequently declared that union members, lawyers, and other professionals cannot be forced to subsidize messages with which they disagree through compulsory union dues or occupational fees.[88] The *Glickman* decision makes little sense. Perhaps the Court simply did not take the constitutional infringement seriously.

Four years after *Glickman*, the Court seemed to change its mind, declaring in *United States v. United Foods*[89] that the government could *not* force mushroom growers to subsidize generic mushroom advertisements. The mushroom company challenging the check-off program "want[ed] to convey the message that its brand of mushrooms is superior to those grown by other producers," explained Justice Anthony Kennedy, while the government wanted to convey the message "that mushrooms are worth consuming whether or not they are branded." While outsiders might think it a minor issue, Kennedy wrote, "First Amendment values are at serious risk if the government can compel a particular citizen, or a discrete group of citizens, to pay special subsidies for speech on the side that it favors."[90]

Kennedy acknowledged that the same factors were present in the mushroom case as in the peach and plum case: Here, too, the law did not bar the growers from expressing their own views, or compel them to express a view; nor did the case involve political statements. But these factors, he declared, "are not controlling." Instead, "[t]he program sustained in *Glickman* differs from the one under review in a most fundamental respect. In *Glickman*, the mandated assessments for speech were ancillary to a more comprehensive program restricting marketing autonomy. Here . . . the advertising itself . . . is the principal object of the regulatory scheme."[91] In other words, the speech restriction in *Glickman* was acceptable because it was imposed by a subsection of a large regulatory scheme, whereas the speech restriction in *United Foods* was unconstitutional because it was imposed by a smaller, stand-alone law.

This distinction is simply bizarre. The First Amendment draws no lines between censorship as part of a "comprehensive" program and censorship adopted as an independent regulation. Certainly, the New Hampshire law that prohibited defacing license plates was part of the state's "comprehensive" motor vehicle code, yet the Court upheld the First Amendment rights of a person who covered up the Live Free or Die motto. And while the Supreme Court held in the famous *Barnette* case that schoolchildren could not be legally required to pledge allegiance to the flag, it is hard to imagine that the Court would have ruled differently if the pledge requirement had been part of a "comprehensive" law like the No Child Left Behind Act. If anything, the view that the "comprehensiveness" of the program makes a difference only encourages the government to increase the amount of regulation or to combine speech restrictions with other kinds of controls in order to escape constitutional restraints.[92]

Despite these theoretical weaknesses, the *United Foods* decision provided some hope to businesses wanting to develop their own individual brands. But that door closed again only four years later in *Johanns v. Livestock Marketing Ass'n*[93] when the Court upheld a system of compelled generic advertising for beef. Rather than return to the *Glickman* rationale—that the compulsion was not really so severe— or the theory of *United Foods*—that the difference turned on the size of the government program at issue—the Court adopted a third approach. This time, the Court found that the speech at issue was not compelled speech by the beef producers at all: it was speech *by the government* that just happened to be funded by a special fee taken from the beef producers. "The message set out in the beef promotions is from beginning to end the message established by the Federal Government," the Court declared,[94] and although citizens "may challenge compelled support of private speech," they "have no First Amendment right not to fund government speech."[95] In *Johanns*, the ranchers argued that theirs was not *simply* a case of government's funding its own expression with tax dollars, because viewers would naturally assume that they endorsed the campaign, which was labeled with the line "Beef: it's what's for dinner." But the Court disagreed. The ads did say they were "funded" by beef producers, but this was not precise enough to establish that viewers would think these particular plaintiffs in *this* case had actually endorsed the ads; and without evidence of "attribution," their rights had not been violated. Instead, the government simply chose to promulgate its own message, with a special fee taken from the plaintiffs.

The problem with this argument is that the same could be said of many coerced speech (or coerced subsidy) cases, including those involving unions or trade organizations. In those cases, the individuals were compelled to pay special assessments to fund public relations campaigns, political lobbying, or other expressive activity that—like the beef program—was not directly attributed to any *particular* individual. Nevertheless, the Court found these schemes to violate the First Amendment.[96] As attorney Daniel Troy notes: "[T]here is no inherent reason why forcing an organization to pay for speech with which it disagrees is worse when the speech is coordinated by a private association rather than by the government. . . . If anything, the imprimatur of legitimacy attached to state-sponsored messages may make the coercion even *more* offensive."[97] Worse still, the beef producers complained that the organization responsible for the ads, the Beef Board, was only nominally supervised by the secretary of agriculture. If that is so, then the board has accomplished what many private-interest groups long for: it has effectively insulated itself from serious oversight on one hand, or from democratic accountability on the other, all while retaining its power to take money away from people for its own use.

What explains the twisted logic of the different commercial speech decisions or the disparate treatment between the generic advertising cases and the union dues cases? Troy offers a dispiriting suggestion: "[E]ven though the Court foreswore any explicit references to the 'lower value' it has accorded commercial expression, the *Johanns* decision nevertheless demonstrates that commercial speech is not being afforded equal protection with other modes of expression, despite the history and explicit text of the First Amendment."[98]

Ultimately, commercial speech is controversial because it lies between the freedom of economic activity, which receives very little respect under the prevailing Progressive-Era approach to constitutional interpretation, and the freedom of expression, which receives very serious protection under that approach. Just as storms develop when opposing air currents collide, so the opposing doctrines of "rational basis scrutiny" and "strict scrutiny" clash in these cases, spreading doctrinal chaos that only expands over time. Progressives exalted the citizen's right to participate in government decision-making as a crucial constitutional privilege—while simultaneously disparaging the right to engage in a gainful trade as merely "the right of industrial combatants to push their struggle to the limits of the justification of self-interest,"[99] a right undeserving of serious legal protection. When the two rights intersect, as they inevitably do, the Progressive model falls apart. Remedying this problem would require rethinking the Progressive model and questioning its assumptions—particularly the assumption that democracy, rather than liberty, is the fundamental purpose of the Constitution's guarantees.[100] But so far, the judiciary shows little inclination to do that rethinking.

10. The Manipulation of Contracts

For most people, the word "contract" brings to mind written documents signed by both sides to an agreement: formal, legally binding arrangements that one enters into when buying a house or a car. But every person makes or acts under dozens, perhaps hundreds, of contracts every day. Consider someone's daily routine. He wakes in the morning in an apartment that he contracted to rent from his landlord. He takes a shower and brushes his teeth using water and light for which he has a contract with the water and power companies. During his commute, he stops for gas and executes a contract with the gas station for fuel. He stops at a drive-in for breakfast and makes a contract to purchase food. He goes to work to fulfill an employment contract with his employer. . . . The list goes on. Any spoken or written agreement for an exchange of values is a contract.

The right to make contracts—sometimes called "liberty of contract"—means simply the right of people to agree to exchanges. It is one of the most important aspects of freedom because it allows a person or a group of people to transform their liberty—their ability to act with their own bodies or their own possessions—into property or opportunities they find useful. Without the freedom to enter into contracts, an individual's liberty would be of little use to him since he could not make agreements to exchange his labor or belongings with others for his basic needs. With that freedom, a person having little material wealth—like Frederick Douglass, free but penniless on the streets of Rochester—can make the exchanges that will allow him gradually to improve his condition. People use their freedom of contract more often than they exercise many other essential liberties. A person might go his entire life without making a political speech or writing to a member of Congress, but no individual other than a monk or a beggar can go long without making a contract to exchange one thing for another.

Yet the freedom of contract has been forcefully attacked throughout the 20th century, and courts have sometimes acquiesced in these attacks, undermining the enforceability and vitality of contracts. Under a variety of legal theories, courts sometimes alter contracts, manipulating their terms or ignoring the parties' contractual obligations out of a misguided sense of doing justice, even when that "justice" contradicts what the parties themselves actually agreed to. Under the theories of "unconscionability," "public policy," or "imbalance of bargaining power," judges sometimes refuse to enforce contracts, or they manipulate the interpretation of contractual terms because they sympathize with the position of one party, or because they believe the other party should bear the cost of an unforeseen circumstance despite an agreement to the contrary. What these theories have in common is the presumption that courts ought to intervene in agreements between parties because those agreements are not the product of "real" choice and because courts can do a better job than the parties themselves of forming a "fair" exchange.

More than a century ago, the Supreme Court warned of the deleterious consequences that would follow if courts interfered with the contractual choices individuals make: "[T]he right of private contract is no small part of the liberty of the citizen," observed Justice George Shiras, and the "most important function of courts" was to "maintain and enforce contracts" and not "to enable parties thereto to escape from their obligation on the pretext of public policy, unless it clearly appear that they contravene public right or the public welfare." Quoting an English judge, Shiras concluded that good public policy required, above all else, that mature adults "have the utmost liberty of contracting, and . . . their contracts, when entered into freely and voluntarily, shall be held sacred, and shall be enforced by courts of justice.'"[1] But in the century that followed, courts developed and implemented a variety of tools for controlling the choices that contracting parties make in order to achieve "preferable outcomes."

The terms "unconscionability," "imbalance of bargaining power," and "public policy" tend to overlap. A contract is said to be unconscionable if it is so unfair that it would "shock the conscience" of the court. For example, a contract might be unconscionable if it includes fine print that no person could read and therefore deprives a person of a right without his knowledge. (As we will see, however, courts tend to blur the distinction between contracts that are "procedurally" unconscionable in this way and contracts that are "substantively unconscionable," which means that they include terms that judges think unreasonable.) Unconscionable contracts are sometimes created when one party is wealthier, more experienced, or better educated and can fool the other side into signing the unfair agreement. This is known as an imbalance of bargaining power: the classic case is one in which one person is at another's mercy and the other side takes advantage of him. A driver whose car has broken down by the side of the road in a desert is essentially at the mercy of a tow truck driver who might charge exorbitant prices for his services. The imbalance in bargaining power is sometimes said to render the resulting contract unconscionable and therefore unenforceable. Finally, a contract is said to contradict public policy if it involves something illegal—say, a murder-for-hire contract—or if the parties agree to do something immoral, dangerous, or otherwise bad for society. Because the definition of public policy is vague, courts have sometimes used this doctrine to justify manipulating contract rights in disturbing ways.

Imbalance of Bargaining Power

In extreme cases, it makes sense for courts to scrutinize a contract closely due to the imbalance of bargaining power or the public policy concerns implicated by the contract. The Roman senator Crassus is said to have become wealthy by running a fire company that would show up at a fire and then negotiate with the homeowner over the price of putting out the fire. The fire would continue to burn while the "negotiations" continued.[2] It does seem unfair to allow Crassus to take advantage of a homeowner's desperation. Yet there is a danger that the exception designed to address such extreme cases could swallow up the basic right of contract.

The core of liberty of contract is the freedom of choice, as opposed to coercion. But the doctrine of unequal bargaining position—also called "economic duress"—often ignores or erodes this distinction. Those who advocate greater government intervention in contracts between unequal parties contend that when a person is in need, that person's choices are not "truly" free. Even contracts that are negotiated under far less pressure than Crassus's firefighting contracts are sometimes characterized as unconscionable and subject to reversal on the theory that every contract ought to be the product of equal bargaining parties, but since parties are never actually equal, no contract is truly consensual. Consent, some New Deal–era writers argued, is "a useless concept in the administration of justice."[3] But discarding the distinction between coercion and consent gives courts supervisory power over virtually any agreement any person might make. Although few legal theorists today are willing to go that far, many have admitted that "a comprehensive and detailed description" of "what precisely is meant by 'inequality of bargaining position'" is "impossible."[4] And without clear definitions of consent or of inequality of bargaining position, no contract is safe from the possibility that a court might annul it on the ground that it was not the product of "true" consent. Doctors, for example, now sometimes find it difficult to enforce agreements involving experimental surgeries or therapies because they know that courts may regard such agreements as the product of unbalanced bargaining power and refuse to enforce them.[5]

Some courts have gone to extreme lengths to absolve contracting parties of the duties they freely undertook. In one 2005 case, for example, a New Jersey court held that a liability waiver signed by a mother on behalf of her 12-year-old son was unenforceable. The mother signed an agreement so that her son could play at a private skateboard park. But when her son broke his leg at the park, the court refused to enforce the waiver because, among other things, "a parent, accompanied by an importunate child," is unable to "rationally calculate[] the risk of injury to the child or its economic cost before bowing to the child's request for entry into a craved pleasure ground and signing the release. . . . The coercive pressures exerted by children in this context are ones that any parent has experienced."[6] In other words, the court would not expect a parent to exert the discipline of saying no to her son, and a child's begging was enough to render the contractual agreement unenforceable.

The concept of unequal bargaining power has given left-leaning activists an opportunity to use courts to make broad changes in the free-market system. Law professor Duncan Kennedy argues that it is a useful tool for "ad hoc . . . intervention" by the government in the service of wealth-redistribution.[7] "Rather than disallowing contracts not in the party's best interest," he writes, a "paternalist court compels the contract she should have made."[8] But Kennedy objects that the inequality theory does not go far enough, because while courts can use the inequality of bargaining power theory to alter contracts as "a weapon in the war against the conservative program of reinforcing all kinds of social hierarchy,"[9] the theory achieves "only rather randomly good results."[10] It would be far preferable, he argues, to "transcend[] . . . pluralism in the name of truth"[11]—that is, simply to dictate to people what sorts of decisions they ought to make. To respect that people make a variety of choices and pursue diverse goals ("pluralism"), or that people have the right to set their own priorities and the moral obligation to suffer the consequences if they make bad decisions—all this is in Kennedy's eyes nothing more than cowardice. When we treat people "as entitled to their mistakes," we are simply "acting to deepen their incapacity,"[12] due to our alienation and fear: we are afraid of the responsibilities that would be entailed by *true* compassion. That sense of alienation is created by capitalism, which forces us into "social segregation and consequent ignorance and fear of one group for another."[13]

Many other lawyers and law professors have urged courts to use the inequality theory to supervise the economic decisions that people choose to make. But the inequality theory has serious flaws. First, every contract involves at least *some* inequality of bargaining position, and often a major one. This hardly makes all such contracts unfair. Everyone shopping at a grocery store is in an unequal position with the grocery store, and grocery stores do not negotiate the prices of products with customers. Nevertheless, consumers freely choose to go to such stores and do not generally consider themselves harmed when they buy groceries. They make these choices because they believe those choices will improve their situation: the relevant issue is not whether the contract is made between equal parties but whether the terms of the contract make each side better off than they were before. The inequality of the parties is irrelevant; in fact, such equality is not only unattainable, it is undesirable. Parties in a state of *exact* equality would have little reason to enter into contracts. Exchanges take place *because* of inequalities: person A has something that person B wants, and he is willing to exchange something for it. Their contract is not based on their relative wealth but on the benefits they seek from that exchange. The buyer at the grocery store says thank you to the cashier because he has received something he wanted in exchange for something he valued somewhat less (his money). He probably would prefer to pay less—but the fact that he agrees to the exchange proves that his position was improved by the bargain in some way. It makes no sense to say that his choice was not "real" because the grocery store is wealthier than he is or because his options were limited. No person can have a theoretically pristine "real" choice from an infinite number of options. The question in any transaction is simply whether that bargain improves the person's position relative to his previous position.

Because virtually every contract is between parties who are unequal in some sense, the unequal bargaining power theory would seem to justify state intervention in almost every contract. But contrary to Professor Kennedy's allegations, it is not callous or cowardly to say that courts should refuse to change the terms of contractual agreements. Instead, enforcing agreements as written is a matter of respect for individual identity and autonomy. Monitoring and correcting the economic choices that people make would transform them into wards of the state, threatening both their freedom and their responsibility. Freedom requires that people shoulder the burdens of their bad decisions just as they enjoy the benefits of wise choices, not only because this provides them with the incentive to make good decisions but also because it would be unfair to require others who *do* chose wisely to pay the price for those who do not. Indeed, it would create precisely the sort of perverse incentives that doomed socialist economies to stagnation and collapse. When a contract involves a wealthy corporation, it is easy to overlook the serious social costs caused by shifting the burden of bad choices to the party that did not agree to undertake that risk, but those costs are real nonetheless. If a bank cannot be sure that it can collect when a borrower defaults on a loan, it will have to make up those costs in some other way, and it will do so by raising interest rates on responsible borrowers. If a car company that finances purchases cannot repossess a car from a person who fails to make payments, it will either raise the price of other cars or stop selling cars on the installment plan entirely, thus raising the cost of living and limiting the freedom of choice for those who would have made their payments. As Judge Susan Graber of the Ninth Circuit Court of Appeals noted in a case involving an insurance contract, "[I]t is not unjust to deny coverage when the insured has not bought coverage for the particular kind of disaster that occurred," even though it may be unfortunate for the person who suffered the disaster. "Indeed, the opposite result is what would be unfair," because forcing an insurance company to pay for a loss not covered by a policy means that "[o]thers who *have* purchased . . . insurance must pay for the claim in the form of increased premiums. Purchasers of flood insurance agree to share only the risk of flood, not any of the many other risks for which other forms of insurance are designed."[14]

Insurance cases, probably more than any other kind, exhibit judicial manipulations of contracts.[15] After a catastrophe occurs, insurance companies often refuse to pay, arguing that the loss was not of the kind covered by the insurance policy. One notorious example occurred in the aftermath of the 1906 San Francisco earthquake, when many insurance companies refused to pay because the policies covered only fire, not earthquake damage, and the destruction—first by earthquake and then by fire—was so extensive that it was impossible to prove what exactly had destroyed many buildings. The insurance companies' actions may have led many people to torch their own shattered homes, thus worsening the firestorm.[16] Frequent complaints about abuses like this led legislatures to establish bureaucracies to oversee the insurance business and prompted courts to regard insurance contracts with particular skepticism. But while it is laudable when government ensures that insurance companies live up to their promises, courts often go too far, requiring coverage for injuries not actually included in the contract.

Take, for example, *E.M.M.I. v. Zurich-American Insurance Co.*,[17] a case involving a jewelry theft. The insurance policy protected a jewelry courier against theft, but only if the theft occurred while the courier was "actually in or upon the vehicle." This provision meant that the policy would not cover any theft that occurred while the courier was stopped at a roadside restaurant or gas station. The policy therefore struck a deliberate balance between risk and security, preventing the courier from recklessly abandoning the jewels but covering any truly unforeseeable theft.

The case began when the courier noticed a peculiar sound coming from the trunk of the car, pulled over, and got out to check the trunk. At that instant, the thief jumped into the car and made off with the jewels. The insurance company refused to pay, contending that the driver was not "actually in or upon the vehicle" when the theft occurred. But the California Supreme Court held that the policy did apply. "Actually in or upon," the court held, did not really mean "actually in or upon"; it meant *sort of* in or upon, or *kind of near*:

"[W]e do not believe a reasonable insured [person] would construe [these words] to mean that the insured must be either inside or on top of the vehicle," the court declared. "To construe . . . the word 'upon,' as applying only to situations in which the insured is inside or physically touching the vehicle would . . . preclude coverage when the insured exits the vehicle and walks a short distance to retrieve the insured merchandise from either the backseat or the trunk."[18] But, of course, that is *precisely* what "actually in or upon" means, and both parties were aware of that when signing. As two of the justices noted in dissent, the phrase "actually in or upon" is "unambiguous. It does not . . . contemplate coverage when the insured or its representative is 'in close proximity' to the vehicle or somewhere nearby at the time of the theft. Rather, the insurer's use of the phrase '*actually in or upon such vehicle*' was deliberate."[19]

Often, judges rule against insurance companies because they believe the companies are wealthier and better able to afford shouldering the losses than is the customer. But the consequences are higher insurance premiums or an economy where insurance coverage is harder to find.[20] Insurance companies "must know with certainty that contract language will be judicially respected. Absent such certainty, only the most cavalier insurer would attempt to write business."[21] When courts impose liability on insurers regardless of contractual language to the contrary, they essentially co-opt insurers to serve as a social security system or a "safety net" that redistributes economic burdens to those the court believes ought to bear them. This makes goods and services more expensive and punishes the prudent. As the California Supreme Court noted more than a decade before the *E.M.M.I.* case: "[C]ertainty in the insurance industry . . . allows insurers to gauge premiums with greater accuracy. Presumably this should reduce costs for consumers because insurers will be able to set aside proper reserves for well-defined coverages and avoid increasing such reserves to cover potential financial losses caused by uncertainty in the definition of coverage."[22]

"Public Policy"

Like "imbalance of bargaining power," the concept of "public policy" has often given judges license to alter contracts in ways they consider preferable. For centuries, courts were asked to void contracts alleged to be bad for society, but for the most part they have resisted doing so on the ground that, as an English judge colorfully put it in 1824, public policy is "a very unruly horse, and once you get astride it . . . [i]t may lead you from the sound law."[23] But while courts for the most part remain careful to avoid pronouncing contracts void on public policy grounds, there are cases in which they have used the theory in disruptive and harmful ways. Take, for example, the Massachusetts Supreme Judicial Court's decision in *R.R. v. M.H.*,[24] involving a surrogacy agreement. Child surrogacy is an increasingly common practice in the United States, where couples who are unable to have a child contract to implant a fertilized egg into the womb of a healthy woman, the surrogate mother. The woman then carries the child to term, turning it over to the contracting parents at birth. In *R.R.*, the parents agreed to pay a surrogate $10,000, along with the health care costs associated with the pregnancy. They also agreed that the birth mother would have contact with the child after it was born. But five months into the pregnancy, the birth mother changed her mind, returned some (but not all) of the couple's money, and refused to give up the child. The contracting parents sued, but the court ruled against them on the ground that the contract was inconsistent with public policy. "[C]ompensated surrogacy arrangements," the court declared, "raise the concern that, under financial pressure, a woman will permit her body to be used and her child to be given away."[25] Relying on New Jersey's famous *Baby M.* case,[26] Chief Justice Herbert Wilkins refused to enforce the contract so as to avoid the possibility that "financial pressure will cause a woman, who may well be a member of an economically vulnerable class, to act as a surrogate."[27]

The *R.R.* and *Baby M.* cases vividly illustrate the evils of paternalistic contract theories: such theories conflict with the principles of liberty and autonomy that underlie both the freedom of contract and sexual privacy. If a woman owns her body and has the right to choose how her body is used—whether it be through working in an office, having a child, attending a protest march, or any other action—she should also have the right to choose whether to participate in a surrogacy contract. Indeed, the Massachusetts court acknowledged that "the mother entered into the agreement on her own volition after consulting legal counsel," that there "was no evidence of undue influence, coercion, or duress," and that she

221

"fully understood [what] she was contracting" to do.[28] For the court to annul her agreement in order to "protect" other women thus restricts their freedom of choice based on the judges' own standards of appropriate conduct.[29] Moreover, contract law already contains rules to protect women against unfair bargaining tactics that might lead to their exploitation. Contracts that are the result of coercion or undue influence can be voided by any court; no special rule banning surrogacy contracts is necessary.

There appears to be no reason to fear the consequences of poor women consciously entering into surrogacy agreements to alleviate their poverty.[30] Women can already sell their blood to blood banks and their eggs to fertility clinics. Like Cosette in *Les Miserables*, they may sell their hair and teeth to support their families; why can they not enter into surrogacy contracts? Childbirth is certainly an emotionally charged subject, and the state has a legitimate role in protecting children from abuse or neglect. But the law does not prevent a woman from giving up her child for adoption, or even from engaging in *non-compensated* surrogacy arrangements. What difference can the presence of compensation make? In the *Baby M.* case, New Jersey's highest court declared that compensated surrogacy contracts are "based on principles directly contrary to our laws" because they "take[] the child from the mother regardless of her wishes and her maternal fitness," all "through the use of money."[31] But it is precisely through the use of money that these agreements do *not* take a child away against a mother's wishes. The mother *agreed* to the exchange. And while such agreements do contemplate the separation of the child from its birth mother, adoptions and noncompensated surrogacy arrangements do so also, and those agreements receive full legal protection. If a woman may make these choices for no compensation, there seems little sense in preventing her from choosing to engage in such acts for money. Moreover, prohibiting contractual surrogacy does not eliminate the practice; it simply drives it underground and makes it more expensive. Many observers have explained that decisions like *Baby M.* and *R.R.* have created a "gray market" in which would-be parents compensate birth mothers in secret, or informally, and at grave risk that the mother might withdraw at any time.[32]

There is much to say for the economic efficiency of surrogacy contracts,[33] but the more fundamental issue is that prohibiting them serves as a paternalistic device for dictating to women how they may or may not use their bodies, and what economic choices they may make, on the basis of what other people consider moral reasons. Although the *Baby M.* case described surrogacy agreements as "degrading" to women, it seems far more degrading to control their freedom of choice so as to protect other people's view of appropriate motherhood.

In *Johnson v. Calvert*,[34] the California Supreme Court rejected the theory that courts should "protect" women from entering into surrogacy agreements. "Although common sense suggests that women of lesser means serve as surrogate mothers more often than do wealthy women," the court noted, there is no reason to believe that such contracts will lead to their exploitation "to any greater degree than economic necessity in general exploits them by inducing them to accept lower-paid or otherwise undesirable employment."[35] Nor is there any reason to believe that such contracts would reduce women to the status of commodities. The opposite seems more likely: the idea that women "cannot knowingly and intelligently agree to gestate and deliver a baby for intending parents carries overtones of the reasoning that for centuries prevented women from attaining equal economic rights and professional status under the law." The court refused to follow Massachusetts and New Jersey in "foreclos[ing] a personal and economic choice on the part of the surrogate mother, and [in denying] intending parents what may be their only means of procreating a child of their own genetic stock."[36]

These cases illustrate how the ambiguity of the term "public policy" allows judges to impose their own social preferences in the place of the actual choices that parties make.[37] As early as 1844, the United States Supreme Court warned that "the great vagueness and uncertainty" of "[t]he question, what is the public policy of a state, and what is contrary to it," would lead to endless "discussion[s] which scarcely come within the range of judicial duty and functions, and upon which men may and will complexionally differ."[38] When courts use vague public policy arguments to manipulate contracts, they not only restrict freedom of choice but also endanger economic stability in general. Few things are more dangerous to an economy than unpredictable legal standards. The function of the "rule of law" is to produce a social and economic order that is regular and thus useful to the people who live within it. This does not mean that the order can never be changed, but when rules are subject to sudden or unpredictable alterations, leading to significant economic costs and benefits, the rule of law breaks down, and with it the ability of contracting people and their businesses to engage in transactions on which society relies.

Imposing unanticipated costs on parties deters investment because people want to be sure about their potential costs and benefits before they invest their time and money.[39] Legal stability promotes business innovation and development by letting firms know what they can and cannot do, and, by eliminating speculation as to what the law will be in the future, it promotes efficiency.[40] Simply put, giving courts a roving commission to do "justice" between contracting parties on the basis of uncertain appeals to the betterment of society does violence to individual choice and weakens economic stability.

Unconscionability

A contract is said to be "unconscionable" if it "shocks the conscience" of the court—that is, if the terms are so outlandishly burdensome that the law simply will not enforce it. Unfortunately, this theory, too, allows judges broad discretion to manipulate the economic agreements between parties and to "do justice" in a subjective, ultimately harmful way. Although lawyers and law professors have published hundreds of articles on the concept of "unconscionability," no clear definition of the term has arisen; one professor acknowledged in 1970 that "we are probably not much more ready now than we were twenty years ago to arrive at comprehensive reasoned elaboration of what is unconscionable."[41] Such vagueness provides a dangerous invitation for judges to act on their own subjective preferences. The unconscionability doctrine is overtly designed to allow courts to interfere with agreements between parties whenever judges consider the exchanges unfair. Thus, like the closely related theory of unequal bargaining position, the theory of unconscionability has often been used to rearrange the contractual agreements into which people have chosen to enter.[42]

Probably the most notorious example of this manipulation was the 1965 case of *Williams v. Walker-Thomas Furniture Co.*[43] The case involved an installment contract in which Ora Lee Williams agreed to pay each month for furniture and other items. A provision in the contract declared that if the buyer failed to make the payments, the company could repossess the property. Moreover, payments were applied pro rata to all furniture bought under the installment plan, meaning that the buyer could not pay off the specific balance due on the refrigerator or the sofa; instead, each payment was divided up and applied equally to the furniture as a whole. As a consequence, if the buyer defaulted, the company could repossess all the furniture. This type of installment contract was commonplace in Washington, D.C., at the time. Although the terms could be harsh for those who defaulted, such contracts did give poor residents credit—and thus furniture—that they could not have obtained otherwise. Without the ability to repossess the property, it is doubtful that the Walker-Thomas company would have been willing or able to provide the easy credit terms that allowed the poor to buy furniture in the first place.[44] There is no evidence that the company unfairly pressured customers or forced them into bargains. But its customers tended to be poor, and many defaulting buyers suffered harsh repossession terms.

Although Ora Lee Williams was probably a welfare recipient, the company's easy credit terms allowed her to purchase some $1,800 worth of furniture and other items—ranging from a wallet and draperies to a washing machine and a stereo—between 1957 and 1962.[45] She made her payments regularly for years but ultimately defaulted, after which Walker-Thomas sought to repossess the furniture.[46] The trial court held that the contract was harsh, but legal, and upheld the company's actions. But on appeal, Judge J. Skelly Wright concluded that the installment contract was so unfair that courts should not enforce it. Unconscionability, he wrote, means the "absence of meaningful choice on the part of one of the parties together with contract terms which are unreasonably favorable to the other party."[47] When a person having "little bargaining power, and hence little real choice, signs a commercially unreasonable contract with little or no knowledge of its terms, it is hardly likely that his consent . . . was ever given to all the terms."[48] Mrs. Williams could not have expected that the contract would impose such severe consequences in the event of default. And because she was in an economically vulnerable position, the court should refuse to enforce the contract's unfair and oppressive terms. The Walker-Thomas company would simply have to bear cost of her default.

225

Many lawyers heralded the decision as a victory for the rights of the poor, whom they pictured as basically victims of an exploitative commercial machine. People like Williams had little bargaining power vis-à-vis large companies like Walker-Thomas, they said, and courts should therefore intervene on their behalf. In his dissenting opinion, Judge John Danaher made an important point: if Williams could not be trusted to make decisions with her money and held to the consequences, good and bad, of making those decisions, she would be little better than a ward of the state, overseen "for her own good" by the government. "Is public oversight to be required of the expenditures of relief funds?"[49] Such a policy would rob her of the liberty to make her own decisions, including possibly unwise ones, and impose a degrading, unequal form of government control over her life. Although couched in humanitarian language, Judge Wright's opinion represented an insidious form of autocratic rule.

Moreover, the *Williams* decision raised the business costs of furniture companies, meaning that those companies became less willing to extend credit to customers. Ultimately, the poor would find it more difficult to obtain furniture and other goods. As one writer has noted recently, "[T]o the detriment of its customers, the furniture company 'certainly tightened up' the amount of credit that it made available to customers after the *Williams* decision, further reducing the credit available to Washington's poor."[50] The court's decision reduced the opportunities for the least well-off to obtain furniture and other amenities that they might otherwise have purchased on credit. There is no doubt that contracts like that used in the *Williams* case can be harsh, but giving credit is risky and costs businesses money. Making it more costly and complicated for them to extend credit to the needy is not wise policy.

What is the proper role of "unconscionability"? Professor Richard Epstein has pointed out that lawyers use the term to describe two types of unfairness—"substantive unconscionability," which occurs when the terms of the contract are unfair, and "procedural unconscionability," which occurs when a contract is the product of unfair negotiations—but only the latter should be a matter of judicial concern.[51] If contracting parties engage in fraud or coercion, their agreement is not a meeting of the minds and should not be enforced. But if it *is* the product of fair negotiations, courts should avoid interceding simply because they think the terms are improper. Contracting parties often reach agreements that outsiders would consider unde-sirable or even absurd; participants on television shows like *Fear Factor* enter into contracts that create national spectacles precisely because the terms are so bizarre. It is not that there is no such thing as a burdensome or unfair contract. But so long as the parties are fully informed about their bargains, and genuinely consent to them, the law should enforce them because no third party is in a better position to make those decisions than the contracting parties them-selves. In short, judges should not "police commerce in terms of commercial decency."[52]

More importantly, there is no a priori "just" arrangement between two parties to a contract. Often they do not know before entering into negotiations exactly what they want the final contract to look like. It is the negotiations process, and respect for each other's rights regarding that process, that establishes what the final agreement will be. Barring coercion or fraud, if the parties truly agree to a con-tract, the result is fair and just by definition.[53] Any free agreement between parties who have not committed an injustice is necessarily a just agreement as far as those parties are concerned.[54]

Allowing the government to dictate the terms of a contract invites abuses that can harm the economy and the rights of parties that courts consider less worthy of protection. This often means, of course, that wealthy and allegedly powerful businesses take the hit. Yet these businesses often operate on slender profit margins in highly com-petitive markets, and executives must carefully choose to avoid risks that could destroy a company and, with it, the hard-earned invest-ments of shareholders. Increasing a business's risks deters it from offering innovative services and pushes investment into safer fields. And again, relieving parties of the burdens they undertook imposes greater costs on more prudent consumers and encourages reckless behavior in the future by those who assume that they will be pro-tected from bad bargains. Doctrines like unconscionability absolve parties of their responsibilities out of a misguided sense of benevo-lence, in a degrading and self-destructive affront to their freedom of choice.[55]

California courts seem especially prone to abuse the "uncon-scionabililty" theory to alter the contracts that even sophisticated, well-educated people have signed.[56] The state's judges often see their role as ensuring that a bargain is substantively "fair" rather than enforcing the parties' freely chosen obligations. One area in which California courts are particularly prone to intercede is arbitration agreements. In 2007, the California Supreme Court used the unconscionability theory to strike down a provision in an employment contract between the Circuit City company and its workers.[57] The provision barred employees from bringing class-action lawsuits against the company and required instead that they submit to private arbitration to handle disputes that might arise during employment.

Companies often prefer arbitration because it is faster, cheaper, and generally overseen by judges specially trained in the field from which the dispute arises.[58] Some lawyers and judges, however, believe that arbitrators are insensitive to the needs of poor or unsophisticated plaintiffs and worry that arbitration agreements often limit the amount of damages available and include restrictive time limits for litigation. These concerns have made California courts jealous to ensure the availability of class-action lawsuits, seeing them as "the only effective way to halt and redress . . . exploitation" by wealthy businesses.[59] Circuit City, however, did not force its employees to give up their rights to bring such lawsuits; instead, the company offered arbitration as an option, providing them at the time of employment with a package of information that included a clear explanation of arbitration procedures. The information packet recommended that employees consult an attorney before signing, and employees were then asked to watch a video that explained what signing the arbitration agreement would mean. Employees had one month after their start dates to opt out of the agreement if they so chose.

Circuit City employee Robert Gentry chose to sign the agreement and waive his right to bring class-action lawsuits against the company. But in 2002, he filed a class-action lawsuit alleging that the company had violated the state's labor code in various ways. Circuit City argued that the case was barred by the arbitration agreement, but the court held the waiver unenforceable. The contract was procedurally unconscionable, the court claimed, because it was not explicit enough about the possible disadvantages to the employee and because employees could not be expected to read and understand a "nine-page single-spaced document" explaining the arbitration process or to consult with an attorney.[60] The Court acknowledged that Circuit City did not compel employees to agree but nevertheless held that employees "felt at least some pressure"[61] to sign it, meaning that the agreement was "not entirely free from procedural unconscionability."[62]

The court's wan statement that the arbitration agreement was "not entirely free" of unconscionability indicates how slim the evidence of unconscionability really was. There was no evidence that Circuit City threatened employees who refused to agree, or that it would have taken any punitive measures toward them. The court's accusation that Circuit City "concealed" the "disadvantageous" terms of the agreement was also flimsy. Nothing in the agreement was dishonest or concealed, and the fact that employees chose to sign without consulting an attorney, or that the company made clear that it preferred arbitration over lawsuits, does not render the agreement unfairly one-sided. *All* parties anticipating a contract will try to make their own preferences clear and will try to convince the other side that the agreement would benefit both sides.

In the end, the court's real concern was the substance of the agreement. Class-action lawsuits are an important tool, the justices wrote, because when people suffer minor injuries, they generally do not find it worthwhile to undergo the time and expense of a lawsuit; only by amassing their damages in a class action can they afford to pursue a remedy in court. Arbitration agreements that eliminate class-action lawsuits thus act like waivers of liability for minor injuries, allowing companies to "'deliberately cheat large numbers of consumers out of individually small sums of money.'"[63] California courts are therefore suspicious of arbitration agreements that waive the opportunity to bring class actions. But although these may be reasonable arguments for enacting laws to prohibit class-action waivers, or even to prohibit arbitration entirely, lawmakers have chosen to do the opposite: they have enacted laws allowing, and even encouraging, private arbitration. By restricting the enforceability of such agreements, the court was undermining these legislative decisions, despite its claim that class-action waivers might be legal under some other circumstances. In fact, given the breadth of the court's decision in the Circuit City case, it is difficult to see what steps a company might now take to execute a valid class-action waiver. As Justice Marvin Baxter concluded in his dissenting opinion, the court simply "elevat[ed] a mere judicial affinity for class actions as a beneficial device for implementing the wage laws above the policy expressed by both Congress and our own Legislature."[64]

The *Gentry* case is a good example of the dangers of the unconscionability theory in general. That theory was devised to protect people who are strong-armed into unfair contracts, not to annul agreements that are freely and knowingly signed by mature adults. Although the terms of some agreements will appear unreasonable to outsiders who disagree with the contracting parties or don't share their priorities, who might conclude that the contracting parties didn't *really* think things through carefully enough, this is not supposed to be sufficient reason to undo an agreement under the unconscionability theory. People who voluntarily sign contracts do so because they believe the benefits outweigh the burdens, and their judgment must be respected: not only are they in a position to know their wants and needs better than anyone else, but their right to choose for themselves—and to be responsible for their choices if they turn out to be bad ones—requires that others not interfere. Yet the California Supreme Court intervened in the *Gentry* case because it considered the bargain that the parties struck to be unfair, even though it was not the product of fraud or manipulation. The court simply imposed its policy preferences on the parties—against their will.

Workers have many options when choosing a place to work; if they do not like one employer's policies, they are free to choose to work elsewhere. Fewer than half the employment contracts in California require arbitration agreements; there was nothing to bar Gentry and his fellow workers from going elsewhere if they thought Circuit City's (voluntary) arbitration scheme was oppressive or unreasonable.[65] They chose to work at Circuit City and to sign the arbitration agreement because they thought, for whatever reason, that it was the best choice for them. They should be held to their word, just as their employer would have been. By annulling the agreement, the California Supreme Court substituted its judgment for the terms of a fairly and openly negotiated contract.

At-Will Employment

"At-will employment" is a term used by courts to describe an agreement between an employer and an employee that allows either side to terminate the relationship at any time and for any reason. The boss may fire the employee whenever he or she wants and the employee is free to quit at any time. Although this form of employment contract has long been the norm in the United States, it has been heavily criticized, and both legislatures and courts often intercede to prevent an employer from firing an employee on the ground that certain management decisions are contrary to public policy. The most obvious example is civil rights legislation prohibiting an employer from firing an at-will employee for racially or sexually discriminatory reasons. By explicitly declaring that these specific, heinous motivations are off-limits, legislatures give employers clear guidelines. Unfortunately, some courts have gone further and manufactured their own, often vague reasons for intervening in at-will employment contracts. Some have even abandoned the at-will contract entirely.

At-will employment benefits workers, employers, and the economy in general. Because it requires little negotiation, transaction costs are kept to a minimum when employees are hired on an at-will basis.[66] The more streamlined hiring process also allows employees and employers a wider range of choices. In a dynamic economy, workers should be free to switch their employment whenever they find other jobs preferable. Today, it seems deeply ironic that in 1986 the Pennsylvania Superior Court approvingly quoted from a report by the New York Bar that "[t]he modern reality of *relative immobility* in the labor market, encouraged by *a web of ties that bind the employee to the job*, places [the at-will employment doctrine] in question."[67] Whatever the circumstances may have been 25 years ago, the American economy has only become more dynamic and employees more willing to change jobs to suit their needs. Nationwide, over the past decade workers have stayed on the job for about three and a half to four years on average, with younger workers changing jobs much more frequently.[68] Had the presumption of at-will employment been abandoned in 1986, many of these workers would have found it harder to locate new jobs, and harder to take those jobs once found. Ten years after the Pennsylvania court's statement, Professor Andrew Morriss, a leading expert on at-will employment contracts, more accurately concluded, "The massive scale of the societal changes at the root of our current economic instability argue against the one-size-fits-all responses offered by the legal system."[69]

At-will contracts allow employers to try out inexperienced, entry-level employees without incurring substantial risks. Business owners can give workers a trial period and decide whether the employee is productive. If they were required to offer jobs only on a permanent or semi-permanent basis, with job security, employers would pay a higher cost for bad hiring decisions. They might be stuck with poorly performing workers or with workers who act dangerously or harass their fellow employees. Businesses would therefore become more stingy about offering people jobs, particularly those people who lack special skills, experience, or personal influence—that is, the workers who are poorest and most in need of work.[70]

The at-will employment contract also provides employees with a check against employer abuses after the contract is formed, and vice versa. As Richard Epstein puts it, "[T]he contract at will provides both employer and employee with a simple, informal 'bond' against future misfeasance of the other side: fire or quit."[71] A wealthy employer may be in a stronger position than the employee to dictate the terms of employment, but he must still compete with other prospective employers who can offer better opportunities to disgruntled workers. Thus, the at-will relationship maximizes an employee's bargaining position. The fact that, for example, the McDonald's Corporation is not on an equal bargaining plane with a minimum-wage worker does not change the fact that if a McDonald's manager abuses the worker, the worker can go to work for Burger King instead. The Utah Supreme Court put it well in a 1998 decision rejecting an employee's argument that the document he signed that acknowledged that he was an at-will employee was unconscionable. "Ryan could have signed the acknowledgment form, received his paycheck, quit [his job], and sought employment elsewhere, as the at-will term permitted him to do," the court noted. "Although Ryan may have wanted to work at [one pharmacy], he was free to seek employment with another pharmacy that did not maintain at-will employment."[72]

Providing workers with job protections they do not bargain for encourages wrongful behavior on both sides. In fact, in the early 20th century, English labor unions successfully lobbied Parliament *in favor* of something very similar to at-will employment because at that time English law required laborers to stay at their jobs on pain of incarceration.[73] Between 1860 and 1875, over 100,000 Englishmen were convicted of the crime of leaving their jobs.[74] Unions pushed for the creation of the "minute contract," which enabled workers to leave a job if an employer mistreated them.

A worse situation was presented in Eastern European communist countries, where workers were guaranteed their jobs regardless of performance. This came at the cost of mobility: employees had no incentive to perform or ability to leave, and employers had no incentive to treat workers well or to eliminate inefficient workers. The result was an attitude well expressed by the Soviet saying, "We pretend to work, and they pretend to pay us."[75] Today, Sweden, Norway, Canada, and Japan provide job security rules that prevent employers from firing workers at will, and these countries have sometimes been offered as examples for the United States to follow.[76] But in none of those places are jobs as easy to find as in the United States. Although Sweden's government claims that its unemployment rate is around 5 percent, this statistic is misleading because it does not include the many government relief programs that subsidize nonworkers without counting them as unemployed—such as early retirement, sick leave, labor market programs, and welfare. The actual joblessness rate in Sweden probably hovers around 15 to 20 percent.[77] Norway performs somewhat better, but its job security laws impose serious and unnecessary costs on Norwegian businesses,[78] and are especially harmful to young job seekers.[79] Canada's unemployment rate has been significantly higher than that in the United States for more than 30 years.[80] And although Japan's unemployment rate has historically been low, recent figures reveal that "the period that people are unemployed [in Japan] continue[s] to lengthen," and that the reason for the growth of unemployment periods is because new jobs are "not available."[81] Meanwhile, many other nations, including France and several Central American countries, have suffered severe economic consequences from the absence of at-will employment.[82]

As these examples reveal, job security has serious downsides. In the United States, unionized industries routinely experience serious inefficiencies as a result of rules that ban the termination of employees who fail to perform or who act inappropriately on the job. Stories of union abuses—forcing businesses to retain employees who have committed serious wrongs—abound. A public employees union in New Jersey, for example, successfully defended a tollbooth worker who was fired for shooting at a car with a paint-ball gun.[83] The Pepsi company was sued when it tried to fire an employee who urinated on the floor of his delivery truck because the employment contract had not specified that such behavior would be cause for termination. The company lost.[84] The list goes on. As one scholar concludes, "If employers can no longer credibly threaten employees with tough disciplinary measures, employees will have little incentive to produce efficiently."[85] Job security encourages employees to shirk their responsibilities or to misbehave, thereby punishing the more efficient and productive employees who might otherwise receive bonuses or raises. New workers also find it more difficult to enter the workforce due to union rules that limit termination: this is because to an employer, each new worker represents a major cost and a long-term risk, and eliminating a current worker means a time-consuming and expensive review procedure, as well as the possibility of a "wrongful termination" lawsuit. The same consequences would probably follow the elimination or restriction of at-will employment contracts. Restricting the at-will contract does not just deter job creation, it also leads to higher prices for consumers. In fact, economists conclude that erosion of the at-will employment contract—either through statutory regulation or through lawsuits for "wrongful termination"—costs Americans millions of jobs and billions of dollars every year.[86]

At-will employment improves the position not only of workers and managers but of consumers in general. The cost of providing securer jobs—and thereby incurring the risk of poor employee performance—is borne by employers who must make up that cost by charging more for products or services. Because at-will jobs tend to be more prevalent in the retail and service industries that serve poor constituencies—rather than the professional services that are patronized by upper- and middle-class consumers—this is an especially serious concern. Increasing the costs on employers ultimately increases the burden on consumers, particularly those with low incomes.[87] Meanwhile, there is little evidence that employers actually mistreat at-will employees or fire them arbitrarily,[88] or that employees themselves wish for the abolition of the at-will employment contract. One study asking workers every year since 1973 what they looked for in a job found that they ranked job security a distant fourth.[89] They were much more concerned about generating a sense of accomplishment or short working hours.

Despite these facts, at-will employment is under fire by scholars who depict it as a Dickensian scheme for empowering abusive bosses, and courts and legislatures have fashioned a variety of exceptions to the at-will doctrine. In the 1908 case of *Adair v. United States*,[90] the Supreme Court explained that the right of an employee to choose where he wants to work "is, in its essence, the same as the right of the purchaser of labor to prescribe the conditions upon which he will accept such labor from the person offering to sell it. So the right of the employee to quit the service of the employer, for whatever reason, is the same as the right of the employer, for whatever reason, to dispense with the services of such employee." Employers and employees have an "equality of right, and any legislation that disturbs that equality is an arbitrary interference with the liberty of contract which no government can legally justify in a free land."[91] If the government could force an employer to retain an employee he no longer wanted or needed, it could also force an employee "against his will, to remain in the personal service of another."[92]

More recent court decisions, beginning especially in the 1980s,[93] have undermined the freedom of choice for both employers and workers by limiting the at-will mechanism. The result is a rash of wrongful termination lawsuits that dry up employment opportunities and raise the cost of living. Some of these cases involve genuine employer wrongdoing, such as firing an employee for refusing to break the law,[94] but in other cases courts have restricted the legitimate right to terminate employees. For example, courts often invoke a "covenant of good faith" when interpreting at-will employment contracts as a means of imposing new duties on employers that were not part of their contracts. And almost every state's courts have found "implied contracts" based on the employer's conduct, which limit the ability to fire an employee despite the fact that no explicit contract ever existed.[95] As a result of these decisions, employers are more reluctant to hire new employees, and longer-tenure employees are likely to keep their jobs even if they fail to perform.

It is impossible to measure the precise economic effect of restrictions on at-will employment, but a thorough 1992 research project by the Rand Corporation found that "aggregate employment averages 2.9 percent lower in years following a state's recognition of tort damages for wrongful termination," and that states recognizing both tort and contract causes of action for wrongful termination would have about 4.7 percent lower employment than states that did not.[96] When state courts adopt limits on the at-will employment contract, aggregate employment drops by 2 to 5 percent—even more in service industries and large businesses. The nonlegal costs of wrongful termination lawsuits can be 100 times greater than the actual legal costs of defending against such lawsuits. "To put this cost in perspective," the Rand authors concluded, "[W]e can use a measure from the general literature on labor demand: a 3-percent decline in aggregate employment is consistent with a 10 percent wage increase."[97] Another survey found much smaller effects but still concluded that adopting exceptions to employment at will caused "a decline of from 0.8 to 1.7 percent in the ratio of employment to population."[98] Still another report found that although joblessness in Montana grew immediately following the state supreme court's abolition of at-will employment, it fell again when the legislature adopted a statute that established complicated procedures for wrongful termination lawsuits. The authors acknowledged that this leveling effect was probably due to "procedural and other limitations on legal claims" under the new statute, which as a practical matter made it impossible for most fired workers to sue.[99] Not only do restrictions on at-will employment dampen job creation, they also change the way that workers are employed. Businesses often turn to temporary workers to fill jobs once staffed by permanent employees. A 2001 report found a 22 percent increase in the use of temps as a result of restrictions on the at-will contract.[100] Because these temporary workers are paid less, employment restrictions operate as a wealth transfer from "low-waged, young, uneducated employees" filling these jobs to their older, better-educated counterparts who remain in salaried positions.[101]

At-will employment is not, as the Pennsylvania court claimed, "an antiquated remnant of a by-gone era."[102] Rather, by making it less expensive and less complicated for workers to obtain employment, the at-will doctrine helps ensure that the right to an honest living is a reality and not an illusion. It is an important protection for both workers and employers who need maximum flexibility to respond to changes in both the economy and in their own personal needs. To put the point simply, *workers are not helped by rules that make it harder and more expensive for employers to hire them,* and this is more and more true in an increasingly dynamic economy.

As is often the case, some courts have tried to remedy the disparities arising from one bad legal rule by adopting an even worse one.

Those employers choosing to hire temporary workers have found themselves losing lawsuits filed by temps who complain that they do not receive the same benefits as permanent employees. In *Vizcaino v. Microsoft Corp.*,[103] temporary employees at Microsoft argued that they were wrongfully denied certain benefits given to permanent employees: in particular, temporary employees (called "freelancers") were not eligible for a retirement program by which Microsoft matched an employee's retirement savings, or for a stock program that allowed permanent employees to buy the company's stock at a discount. The freelancers were never misled; they knew when they entered their jobs that they were ineligible for these benefits.[104]

Nevertheless, a group of them sued, arguing that they were entitled to the benefits, and the Ninth Circuit Court of Appeals agreed with them. Judge Stephen Reinhardt wrote the opinion declaring that Microsoft's employment benefit documents were ambiguous because the documents declared eligible all "common law employees." A reasonable person, Reinhardt continued, might have thought that this meant that freelancers, too, were eligible for benefits, and "[t]he fact that Microsoft did not intend to provide benefits to persons who [*sic*] it thought were freelancers or independent contractors sheds little or no light on that question."[105] Although Microsoft separated freelancers from other employees; paid them out of different funds, gave them different badges, different e-mail addresses, and different training, and even though the freelancers repeatedly testified that they knew they were ineligible for the benefits, the court declared them eligible anyway. As Judge Stephen Trott wrote in dissent, the court was engaged in "head-in-the-sand thinking," designed to reverse the clear import of Microsoft's employment contracts. "If I *know* I have a 'no benefits' contract," asked Trott, "what good does it do to ask what the ordinary average Babbitt . . . might believe after reading a Random House dictionary? These plaintiffs were university educated. One had a law degree. They *knew* what they were getting into."[106]

As one law professor later wrote, Judge Reinhardt abused the traditional tools of contractual interpretation in his *Vizcaino* opinion, using "the maxims of statutory construction not to determine what the parties had actually agreed to—that was undisputed—but to conclude that the plaintiffs were entitled to benefits even though they [were] not." Thus, the decision "stretched contract law to the breaking point to get to its conclusion."[107] But while *Vizcaino* was one of the more extreme examples of courts' abusing their powers to reach a desired conclusion, the cause of its tortured reasoning was clear from the outset. As Judge Trott pointed out, the decision's language indicated the sort of anti-business bias that often motivates courts to manipulate the meaning of contracts. Reinhardt's "choice of words" seemed designed to "clothe Microsoft with a Dickensian anti-labor attitude," he wrote. "Such characterizations spring full-bloom from the first sentence of the majority's opinion where 'avoiding payment of employee benefits' and 'increasing profits' foreshadow the negative coloration of the infidel Microsoft's role in this drama."[108] Yet Microsoft was always clear about its policies, and the employees admitted that they accepted those policies when choosing to work for the company. "Thus, the majority seems to overlook the constitutional right of private parties freely to enter into contracts of their own choice and benefit."[109]

The right to make contracts, and especially employment contracts, is central to individual liberty and the values of self-determination and free choice. But for contract law to work as it ought to, the rights of both parties must be respected. When courts put their thumbs on the scales, society ultimately loses because parties will be more reluctant to enter into agreements and courts themselves lose credibility as impartial administrators of justice. This drives up the costs of making contracts and decreases economic efficiency as companies devote time and energy to defending themselves from lawsuits rather than providing the public with goods and services. Worst of all, it makes it more difficult for workers to find good jobs, as employers—understandably wary of the costs associated with hiring a full-time employee—turn instead to temporary labor or choose to do business in states where employment is not fraught with the same costs and risks. When people and businesses choose to enter into contracts, their choices should be respected, regardless of whether others consider the results to be unequal or unfair. The point of freedom of contract—the point of freedom itself—is not to accomplish some ill-defined equality of result but to allow each person to pursue happiness as best he or she can without the interference of those who think they can choose better.

11. The Abuse of Tort Law

The abuse of tort law by mercenary lawyers poses a major threat to American businesses and therefore to the economic liberties of everyone. Every year, frivolous or misguided "deep-pockets" lawsuits against companies cost more than $865 billion.[1] Much has been written on the "jackpot justice" attitude that spawns professional plaintiffs and saps the nation's economic vitality.[2] Here we can consider only some of the more egregious examples.

Public Nuisance

Recent years have seen a trend not only of private but of massive *government*-initiated tort lawsuits against tobacco companies, gun manufacturers, carmakers, and other "politically incorrect" businesses. Cases in Rhode Island, Illinois, and New Jersey have targeted former manufacturers of lead paint for millions of dollars in damages on the ground that lead paint causes illnesses, despite the fact that lead paint was both legal and common when the companies sold it. When it is not properly maintained, lead paint flakes can rub off and be ingested, particularly by children, leading to severe health problems, which is why the federal government banned it in 1978. But many buildings in America are still covered in lead paint, and some state officials have seen this as an opportunity to bring lucrative lawsuits arguing that the paint companies are responsible for a "public nuisance." These lawsuits demand enormous damage awards to reimburse the states for the money they claim to have spent providing health care to people who have become ill from lead exposure and cleaning up sites contaminated with lead paint.

Whether these lawsuits are really motivated by a concern for the public welfare or by simple greed,[3] they pose a serious danger to economic freedom because of the legal theory behind them: the concept of public nuisance is simply so vague that nobody knows what that phrase means. And without clear standards to define the term, government and private attorneys can exploit that ambiguity to extort enormous sums from any business that produces an arguably unsafe or undesirable product.

For decades, law professors and other experts have described the concept of "public nuisance" by using terms like "mystery,"[4] "quagmire,"[5] a "'wilderness' of law,"[6] a "sprawling doctrine,"[7] a "legal garbage can" full of "vagueness, uncertainty and confusion,"[8] a "mongrel" doctrine "intractable to definition,"[9] and "confused beyond repair."[10] Others acknowledge that "no judicial consensus has emerged on some of the core issues that should establish the parameters of the tort of public nuisance."[11] Many courts have agreed. Nuisance "'has meant all things to all people,'" wrote the California Court of Appeal in 1994, quoting the torts expert W. Page Keeton, "'and has been applied indiscriminately to everything from an alarming advertisement to a cockroach baked in a pie.'"[12]

One common definition given to "public nuisance" is "an unreasonable interference with a right common to the general public."[13] But the statutes and judicial decisions of various states contain so many differences that Supreme Court Justice Harry Blackmun confessed in 1992 that courts have "search[ed] in vain" for "anything resembling a principle in the common law of nuisance."[14] This vagueness has led some courts to block the government from using public nuisance theories to shut down adult businesses, censor objectionable books, or prohibit assemblies in public parks.[15] In one especially odd New Jersey case, a court held that one variety of public nuisance theory, known as "common scold"—an antiquated concept that made it a crime for a woman to be obnoxiously critical—was unconstitutional because, among other things, it was too vague for anybody to know what it actually means.[16] Yet this same vagueness attracts ambitious attorneys who want to use other kinds of public nuisance arguments to sue industries that are seen as harming the public in some way.[17]

Recognizing the danger of using incomprehensible legal theories, previous generations of lawyers tried to draw some boundaries around "public nuisance" to prevent it from swallowing up areas of the law where it did not really belong. For example, the authors of the *Restatement of Torts* provided explanations and notes defining "unreasonableness" as action that is either intentionally wrong or, if unintentional, is "otherwise actionable" in that it is "negligent or reckless" or "abnormally dangerous."[18] These lawyers were especially sensitive to the fact that the "unreasonableness" requirement must be carefully applied because without it, courts would be "acting without an established and recognized standard," leading to "potentially widespread damage liability."[19] In addition, the *Restatement*'s authors took note of the standards older common-law courts used for determining when behavior was unreasonable, including "[w]hether the conduct involves a significant interference with the public health, the public safety," or is "proscribed by a statute, ordinance or administrative regulation."[20] Without these boundaries, the public nuisance theory could be expanded to allow government to prosecute "bad action" or "improper conduct"—something courts have often said would be unconstitutionally vague.[21]

The authors also defined a "common right" or a "public right" as a right "common to all members of the general public. It is collective in nature and not like the individual right that everyone has not to be . . . injured,"[22] thus making clear that a "public right" is more than just an aggregate of private rights by a large number of people.[23] A "public right" instead refers to the citizen's right to access a public good—that is, a common resource like the air or the ocean, which can be used simultaneously by many people without intruding on one another's rights.[24] Because the concept of public nuisance—which was originally a crime—has for centuries provided a basis for government to obtain injunctions to stop wrongful behavior, the *Restatement*'s authors acknowledged that there is no historical tradition that allows government to seek money damages for public nuisances.[25] Thus, in a section entitled "Who Can Recover for Public Nuisance," they explained that private individuals may "recover damages in an individual action for a public nuisance" under certain circumstances, and public authorities may abate public nuisances through injunctions;[26] nowhere do they suggest that public officials could bring public nuisance suits for money.

In the past, courts rejected attempts to broaden the applicability of public nuisance theory through litigation. In 1971, for example, the California Court of Appeal threw out a lawsuit by environmental activists who sued automobile manufacturers for causing air pollution.[27] The plaintiffs asked for damages on the grounds that the companies had harmed the environment by manufacturing pollution-causing devices. But noting that a ruling for the plaintiffs would mean "judicial regulation of the processes, products and volume of business of the major industries of the country," the court dismissed the case. Judges, it warned, have no authority to "do what the elected representatives of the people have not done: adopt stricter standards over the discharge of air contaminants in this country, and enforce them with the contempt power of the court."[28] Recently, the same court rejected a similar lawsuit against gun manufacturers on the ground that "[m]erely engaging in what plaintiffs deem to be a risky practice, without a connecting causative link to a threatened harm, is not a public nuisance."[29] It warned that if the nuisance tort were stretched to allow lawsuits against gun makers, "[a]ny manufacturer of an arguably dangerous product that finds its way into California can be hauled [sic] into court." Manufacturers of many products might be held liable not for making faulty products but for marketing and selling their products in ways that might attract criminals or vulnerable consumers to use or abuse them. This was simply not a proper role for the broad catchall language of public nuisance, which the court described as "'a peculiarly blunt and capricious method of regulation, depending . . . on the vicissitudes of the legal system, which make results highly unpredictable in probability and magnitude.'"[30]

The constitutional ramifications of this vagueness are troubling. Courts have often held that the due process cause requires laws to be clear enough to afford a reasonable person some ability to predict whether his actions will violate the law.[31] This requirement of clarity also applies where the defendant is a business.[32] Although the Court has sometimes said that businesses are entitled to less legal clarity than are individuals,[33] that theory is based on the presumption that businesses can more easily afford expert legal advice; yet even experts cannot say what "public nuisance" means.

Moreover, the Court has repeatedly held that the due process clause does not allow courts to impose crushing and unpredictable tort judgments on businesses. In *BMW v. Gore*,[34] a jury awarded the buyer of a new car $4,000 in compensatory damages because the retailer scratched and secretly repainted the car before delivery. The jury then imposed $4 million in punitive damages. The Supreme Court overturned this, concluding that the amount was so excessive that it violated "[e]lementary notions of fairness enshrined in our constitutional jurisprudence." Those principles require that a person or business "receive fair notice not only of the conduct that will subject [them] to punishment" but "also of the severity of the penalty."[35] A few years later, in *State Farm v. Campbell*,[36] the Court invalidated a $145 million punitive damages award against an insurance company because the damages were so excessive compared with the plaintiff's injury as to violate basic fairness requirements and therefore fell short of the requirement of due process of law.[37] These cases confirm that the principles of due process—including the fundamental rule that legal lines must be clear enough to permit people to know ahead of time what actions will incur punishment—apply both to individuals and to businesses, and not only to the *statutes* that legislatures enact but also to common-law legal theories like public nuisance. If the law is too vague for reasonable people to understand what acts are allowed and what acts the state will punish, then the law is unconstitutionally vague.

State officials who bring nuisance cases against car companies and lead paint makers are exploiting an already vague and potentially dangerous tort in ways that make it even more ambiguous and are likely to expose businesses to liability for excessive damages.[38] Ignoring the traditional rule that government may not obtain money damages under this tort, public officials now seek tremendous amounts of money from private businesses, money that will only tantalize them with thoughts of more money in the future. And perhaps worst of all, many such lawsuits are based on conduct that was *lawful and reasonable* when the defendants engaged in it. In 2006, California's attorney general filed a public nuisance case in federal court against General Motors and other carmakers, arguing that the companies were contributing to global warming by making and selling automobiles. The public nuisance tort is supposed to cover only conduct that is unreasonable, but there is nothing unreasonable about selling cars—indeed, as the carmakers pointed out in their brief to the trial court, the state of California itself operates a fleet of over 100,000 automobiles. Likewise, there was nothing illegal or unreasonable about making and selling lead paint at the time that the targeted companies did so. The states suing these paint makers never alleged that they defrauded the public or covered up the hazards associated with the use of their products. Rather, they sued despite the fact that the companies' conduct was legal.

If the lawful sale of a legal product can later serve as grounds for future liability of potentially unlimited severity, companies will be unable to escape devastating—and economically wasteful—liability. This is true not only of paint, firearms, and cars but also of such potentially dangerous but still lawful products as alcohol, caffeine, or fast food, which might well be targets in the future.[39] It is easy to foresee a flood of cases against everything from adult magazines to music with violent lyrics, to sellers of alcohol or caffeinated beverages, to beneficial industries that have harmful or polluting side effects, like power companies, pharmaceutical makers, or even movie studios whose films might glorify and "encourage" reckless driving, violence, or unsafe sex. Unable to predict what conduct will expose them to liability, businesses will take extensive steps to avoid that liability; they will curtail research, development, and economic expansion and will divert resources to insuring against lawsuits.

Sensing the threat posed by an unbridled public nuisance tort, an Illinois appeals court, the New Jersey Supreme Court, and the Rhode Island Supreme Court recently rejected lawsuits against former lead paint makers. To allow government to sue companies that "produced a legal product decades ago that was used by third parties who applied the product," wrote the Illinois judges, would seriously undermine important public policy concerns.[40] The New Jersey Supreme Court was more explicit.[41] Recognizing that the tort of public nuisance was "'vaguely defined' and 'poorly understood,'"[42] the court was skeptical of the government's attempt to go beyond even the loose common-law standards that "define it as a cognizable theory of tort law." Doing so might have "disastrous consequences" because if "merely offering an everyday household product for sale can suffice for the purpose of interfering with a common right," the concept of public nuisance would even apply to "ordinary consumer products which, although legal when sold, and although sold no more recently than a quarter of a century ago, have become dangerous through deterioration and poor maintenance by the purchasers."[43] If that were to happen, "nuisance law would become a monster that would devour in one gulp the entire law of tort."[44] The Rhode Island Supreme Court recently agreed. After the state's longest civil trial, a jury found Sherwin-Williams and other paint companies liable for causing the state's children to be exposed to lead paint.[45] The judge ordered the companies to pay the cost of eliminating the paint throughout the state, which will cost anywhere from $1.37 billion to $3.47 billion.[46] But in July 2008, the state's highest court threw out the lawsuit on the grounds that lead paint was legal when it was sold but the paint companies were not responsible for its deterioration. "In declining to adopt such a widespread expansion of [public nuisance] law," the court observed, "we are mindful of the words of Edmund Burke that 'bad laws are the worst sort of tyranny.'"[47] Unfortunately, these decisions have not put a stop to public nuisance lawsuits against lead paint manufacturers: shortly before the New Jersey decision was issued, an appeals court in California reinstated a lawsuit against paint makers that had been dismissed by a trial judge,[48] and similar cases continue in Mississippi, Texas, Ohio, and Missouri, wasting taxpayer dollars and dangerously expanding an already vague concept of tort law.[49]

California's Vague Business Torts

Legislatures and courts often struggle to make the law flexible enough to protect people but precise enough to prevent abusive and opportunistic lawsuits. But in some cases, states have enacted laws so broadly written that almost anyone can sue almost anyone else for almost anything at all.

One of the worst offenders is California's Unfair Competition Law, also known as "section 17200,"[50] which is so ambiguous that it covers almost anything that plaintiffs think "unfair." Courts acknowledge that the term "unfair" is "not precisely defined in the statute, and the courts have struggled to come up with a workable definition."[51] The statute's language is so unclear that, as one expert on the abuse of tort law points out, even "compliance with the law is not necessarily a defense since business practices that are not 'unlawful' may still be 'unfair.'"[52] Under this law, courts have almost unlimited discretion to decide what commercial conduct is allowable or not.[53]

Worse, almost anybody can be a plaintiff. In 1995, law professor Robert Fellmeth warned that the extremely broad standing rules attached to section 17200 meant that any member of the public was entitled to sue, even if he or she had not been injured by the business practice at issue.[54] In fact, the rules were so lax that a plaintiff could bring a section 17200 claim on the ground that the defendant had violated *another* law, even if the plaintiff could *not* have sued under that other law.[55] For example, even though certain federal environmental statutes specify that only federal government officials may use them as grounds for a lawsuit, California courts nevertheless allowed any person to sue under these laws because the violation of a federal law also qualifies as an "unfair" business practice.[56] "No statute of which we are aware," wrote Fellmeth, "confers the kind of unbridled standing to so many without definition, standards, notice requirements, or independent review." The law was "headed toward the worst of all possible legal worlds: abuse of process as unqualified person[s] disingenuously invoke the interests of the general public, extortionate nuisance lawsuits with high exposure, confusion and duplication of litigation resources, and uncertain finality."[57]

The years that followed proved Fellmeth right. The number of frivolous, expensive, time-consuming section 17200 cases is legion. One plaintiff alleged that an airline engaged in unfair competition by failing to provide enough legroom for extraordinarily tall passengers.[58] Another plaintiff alleged that it was "unfair" for a hotel to charge a fee for room service.[59] A class-action suit alleged that the makers of the Brita water filters engaged in an unfair business practice because the instruction booklet said that consumers would have to replace their filters more often than is actually necessary, meaning that a gallon of filtered water cost 17 cents more than it otherwise would.[60] Another plaintiff sued a movie company for advertising its films with praise from fake movie critics[61]—a lawsuit described by a dissenting justice as "the most frivolous case with which I have ever had to deal."[62] Still another argued that it was "unfair" for a grocery store to place anti-theft tags on its Sudafed and other over-the-counter medications because that made it hard to read the warning label, which made him "feel that he could not safely use the Sudafed."[63] And one group of plaintiffs argued (successfully) that the Kwikset corporation had committed an unfair business practice by labeling its locks "made in the U.S.A.," when the tiny screws holding the locks together were actually made in Taiwan.[64] Plaintiffs often try to use the Unfair Competition Law to advance their political agendas; they've argued that it was an unfair business practice for an adult cable television channel to make money by selling pornographic cable television programming,[65] or for a clinic to make money by providing abortions,[66] or for a corporation to defend itself against

246

allegations that it abuses workers.[67] In one case, the court was even forced to explain that the law did not prohibit retailers from selling at a profit.[68] As Michael Greve has concluded: "California courts have created multiple vehicles to facilitate generous monetary relief. In short, '[t]he only apparent limitation upon the practical reach of the UCL is the imagination of man (and woman).'"[69]

Although courts have ultimately ruled against most of these frivolous complaints, they have done so only after time-consuming and expensive litigation, regularly costing businesses hundreds of thousands of dollars even when they win. Most abuses of section 17200 go unreported because California's trial courts do not publish their decisions. Only those cases that make it to the appellate court level are preserved for researchers, so the true effects of this law are impossible to measure, particularly its effect on the small businesses intimidated into settlements because they cannot afford to go to court. These companies often simply pay whatever the aggressive plaintiff's attorney demands to make the case go away.

In one highly publicized incident, the California attorney general brought an action to stop a law firm known as the Trevor Law Group from abusing the Unfair Competition Law. The court ruled in his favor, concluding that the firm had engaged in "a kind of legal shakedown scheme" whereby "[a]ttorneys form[ed] a front 'watchdog' or 'consumer' organization . . . scour[ed] public records on the internet for what are often ridiculously minor violations of some regulation or law by a small business, and sue[d] that business in the name of the front organization."[70] Trevor had filed cases against dozens of small manicure shops for reusing the same bottles of nail polish on different customers (which is not illegal[71]). Most of these businesses—often family owned and staffed by unskilled immigrants—paid Trevor off at a few thousand dollars each rather than go to court.[72] But while the attorney general managed to shut down one outstanding abuser, others continue to harass California businesses because the law is so vague that courts find it difficult to dismiss even ridiculous cases. Unfair business practice litigation in California has degenerated into a feeding frenzy for attorneys who use the law to shake down businesses, particularly small businesses that cannot afford to defend themselves.[73]

In 2004, voters enacted Proposition 64, which restricted some of the law's abuses by requiring plaintiffs to show that they had actually been injured before bringing a lawsuit.[74] But because the definition of injury is itself so broad—even a tiny amount of money can qualify—this initiative sets up only a minimal protection against abuses.[75] And the amendment did nothing to clarify what qualifies as an "unfair" practice or limit the amounts that lawyers and plaintiffs can demand for trifling or nonexistent violations.

Moreover, other similar laws remain unchanged, allowing plaintiffs to bring other kinds of frivolous cases against businesses. The state's Proposition 65, for example, requires businesses to post signs warning the public that certain harmful chemicals (including lead in crystal or carbon monoxide in automobile exhaust) can be found on the property. This law creates a special incentive for abuse because it provides that individuals who bring successful lawsuits are entitled to receive 25 percent of all civil penalties recovered in a lawsuit, and defendants can be liable for up to $2,500 per day per violation.[76] As a result, Proposition 65 has become one of the most common tools for extorting money from businesses in the guise of protecting public health and safety, something the state's lawyers have come to call "greenmail."[77]

In one 2006 case, Justice David Sills of the California Court of Appeal explained at length how unscrupulous lawyers masquerading as public-interest law firms use Proposition 65 and the Unfair Competition Law "to precipitate payoffs by private businesses for alleged violations of law having no real relationship to a true public interest."[78] The "Consumer Defense Group," which filed the lawsuit, was really a "straw plaintiff[]" created by enterprising attorneys who saw Proposition 65 as an opportunity for lucrative litigation.[79] This group targeted apartment owners for Proposition 65 lawsuits for two reasons: "One, each apartment had . . . parking facilities! Thus the apartment allegedly 'exposed' tenants and visitors to carcinogens in auto exhaust. . . . Two, each apartment did not prohibit tobacco smoking," meaning that "somewhere on the property the apartment allegedly 'exposed' its tenants and visitors to second-hand tobacco smoke."[80]

Justice Sills provided a step-by-step illustration of how such cases work. First, create "a 'consumer' organization that you of course control." Second, locate a "'target' business" and fill out the necessary forms, which are "intended to frighten all but the most hardy of targets (certainly any small mom and pop business) into a quick settlement when they get it." The business then offers settlement to get out of a lawsuit, and the plaintiff can keep the monetary reward by depositing it with his sham consumer-interest group.[81] In this way, the attorneys behind the Consumer Defense Group had "attempted to . . . shake [apartment owners] down for attorney fees based on the absence of Proposition 65 warnings based on so-called 'exposures' such as the absence of an absolute prohibition of smoking on the premises."[82] The court described this as "extortion."[83] Unfortunately, while Justice Sills dismissed this especially egregious case, most such lawsuits are settled out of court by businesses that would rather pay a plaintiff to go away than undergo the time and expense of defending themselves in court.[84] These lawsuits transfer millions of dollars every year from productive businesses to the pockets of attorneys and plaintiffs who threaten to sue over practices that often pose no realistic threat to the safety of Californians.[85]

Civil Rights Laws

Civil rights statutes are also frequently abused by opportunistic litigants who seek not to prevent wrongful discrimination but to enrich themselves at others' expense, often over the most minor infractions. Again, California is a frequent source of such abuse. Under the Unruh Civil Rights Act, for example, it is illegal for the state's businesses to offer discounts to women: "ladies' nights" at bars are illegal.[86] In a 2007 case, the California Supreme Court held that a man who "suffers" from this sort of discrimination by being required to pay the regular price on a ladies' night does not even have to ask the manager to give him a similar discount before filing a lawsuit for "discrimination."[87] Other abuses abound, enriching professional plaintiffs and the bounty-hunter attorneys who represent them.

One such legal organization, Consumer Cause, Inc., has a particular fondness for abusing the civil rights laws.[88] The organization's founder, Morse Mehrban, is a well-known "bounty-hunter" lawyer who was recently fined $20,000 for misappropriating part of the $600,000 he obtained in a flurry of Proposition 65 lawsuits.[89] Consumer Cause's only shareholder is Mehrban's mother; his father is the treasurer, and his wife is the only employee.[90] Nevertheless, Mehrban's group masquerades as a civil rights organization for purposes of financial gain. It recently represented Marc Angelucci, himself an attorney who often collaborates with Mehrban in challenging the constitutionality of domestic violence laws on the ground that they discriminate in favor of women.[91] In 2004, Mehrban and Angelucci sued a nightclub that advertised discounts for ladies' nights, offering, of course, to drop the case if the club would make out a check for $5,000.[92] The club agreed, and the case settled, whereupon Mehrban and Angelucci filed a motion for attorney's fees. But the court rejected this request, noting that the club had not actually operated a ladies' night for almost a year before the lawsuit was filed. "It appears," wrote the court, "that Consumer Cause based its complaint on information published in various editions of the *L.A. Downtown News*," which "incorrectly stated that admission 'is free for women on Fridays before 10 p.m.'" Mehrban and Angelucci had filed the case without even making "at least some preliminary investigation."[93] Undeterred, Mehrban, Angelucci, and Consumer Cause continue to file lawsuits against bars that offer ladies' nights.

In just two years, the organization filed more than 130 cases against companies in the Fresno area alone.[94] Among its many other lawsuits was a 1999 case against hotels and gas stations for selling cigars without posting Proposition 65 warnings about the chemicals in tobacco smoke.[95] The trial judge, Los Angeles County Superior Court Judge Brett Klein, asked Mehrban in court how the damages or a settlement would be spent if Consumer Cause prevailed.[96] Mehrban answered that money from his Proposition 65 cases is deposited into a "trust fund . . . established by Consumer Cause, Inc." and withdrawn to pay Mehrban for his legal services. This, he said, was the trust fund's only expense, except for "expenses maintaining a corporate structure."[97] Judge Klein dismissed the case, noting that it was

> brought in the private interest, not in the public interest.... There are many nouns that one might attempt to use, metaphorically, to describe what this case is about. "Bounty hunter," the term used by defendants in their papers, is not one that I would use. I think, rather, the most appropriate metaphorical term would be "racketeering."[98]

In 2007, Mehrban and Angelucci prevailed in a lawsuit filed against another Southern California nightclub for offering discounts on ladies' night. The lower court held that Angelucci (who once again served as the plaintiff) was at least required to ask the owner to give him the discount before he could claim that he had been discriminated against, but the state supreme court overruled this. Any price differential at all, it declared, is alone grounds for a lawsuit.[99]

Another infamous tool for exploitation by attorneys and plaintiffs is the Americans with Disabilities Act. The ADA requires businesses to ensure that their facilities are "accessible" to people with disabilities, meaning that companies must install expensive wheelchair ramps, elevators, toilet facilities, and even new door handles to replace the knobs that are unusable by people who lack full use of their hands. In fact, the ADA is "potentially the most expensive business mandate in history."[100] A world in which buildings are more easily accessed by people with physical handicaps is certainly desirable, but imposing these severe costs on businesses makes it harder for entrepreneurs to start and run businesses, raises costs to consumers, and unfairly requires private companies to pay for public benefits that should be paid for by taxpayers if they consider these benefits worthwhile.

Troublesome as these requirements are, many companies have managed to deal with them. More troubling is the vagueness of the law's wording, which declares that businesses must provide "reasonable accommodations" to people with disabilities. In some cases, this requirement has been taken to a ridiculous extreme. The United States Supreme Court has held, for example, that the ADA requires professional golfing tournaments to change rules against golf carts because they discriminated against players who found walking difficult.[101] In other cases, plaintiffs with learning disabilities—including medical students—have demanded and received extra time to take tests.[102] In still others, movie theaters were found liable for violating the act because the seats they provided for people in wheelchairs did not enjoy the same viewing angles as other seats.[103] Courts have even held that because certain dangerous mental disorders qualify as disabilities under the ADA, employers must provide expensive "accommodations," such as paying for treatment programs for alcoholic or drug-abusing employees instead of firing them. When the Coca-Cola company discharged an executive who engaged in "violent and threatening behavior," the executive sued, arguing that the company had discriminated against him as an alcoholic, in violation of the ADA. A jury awarded him $7.1 million.[104] What may be even worse, the proliferation of mental disorders described in the psychological literature—and the vagueness with which they are defined—means that nearly any employee with a difficult personality can claim to be suffering from a disability covered by the ADA. As ADA expert Walter Olson points out, there's "narcissistic personality disorder," which is characterized by an excessive need for approval and little attention for the needs of others, or "avoidant personality disorder," which manifests itself through an extreme sensitivity to criticism. At one time, hostile, abusive, or lazy employees, or those who were just not right for the job, could simply have been discharged, but now an employee can claim to be suffering from a disorder and sue for discrimination if he is fired, or even if he is merely transferred to a less desirable position or receives any other treatment he perceives as negative.[105]

It is not always clear what a "reasonable accommodation" under the act might be. Businesses must install wheelchair ramps, to be sure. But one ADA practitioner also recommends abolishing "busy or changing patterns" in carpets and eliminating harsh light and unusual fonts on signs to accommodate people with poor eyesight.[106] One worker who suffered from asthma successfully sued a telephone company that installed and removed office equipment, a job that generally involves a lot of dust and is therefore bad for asthmatics. When the company discharged the asthmatic, the court found it in violation of the ADA for not accommodating her condition.[107] In May 2007, a worker who claimed to suffer from "seasonal affective disorder"—meaning that her mood was unduly affected by weather conditions—sued her employer for $33 million because she didn't get a desk next to a window.[108]

As legal historian Lawrence Friedman once noted, vague language in a law is essentially a delegation to courts. "Such a law buys time; it is a compromise between those who want sharp, specific action, and those who stand on the status quo."[109] The problem is that the costs of those compromises fall unfairly on those who run businesses, and vagueness encourages litigation by mercenary plaintiffs. Lawsuits are not only extremely easy to formulate but also come with built-in incentives: because the ADA is considered a civil rights law, attorneys who win such cases can demand attorney's fees in addition to their share of damages. Suing under the ADA is so lucrative, in fact, that some plaintiffs seem to make a living merely by filing lawsuits. Jarek Molski, a well-known professional plaintiff, filed more than

700 lawsuits under the act in courts throughout California, nearly all of which were settled out of court for a payoff.[110] In 2005, a federal court dismissed one of his cases, noting that although civil rights laws are "intended to achieve the prompt remediation" of discrimination, Molski's "true motive" was "to extort a cash settlement."[111] In another decision, the court pointed out: "Almost as startling as the sheer number of complaints Molski has filed, is the number of those claims that settle. Of the hundreds of cases Molski has filed in this district, not one has ever been litigated on the merits."[112] Instead, businesses generally paid to settle the case before trial. "Molski's m.o. is clear," the judge concluded, "sue, settle, and move on to the next suit."[113] Lawsuits like these justify Walter Olson's concern that "[n]o degree of good faith can keep [businesses] from being taken to court and sometimes losing."[114]

The number of federal discrimination lawsuits increased 2,200 percent between 1969 and 1994.[115] They now account for one-fifth of all lawsuits filed in the United States.[116] A startling number of these are later determined to be frivolous.[117] As many experts have noted, in many of these cases "the suits are not, in any realistic sense, brought either by or on behalf of" the plaintiffs but rather "as a practical matter, it is the private attorneys who initiate suit and who are the only ones rewarded for exposing the defendants' law violations."[118] And although defendants often manage to defend themselves from the most absurd cases, the defense still costs so much money in attorney's fees, court costs, and time that even defendants who win actually lose.

Although complaints about the abuse of civil rights laws abound, it bears emphasizing that many of these cases, while seemingly frivolous, are actually *warranted* by the language of the statutes under which they are brought. Businesses without wheelchair ramps or with doors too narrow for wheelchairs to enter really *are* in violation of the law, as are California companies that offer free chocolates to women or ladies' night discounts. Many of these violations may seem petty, but they are nevertheless actual violations, and attorneys who file enforcement actions with the unseemly motive of personal gain are rarely doing anything technically illegal. The fact that the Trevor Law Group brought so many cases in hopes that defendants would settle distinguishes it only in degree from the litigator who targets only a single business. Nor does the motive of filing a lawsuit prove that the claims are not substantiated by the law. A desire for personal gain instead of for "doing justice" may not play well in the media, but civil rights laws are tailored to self-interested motives because they provide for attorney's fees as an incentive to *encourage* the filing of lawsuits. Opportunistic plaintiffs who comply with the literal language of a statute when filing a case are not to be blamed for their opportunism any more than a taxpayer who takes advantage of a legal deduction for his own personal gain, or a property owner who uses the threat of a lawsuit to obtain a concession from a neighbor. The fault for profit-seeking ADA plaintiffs lies in the vague language of a law that gives them the opportunity to extort businesses with legal threats. Without fixing this problem, the danger of jackpot justice will remain. The successful prosecution of the Trevor Law Group may have sent a warning shot across the bow of one of the largest pirate ships, but it will probably not deter others from searching for treasure in the future.

12. Regulatory Takings

The Fifth Amendment declares that government may not take private property for public use unless it pays the owner "just compensation." The most obvious example of such a taking is when government uses the power of "eminent domain" to seize the title to land that it needs for a freeway, firehouse, or other public project. While virtually everyone agrees that these are "public uses," local governments also frequently take land to benefit private parties. This became a major controversy in 2005 when the Supreme Court decided *Kelo v. New London*,[1] allowing a small Connecticut city to condemn several homes and other properties and transfer them to private developers to construct condominiums and shopping centers. This, the Court said, was constitutionally permitted notwithstanding the Constitution's restriction of eminent domain to "public uses." The justices reasoned that the term "public use" is synonymous with "public benefit," so government can take property for any project that benefits the public. But since the rational basis test gives bureaucrats practically unlimited power to determine what does and does not benefit the public, this essentially meant that lawmakers can redistribute property for whatever purpose they consider a good idea—including taking property from one owner and giving it to another to use for his own private profit.[2] This decision led to a nationwide outcry and efforts in almost all the states to restrict the use of eminent domain.[3] Private property, many people argued, should be taken only for genuinely public uses, such as highways or post offices, and not for a private enterprise, even if that enterprise might somehow benefit the public in some indirect way.

But there is another, subtler way in which government takes private property: so-called regulatory takings, which occur when the government restricts an owner's rights to use his or her land. The question of whether and when a property owner should be compensated for this kind of taking is a center of controversy. And because these regulations often affect businesses, and particularly the real

255

estate and housing markets, the subject of regulatory takings is of central importance to economic freedom in the United States.

Why Are There "Regulatory" Takings?

The concept of regulatory takings addresses an ambiguity in the Fifth Amendment. Although that amendment requires the government to compensate property owners when it takes away their property, it does not define the word "take." If the amendment required compensation only for the use of eminent domain, clever government officials could get around the compensation requirement simply by enacting laws that require property owners to do with their land what the government wants them to do (or to refrain from doing that which the government disapproves), rather than actually taking away the title to the land. If the government wanted to provide the public with, say, a public park, it could either seize the property through eminent domain and compensate the owner or decree that the owner must turn his land into a park and *not* compensate the owner. It is obvious which option the government would choose. Without a remedy for such nonpossessory takings, landowners would be entirely at the government's mercy.

In 1871, the United States Supreme Court began closing this loophole in a case called *Pumpelly v. Green Bay Company*.[4] Pumpelly, a Wisconsin property owner, sued the Green Bay Company for flooding his land during the construction of a canal. Since the company was a government entity, Mr. Pumpelly argued that this action had taken his land without just compensation, in violation of the Wisconsin state constitution.[5] But the company argued that it had not actually *taken* anything; it had only flooded the land; Pumpelly still *owned* the property, even if it was now under water.

The Supreme Court rejected this facile argument. "It would be a very curious and unsatisfactory result," the justices wrote, if the government could "destroy [property's] value entirely, . . . inflict irreparable and permanent injury to any extent, . . . [and,] in effect, subject it to total destruction without making any compensation, because, in the narrowest sense of that word, it is not *taken* for the public use."[6] Such a rule would allow government much greater control over property than the amendment's authors intended; states could evade a constitutional protection that was meant to secure the rights of citizens.

Three years later, the Michigan Supreme Court reiterated the point. "It is a transparent fallacy to say that this is not a taking of his property, because the land *itself* is not taken," the court noted, or "because the title, nominally, still remains in [the owner], and he is merely deprived of its beneficial use."[7] The fallacy lay in ignoring the fact that the right to use is a necessary component of property rights: the right to own something is not simply the right to lay claim to a physical object but the right to operate, apply, work, sell, or manipulate that object. One with no right to use a hammer, or a car, or land, or who lacks the power to sell, give away, trade, or exclude others from these things, would gain little by claiming to "own" them. So for the government to take away use rights *does* mean to "take" the property at issue. As the Michigan court remarked, property "does not consist merely of the right to the ultimate particles of matter of which it may be composed."[8] To speak of "ownership" as divorced from the right to use property would be to speak of "a purely metaphysical abstraction, as immaterial and useless to the owner as 'the stuff that dreams are made of[.]'"[9]

At the same time, courts also recognized that government had extensive power to regulate property to protect public health, safety, and welfare, even if such regulations had severe negative effects on property values. In *Mugler v. Kansas*,[10] the Court upheld a law prohibiting the making or selling of alcohol without a license. When Peter Mugler continued to operate his brewery, he was brought up on charges and, citing the *Pumpelly* case, argued that the law deprived him of the right to use his property. The Supreme Court disagreed. "The question in *Pumpelly v. Green Bay Co.*, arose under the state's power of eminent domain," wrote Justice John Marshall Harlan, "while the question now before us arises under what are, strictly, the police powers of the state, exerted for the protection of the health, morals, and safety of the people."[11] If the state exercised its police powers, it was not required to compensate property owners, even if those powers led to a drastic diminution in the value of the property. Such laws did not appropriate property for the benefit of the public, but merely declared "that its use by any one, for certain forbidden purposes, is prejudicial to the public interests."[12]

Harlan recognized that the dividing line between police power regulations (not requiring compensation) and the use of eminent domain (where compensation was required) was not always clear, but he tried to explain the distinction: "The exercise of the police power by the destruction of property which is itself a public nuisance, or the prohibition of its use in a particular way, whereby its value becomes depreciated, is very different from taking property for public use. . . . In the one case, a nuisance only is abated; in the other, unoffending property is taken away from an innocent owner."[13] Yet alcohol had not been a nuisance in Kansas when Peter Mugler began manufacturing it. Could the state convert it into a nuisance by mere fiat, thus eliminating the rights Mugler legitimately expected to exercise? Harlan said yes and relied on *Stone v. Mississippi*[14] to do it: "[T]he supervision of the public health and the public morals is a governmental power, 'continuing in its nature,'" he wrote, and "'for this purpose, the largest legislative discretion is allowed, and the discretion cannot be parted with any more than the power itself.'"[15] In other words, states had unlimited power to declare that something that was once legal was now an illegal public nuisance, thereby eliminating a person's property rights and taking previously "unoffending" property "away from an innocent owner" without compensation.[16]

Taken together, *Pumpelly* and *Mugler* set the stage for serious legal confusion about the nature of property rights. At what point does a noncompensable regulation, purportedly in the service of public health and safety, go beyond that limit and end up confiscating private property, activating the just-compensation requirement? In the 1922 case of *Pennsylvania Coal v. Mahon*,[17] Justice Oliver Wendell Holmes acknowledged that this line was not clearly drawn. The "seemingly absolute protection" given to property owners by the takings clause was "qualified by the police power," he wrote, which led to a "natural tendency . . . to extend the qualification more and more until at last private property disappears." But government control over property "cannot be accomplished in this way under the Constitution." Whatever confusion might exist as to the boundary between the police power and eminent domain, "[t]he general rule at least is that while property may be regulated to a certain extent, if regulation goes too far it will be recognized as a taking."[18]

"Goes too far" is not very helpful as a legal rule; but in the more than 80 years since *Mahon* was decided, the Supreme Court has never formulated a clearer one. Some scholars have proposed helpful suggestions. Professor Richard A. Epstein, for example, argued in his pathbreaking book *Takings: Private Property and the Power of Eminent Domain* that the police power, by which the state protects individuals from aggression or injury by others, differs categorically from eminent domain, which the state uses to take property to provide some sort of public benefit or public good to which people would not otherwise be entitled. The police power is the state's power to use coercion in defense of individual rights, arising from the classical liberal principle that people have the right to defend themselves from direct injuries and can entrust the state to help protect them. That power imposes no obligation on the state to compensate the affected person, who has not been deprived of any rightful freedom. In Epstein's formulation, "the police power gives the state control over the full catalogue of common law wrongs involving force and misrepresentation, deliberate or accidental, against other persons, including private nuisances."[19] But no one has a natural right to benefit himself by compelling another person to give up his land; thus, the government must pay compensation when it seizes property to provide amenities that go beyond merely protecting of the rights of the innocent.

The distinction between the police power and eminent domain makes sense of an otherwise curious paradox in the law of takings: the government can entirely deprive a criminal of his property—for instance, the gun with which he commits a robbery—without compensating him at all. But it cannot deprive an innocent person of even a minor property right through eminent domain without compensation. This contradiction is only apparent because the seizure of property used in a crime is an exercise of the police power that protects the rights of the innocent and therefore requires no compensation, whereas a small encroachment on the property of an unoffending citizen as a means to provide the public with some desirable benefit is an exercise of the eminent domain power: it injures one who has violated nobody's rights, and that person deserves to be made whole.

Epstein's theory is clear, principled, and persuasive. But it has not been adopted by the legal community and has been criticized by courts and commentators who argue that the dividing line between eminent domain and the police power is often far from obvious. But while there will always be hard cases, a clear conceptual distinction is important for counteracting the "natural tendency" to expand the police power, as Holmes warned, until private property disappears.

Modern Attempts to Explain What "Goes Too Far"

Today, there are three basic kinds of regulatory takings. The first two, known as "categorical" takings, always entitle the property owner to compensation, at least in theory. If these two categories do not apply, however, a regulatory takings case will fall into the third category, analyzed under the so-called *Penn Central* test—an incoherent test with few meaningful guiding principles, under which property owners virtually never obtain compensation.

The first category was delineated in *Loretto v. Teleprompter Manhattan CATV Corp.*,[20] in which the Supreme Court held that an apartment owner who was forced to install cable television equipment on her building was entitled to compensation despite the fact that the equipment was very small and constituted a very minor physical infringement on her property. The Court explained that a law requiring a person to admit something onto her land against her will was an "occupation" that "denies the owner any power to control the use of the property."[21] Since the right to exclude others from one's property is so essential to the concept of ownership, the government may not deprive a person of that right without just compensation.

The second categorical taking comes from the Supreme Court's decision in *Lucas v. South Carolina Coastal Council.*[22] This case involved a state law that prohibited a developer from constructing anything on the shorefront property on which he intended to build a home. The Court held that because the restriction blocked "all economically beneficial or productive use" of the land, the owner was entitled to just compensation.[23] Such a regulation, after all, was tantamount to the outright expropriation of his property.

These two categories were supposed to make it easier to identify the circumstances in which property owners were due compensation from the government, but they suffer from some major logical flaws that undermine their power to protect property owners. The *Loretto* decision, for example, noted that the cable television equipment was a *"permanent* physical invasion" of Ms. Loretto's property.[24] *Temporary* invasions, therefore, have often been held not to constitute a taking, even where those invasions are far more severe than the ones at issue in *Loretto*.[25] Perhaps the most egregious example arose in *Yee v. Escondido*,[26] when owners of mobile home parks challenged the constitutionality of a California law prohibiting them from evicting people who lived on their land. These mobile homes—something of a misnomer since they are usually too large to actually move—were owned by their residents, but the ground underneath them was not. The land was leased from the owner of the mobile home park, who also provided other facilities for residents and charged a monthly rent. Because the state law prohibited these owners from evicting residents except under specified circumstances, the owners argued that the law essentially created a permanent physical occupation of their land similar to the occupation allowed in *Loretto*. The Supreme Court rejected this argument. The owners "voluntarily rented their land" to the residents, wrote Justice O'Connor, and "neither the city nor the State compels petitioners, once they have rented their property to tenants, to continue doing so. To the contrary, the Mobile-home Residency Law provides that a park owner who wishes to change the use of his land may evict his tenants, albeit with 6 or 12 months notice."[27] Forcing an owner to wait a year before evicting an unwanted tenant was not a taking; instead, the law "merely regulate[d] petitioners' *use* of their land."[28]

The government had made the same argument in *Loretto*, claiming that the cable-installation requirement was not really compulsory since the apartment owners could simply stop renting out property if they did not want to abide by that requirement. The Court had rejected that argument in a footnote. But in *Yee*, the Court brushed aside its previous opinion "because there has simply been no compelled physical occupation giving rise to a right to compensation that [the mobile home park owners] could have forfeited. Had the city required such an occupation, of course, [they] would have a right to compensation, and the city might then lack the power to condition petitioners' ability to run mobile home parks on their waiver of this right. But because the ordinance does not effect a physical taking in the first place, this footnote in *Loretto* does not help [them]."[29] Thus, the distinction between *Loretto* and *Yee* rested on the fact that in the former case the law required an owner to *accept* an invasive occupation of the property, while in *Yee* it simply required the owner to *maintain* a person on the property even after the owner no longer wanted to. That distinction, however, is an illusion: the law of trespass holds that anyone who stays after an owner orders him to leave is guilty of a tort or a crime.

Even more abused is the *Lucas* category of takings. Although the Court claimed that a law that completely deprives a person of the value of his property requires compensation, it has never required compensation for anything less than the *total* value. This has simply served as an invitation for politicians to adopt laws imposing severe, but not *total* deprivations. In one case in Rhode Island, for example, the government prohibited a property owner from constructing condominiums on his land—land that, without the restriction in place, was worth more than $3 million.[30] But the government was willing to let him construct a single home on the property, which would make the land worth about $200,000.[31] Thus, although the law deprived him of at least $2.8 million, the government was not required to compensate him at all for this loss. By leaving a token value to a property owner, the government can evade the compensation requirement even for such devastating takings.

Weakened as these two categories are, they provide more hope for property owners than the third group of regulatory takings. If a case does not fall within the first two categories, it is viewed through the analysis created in *Penn Central Transportation Company v. City of New York*.[32] The *Penn Central* test is actually not a test at all, but an "essentially ad hoc, factual inquir[y]"[33] in which judges weigh various factors and intuit when a regulation "goes too far." These factors are first, the economic impact of the regulation on the property owner; second, the extent to which the regulation interferes with "reasonable, investment-backed expectations"; and third, the "character" of the government action.

It is an indication of the hollowness of this test that in the three decades since it was invented, the Supreme Court has never found that it entitled a property owner to compensation. Moreover, as Pacific Legal Foundation attorney R. S. Radford puts it, "In keeping with what had become a long tradition . . . none of [its] terms were ever defined, either in *Penn Central* or in any subsequent case."[34] For example, it is unclear what the "character of the government action" means. From the few cases that have tried to answer this question, it seems to mean that a law that exceeds the government's legitimate powers, or a law that is somehow "unfair," would exceed the police power and constitute a taking. But other parts of the Constitution—particularly the due process of law clause—already prohibit the government from going beyond its legitimate powers or acting in a fundamentally unfair way. In one 1998 case, the justices were divided over whether a law requiring a company to pay pensions that it and its employees had not agreed to was a regulatory taking. Applying the *Penn Central* test, Justice O'Connor found that the "character" of the government action was "quite unusual" because it "implicate[d] fundamental principles of fairness underlying the Takings Clause."[35] But Justice Anthony Kennedy pointed out in a separate opinion that questions of fairness are normative concepts that apply through the due process clause, not through the takings clause, and the Fifth Amendment declares that government may *never* take property in violation of the basic standards of fairness and equality that make up "due process of law."[36] Only if a taking meets these standards may the government condemn property, and it must then pay just compensation.

The other *Penn Central* factors are equally problematic. Courts apply them in an unprincipled and inconsistent way, depending on the judges' own conceptions of fairness, without clear guidelines. Because courts will compensate an owner only for "reasonable, investment-backed expectations," cases often turn on whether the judge thinks the investment was "reasonable." If a property owner was aware of the existence of a restriction on the property before he purchased it, a judge is likely to find that the owner's expectations were not reasonable. In a 1999 case, a property owner lost despite the fact that the law was enacted *after* he purchased the property, because the court found that "public concern about the environment resulted in numerous laws and regulations affecting land development" in the past, and thus the property owner should have known that "rising environmental awareness" would "translate[] into ever-tightening land use regulations" later restricting his right to use his property.[37] As Professor Steven Eagle, a leading authority on regulatory takings, explains, this focus on the "reasonableness" of a property owner's expectations creates a "vicious circuity: 'A person's property is limited by an official's determination of his reasonable expectations, and his expectations are limited by the most recent statute, ordinance, or administrative ruling redefining his rights.'"[38]

Under the *Penn Central* analysis, inconsistency is inevitable. Sometimes, writes former U.S. attorney general William P. Barr, regulations "that cause massive economic harm to the owner are held not to go too far, whereas others with only a slight impact are found to constitute regulatory takings. . . . As it turns out, the Court has usually not considered it unfair or unjust to force owners to bear fairly heavy burdens, at least if the owner is rich."[39] In general, no matter how severe the economic impact of a regulation, so long as it falls short of a total deprivation under *Lucas*, the other two *Penn Central* factors—interference with investment-backed expectations and the character of the government action—typically cut off a person's hope of recovery.

Why the Controversy over Regulatory Takings?

It seems obvious that the government should compensate owners for certain violations of their property rights. "Viewshed ordinances," for example, are laws that prohibit construction so as to preserve a pleasant view of a hillside or a coastline for the benefit of the general public. In years past, if the government wanted to provide such a benefit, it would condemn the property or part of the property through eminent domain. The owner would be compensated and the public would receive the benefit in precisely the same way that other public recreational facilities are provided. Due to the vague and confusing standards used in regulatory takings cases, however, local governments can use viewshed ordinances instead, to provide the public with a view seemingly "free of charge." Of course, it is not actually free because the cost is simply borne by the property owner instead of the taxpayer—a condition that courts have long said is precisely what the takings clause was intended to prohibit: "The Fifth Amendment's guarantee that private property shall not be taken for a public use without just compensation was designed to bar Government from forcing some people alone to bear public burdens which, in all fairness and justice, should be borne by the public as a whole."[40]

The issue of regulatory takings is controversial because government today imposes so many restrictions on property owners that it simply cannot afford to compensate them. Debates over regulatory takings law generally boil down to that simple problem: federal, state, and local governments take so much property away from people that there is just not enough money to make them whole. As Douglas Kendall, executive director of the far-left Community Rights Counsel, has acknowledged, environmentalists "realize that a compensation requirement would essentially gut their efforts to protect endangered species and sensitive ecosystems, because the funds necessary to compensate these landowners simply do not and will not ever exist."[41] And Glenn Sugameli, an attorney for the National Wildlife Federation, opposes compensation for regulatory takings because they would be "so prohibitively expensive as to force repeal of [environmental] protections."[42] Thus, the argument goes, since the government cannot afford to pay people for the injuries it inflicts on them, it should not have to pay for those injuries at all. This argument would seem to lack moral persuasiveness. Yet lawyers and judges have frequently employed it to refuse compensation to property owners whose rights were nullified by government action. In one particularly severe case in the Lake Tahoe area, in which hundreds of property owners were prohibited from constructing on their land for decades, the Supreme Court eventually denied compensation, noting, "A rule that required compensation for every delay in the use of property would render routine government processes prohibitively expensive," and quoting Oliver Wendell Holmes, "'Government hardly could go on if to some extent values incident to property could not be diminished without paying for every such change in the general law.'"[43]

There are several problems with the argument that government should not have to pay for projects that cost too much. First, there is the obvious moral objection: taking things without paying for them is wrong. It commits an injustice against an innocent party. While clever rationalizations for such injustices might be devised—arguing that there is really no such thing as private property, for example— these are nothing more than excuses for injustice, and they set a dangerous precedent for the violation of other rights. If property can be taken without payment because providing the public with certain public amenities is just too important a goal, then why could the same rationale not be used to justify silencing dissenters, or depriving people of their religious freedom? In the past, arguments that the "public good" justified overriding individual rights led to horrendous abuses. When the Roosevelt administration interned Japanese Americans in camps during World War II, it had one of the strongest possible arguments for the "importance" of its policies: the United States was involved in the most horrific war in its history at the time, and one of its enemies was the Empire of Japan. But few today would agree that the government was justified in violating individual freedom. Indeed, the government later formally apologized to and compensated the Japanese Americans it had wronged.

Secondly, those who oppose compensation for regulatory takings often argue that such compensation would violate democratic principles by restricting the ability of the majority to regulate the use of property. But, in fact, such compensation would actually be good for democratic decisionmaking. At present, bureaucrats can adopt government programs without concern for the costs of those programs because the money does not come out of taxpayer funds. The costs still exist and are still borne by somebody, but because they are not borne by society in general, voters and taxpayers do not know what they are. As New York's highest court explained, the problem with uncompensated regulatory takings is that there

> is no attempt to share the cost of the benefit among those benefited, that is, society at large. Instead, the accident of ownership determines who shall bear the cost initially. Of course, as further consequence, the ultimate economic cost of providing the benefit is hidden from those who in a democratic society are given the power of deciding whether or not they wish to obtain the benefit despite the ultimate economic cost, however initially distributed. In other words, the removal from productive use of private property has an ultimate social cost more easily concealed by imposing the cost on the owner alone. When successfully concealed, the public is not likely to have any objection to the "cost-free" benefit.[44]

If government must compensate for the injuries it causes, voters would be better able to make wiser choices about the uses of state power and about the wisdom of bureaucratic plans.[45]

Moreover, if democratic principles justify depriving individuals of property rights without just compensation, then why would the same argument not apply to other forms of government liability? Why compensate for eminent domain, for example? It is obviously expensive for government to pay for actually seizing property directly through eminent domain, which limits what the majority can do. Yet nobody argues for eliminating the compensation requirement when government uses eminent domain to take land directly. Government is also liable when it deprives people of other civil rights. In *Owen v. City of Independence, Missouri*,[46] the Supreme Court explained the reasons why cities must compensate people whose civil rights they violate. It would be "'uniquely amiss'" if the government itself, to which people "look for the promotion of liberty, justice, fair and equal treatment," could "disavow liability for the injury it has begotten," wrote Justice William Brennan.[47]

Requiring government to pay for the wrongs it commits creates an incentive for wise and careful decisionmaking: "[C]onsideration of the municipality's liability for constitutional violations is quite properly the concern of its elected or appointed officials. Indeed, a decisionmaker would be derelict in his duties if, at some point, he did not consider whether his decision comports with constitutional mandates and did not weigh the risk that a violation might result in an award of damages from the public treasury."[48] And when officials "harbor doubts about the lawfulness of their intended actions," the possibility that the city might face damages for wrongful conduct might lead them "to err on the side of protecting citizens' constitutional rights" or "encourage those in a policymaking position to institute internal rules and programs designed to minimize the likelihood of unintentional infringements on constitutional rights."[49]

Finally, it would be unfair to abandon the person whose rights have been violated to carry the whole cost of a wrongful act by government. It is "fairer to allocate any resulting financial loss" to the government and the taxpayers rather than to "those whose rights . . . have been violated."[50] The public is ultimately responsible for the wrongs committed by government, and it is proper for the general public to pay. The *Owen* decision was joined by Justices Thurgood Marshall, William O. Douglas, Harry Blackmun, John Paul Stevens, and Byron White—many of whom refused to apply the same logic to government actions violating private property rights.[51]

The argument that government should not have to compensate for regulatory takings because it would restrict the discretion of bureaucrats would also justify insulating government from liability for anything.[52] Indeed, under that principle, private corporations should also be immune from tort liability since corporate officers also need to make difficult decisions and it would be easier for them to do so if they did not need to worry about being required to pay damages for injuring people. Courts have never adopted this argument because the whole point of tort law is that private parties must pay people back for harming them or depriving them of their rights. For the same reason, government ought to compensate property owners when it takes their property rights away. The argument that government should be subject to different rules than private parties is repulsive in a nation whose fundamental creed is that "all men are created equal."

Tactics for Denying Compensation to Property Owners

Law professors and judges have concocted a variety of mechanisms to avoid compensating landowners who are barred from using their property as they had hoped to do.

The most obvious method is to exploit the vague language of *Penn Central*, declaring a property owner's plans "unreasonable" and therefore not subject to just compensation. But a more complicated mechanism involves changing the court's perspective on the size of the taking itself—the so-called relevant parcel problem. Here, the question is whether a regulation takes the complete value of a section of the property (requiring compensation under *Lucas*) or whether that section of property is only part of a larger landmass, the value of which has merely been *decreased*, not eliminated, by the regulation at issue. If, say, a law prohibits any development of 9 acres on a parcel of land 10 acres in size, is this a complete (and compensable) taking of the 9 acres? Or is it only a noncompensable diminution in the value of the 10-acre whole? By shifting the frame of reference to the larger parcel, a court can declare that all but the most oppressive regulation is merely a noncompensable decrease in value.[53] Of course, this problem of definition is a serious one, but Professor Eagle convincingly argues that the "relevant parcel" in a takings case should be any "commercial unit,"[54] meaning that any portion of the property that might otherwise be bought and sold on a free market (such as easements or mineral rights) should be considered a compensable property right, even if it does not make up the entire interest possessed by the owner. At present, the law focuses instead on the economic impact on the property owner instead of the nature of the interest that the state has confiscated. Yet the Constitution does not protect the property owner merely from "heavy" or "extreme" burdens; it protects a property owner from *any* deprivation of property for public use.

Another technique for avoiding compensation is time limits. In some cases, courts have held that if a property owner was aware of a regulation's existence when he purchased the property, he cannot seek compensation no matter how much it limits his rights. This theory, known as the "notice rule," originated in a misapplication of the Supreme Court's decision in *Ruckleshaus v. Monsanto*,[55] which held that a chemical company was not entitled to compensation when it was forced to disclose its secret formulas to the public in exchange for a government license. The Court explained that the Monsanto company knew of the existence of the disclosure requirement when it sought the license, and therefore it essentially consented to the taking of its trade secrets. In later cases, the Court clarified that this "constructive consent" rule applied only when the complaining party was seeking a government *privilege* and not when he or she was simply seeking to exercise a property right. In *Nollan v. California Coastal Commission*,[56] for example, a California couple sued when the government forced them to give up some of their property in exchange for a building permit. The government argued that, like the Monsanto company, the Nollans were aware of the requirement when they bought the land and were therefore not owed compensation. But the Court rejected this argument because the *Monsanto* "notice rule" applied only to those who were seeking a *"valuable Government benefit"* and not to "the right to build on one's own property." That right "cannot remotely be described as a 'governmental benefit.'"[57] *Nollan* represented a significant step: it would be all too easy for the government to characterize any property right—which the government must compensate for taking—as a privilege for which the government can require the *citizen* to pay.

This is precisely what the state of Massachusetts argued in a 2002 case in which the state forced tobacco companies to disclose their ingredients for the privilege of doing business in the state. The tobacco companies argued that requiring the disclosure of this valuable information essentially constituted a taking of their property, but the government argued that the companies were aware of this requirement when they chose to do business in Massachusetts, and therefore they were not entitled to compensation: they had consented to the taking. At first, the trial court rejected this argument as a misapplication of the *Monsanto* notice rule: "'[P]ermission to continue operating a lawful business is not the type of government benefit'" to which the notice rule could apply, the court concluded.[58] The idea that a business's awareness of the existence of a confiscatory rule could alone cut off the right to just compensation "rests on the positivist notion that since, in a broad sense, all property rights emanate from the State, the State is free to take them away whenever it determines to do so. That proposition must be rejected."[59] That decision was initially reversed by a three-judge panel of the First Circuit Court of Appeals, which declared that the notice/consent rule *did* bar the plaintiff's claims because "the ability to market tobacco products in Massachusetts" *was* a privilege for which the state could demand concessions from the tobacco companies.[60] This decision was again overturned, this time by the full First Circuit, which reinstated the trial court's decision and found that the notice rule did not apply. "[A]llowing a manufacturer to simply sell its legal product" is a right inhering in ownership, "similar to building on one's land," and not "a valuable government benefit" that can be conditioned on the taking of property.[61] The state's attempt to "condition the right to sell tobacco on [a] forfeiture" was "an unconstitutional taking of the tobacco companies' products."[62]

Similar confusion reigns in other courts. In 2000, the Rhode Island Supreme Court held that when a property owner bought land subject to a confiscatory land-use regulation, he could not seek just compensation for that taking.[63] The United States Supreme Court reversed that decision, however, holding that judges cannot throw out a person's case simply because the law was in place years before the lawsuit.[64] Justice Sandra Day O'Connor wrote a separate opinion in the case arguing that the timing of a regulation could be considered among the other vague factors in the *Penn Central* "reasonableness" analysis.[65] Unfortunately, this has meant that courts continue to decide that a property owner's expectations were not "reasonable" or that the property owner "consented" to the taking just because he or she knew of its existence before buying the land or trying to sell property.[66] In the raisin-confiscation case discussed in chapter 7, for example, a federal judge found that farmers who tried to sell raisins in the interstate market could not challenge the seizure of their crops because they were aware of the confiscation requirement when they began selling raisins.[67]

Perhaps the most absurd use of time limits to eliminate the rights of property owners came in the Lake Tahoe case. There, the government enacted a series of supposedly "temporary" moratoriums, barring property owners for more than two decades from constructing anything on their land. According to the *Lucas* decision, a moratorium that prohibits all economically viable use of land should entitle the owner to compensation, and according to a case called *First English*,[68] even temporary takings of property require just compensation. But in *Tahoe-Sierra*, which involved a combination of total and (allegedly) temporary deprivations of the right to use land, the Court found that the government owed the owners *no* compensation. The Court began by carefully narrowing the question in the case. Although the plaintiffs complained about the systematic, long-standing deprivation of their property rights, the Court addressed only "whether a moratorium on development imposed during the process of devising a comprehensive land-use plan constitutes a *per se* taking."[69] It did not, declared Justice John Paul Stevens. After all, compensating owners for such moratoriums would cost too much.

Those who oppose compensating property owners for regulatory takings have adopted several other tactics beyond procedural tricks. Some argue that the Founders never intended the Fifth Amendment's just compensation clause to require payment for regulatory takings because colonial land-use law imposed restrictions on people's property use, and none of the Founders suggested that owners should be compensated for these restrictions.[70] Others point out that early American decisions did require compensation for a wide variety of non-eminent-domain takings, including what would today be called regulatory takings.[71] It should not be surprising that at the time of the Constitution's ratification, more than a century before the creation of the modern regulatory state, the Founders would not have provided clearer restrictions on land-use regulation. Zoning and other land-use planning devices were unknown to them and to the authors of the Fourteenth Amendment, just as infrared cameras and telephone eavesdropping devices were unknown to the authors of the Fourth Amendment's warrant requirement. Yet just as the *principles* of the warrant requirement apply to technologically advanced versions of "searching,"[72] so the principle of just compensation applies to modern regulations that confiscate the value of a person's property. Moreover, as Professor Kris Kobach notes, state courts before the Civil War were already requiring compensation for takings that fell short of outright seizure,[73] and we have seen how the United States Supreme Court agreed in 1871 that acts that diminished the value of land entitled the owner to just compensation.

Even more startling is the theory of "givings," increasingly popular among defenders of government control over land use.[74] According to this argument, government *creates* whatever value property has by eliminating restrictions on its use or granting licenses allowing an owner to put land to a profitable purpose. It is therefore the *property owner* who owes compensation, not the other way around.[75] "Givings" advocate Reza Dibadj acknowledges the underlying purpose behind the theory: "Provided we are willing to refocus the debate, there are ways to regulate without giving the public's house away."[76] In other words, shifting the burden to property owners gives bureaucrats greater power to control the uses of property without having to compensate those on whom those burdens fall.

But the givings theory ignores the fundamental status of individual freedom. Advocates of givings theory hold that freedom is simply created by government decisions that give a person independence from the interference of others. As law professor Cass Sunstein pronounces, the "voluntary private sphere [is] actually itself a creation of law."[77] Since both freedom and its opposite are equally the creations of government, therefore, it is not possible to argue that government is doing anything *wrong* or taking anything *away* when it prohibits or restricts the scope of liberty people previously enjoyed; it is merely redesignating the contours of the choices society allows people to make. Proposed government actions cannot be judged against a baseline of freedom because there is no such baseline: the choice between liberty and restriction is morally neutral and is made solely on a utilitarian basis.

Few property owners—indeed few owners of any rights—would fall for such sophistry. The concept of property is logically prior to regulation, just as production is prior to distribution, to say nothing of redistribution. Building permits and land-use regulations do not exist in a state of nature, but property does because individuals create property through labor in interaction with nature.[78] To say that property is created by the state's choice not to deprive people of it

272

is like saying that one's property rights are merely the function of a burglar choosing *not* to steal one's things, or that government's choice not to censor or to persecute dissenters is the *source* of the rights of free speech or freedom of religion. More than three centuries ago, when Sir Robert Filmer advanced a similar argument in his treatise *Patriarcha*, John Locke replied: "His system lies in a little compass; it is no more but this, 'That all government is absolute monarchy.' And the ground he builds on is this, 'That no man is born free.'"[79] If one holds that people *are* born free, in rightful possession of themselves and their faculties, then liberty—and the private property rights that arise from liberty—cannot be a gift of society.

As with the rational basis test, the givings theory shifts the burden of proof in violation of logic. The person who asserts a claim ought to muster the reasons supporting the claim; when such reasons are not forthcoming, the claim should not be believed. Likewise, when neighbors (or the government) assert the right to restrict a person's liberty or property rights, the onus is on them to substantiate their claim, not on the right-possessor to justify why he should be free. Those like Sunstein who argue that demands of privacy must be "defended" against the presumption that government may regulate[80] are imposing on the individual a logically impossible task. As philosopher Anthony de Jasay explains:

> The presumption of liberty implies that the act will remain free and will not be stopped until the affirmation of its objectionable nature is not only made, but also verified. The opposite presumption would stop the actor doing the act in question until he could show it to be proof against possible objection. There is an indefinitely large number of potential objectors having a potentially infinite number of objections, some of which may be sufficiently strong. To falsify the hypothesis that the act is objectionable, and therefore not one of the actor's liberties, is a needle-in-the-haystack type of task, very difficult and costly if the set of potential objections is large, and logically impossible if the set is not finite (which, in a strict sense, it never is). Taking the haystack apart blade by blade to falsify the supposition of its harboring a needle would take long enough to mean an indefinite suspension of the act whose free performance depended on there being a needle. Taken literally, the presumption that every act may be harmful and hurt some interest would freeze everything into total immobility.[81]

The fact that a person must be presumed free unless good reasons exist for limiting his freedom is the reason for the criminal law maxim that a defendant is innocent until proven guilty, and for the same reason, the law must not presume that people are fundamentally unfree prior to the state's creating their liberty or property rights.[82] As Jasay concludes, the presumption that people are basically free "is hardly a matter of ethics, of a liberal temperament, or even of efficient social and economic organization. It is a matter of epistemology."[83] Yet the givings theory adopts the opposite presumption: it holds that people are basically unfree; that they are endowed by the state with certain malleable rights, and that owners of property or of other rights are deprived of nothing if the government eliminates those rights.

Yet "givings" theory compounds its fallacies. In no area of private law may a person demand a fee in exchange for *not taking away someone else's property*. In the 1987 *Nollan* case, the Supreme Court accurately characterized such a demand as "extortion."[84] Extortion is wrongful because it puts an innocent person to the choice between two things—"your money or your life"—when that person has the right to both. And because government is only a group of individuals, it cannot have any greater right to extort citizens than can the individuals who compose it.[85] But the givings theory holds that because the state creates property rights by refraining from taking away those rights, a landowner must pay for that grace. Extortion therefore becomes wise government policy.

Exactions

Perhaps the fastest-growing area of regulatory takings law involves "exactions": demands government makes of landowners in exchange for permission to use their property. These demands can take the form of land, cash, or the waiver of other rights, and local governments frequently impose these burdens as a way to increase revenue without taking the politically unpopular step of raising taxes. Often these cases consist of outright attempts to extort money from property owners under the pretext of protecting the public.

If a developer plans to construct hundreds of new homes whose occupants will overload the public streets, it might be rational for the government to require the developer to mitigate this effect by improving the affected roads. But all too often, a property owner's application for a building permit gives local bureaucrats the opportunity to demand crippling and wholly arbitrary payoffs from the owner. In a 2004 case in the Sacramento suburb of Elk Grove, California, Jonette Banzon and her husband Mohammed Ahmad were ordered to pay more than $240,000 for a permit to construct a $500,000 home. After they filed a lawsuit, the city decreased the demand and the couple settled out of court.[86] Such fees are quite common and are increasing. A 2007 survey found that development fees had increased by 77 percent nationwide in the previous four years, adding an average of more than $10,000 to the cost of a home.[87] In some California communities,[88] the costs are far greater: a 1999 report by the nonpartisan Public Policy Institute of California found that residential development fees average between $20,000 and $30,000 per home.[89] In the community of Antioch, development fees accounted for more than 19 percent of the entire cost of a home.[90] And a 2001 report found that in Contra Costa County, the construction of a 45-unit apartment building cost $920,000 in development fees alone—not counting the actual costs of building materials or labor.[91] Obviously, these fees have a significant effect on the supply of housing and are among the biggest reasons for the high prices of new homes.[92]

In the *Nollan* case, the Supreme Court sought to limit the abuse of development fees by holding that when government demands a concession from a homeowner in exchange for a building permit, the demand must have a meaningful connection (or "nexus") to ameliorating some public problem arising from the development.[93] In that case, the California Coastal Commission told the Nollan family that if they wanted a building permit, they would first have to sign over an easement allowing the general public to walk across their yard to a beach. The commission claimed that the Nollans' new home would block the view of the ocean from the highway and that this would create a "psychological barrier" between the general public and the sea.[94] But as the Court noted, the easement that the commission demanded bore no relationship to this "barrier": "It is quite impossible to understand how a requirement that people already on the public beaches be able to walk across the Nollans' property reduces any obstacles to viewing the beach created by the new house."[95] The absence of a connection between the effect of the construction and the demand the government made on them showed that the commission was actually using its regulatory power as a lever to force the Nollans to give up something the commission wanted, unrelated to government's legitimate regulatory powers.[96] The Court used an analogy to explain the commission's abuses: If government were to prohibit yelling "fire!" in a crowded theater, such a law would doubtless be a constitutional exercise of police powers. But if the government sold permits *allowing* people to shout "fire!" if they paid the government $100, the otherwise legitimate rule would be perverted into a money-making scheme that violated the Constitution's prohibition on taking property without compensation.[97]

Despite the *Nollan* decision, local governments continue to abuse their power by demanding payments from property owners in exchange for the permission to exercise the rights of ownership.[98] In one case, a San Francisco hotel was forced to pay the government more than $500,000 for permission to offer its rooms to the general public instead of serving as a long-term residential hotel. The California Supreme Court declared that the hotel was not entitled to compensation even though, as Justice Janice Rogers Brown explained in her dissent, the government was basically seizing the hotel and selling it back to the owners at extortionate rates.[99] A more extreme case occurred in New York a year after the Supreme Court's infamous *Kelo* eminent domain decision. Property owner Bart Didden owned land that he intended to lease to CVS to operate a pharmacy,[100] but city officials wanted to develop the neighborhood, so they decided to condemn it, *Kelo*-style, and transfer it to a private developer. Although the developer planned to lease the land to a Walgreen's pharmacy instead of CVS, he approached Didden with a deal: If Didden would agree to pay him more than $800,000, he would not move to have the property condemned. Didden indignantly refused, and the next day the city seized his land. Federal courts refused to hear the case.[101]

Probably most disturbing of all is the case of Craig and Robin Griswold, two Southern California property owners who were told that if they wanted a building permit, they would have to relinquish their *constitutionally protected right to vote*. Article XIIID of the California Constitution guarantees homeowners the right to vote on whether their property should be "assessed" fees for local improvements, such as street lights and sidewalks. Without holding an election, the government may not impose an assessment. But the

Griswolds' hometown of Carlsbad enacted an ordinance requiring property owners who apply for building permits and whose construction projects the city estimates to cost above a certain amount to either pay an assessment fee up front—nearly $115,000 in the Griswolds' case—or sign a waiver giving up the right to vote on assessments. What's more, the waiver runs with the land and will bind anyone to whom the Griswolds might sell their land. Although the Griswolds filed a lawsuit against the city, it was dismissed on technical grounds and is currently on appeal.[102] When asked why the city would do this, the city attorney told reporters that the Griswolds were wrong to think their rights had been violated: "In this state," he said, "development is a privilege."[103]

The Future of Regulatory Takings Law

In the 1980s and early 1990s, there was hope among some property rights activists that the Supreme Court under Chief Justice William Rehnquist would be more sympathetic to the rights of exploited property owners. Initially, some of the Court's decisions, including *Nollan*, substantiated that hope, but by 2005, when Chief Justice Rehnquist was succeeded by Chief Justice John Roberts, it was clear that the revival had not come. Indeed, in the last years of Rehnquist's life, the Court turned away from even the minor advances it had made in protecting the rights of property owners. Most obvious were the *Kelo* and *Tahoe-Sierra* cases, which ignored constitutional restrictions on government's power to confiscate private property. But the Court also seemed to limit the *Nollan* case when it decided that property owners could not challenge the constitutionality of land-use restrictions on the ground that they failed to "substantially advance" the government's asserted goals. Instead, the justices said, this argument could only be advanced under the Constitution's due process clause—meaning that courts would apply the flaccid "rational basis" test when evaluating those restrictions.[104] In another case, the Court reinforced a procedural technicality that generally bars property owners from asking federal judges to hear their cases—a rule that only applies to property owners and generally leaves them no realistic chance of obtaining compensation for their injuries.[105] The supposedly far-right Rehnquist Court actually accomplished little in the way of enforcing the Constitution's protections for property rights.[106]

It remains to be seen whether the Roberts Court will be more sympathetic to Americans who own private property and want to build on it. So far, the Roberts Court has decided few property rights cases, and those have gone badly for owners. In a 2007 decision, the Court refused to allow a Wyoming rancher to sue the government when it engaged in a years-long campaign of harassment against him in an attempt to coerce him into giving up his land for free.[107] And a case regarding whether the federal government has power under the Clean Water Act (which allows government to regulate the pollution of "navigable waters") to control the use of land miles away from the nearest navigable waterway ended in a confusing split decision that left citizens with little guidance as to what federal officials can and cannot regulate.[108] Given the fact that Roberts represented the government in the 2002 *Tahoe-Sierra* case, and given his pledge to Congress during his confirmation hearings that he would operate with "judicial modesty" (meaning he would not disturb the Court's expansive and misguided interpretations of federal power[109]), it seems unlikely that the near future holds much hope for property owners.[110]

13. The Future of Economic Liberty

Constitutional protections for economic liberty suffered a severe blow in the 1930s when the U.S. Supreme Court essentially stopped paying serious attention to such matters. Instead, the justices relegated the freedom of contract, property rights, and other economic rights to the realm of "rational basis scrutiny" where elected legislatures and unelected administrative agencies are given virtually free rein. Legal historians have sometimes argued that this sudden reversal of constitutional precedent came in reaction to President Roosevelt's 1937 plan to "pack the Court" with sympathetic new justices who would support his New Deal programs. These historians have pointed in particular to four decisions in 1937 and 1938—*Helvering v. Davis*,[1] *NLRB v. Jones & Laughlin Steel Corp.*,[2] *West Coast Hotel Co. v. Parrish*,[3] and *United States v. Carolene Products Co.*[4]—as signaling the advent of the New Deal regime under which we still live today. By caving in to Roosevelt's threats, the Court managed to evade the plan to add more justices—leading to the quip that the justices' sudden reversal was the "switch in time that saved nine."[5] This is an exaggeration, but it contains a basic truth.

It is an overstatement because the court-packing plan had little chance of succeeding, but also because the foundations for the New Deal's jurisprudential revolution were laid decades before by the Progressive intellectuals: social scientists, philosophers, lawyers, and judges who rejected the individualistic natural rights foundations of the Constitution and its protections for economic liberty. In place of these foundations, the Progressives substituted a collectivist political philosophy that reinterpreted rights as permissions and elevated "democracy" over liberty as a constitutional value. By "democracy," the Progressives did not necessarily mean majority rule or the American political tradition of government by consent; they meant public decisionmaking, often by allegedly expert administrative agencies that would impose scientific plans for the organization of society instead of the supposedly chaotic and haphazard mechanisms of the free market. It took many years of test cases, dissenting opinions, and debates in legal periodicals before the courts began embracing Progressive theories. The culmination of Progressivism began in a series of decisions in the mid-1930s, most notably *Nebbia v. New York*[6] and *Home Building & Loan Assoc. v. Blaisdell*,[7] three years before the Court-packing plan was unveiled. The cases that invalidated such New Deal programs as the Agricultural Adjustment Act[8] and the National Industrial Recovery Act[9] were significant but only temporary setbacks for Progressives. The 1937 and 1938 cases finally set the course for the rest of 20th-century jurisprudence by eviscerating the constitutional scheme of enumerated powers and splitting the Bill of Rights into "fundamental" rights and "nonfundamental" rights.

Thus, while the "switch in time" is a myth, it is nevertheless true that the overthrowing of constitutional protections for economic liberty was sudden by legal standards. Within a decade, the Court abandoned the principles of classical liberalism and officially embraced the doctrines of Progressivism. Cass Sunstein, an enthusiastic defender of the New Deal legacy, acknowledges that these cases "altered the constitutional system in ways so fundamental as to suggest that something akin to a constitutional amendment had taken place."[10] Yet this alteration did not include any actual constitutional amendment, and it occurred mostly within the elite circles of intellectuals whose utopian theories have been largely discredited since then.[11] Nevertheless, the New Deal revolution was in line with worldwide intellectual trends at the time. In the early 20th century, and especially the 1930s, countries in Europe and North America were abandoning classical liberal doctrines in favor of authoritarian and collectivist theories of politics and economics. European governments embraced—and social scientists applauded—fascism, communism, and allied ideologies, and similar if less extreme effects were felt in Canada and the United States. In 1934, Yale professor Francis W. Coker concluded that the philosophical debate was over, and freedom of economic choice had lost: "[T]he American courts have enunciated a broad and positive collectivist doctrine" affirming government regulation, he noted,[12] and there was "no important economic group that now holds in practice to any anti-interventionist conception of the proper sphere of state activity in the economic field."[13] An admirer of the Roosevelt administration's "rapid advances in collectivism,"[14]

Coker predicted that if its economic and social controls "work passably well in the emergency [of the Great Depression], they will in many particulars became [*sic*] permanent parts of governmental policy."[15] His prophecy proved correct. "[I]n this day and age," wrote law professor Gary Lawson 60 years later, "discussing the doctrine of enumerated powers is like discussing the redemption of Imperial Chinese bonds. There is now virtually no significant aspect of life that is not in some way regulated by the federal government."[16]

The legacy of this intellectual shift, both in America and in European democracies, has left some interesting consequences in its wake. In his thorough history of the decline of freedom of contract in English law, Professor P. S. Atiyah noted a "strange paradox" that is equally present in contemporary American law.[17] During the 19th century, he explained, "a close association was perceived between the role of the individual in the political sphere and his role as a consumer in the economic sphere."[18] In both realms, individuals were believed to be sovereign, having the same sorts of rights to make their own choices and the same obligations to live up to their responsibilities. Freedoms of speech and press, private property rights, and the right to earn a living in a gainful trade were seen as essentially equal kinds of claims to individual autonomy. But beginning with the rise of collectivist theories at the opening of the 19th century, "the sovereignty of the consumer in the economic sphere" was "almost entirely eroded." Today, individuals are presumed to be competent to vote on important matters of public policy and are even courted by politicians who seek to provide the public with virtually any policy that voters demand. Yet the opposite attitude prevails in economic matters, where political leaders view people as incapable of making responsible decisions on their own. "Few people accept that the public as consumers (rather than as voters) know their own interests best, and can, therefore, be safely left to judge (for example) of the quality of the products offered them for sale."[19] In short, economic freedom is perceived as a dangerous threat, while the right to political participation is seen as a fundamental right of all mature adults. When the two come into conflict, as they often do, courts take pains to protect participatory rights, often ignoring the right to make economic choices. Sometimes, they even denigrate such freedom. Collective decisions are seen as the source, validation, and limit of individual rights.

Americans have not adopted this view consistently—certain "fundamental" rights are still protected by courts, even though they are not related to political activity. These are the so-called privacy rights. The right to make personal sexual choices, for instance, is strongly protected under such court decisions as *Lawrence v. Texas*,[20] even though it does not contribute to "democratic participation." This category of rights is protected, as Justice Harry Blackmun once wrote, because "they form so central a part of an individual's life," and because "a person belongs to himself and not others nor to society as a whole."[21] Ironically, this is the language of natural rights, which most of today's lawyers and judges have repudiated, and which ought also to include the freedom to make economic choices.[22] Certainly, if the Constitution protects rights that are so central to individual life, and if individuals belong to themselves and not to others, there is no sense in disparaging their right to buy and sell property, or to work for or run a business. Judges who have supported privacy rights, but not property rights or economic freedom, have struggled to formulate some justification for this difference in treatment, but have failed. In fact, their attempts have only led to more confusion.

The controversial case of *Griswold v. Connecticut*[23] demonstrates the perverse results of this "double standard" in constitutional rights. In that case, Justice William O. Douglas, a Roosevelt appointee and lifelong defender of the New Deal legacy, struck down a state law that prohibited doctors from advising married couples about contraceptives. Although the Constitution does not explicitly declare that married couples have the right to use contraceptives, Douglas found that this right was constitutionally protected because "specific guarantees in the Bill of Rights have penumbras, formed by emanations from those guarantees that help give them life and substance."[24] When viewed together, the Third, Fourth, Fifth, and Ninth Amendments, which refer to rights of security in the home or to unenumerated rights "retained by the people," create in Douglas's words "a zone of privacy which government may not force [a person] to surrender to his detriment."[25]

Douglas's notion of emanations and penumbras has been ridiculed and parodied many times, but it represented a clumsy attempt to provide constitutional protection for rights he held dear and that did not relate to political participation, while clinging to the Progressive notion that rights are nothing more than permissions government may grant or withhold for the betterment of society. The reason this effort was unconvincing is that privacy and economic freedom involve the same basic principle: the right of an individual to choose for himself how to pursue happiness while respecting the rights of others to do the same. Douglas's contorted vocabulary was the consequence of trying to embrace one and push away the other when the two are logically inextricable. Since *Griswold*, even more embarrassments and paradoxes have arisen from judicial attempts to explain why some rights are fundamental privacy rights—even when they lack traditional standing in American legal history—but others are "nonfundamental," economic matters that government can control almost at will. As Justice Thomas pointed out in the *Kelo* case, courts now hold the privacy of acts in the home to be sacrosanct—but impose almost no restrictions on the government's efforts to seize the home itself.

At bottom, the difference in treatment between some rights and others is rooted not in principle or consistency but in power. As Michael McGerr notes in his history of Progressivism, the advocates of the New Deal and Great Society programs "knew, better than the old progressives, how much the people were eager for Washington to help ensure their prosperity." Post–New Deal political and judicial leaders believed that government should "make sure Americans could afford pleasure, and then get out of the way."[26] Government relies on the denigration of economic liberty to perpetuate its redistributive programs. Unfortunately, property owners and business owners have largely failed to stand up for their rights.

Thanks to the New Deal revolution, any discussion of economic liberty and the law tends to involve a long discussion of legal history. Bernard Siegan's pioneering book, *Economic Liberties and the Constitution*, and his subsequent works, such as *Property Rights from Magna Carta to the Fourteenth Amendment*, were largely investigations into nearly forgotten precedents protecting these rights. This use of the historical perspective is necessary because much of the Progressive revolution was devoted to obscuring or rewriting legal history. In the 1930s, writers like Irving Brant,[27] Dean Alfange,[28] Alphaeus Thomas Mason,[29] and others crafted an interpretation of the Constitution that ignored legal protections for property and economic liberty. Brant, for example, wrote a hysterical polemic in 1937 entitled *Storm over the Constitution*, with an introduction by Vice President Henry A. Wallace, arguing that the New Deal was compatible with the intentions of the Constitution's authors and that in those rare cases when the two conflicted, historical necessity overrode the Constitution's language. "By every definition that can be found in the records of the Federal Convention," Brant wrote, "the implications of national power in our Constitution are broad enough for national necessity. . . . The power is in the Constitution. The framers put it there, and when we deny its existence, we deny their work."[30] Thus, opponents of the New Deal who complained that the government was violating basic constitutional principles were really just "avoid[ing] living issues."[31] The Framers "intended the powers of the federal government to be broad enough to achieve the purposes stated in the preamble,"[32] and Supreme Court decisions striking down New Deal programs were simply the work of reactionaries opposed to the progress of "economic democracy."

Brant and other Progressives managed to persuade important legal thinkers either that constitutional protections for economic liberty were modern usurpations by judges beholden to the capitalist class or that such protections had been superseded by the imperatives of modern society. Their success has never been undone, and today, prominent historians still contend that the right to earn a living is not a legitimate constitutional right at all. Paul Kens, for example, claims that Stephen Field's dissent in the 1873 *Slaughterhouse Cases* "invented a new right. Nowhere does the Constitution expressly guarantee a right to engage in a trade or profession."[33] Kens ignores the legal history, well known to lawyers of Field's day, that secured this right as far back as the 17th-century *Case of the Monopolies*.[34] And while the Constitution may not include the words "right to earn a living," many other rights that are not "expressly" guaranteed in the Constitution are universally recognized as part of the "liberty" protected by the Fifth and Fourteenth Amendments. Be that as it may, scholars like Siegan have demonstrated that few rights are as firmly situated in American history as the right to earn a living without unreasonable interference by government. Since the Supreme Court has explained that the "liberty" protected by the Constitution includes rights "deeply rooted in this Nation's history and tradition,"[35] there can be little serious dispute that economic freedom, including the right to engage in a trade or a profession, is a constitutional right.

Much progress has been made recently in vindicating this history. Although the Progressive consensus against *Lochner* prevailed virtually unchallenged for more than 75 years, until it was first questioned publicly by William Letwin in 1979[36] and Siegan in 1980,[37] a new generation of academics has reevaluated this understanding in the years since. David E. Bernstein—the nation's leading authority on the case—observes that "[s]cholars from across the political spectrum increasingly argue that in completely abandoning *Lochner*, the Court has left important economic rights vulnerable to government overreaching."[38] Prominent academics are challenging the consensus view and arguing that, as a matter of both history and legal and political philosophy, protections for economic freedom are essential to the American constitutional order. And organizations like the Pacific Legal Foundation and the Institute for Justice have brought legal challenges setting important new precedents in defense of economic liberty. Meanwhile, scholars in the law and economics movement have made dramatic advances in articulating a scholarly defense of free-market economics and the legal institutions that foster economic freedom.[39]

But defenders of the right to earn a living must not be lulled into thinking of themselves as devotees of the past, or as advocates for a "return" to some historical idyll. The fact is that economic liberty has never been thoroughly and consistently protected in American law. During the 19th century, minority groups and women were almost entirely deprived of economic freedom. Bribed legislators gave monopolies to favored businesses and steered government contracts to their friends. The government routinely granted subsidies and favors to "private" enterprises through direct grants and shady secret deals and by allowing them certain government powers, such as the power of eminent domain. Simply put, there was never any "golden age" of economic freedom in American history. In some ways, entrepreneurs and companies were freer in the past, but in other ways, they were much more restricted. Defenders of limited government do themselves a profound disservice, therefore, when they describe themselves as advocating a return to an older understanding of the Constitution. Like other constitutionally protected freedoms, economic liberty is not backward looking, and its defenders are not demanding to "turn back the clock." They are seeking a promise that was never fully honored by American law. To paraphrase philosopher Ayn Rand, defenders of economic freedom are not seeking to restore freedom, but to discover it.

An immigrant living in Florida who seeks to open a taxi company but finds his opportunity stifled by unresponsive bureaucrats and intrusive regulations that benefit only established taxi companies is not looking to the past or longing for some golden age. He is looking forward to the American dream—a dream pursued but never fully implemented by America's Founders or by the generations that followed. He is looking for the right to pursue happiness. In our age, that right is more widely available to a broader class of people—men and women of more races and conditions—than ever before. Yet in many ways, it is still obstructed by outdated bureaucratic machinery that was put in place in the time of our grandparents. The regulation of taxicabs, like the rational basis test itself, is the rusty relic of an age when American intellectuals thought economic freedom had proved itself unworkable and the shining future would be centrally planned and bureaucratically controlled. Subsequent decades have vindicated the freedom of choice: the fall of communism, the enormous expansion of free markets in the post–World War II era, the undreamed-of possibilities of the information age, of Internet commerce, and globalization have proved them wrong. Yet the fossils of the regulatory state remain in place, thwarting the dreams of those who want only to earn an honest living without unreasonable government interference.

The future of economic liberty will depend in part on a reevaluation of inherited prejudices about *Lochner* and similar cases.[40] For one thing, it will require lawyers, judges, and academics to reject the antiquated assumption that judicial protections for economic freedom benefit only greedy corporate interests at the expense of workers and the underprivileged. In fact, "big business" has rarely been fond of the free market. It is the *innovator* who seeks economic freedom—the person with a new idea. Whether it be the pest control technician who wants to try a new method for preventing pigeons from landing on buildings, or the hair braider who wants to open a new shop to do hairstyles that consumers had never seen before, it is the newcomer who seeks economic freedom. And it is often the old, established businesses that want to be protected against new competition. Picturing the revival of economic liberty as a return to the past means getting the truth entirely backward. It is the *future* that needs freedom.

Implementing constitutional protections for economic freedom will require a reevaluation of the relative positions of democracy and liberty in the American constitutional order. This will be difficult for some, but it is already starting. Prominent liberal lawyers like Professor Laurence Tribe,[41] former Clinton administration solicitor general Walter Dellinger,[42] and former American Civil Liberties Union president Nadine Strossen[43] have joined libertarian writers like Richard A. Epstein,[44] Randy E. Barnett,[45] and Clint Bolick[46] in arguing that the right to economic freedom deserves respect and judicial protection, just as do freedom of speech, freedom of the press, or freedom of religion.

One area in which change can already be detected is in the reevaluation of the *Slaughterhouse Cases*. There, the Supreme Court declared that the Fourteenth Amendment's privileges or immunities clause only protects a narrowly defined class of rights that owe their existence to the federal government—a class that did not include the right to work in a common occupation. There is a strong consensus among legal academics that the decision was wrong and that, whatever else might be said about the privileges or immunities clause, it was intended to provide a far broader scope of protection than the *Slaughterhouse* Court recognized.[47] Liberal law professor Akhil Amar contends that the Supreme Court, by "strangling the privileges-or-immunities clause in its crib," delayed the implementation of important civil rights milestones,[48] and the conservative dean of Chapman University Law School, John C. Eastman, agrees, writing that *Slaughterhouse* was "flatly inconsistent with the original understanding of the Privileges or Immunities Clause."[49]

The academic rejection of *Slaughterhouse* has become so strong that the Supreme Court has also indicated a willingness to reconsider the decision. In *Saenz v. Roe*,[50] for almost the first time in 125 years, the Court held a state law unconstitutional for violating the Fourteenth Amendment's privileges or immunities clause.[51] "Legal scholars agree on little beyond the conclusion that the clause does not mean what the Court said it meant in 1873," wrote Justice Clarence Thomas in a separate opinion.[52] The Court's decision did not address specifically what sorts of rights are protected by the clause, merely observing that there are "fundamentally differing views" about what it covers.[53] Nor did the decision discuss whether or to what degree the clause protects economic liberty. But the Court's willingness to cite it at all signaled its potential for protecting individual rights. Justice Clarence Thomas has shown particular interest in such arguments, indicating in at least one other case that he believes the clause ought to protect far more rights than the Court has been willing to acknowledge.[54] This is hardly surprising, as Thomas published an important law review article about the clause years before being appointed to the federal bench.[55]

Some defenders of economic liberty look to the overruling of *Slaughterhouse* as the only realistic chance of reinvigorating constitutional protections for economic freedom, given the disdain with which *Lochner* and similar cases are still viewed by most lawyers, judges, and law professors.[56] This option is viable given that the Supreme Court has since abandoned the view expressed in *Slaughterhouse* that the right to earn a living is not a federally protected right. It and other federal courts have acknowledged, albeit rarely, that the right is protected by the federal Constitution.[57] Thus, there is no legal reason why, even without overruling *Slaughterhouse*, the clause would not protect economic freedom against state interference.

But there are two political reasons why a revival of the privileges or immunities clause might still be a long way off. First, many defenders of the modern regulatory welfare state, perhaps the largest single obstacle to economic freedom, have shown a willingness to preserve the New Deal legacy at virtually any cost. In many instances, this had led to contorted legal arguments or even to the outright ignoring of the Constitution's language. Professor Bruce Ackerman has even devised an argument that the New Deal era worked a kind of invisible constitutional amendment that legitimizes government programs that lack any actual footing in the Constitution's text and history.[58] Others reveal an even more explicitly result-oriented approach. David Skillen Bogen, author of *Privileges and Immunities: A Reference Guide to the United States Constitution*, warns that the reversal of *Slaughterhouse* "threatens . . . to bring back the infamous *Lochner* decision," and therefore that courts should hesitate to enforce the privileges or immunities clause.[59] And Michael Kent Curtis, perhaps the nation's leading authority on the history of the clause, wrote a law review article of more than 100 pages trying to devise an argument for overturning *Slaughterhouse* without reviving serious protections for economic freedom.[60]

Such arguments cannot escape the fact that, as Randy E. Barnett has put it, "the privileges or immunities protected from abridgement by the Fourteenth Amendment . . . included the 'right . . . to make and enforce contracts'—the very right protected by the Court in *Lochner v. New York*."[61] Nevertheless, they demonstrate that the legal academy and almost all political leaders in the United States are willing to indulge even questionable theories to support the continued viability of the government apparatus that routinely intrudes on economic freedom. As Professor Gary Lawson concludes, "[E]ssential features of the modern administrative state have, for more than half a century, been taken as unchallengeable postulates by virtually all players in the legal and political worlds," and there is "no reasonable prospect that this circumstance will significantly improve in the foreseeable future."[62] Judges committed to preserving the modern regulatory state at all costs, and armed with the powerful tool of rational basis scrutiny, can find easy opportunities for quashing appeals for economic freedom. The decision in *Powers v. Harris*,[63] in which the Tenth Circuit Court of Appeals declared economic protectionism alone to be a legitimate state interest under the Fourteenth Amendment, is the most extreme example of this kind of thinking. Because "adopting a rule against the legitimacy of intrastate economic protectionism and applying it in a principled manner would have wide-ranging consequences," the court simply rejected the proposition that economic regulations should actually advance some general public good.[64]

Defenders of economic liberty therefore face an extremely difficult battle in a field that is more uneven than any other *ever* faced in the history of American law. Even at the lowest point of the days of slavery, some American courts were willing to declare slavery unconstitutional.[65] And even in the era of Jim Crow, many legal academics and leading judges considered segregation unconstitutional and were willing to take steps to end it. But while more legal scholars are open to viewing *Lochner* favorably and to questioning the viability of *Slaughterhouse* and New Deal–era precedents, they remain a minority in the academy, and virtually no federal judge is willing to challenge the Progressive consensus openly. Moreover, the consuming disfavor with which economic freedom is treated today in both the legal academy and the judiciary is supported by entrenched economic interests that have grown up around various institutions that depend on violations of economic freedom, institutions that will fight hard to retain their legal privileges and monopolies. As public choice theory suggests, organized professions that for

70 years have enjoyed the power to eliminate competition through licensing, zoning, and other laws will spare little effort in defending their turf. When Senator Joseph Biden demanded at a confirmation hearing to know whether Supreme Court nominee Clarence Thomas believed in the theories advanced in Richard A. Epstein's book *Takings*, the message was clear: powerful interests will do whatever they can to perpetuate the Progressive apparatus of restrictions on economic liberty.[66]

Aside from this overwhelming bias against economic freedom, there is the allied effort by some academics to overturn *Slaughterhouse* in a way that will actually *increase* restrictions on economic freedom. Lawyers like Erwin Chemerinsky, Charles Black, Peter Edelman, and Frank Michelman have argued that the privileges or immunities clause ought to be revived, not to protect the right to earn a living but to provide a constitutional basis for welfare payments.[67] In brief, they argue that among the "privileges or immunities" of citizens is the right to receive the money earned by others and taken from them by force. It need hardly be said that the advent of a constitutional right to welfare would work an enormous change on the American nation. Such a right is fundamentally incompatible with the freedoms guaranteed in the Constitution—particularly economic liberty and property rights—since a right to such payments would mean that some people are entitled *by right* to the earnings of others.[68] A right to welfare would lead government beyond the "negative rights" conception that underlies the Bill of Rights—a conception called "negative" because it requires people only to refrain from interfering with one another's expression or religion or property—and into the realm of "positive rights," where one person may demand certain goods and services from another. If person A has a right to the wealth created by person B, that means he may coerce B by taking from him the fruits of his labor or even forcing him to work against his will. As philosopher Robert Nozick observed, the theory of "distributive justice" underlying the modern welfare state "involve[s] appropriating the actions of other persons. Seizing the results of someone's labor is equivalent to seizing hours from him and directing him to carry on various activities. . . . This process . . . makes them a *part*-owner of you; it gives them a property right in you. . . . These principles involve a shift from the classical liberals' notion of self-ownership to a notion of (partial) property rights in *other* people."[69] Indeed, not long ago the Canadian government even considered *forcing* doctors to work in certain "underserved" areas in order to provide citizens with a "right" to health care.[70] Needless to say, the advent of a constitutional right of some Americans to the wealth earned by others—and thus, a legally enforced power to override the economic choices of others—would contradict the fundamental right to the pursuit of happiness.[71] As Thomas Jefferson wrote almost two centuries ago, "To take from one, because it is thought his own industry and that of his fathers has acquired too much, in order to spare to others, who, or whose fathers have not, exercised equal industry and skill, is to violate arbitrarily the first principle of association, the guarantee to everyone the exercise of his industry and the fruits acquired by it."[72]

To be sure, government by statute already routinely takes money from some and transfers it to others, but it is precisely the fact that such transfers infringe on the rights of productive workers that raises moral and political objections to those programs. What is more, transforming welfare from charity into a constitutional right would make it extraordinarily difficult to implement changes like the Clinton administration's successful welfare reforms and would radically alter the nature of constitutional liberty. It would also likely lead to an exodus of productive enterprises from the United States— a "brain drain" similar to that already experienced in Canada and other countries where socialized medicine has driven doctors to leave for countries where their freedoms are more respected.[73]

Disturbing as the prospect is, there is a colorable legal argument for some form of a constitutional right to welfare. A clause in the Articles of Confederation required the states to respect the privileges and immunities of citizens, "paupers, vagabonds, and fugitives from justice excepted."[74] The fact that this phrase was eliminated by the Constitutional Convention in 1787, and by the Fourteenth Amendment Congress in 1868, leads advocates of a constitutional right to welfare to argue that the amendment lacking that clause should be read to require the provision of "food, shelter, and medical care" to all "paupers" or others the state regards as needy.[75] This threat has led some otherwise sympathetic scholars to view the possibility of a revived privileges or immunities clause with skepticism—what John Eastman calls the "Justice Brennan Problem." Many conservatives and libertarians, he writes, "are not willing to give any credence to

291

a natural rights jurisprudence" because it might "become the departure point for Justice Brennan's, or now Justice Stevens's, liberalism—a liberalism that purports to be grounded in natural rights but actually ignores the tenets of such rights."[76]

Thus, it is understandable that conservatives and libertarians might hesitate to join in seeking to revive the privileges or immunities clause. Yet that hesitation is ultimately unjustified. After all, those who believe the Constitution should guarantee welfare rights will pursue that goal regardless of whether or not free-market advocates promote a restoration of the privileges or immunities clause; already they have made significant advances in that direction under the due process clause and other constitutional provisions.[77] For defenders of economic liberty to avoid using the privileges or immunities clause as it was intended out of fear that others might *mis*-use it would do little to forestall the movement for the constitutionalization of welfare, but it would abandon an important and legitimate tool that might do much good in protecting economic freedom. History always moves forward; the question is what can be accomplished in the interim.

In the end, the cause of economic liberty—of the American dream itself—will prevail only if its advocates are willing to take the time not only to litigate in courts but also to educate their fellow citizens. The Progressive movement was enormously successful in inculcating what was then a new principle in American culture: the notion that one person has a right to control how another person uses his property or freedom. The elevation of collective decisionmaking over the right to make one's own choices—of "democracy" over liberty—took many decades. But once the Progressives prevailed, they taught their principles to a new generation of Americans, and that generation taught their children, and so on to the present day. Thus, many American adults no longer understand the basic economic and moral foundations of the free market. Moreover, most lawyers and judges do not know the history of the Progressive legal theories that they were taught in law school. Many have never even considered the issue, and given the habitual conservatism of the law, it is especially hard for them to understand why economic freedom might deserve greater protection than it currently receives. To them, the legacy of the New Deal is a palimpsest: simply the background that they take for granted. The idea that economic freedom would be protected by the Constitution in the same way that it protects rights of religious freedom or privacy strikes many of them as bizarre. Thus, in the end, it is only cultural and social change that can revive the freedom of economic choice. Only when Americans, and particularly the legal elite, come to recognize the fundamental importance of that liberty and the unfairness of laws that limit it, will the nation be prepared to extend full protection to the fundamental human right to earn a living.

Notes

Preface

1. Although the Institute ended up not taking the case, it was litigated. The taxi drivers lost. *Restrepo v. Miami-Dade County*, 2002 WL 548821 (S.D. Fla. 2002). See also *South Florida Taxicab Ass'n v. Miami-Dade County*, 2004 WL 958073 (S.D. Fla. 2004).

2. Rick Bragg, "For Black Taxi Company in Miami, a County Law Is the Latest Threat," *New York Times*, June 8, 1999, p. A20.

3. Steven Oxenhandler, "Taxicab Licenses: In Search of a Fifth Amendment, Compensable Property Interest," *Transportation Law Journal* 27 (2000): 113–58.

4. Carol Marbin Miller, "Taken for a Ride? Taxi Drivers Renew Fight over Ordinance They Say Favors Cab Owners," *Broward Daily Business Review*, March 30, 2000, p. 1.

5. *Restrepo*, 2002 WL 548821 at *1.

6. Francis X. Gilpin, "Taxi Stand," *Sarasota Weekly Planet*, January 10, 2002, http://tampa.creativeloafing.com/gyrobase/Content?oid=oid%3A1315; and Rebecca Wakefield, "Calling All Cabbies: Battered by a Corrupt Industry, Miami's Independent Taxi Drivers Consider Unionizing," *Miami New Times*, October 25, 2000, http://www.miaminewtimes.com/2001-10-25/news/calling-all-cabbies/.

7. Greg Bensinger, "Taxi Medallions Fetch a Record $600,000 Each," *New York Sun*, May 30, 2007, http://www.nysun.com/article/55479.

8. John Kreiser, "Crabby Cabbie: A New York Original," CBS News Assignment America, June 23, 2006, http://www.cbsnews.com/stories/2006/05/12/assignment_america/main1616300.shtml; and "Ray Kottner's Free Taxi Locked Up," UPI, July 21, 2007, http://www.upi.com/NewsTrack/Quirks/2007/07/21/ray_kottners_free_taxi_locked_up/2092/.

9. Walter E. Williams, *The State against Blacks* (New York: New Press, 1982), pp. 86–87.

10. "County Relaxes the Rules for Inner-City Cab Service," *South Florida Sun-Sentinel*, June 27, 1999, p. B9.

11. Bill Varian, "Limo Owner's Cut Rates Imperil His Business," *St. Petersburg Times*, October 8, 2003, p. B1.

12. Gregory Cox, Hillsborough County Transportation Commission, letter to Hilary Black, August 11, 2003 (on file with author).

13. James Chan, *Spare Room Tycoon* (London: Nicholas Brealey Publishing, 2000).

14. See, for example, *Jones v. Temmer*, 829 F. Supp. 1226 (D. Colo. 1993), *vacated as moot*, 57 F.3d 921 (10th Cir. 1995).

15. Kenneth L. Karst, *Belonging to America: Equal Citizenship and the Constitution* (New Haven, CT: Yale University Press, 1989), p. 179.

16. See, for example, *FCC v. Beach Communications, Inc.*, 508 U.S. 307, 315 (1993) (It is "entirely irrelevant whether the conceived reason for the challenged [law] actually motivated the legislature," or whether it had any genuine facts to support its action).

17. *West Virginia State Board of Education v. Barnette*, 319 U.S. 624, 638 (1943).

18. *Washington v. Seattle School Dist. No. 1*, 458 U.S. 457, 486 (1982) (quoting *San Antonio Independent School Dist. v. Rodriguez*, 411 U.S. 1, 28 [1973]).

19. *Lochner v. New York*, 198 U.S. 45 (1905).

Chapter 1

1. See, for example, Ayn Rand, *Atlas Shrugged* (New York: Random House, 1957); Ayn Rand, *Capitalism: The Unknown Ideal* (New York: Signet, 1967); Robert Nozick, *Anarchy, State and Utopia* (Cambridge, MA: Harvard University Press, 1974), chap. 7; David Boaz, *Libertarianism: A Primer* (New York: Free Press, 1997), pp. 80–82; Tibor R. Machan and James E. Chesher, *A Primer on Business Ethics* (Lanham, MD: Rowman & Littlefield, 2003); Tibor Machan, *The Passion for Liberty* (Lanham, MD: Rowman & Littlefield, 2003), chap. 3; and Tara Smith, "Money *Can* Buy Happiness," *Reason Papers* 26 (2003): 7–19. See also Anthony de Jasay, *Choice, Contract, Consent: A Restatement of Liberalism* (London: Institute of Economic Affairs, 1991), pp. 93–103.

2. *Meyer v. Nebraska*, 262 U.S. 390, 399 (1923). See also *Yu Cong Eng v. Trinidad*, 271 U.S. 500, 526–27 (1926); *Nebbia v. People of New York*, 291 U.S. 502, 547 (1934) (McReynolds, J., dissenting); *Senn v. Tile Layers Protective Union, Local No. 5*, 301 U.S. 468, 487 (1937) (Butler, J., dissenting); *Board of Regents of State Colleges v. Roth*, 408 U.S. 564, 572 (1972); and *Roe v. Wade*, 410 U.S. 179, 214 (1973) (Douglas, J., concurring).

3. *City of Memphis v. Winfield*, 27 Tenn. (8 Hum.) 707 (1848). Winfield's lawyer was the prominent attorney E. M. Yerger, who years later would move to Mississippi and end up as a publisher and editor of the *Jackson News*. At the end of the Civil War, Yerger fatally stabbed Union Colonel Jasper Crane, who was in command of the occupying forces of Jackson. Convicted by a military tribunal, Yerger would appeal to the U.S. Supreme Court to challenge the constitutionality of such tribunals in *Ex parte Yerger*, 75 U.S. (8 Wall.) 85 (1868). See John W. Green, "Four Attorneys-General and Reporters," *Tennessee Law Review* 19 (1947): 3; and James Wilford Garner, *Reconstruction in Mississippi* (New York: Macmillan, 1901), pp. 170–71.

4. Turley (1800–1851) joined the state supreme court at the age of 35. Highly educated and a quick thinker, he was said to sometimes make up his mind so quickly that he would walk out of conferences and leave his colleagues to discuss the case among themselves. "Precedents with him had no weight, unless supported by reason. It was not his habit to base his decisions on former cases, but to argue out the proposition from original premises, citing precedents only to illustrate his conclusions." Albert D. Marks, "The Supreme Court of Tennessee Part II: Under the Constitution of 1834," *Green Bag* 5 (1893): 175. He died in a freak accident when he tripped on a street and stabbed himself with his cane. Ibid., 176.

5. *Winfield*, 27 Tenn. (8 Hum.) at 709–10.

6. *Allen v. Tooley*, 80 Eng. Rep. 1055, 1055 (K.B. 1614).

7. Frederick Douglass, *The Life and Times of Frederick Douglass*, reprinted in *Douglass: Autobiographies*, ed. Henry Louis Gates Jr. (New York: Library of America, 1994), p. 654.

8. Charles Sumner, "The Barbarism of Slavery," *Congressional Globe*, 36th Cong., 1st sess. (1860), p. 2592 (emphasis in original).

9. Abraham Lincoln, Speech at Chicago, Ill. (July 10, 1858), in *The Collected Works of Abraham Lincoln*, ed. Roy P. Basler (Camden, NJ: Rutgers University Press, 1953), vol. 2, p. 500.

10. Alexis de Tocqueville, *Democracy in America*, trans. George Lawrence and ed. J. P. Mayer (New York: Harper Perennial, 1969), pp. 345–46.

11. Civil Rights Act of 1866, 14 Stat. 27–30, codified as amended at 42 U.S.C. § 1981.

12. *Slaughterhouse Cases*, 83 U.S. (16 Wall.) 36, 109–10 (1872) (Field, J., dissenting).

13. Ibid. at 100.

14. John E. Nowak, "The 'Sixty Something' Anniversary of the Bill of Rights," *University of Illinois Law Review* 1992: 452.

15. *Barsky v. Board of Regents*, 347 U.S. 442, 472 (1954) (Douglas, J., dissenting).

16. Arthur S. Miller, "Pretense and Our Two Constitutions," *George Washington Law Review* 54 (1986): 384.

17. Peter Irons, *God on Trial* (New York: Viking, 2007), p. 17.

18. Kenneth L. Karst, *Belonging to America: Equal Citizenship and the Constitution* (New Haven, CT: Yale University Press, 1989), p. 179.

19. Robert Green McCloskey, *American Conservatism in the Age of Enterprise 1865–1910* (New York: Harper Torchbooks, 1951), pp. 84, 174.

20. I am certainly not the first to reject the consensus view on these issues. The works of Professors Bernard Siegan and David E. Bernstein are the leading sources in presenting a more balanced interpretation. See especially Bernard Siegan, *Economic Liberties and the Constitution* (Chicago: University of Chicago Press, 1980); and David E. Bernstein, "*Lochner* Era Revisionism, Revised: *Lochner* and the Origins of Fundamental Rights Constitutionalism," *Georgetown Law Journal* 92 (2003): 1–60. See also Hadley Arkes, *The Return of George Sutherland* (Princeton, NJ: Princeton University Press, 1994); G. Edward White, *The Constitution and the New Deal* (Cambridge, MA: Harvard University Press, 2000), especially chapter 8; James A. Dorn and Henry G. Manne, eds., *Economic Liberties and the Judiciary* (Fairfax, VA: George Mason University Press, 1987); and Manuel Cachán, "Justice Stephen Field and 'Free Soil, Free Labor Constitutionalism': Reconsidering Revisionism," *Law and History Review* 20 (2002): 541–76.

21. Obviously, a full vindication of these arguments would be out of place here. Good defenses of these propositions are to be found in F. A. Hayek, *Law, Legislation and Liberty*, 3 vols. (Chicago: University of Chicago Press, 1979); Ludwig von Mises, *Liberalism: The Classical Tradition* (Irvington-on-Hudson, NY: Foundation for Economic Education, 1996); Henry Hazlitt, *Economics in One Lesson* (New York: Three Rivers Press, 1979); Rand, *Capitalism: The Unknown Ideal*; Virginia Postrel, *The Future and Its Enemies* (New York: Free Press, 1998); and David Boaz, *Libertarianism: A Primer* (New York: Free Press, 1997).

22. See, for example, McCloskey, *American Conservatism*, pp. 26–30.

23. James W. Ely Jr., "Rufus Peckham and Economic Liberty," Vanderbilt Public Law Research Paper no. 08-04, http://ssrn.com/abstract=1105065.

24. Thomas C. Leonard, "Origins of the Myth of Social Darwinism: The Ambiguous Legacy of Richard Hofstadter's *Social Darwinism in American Thought*," *Journal of Economic Behavior and Organization* 71 (2009): 37–51. See also James W. Ely Jr., "Economic Due Process Revisited," *Vanderbilt Law Review* 44 (1991): 219.

25. Louis Menand, *The Metaphysical Club* (New York: Farrar, Strauss, & Giroux, 2001), p. 302. See also Bernstein, "*Lochner* Era Revisionism," 8–9.

26. The cases were *United States v. Martin*, 94 U.S. 400, 403 (1876); *Union Refrigerator Transit Co. v. Commonwealth of Kentucky*, 199 U.S. 194, 203 (1905); *German Alliance Ins. Co. v. Lewis*, 233 U.S. 389, 416 (1914); and *Pollock v. Farmers' Loan & Trust Co.*, 157 U.S. 429, 559 (1895), in which both the majority and the dissent cited Smith. See *Pollock*, 157 U.S. at 631, 640 (White, J., dissenting).

27. I use the term "justice" in its precise sense. The term has, unfortunately, often been abused in the name of "social justice," a meaningless concept. See Hayek, *Law, Legislation and Liberty*, vol. 2.

28. *Adkins v. Children's Hospital*, 261 U.S. 525 (1923).

29. *Washington v. Glucksberg*, 521 U.S. 702, 760 (1997) (Souter, J., dissenting).

30. Arkes, *The Return of George Sutherland*, p. 13. The effects of these minimum wage laws were, in fact, to increase unemployment for women. Clifford F. Thies, "The First Minimum Wage Laws," *Cato Journal* 10, no. 3 (Winter 1991): 715–46. Michael McGerr notes that the American Federation of Labor sought "[t]o shore up male wages [by] . . . favor[ing] equal pay for women. Of course, if men and women received the same wages, then men were more likely to get the jobs." McGerr, *A Fierce Discontent: The Rise and Fall of the Progressive Movement in America, 1870–1920* (New York: Free Press, 2003), p. 132.

31. *Muller v. Oregon*, 208 U.S. 421 (1908).

32. Brief of Defendant in Error, State of Oregon, *Muller v. Oregon* (1908 WL 27605), p. 11. See also David E. Bernstein, "*Lochner*'s Feminist Legacy," *Michigan Law Review* 101 (2003): 1960–86; and David P. Bryden, "Brandeis's Facts," *Constitutional Commentary* 1 (1984): 303–21.

33. Brief of Defendant, *Muller*, p. 19.

34. *Lochner v. New York*, 198 U.S. 45 (1905).

35. *Muller*, 208 U.S. at 420.

36. Ibid. at 421–22.

37. Ruth Bader Ginsburg, "Constitutional Adjudication in the United States as a Means of Advancing the Equal Statute of Men and Women under the Law," *Hofstra Law Review* 26 (1997): 269–70.

38. David E. Bernstein, "The Feminist 'Horseman,'" *Green Bag (Second Series)* 10 (2007): 380.

39. *Adkins*, 261 U.S. at 553.

40. Ibid. at 553.

41. Ibid. at 554–55.

42. James Madison, "Charters," in *Madison: Writings*, ed. Jack Rakove (New York: Library of America, 1999), p. 502.

43. *Adkins*, 261 U.S. at 546.

44. Thomas Reed Powell, "The Judiciality of Minimum Wage Legislation," *Harvard Law Review* 37 (1924): 555.

45. Ibid., 556.

46. See Timothy Sandefur, "The Wolves and the Sheep of Constitutional Law: A Review Essay of Kermit Roosevelt's *The Myth of Judicial Activism*." *Journal of Law and Politics* 23 (2007): 1–40.

47. George Anastaplo, *The Constitution of 1787: A Commentary* (Baltimore: Johns Hopkins University Press, 1989), p. 19.

48. Roscoe Pound, "Liberty of Contract," *Yale Law Journal* 18 (1909): 454.

49. Ibid., 457.

50. Ibid., 467.

51. Charles Edward Merriam, *A History of American Political Theories* (New York: Macmillan, 1903), p. 313.

52. Ibid., p. 311.

53. *Duplex Printing Press Co. v. Deering*, 254 U.S. 443, 488 (1921) (Brandeis, Holmes, and Clark, JJ., dissenting).

54. See Timothy Sandefur, "Mine and Thine Distinct: What *Kelo* Says about Our Path," *Chapman Law Review* 10 (2006): 19–26.

55. Thomas G. West, "Progressivism and the Transformation of American Government," in *The Progressive Revolution in Politics and Political Science: Transforming the American Regime*, ed. John Marini and Ken Masugi (Lanham, MD: Rowman & Littlefield, 2005), p. 16.

56. Gabriel Kolko, *The Triumph of Conservatism: A Reinterpretation of American History* (Chicago: Quadrangle Books, 1963), p. 3.

57. The classic treatments of economic decisionmaking in the economic as opposed to the political arena are the works of Ludwig von Mises and Friedrich Hayek, particularly Ludwig von Mises, *Human Action*, 4th ed. (Irvington-on-Hudson, NY: Foundation for Economic Education, 1996). A briefer version is provided in his book *Liberalism: The Classical Tradition* (Irvington-on-Hudson, NY: Foundation for Economic Education, 1996), pp. 70–75. Hayek's most famous discussion of the issue is "The Use of Knowledge in Society," *American Economic Review* 35, no. 4 (1945): 519–30.

58. Kolko's *Triumph of Conservatism* is the most thorough assessment of the Progressive legacy from this perspective.

59. *A.L.A. Schechter Poultry Corp. v. United States*, 295 U.S. 495 (1935).

60. *United States v. Carolene Products Co.*, 304 U.S. 144, 152–53 (1938).

Chapter 2

1. Sir Edward Coke traced it back at least to the case of John Peachie (or Pecchie), whose royal monopoly on the sale of wine in London was struck down by a court in 1377. Edward Coke, *The Third Part of the Institutes of the Laws of England*, facsimile of 1797 edition (Buffalo, NY: William S. Hein Co. 1986), p. 181. See also William Holdsworth, *A History of English Law*, 3rd ed. (London: Methuen, 1945), vol. 4, p. 344, n. 6.; and William Letwin, *Law and Economic Policy in America: The Evolution of the Sherman Antitrust Act* (Chicago: University of Chicago Press, 1965), pp. 20–22.

2. Timothy Sandefur, "The Right to Earn a Living," *Chapman Law Review* 6 (2003): 207–78.

3. Jacob I. Corré, "The Argument, Decision, and Reports of *Darcy v. Allen*," *Emory Law Journal* 45 (1996): 1275–76.

4. *Darcy v. Allen*, 77 Eng. Rep. 1260 (1603).

5. *The Case of the Tailors of Ipswich*, 77 Eng. Rep. 1218 (K.B. 1615).

6. Ibid. at 1218.

7. Catherine Drinker Bowen, *The Lion and the Throne: The Life of Edward Coke* (Boston: Little, Brown, 1957), p. 304.

8. Adam Smith, *An Inquiry into the Nature and Causes of the Wealth of Nations* (Indianapolis: Liberty Classics, 1976), vol. 2, pp. 647–48.

9. See Barbara Malament, "The 'Economic Liberalism' of Sir Edward Coke," in *Law, Liberty, and Parliament: Selected Essays on the Writings of Sir Edward Coke*, ed. Allen D. Boyer (Indianapolis: Liberty Fund, 2004), p. 186.

10. *Chesman et ux v. Nainby*, 93 Eng. Rep. 819, 821 (K.B. 1727).

11. Letwin, *Law and Economic Policy in America*, p. 28.

12. Bowen, *The Lion and the Throne*, p. 462; Statute of Monopolies, 21 Jac. 1 c. 3.

13. James Kent, *Commentaries on American Law*, 12th ed., facsimile of 1873 edition, ed. O. W. Holmes Jr. (Littleton, CO: F. B. Rothman, 1999), vol. 2, p. 272, n. (c).

14. Coke, *Third Part of the Institutes*, p. 181.

15. Edward Coke, *The Second Part of the Institutes of the Laws of England*, p. 47.

16. Ibid.

17. J. A. Guy, "Origins of the Petition of Right Reconsidered," in Boyer, *Law, Liberty, and Parliament*, p. 328.

18. Bowen, *The Lion and the Throne*, pp. 532–34.

19. Jefferson to John Page, December 25, 1762, in *Jefferson: Writings*, ed. Merrill Peterson (New York: Library of America, 1984), p. 735.

20. Jefferson to James Madison, February 17, 1826, in Peterson, *Jefferson: Writings*, p. 1513.

21. *Weaver of Newbury's Case*, 72 Eng. Rep. 962 (K.B. 1616?).

22. *The Case of the Bricklayers*, 81 Eng. Rep. 871 (K.B. 1624).

23. See, for example, *Mounson v. Lyster*, 82 Eng. Rep. 122 (K.B. 1632).

24. *Colgate v. Bacheler*, 78 Eng. Rep. 1097 (K.B. 1602).

25. As the court explained in *The City of London's Case*, "The King may erect *guildam mecatoriam, i.e.*, a fraternity or society or corporation of merchants, to the end that good order and rule should be by them observed for the increase and advancement of trade and merchandise, and not for the hindrance of it." 77 Eng. Rep. 658, 663 (K.B. 1610).

26. Letwin, *Law and Economic Policy in America*, pp. 46–52.

27. *Allen v. Tooley*, 80 Eng. Rep. 1055, 1057 (K.B. 1614).

28. Ibid. at 1055.

29. Ibid. at 1059.

30. Thomas Jefferson, "Thoughts on Lotteries" (February 1826), in *The Writings of Thomas Jefferson*, ed. Albert Ellery Bergh (Washington: Thomas Jefferson Memorial Association, 1907), vol. 17, p. 449.

31. Jefferson to Joseph Milligan, April 6, 1816, in Bergh, *The Writings of Thomas Jefferson*, vol. 14, p. 466.

32. "Property" (March 29, 1892) in *Madison: Writings*, ed. Jack Rakove (New York: Library of America, 1999), p. 516.

33. Thomas G. West, *Vindicating the Founders: Race, Sex, Class, and Justice in the Origins of America* (Lanham, MD: Rowman & Littlefield, 1997), pp. 38–39.

34. Virginia Declaration of Rights (1776), para. 1 (emphasis added).

35. James Madison, Speech in the Virginia Constitutional Convention (1829), in Rakove, *Madison: Writings*, p. 824.

36. West, *Vindicating the Founders*, p. 39.

37. Smith, *The Wealth of Nations*, vol. 1, p. 138.

38. Ibid., vol. 2, p. 660.

39. Ibid., vol. 2, pp. 647–48.

40. Ibid., vol. 2, p. 654.

41. Ibid., vol. 1, p. 140.

42. William Blackstone, *Commentaries on the Laws of England* (London: A. Strahan, 1809), vol. 1, p. 470.

43. *Encyclopedia Britannica* (Edinburgh: Bell & MacFarquar, 1771), vol. 2, p. 281. In fact, some American cities are still referred to as "municipal corporations." See, for example, *Chicago Title Land Trust Co. v. Board of Trustees of Village of Barrington*, 878 N.E.2d 723, 724 (Ill. App. 1st Dist. 2007).

44. Robert Hessen, *In Defense of the Corporation* (Stanford, CA: Hoover Institution Press, 1979), pp. 3–33; and Margaret M. Blair, "Locking in Capital: What Corporate Law Achieved for Business Organizers in the Nineteenth Century," *UCLA Law Review* 51 (2003): 414–23.

45. "What frequently distinguished incorporated from unincorporated joint-stock companies [in the 18th century], therefore, was that the former were owned by politically well-connected merchants who had paid a handsome price to secure a monopoly, while the latter lacked the money or connections to gain similar privileges." Paul G. Mahoney, "Contract or Concession? An Essay on the History of Corporate Law," *Georgia Law Review* 34 (2000): 887.

46. Jefferson to George Logan, November 12, 1816, in *The Works of Thomas Jefferson*, ed. Paul Leicester Ford (New York: G. P. Putnam's Sons, 1905), vol. 12, p. 44.

47. Jefferson to James Madison, December 20, 1787, in Peterson, *Jefferson: Writings*, p. 916.

48. Madison to Thomas Jefferson, October 17, 1788, in Rakove, *Madison: Writings*, p. 423.

49. Madison, Detached Memorandum on Monopolies, Corporations, Ecclesiastical Endowments (1819), in Rakove, *Madison: Writings*, p. 756.

50. Adrienne Koch, *James Madison's Notes of Debates in the Federal Convention* (New York: W. W. Norton, 1966), pp. 638–39.

51. Gordon S. Wood, *The Radicalism of the American Revolution* (New York: Knopf, 1992), p. 321.

52. Ibid., p. 318.

53. Thomas Bowden, "Antitrust: The War against Contract," in *The Abolition of Antitrust*, ed. Gary Hull (New Brunswick, NJ: Transaction, 2005), p. 105; Franklin A. Gevurtz, "The Historical and Political Origins of the Corporate Board of Directors," *Hofstra Law Review* 33 (2004): 108–9; and Blair, "Locking in Capital," 425–27.

54. Lawrence Friedman, *A History of American Law*, 3rd ed. (New York: Simon & Schuster, 2001), p. 137.

55. *Swan v. Williams*, 2 Mich. 427, 434 (1852).

56. Cal. Corporations Code §§ 209, 2005(d).

57. Roger Pilon, "Corporations and Rights: On Treating Corporate People Justly," *Georgia Law Review* 13 (1979): 1297.

58. *Dartmouth College v. Woodward*, 17 U.S. (4 Wheat.) 518 (1819).

59. *Charles River Bridge v. Warren Bridge*, 36 U.S. (11 Pet.) 420 (1837).

60. Ibid. at 545–46.

61. Ibid. at 548.

62. Ibid. at 549.

63. Ibid. at 552–53.

64. Stanley Kutler, *Privilege and Creative Destruction: The Charles River Bridge Case* (New York: W. W. Norton, 1978), p. 94.

65. Ibid., pp. 94–95.

66. Ibid., p. 137.

67. William H. Page, "Ideological Conflict and the Origins of Antitrust Policy," *Tulane Law Review* 66 (1991): 31.

68. *Kelo v. New London*, 545 U.S. 469 (2005).

69. See, for example, *Slaughterhouse Cases*, 83 U.S. (16 Wall.) 36, 87–88 (1872) (Field, J., dissenting); and *Munn v. Illinois*, 94 U.S. (4 Otto) 113, 148–49 (1876) (Field, J., dissenting).

70. Timothy Sandefur, "A Gleeful Obituary for *Poletown Neighborhood Council v. Detroit*," *Harvard Journal of Law and Public Policy* 28 (2005): 654–60; and Timothy Sandefur, "Mine and Thine Distinct: What *Kelo* Says about Our Path," *Chapman Law Review* 10 (2006): 15–34.

71. Ralph Nader, Mark Green, and Joel Seligman, *Taming the Giant Corporation* (New York: W. W. Norton, 1976).

72. Hessen, *In Defense of the Corporation*. See also Robert Hessen, "A New Concept of Corporations: A Contractual and Private Property Model," *Hastings Law Journal* 30 (1979): 1327–50.

73. Hessen, *In Defense of the Corporation*, p. 17.

74. For a fuller discussion, including a proposal for compulsory insurance as a better substitute for limited liability, see Pilon, "Corporations and Rights," 1309–10.

75. Hessen, *In Defense of the Corporation*, p. 115.

76. Ibid. , pp. 16–22.

77. *Santa Clara County v. Southern Pacific Railroad*, 118 U.S. 394 (1886).

78. *Railroad Tax Cases*, 13 F. 722, 746–47 (C.C.D. Cal. 1882).

79. Ibid. at 747–48.

80. Ibid.

81. Robert L. Raymond, "The Genesis of the Corporation," *Harvard Law Review* 19 (1906): 353.

82. Milton Friedman, "The Social Responsibility of Business Is to Increase Its Profits," *New York Times Magazine*, September 13, 1970. Interesting responses to Friedman are found in Roger Donaway, "Private I: Was Milton Friedman Pro-Capitalist?" *New Individualist*, April 2007; and Roger Donaway, "Private I: The Lengthened Shadow of a Businessman," *New Individualist*, May 2007.

83. Norman Barry, "The Stakeholder Concept of Corporate Control Is Illogical and Impractical." *Independent Review* 6 (2002): 550.

84. Raymond, "The Genesis of the Corporation," 361.

Chapter 3

1. Samuel Eliot Morison, *The Oxford History of the American People* (New York: New American Library, 1972), vol. 3, pp. 104–6.

2. Some historians have argued that "free labor ideology" was a creation of the Jackson era. See, for example, Eric Foner, *Free Soil, Free Labor, Free Men: The Ideology of the Republican Party before the Civil War* (New York: Oxford University Press, 1970). In fact, it was a contemporary articulation of the classical liberal principles of the Declaration of Independence. See, for example, Harry V. Jaffa, *Crisis of the House Divided* (Chicago: University of Chicago Press, 1959); and Harry V. Jaffa, *A New Birth of Freedom* (Lanham, MD: Rowman & Littlefield, 2000).

3. Sixth Debate with Stephen Douglas (October 13, 1858), in *Abraham Lincoln: Speeches and Writings*, ed. Don Fehrenbacher (New York: Library of America 1989), vol. 1, p. 734.

4. Civil Rights Act of 1866, 14 Stat. 27 (1866), codified as amended at 42 U.S.C. §§ 1981–82.

5. *Corfield v. Coryell*, 6 F. Cas. 546 (C.C.E.D. Pa. 1823) (No. 3230).

6. Ibid. at 551–52.

7. See *Congressional Globe*, 39th Cong., 1st sess., p. 2765 (1866); and *Congressional Globe*, 42d Cong., 1st sess., App. p. 69 (1871).

8. *Congressional Globe*, 42d Cong., 1st sess., App. p. 86 (1871).

9. *Congressional Record*, vol. 1, p. 363 (1874).

10. *Congressional Globe*, 42d Cong., 2d sess., p. 844 (1872).

11. *In re Parrott*, 1 F. 481, 506 (C.C.D. Cal. 1880).

12. *Slaughterhouse Cases*, 83 U.S. (16 Wall.) 36 (1873).

13. See Ronald M. Labbé and Jonathan Lurie, *The Slaughterhouse Cases: Regulation, Reconstruction, and the Fourteenth Amendment* (Lawrence: University Press of Kansas, 2003), pp. 82–84.

14. *Slaughterhouse*, 83 U.S. (16 Wall.) at 74.

15. Ibid. at 77.

16. Ibid. at 79.

17. Ibid. at 96 (Field, J., dissenting).

18. Ibid. at 101–5 (Field, J., dissenting).

19. Ibid. at 110 (Field, J., dissenting).

20. Ibid. at 92–93 (Field, J., dissenting).

21. *Bradwell v. People of State of Illinois*, 83 U.S. (16 Wall.) 130, 139 (1872).

22. The Court did rely on the clause in the case of *Colgate v. Harvey*, 296 U.S. 404 (1935), but overruled that case soon thereafter in *Madden v. Kentucky*, 309 U.S. 83 (1940).

23. Paul Kens, *Justice Stephen Field: Shaping Liberty from the Gold Rush to the Gilded Age* (Lawrence: University Press of Kansas, 1997), p. 8. See also James May, "Antitrust in the Formative Era: Political and Economic Theory in Constitutional and Antitrust Analysis 1880–1918," *Ohio State Law Journal* 50 (1989): 283–88.

24. Michael McGerr, *A Fierce Discontent: The Rise and Fall of the Progressive Movement in America 1870–1920* (New York: Free Press, 2003), p. xiv.

25. Alex Epstein, "Vindicating Capitalism: The Real History of the Standard Oil Company," *Objective Standard* 3, no. 2 (Summer 2008): 29–65.

26. Henry D. Lloyd, "The Story of a Great Monopoly," *Atlantic Monthly*, March 1881, p. 325.

27. Ibid., p. 327.

28. McGerr, *A Fierce Discontent*, pp. 56–59.

29. May, "Antitrust in the Formative Era," 287.

30. Milton and Rose Friedman, *Free to Choose* (San Diego: Harvest, 1990), p. 93.

31. McGerr, *A Fierce Discontent*, pp. 48–50; and Tom Peyser, "Looking Backward at *Looking Backward*," *Reason*, August–September 2000, http://www.reason.com/news/show/27797.html.

32. Henry D. Lloyd, "Lords of Industry," *North American Review*, June 1884, p. 552. See also Elizabeth Sadler, "One Book's Influence: Edward Bellamy's *Looking Backward*," *New England Quarterly* 17, no. 4 (December 1944): 530–55.

33. Lloyd, "Lords of Industry," pp. 551–52.

34. Ibid.

35. Theodore Roosevelt, 1906 State of the Union address, in *A Compilation of the Messages and Papers of the Presidents*, ed. James D. Richardson (Washington: Bureau of National Literature and Art, 1908), vol. 11, p. 1202.

36. John Dewey, "The Future of Liberalism," *Journal of Philosophy* 32, no. 9 (1935): 225–30.

37. Charles Paul Freund, "Our Secret Pledge," *Reason*, June 27, 2002, http://reason.com/news/show/33640.html.

38. McGerr, *A Fierce Discontent*, p. 214.

39. Eric R. Claeys, "*Euclid* Lives? The Uneasy Legacy of Progressivism in Zoning," *Fordham Law Review* 73 (2004): 751–53; and Wendell E. Pritchett, "The 'Public Menace' of Blight: Urban Renewal and the Private Uses of Eminent Domain," *Yale Law and Policy Review* 21 (2003): 1–52.

40. Woodrow Wilson, "Position and Importance of the Arts Course as Distinct from the Professional and Semi-Professional Courses," *Journal and Proceedings of the Association of American Universities Sixth Annual Conference* (Chicago: University of Chicago Press, 1905), p. 74.

41. U.S. Const. Amends. XVII, XVIII.

42. Thomas Jefferson, First Inaugural Address (1800), in *Jefferson: Writings*, ed. Merrill Peterson (New York: Library of America, 1984), p. 494.

43. Woodrow Wilson, "Leaders of Men" (1890), reprinted in *Woodrow Wilson: The Essential Political Writings*, ed. Ronald J. Pestritto (Lanham, MD: Lexington Books, 2005), p. 214.

44. See, for example, Robert Green McCloskey, *American Conservatism in the Age of Enterprise 1865–1910* (New York: Harper & Row, 1951), pp. 26–30.

45. David E. Bernstein, "*Lochner* Era Revisionism, Revised: *Lochner* and the Origins of Fundamental Rights Constitutionalism," *Georgetown Law Journal* 92 (2003): 7–9.

46. *Lochner v. New York*, 198 U.S. 45, 75 (1905) (Holmes, J., dissenting). Holmes wrote the majority opinion in *Buck v. Bell*, 274 U.S. 200 (1927), upholding a state's authority to enforce a eugenics program whereby women who were thought to be of insufficient intelligence were sterilized against their will. For more on Holmes's peculiar fondness for eugenics, see Albert W. Alschuler, *Law without Values: The Life, Work, and Legacy of Justice Holmes* (Chicago: University of Chicago Press, 2000), pp. 27–29, 65–67.

47. Eric Foner, *The Story of American Freedom* (New York: W. W. Norton, 1998), p. 122.

48. *Slaughterhouse*, 83 U.S. (16 Wall.) at 105 (Field, J., dissenting).

49. As William Bernstein puts it, "Nineteenth century Britain never was the gauzy Valhalla of laissez-faire that has been romanticized by modern libertarians. . . ." *The Birth of Plenty: How the Prosperity of the Modern World Was Created* (New York: McGraw-Hill, 2004), p. 341.

50. Paul Johnson, *A History of the American People* (London: Weidenfeld & Nicholson, 1997), pp. 443–45.

51. Vincent P. DeSantis, *The Shaping of Modern America: 1877–1920*, 2nd ed. (Arlington Heights, IL: Forum Press, 1989), p. 5.

52. May, "Antitrust in the Formative Era," 288.

53. William H. Page, "Ideological Conflict and the Origins of Antitrust Policy," *Tulane Law Review* 66 (1991): 30–31.

54. *Congressional Record*, vol. 21, p. 2456 (1890).

55. Ibid., p. 2457.

56. Ibid.

57. Ibid.

58. Ibid., p. 2569.

59. See William Letwin, *Law and Economic Policy in America: The Evolution of the Sherman Antitrust Act* (Chicago: University of Chicago Press, 1965), pp. 253–55.

60. 26 Stat. 209, codified as amended at 15 U.S.C. § 1 (2003).

61. See, for example, William D. Guthrie, "Constitutionality of the Sherman Anti-Trust Act of 1890," *Harvard Law Review* 11 (1898): 80–94.

62. Ibid., 80. See also Edward B. Whitney, "Constitutional Questions under the Federal Anti-Trust Law," *Yale Law Journal* 7 (1898): 290.

63. See Dominick T. Armentano, *Antitrust Policy: The Case for Repeal* (Washington: Cato Institute, 1986); Gary Hull, ed., *The Abolition of Antitrust* (New Brunswick, NJ: Transaction, 2005); Edwin S. Rockefeller, *The Antitrust Religion* (Washington: Cato Institute, 2007); and D. T. Armentano, "Efficiency, Liberty, and Antitrust Policy," in *Economic Liberties and the Judiciary*, ed. James. A. Dorn and Henry G. Manne (Washington: Cato Institute, 1987), pp. 309–16.

64. *United States v. Aluminum Co. of America*, 148 F.2d 416 (2d Cir. 1945).

65. Ibid. at 430–31.

66. Ibid. at 429.

67. Ibid. at 431.

68. Ibid. at 432.

69. Alan Greenspan, "Antitrust," in *Capitalism: The Unknown Ideal*, ed. Ayn Rand (New York: New American Library, 1967), p. 71.

70. *Olympia Equipment Leasing Co. v. Western Union Telegraph Co.*, 797 F.2d 370, 375–76 (7th Cir. 1986); and *United States v. Syufy Enterprises*, 903 F.2d 659, 668 (9th Cir. 1990).

71. *Syufy Enterprises*, 903 F.2d at 668 (emphasis in original).

72. Richard O. Zerbe Jr., Letter to the Editor, *Regulation*, Spring 2006, pp. 1–2; and Louis B. Schwartz, "'Justice' and Other Non-Economic Goals of Antitrust," *University of Pennsylvania Law Review* 127 (1979): 1078.

73. *Olstad v. Microsoft Corp.*, 284 Wis. 2d 224, 230 (2005).

74. Ibid.

75. Brief of Appellant, *Olstad v. Microsoft Corp.*, No. 03-1086, 2003 WL 23837568 at *1.

76. See Penelope A. Preovolos, "Unfair Practices and Predatory Pricing," paper presented at the 47th Annual Practicing Law Institute Advanced Antitrust Seminar, New York, January–February 2008, p. 212.

77. *In re Midwest Oil of Minnesota, LLC*, No. 3-1011-16696-2 (August 16, 2006) (on file with author). See also Tom Ford, "Midwest Oil Fined for Selling Gas Too Cheaply," *Minneapolis Star Tribune*, February 24, 2006, p. 1D (2006 WLNR 3234771).

78. *In re Midwest Oil*, p. 3.

79. Frank H. Easterbrook, "Predatory Strategies and Counterstrategies," *University of Chicago Law Review* 48 (1981): 275.

80. See Roland H. Koller II, "The Myth of Predatory Pricing: An Empirical Study," *Antitrust Law and Economic Review* 4 (1971): 105 ("the standard theoretical analysis in this area treats predation as a form of non-maximizing (irrational) behavior and thus

an unlikely occurrence in the real world"); James C. Miller III and Paul Pautler, "Predation: The Changing View in Economics and the Law," *Journal of Law and Economics* 28 (1985): 495–502; and Robert H. Bork, *The Antitrust Paradox: A Policy at War with Itself* (New York: Free Press, 1993), p. 154 ("predation by such techniques is very improbable . . . [and prohibiting price-cutting] would do much more harm than good").

81. John S. McGee, "Predatory Price Cutting: The Standard Oil (N.J.) Case," *Journal of Law and Economics* 1 (1958): 168.

82. See, for example, Kenneth G. Elzinga, "Predatory Pricing: The Case of the Gunpowder Trust," *Journal of Law and Economics* 13 (1970): 223–40.

83. Koller, "The Myth of Predatory Pricing," 105; Epstein, "Vindicating Capitalism," 46.

84. Koller, "The Myth of Predatory Pricing," 122.

85. *Matsushita Electric Industries v. Zenith Radio*, 475 U.S. 574 (1986).

86. *Brooke Group v. Brown & Williamson Tobacco*, 509 U.S. 209 (1993).

87. *Brooke Group*, 509 U.S. at 224.

88. Ibid. at 225.

89. See Daniel A. Crane, "The Perverse Effects of Predatory Pricing Law," *Regulation*, Winter 2005–2006, p. 26.

90. Rockefeller, *The Antitrust Religion*, p. 8.

91. *Nestle Holdings, Inc./Dreyer's Grand Ice Cream Holdings, Inc.*, FTC Docket no. C-4082, http://www.ftc.gov/os/caselist/0210174.htm (accessed February 27, 2006). See also *In re Super Premium Ice Cream Distribution Antitrust Litigation*, 691 F. Supp. 1262, 1268 (N.D. Cal. 1988); and *Winter Hill Frozen Foods and Services, Inc. v. Haagen-Dazs Co., Inc.*, 691 F. Supp. 539, 547–48 (D. Mass. 1988).

92. *FTC v. Whole Foods Market, Inc.*, 2008 WL 5101226 (D.C. Cir. November 21, 2008).

93. *Fisherman's Wharf Bay Cruise Corp. v. Superior Court*, 114 Cal. App. 4th 309 (2003).

94. Ibid. at 323.

95. Ibid. at 330.

96. *Parker v. Brown*, 317 U.S. 341 (1943).

97. *City of Columbia v. Omni Outdoor Advertising, Inc.*, 499 U.S. 365, 377 (1991).

98. *American Tobacco Co. v. United States*, 328 U.S. 781, 809 (1946).

99. Paul E. Slater, "Antitrust and Government Action: A Formula for Narrowing *Parker v. Brown*," *Northwestern University Law Review* 69 (1975): 73.

100. *Omni Outdoor*, 499 U.S. at 379 (emphasis added).

101. David Joseph White, "Participant Governmental Action Immunity from the Antitrust Laws: Fact or Fiction?" *Texas Law Review* 50 (1972): 482.

102. *Sea-Land Service, Inc. v. Alaska Railroad*, 659 F.2d 243 (D.C. Cir. 1981), *cert. denied*, 455 U.S. 919 (1982).

103. Ibid. at 247.

104. Thomas R. LaGreca, "Comment: The Federal Government's Antitrust Immunity—Trade as I Say, Not as I Do," *St. John's Law Review* 56 (1982): 533.

105. *United States v. Trans-Missouri Freight Ass'n*, 166 U.S. 290 (1897).

106. *U.S. Postal Service v. Flamingo Industries*, 540 U.S. 736 (2004).

107. Postal Reorganization Act, Pub. L. No. 91-375, 84 Stat. 719 (codified as amended at 39 U.S.C. § 101 *et seq.*).

108. 39 U.S.C. § 201.

109. 39 U.S.C. § 401(1); *Franchise Tax Board of California v. U.S. Postal Service,* 467 U.S. 512, 519 (1984).

110. *Franchise Tax Board,* 467 U.S. at 520.

111. *Antitrust Exemptions and Immunities,* Hearing before the Subcommittee on Monopolies and Commercial Law of the House Committee on the Judiciary, 95th Cong., 1st sess., March 29, 1977, pp. 1890–91.

112. *Flamingo Industries (USA) Ltd. v. U.S. Postal Service,* 302 F.3d 985, 989 (9th Cir. 2002), *rev'd,* 540 U.S. 736 (2004).

113. Ibid. at 993.

114. *Loeffler v. Frank,* 486 U.S. 549, 558 (1988); and *Franchise Tax Board,* 467 U.S. at 520.

115. 39 U.S.C. § 201.

116. See 22 U.S.C. § 2452. Brief of Respondent, *USPS v. Flamingo Industries* (no. 02-1290), p. 18, n. 7.

117. 36 U.S.C. § 2301.

118. *Mail Order Ass'n of America v. USPS,* 986 F.2d 509, 519 (D.C. Cir. 1993) (citations omitted).

119. Brief of Respondent at 20 (citing 17 U.S.C. § 105).

120. Ibid., p. 21 (citing USPS, SEC No-Action Ltr., 1971 SEC No-Act. LEXIS 2205 (August 27, 1971)).

121. *Flamingo Industries,* 540 U.S. at 746.

122. Ibid.

123. Ibid. at 747.

124. *United States v. Trans-Missouri Freight Ass'n,* 166 U.S. 290 (1897).

125. *Mail Order Ass'n,* 986 F.2d at 519 (citations omitted).

126. *Hoover v. Ronwin,* 466 U.S. 558, 584 (1984) (Stevens, J., dissenting). Again, it is not my purpose to defend antitrust jurisprudence, which has generally been far less concerned with protecting the consumer or the free market than with regulating private economic behavior, frequently in unfair and irrational ways. See Steven Semeraro, "Demystifying Antitrust State Action Doctrine," *Harvard Journal of Law and Public Policy* 24 (2000): 205, n. 1 (citing sources on irrationality of antitrust law).

127. See *Flamingo Industries,* 302 F.3d at 993.

128. *Flamingo Industries,* 540 U.S. at 748.

129. Although private companies like UPS and Federal Express also carry packages, the federal Private Express Statutes still make it illegal for private companies to carry letters. 18 U.S.C. § 1696. Private companies may carry mail only if "the amount of postage which would have been charged on the letter if it had been sent by mail is paid by stamps, or postage meter stamps, on the envelope." 39 U.S.C. § 601(a)(2). The federal government regulates shippers to enforce these and other regulations. Ironically, the USPS transports mail by contract with FedEx Express and is FedEx's single largest customer. See USPS press release, "U.S. Postal Service, FedEx Express Agree to New Contract for Air Transportation of Mail," August 1, 2006, http://www.usps.com/communications/news/press/2006/pr06_048.htm.

130. *City of Lafayette v. Louisiana Power & Light Co.,* 435 U.S. 389, 419–20 (1978) (opinion of Burger, C.J.).

131. *Cooper Corp.*, 312 U.S. at 604–5; see also *FTC v. Ticor Title Ins. Co.*, 504 U.S. 621, 633 (1992) (Antitrust immunity for government "is conferred out of respect for ongoing regulation by the State, not out of respect for the economics of price restraint.").

132. Letter from Gregory B. Cox, executive director, Hillsborough County Public Transportation Commission, to Elise Batel Lynn, August 11, 2003, at p. 2 (on file with the author).

133. *Lafayette v. Louisiana Power & Light Co.*, 435 U.S. 389, 412 (1978); and *Town of Hallie v. City of Eau Claire*, 471 U.S. 34, 38–39 (1985).

134. *Unity Ventures v. Lake County*, 631 F. Supp. 181 (N.D. Ill. 1986) (reversing the 1984 jury verdict against the city); and Carol F. Lee, "The Political Safeguards of Federalism? Congressional Responses to Supreme Court Decisions on State and Local Liability," *Urban Lawyer* 20 (1988): 313–14.

135. Thomas William Mayo, "The Local Government Antitrust Act: A Comment on the Constitutional Questions," *Journal of Air Law and Commerce* 50 (1985): 807.

136. 15 U.S.C. § 35.

137. *United States v. Topco Associates, Inc.*, 405 U.S. 596, 610 (1972).

138. James Kent, *Commentaries on American Law*, 12th ed., facsimile of 1873 edition, ed. O. W. Holmes Jr. (Littleton, CO: F. B. Rothman, 1999), vol. 2, p. 272, n. (c).

139. *United States v. Trans-Missouri Freight Ass'n*, 166 U.S. 290 (1897).

140. *Eastern Railroads Presidents Conference v. Noerr Motor Freight, Inc.*, 365 U.S. 127 (1961); and *United Mine Workers v. Pennington*, 381 U.S. 657 (1965).

141. *Noerr*, 365 U.S. at 140.

142. Ibid. at 137–38.

143. Ibid. at 137.

144. *In re Greene*, 52 F. 104, 115–16 (C.C.S.D. Ohio 1892); and *United States v. Trans-Missouri Freight Ass'n*, 53 F. 440 (C.C.D. Kan. 1892), *rev'd*, 166 U.S. 290 (1897).

145. Gary Minda, "Interest Groups, Political Freedom, and Antitrust: A Modern Reassessment of the *Noerr-Pennington* Doctrine," *Hastings Law Journal* 41 (1990): 908–9.

146. See also Milton Handler and Richard A. De Sevo, "The *Noerr* Doctrine and Its Sham Exception," *Cardozo Law Review* 6 (1984): 1–69; and Daniel R. Fischel, "Antitrust Liability for Attempts to Influence Government Action: The Basis and Limits of the *Noerr-Pennington* Doctrine," *University of Chicago Law Review* 45 (1977): 80–122.

147. George Riesman, *Capitalism: A Treatise on Economics* (Ottawa: Jameson Books, 1996), p. 356; Friedrich Hayek, *The Constitution of Liberty* (Chicago: University of Chicago Press, 1960), pp. 273–75; and Murray Rothbard, *Man, Economy, and State* (Los Angeles: Nash Publishing, 1970), p. 626.

148. *Loewe v. Lawlor*, 208 U.S. 274 (1908).

149. Dallas L. Jones, "The Enigma of the Clayton Act," *Industrial and Labor Relations Review* 10 (1956): 202 ("As a result of Danbury and other adverse decisions, the [American Federation of Labor] initiated a vigorous political campaign to secure support to amend the law.").

150. Richard A. Epstein, *How the Progressives Rewrote the Constitution* (Washington: Cato Institute, 2006), p. 86.

151. Ibid., p. 89.

152. Mark Twain, "Life on the Mississippi," in *Mark Twain: Mississippi Writings*, ed. Guy Cardwell (New York: Library of America, 1982), pp. 327–28.

153. George B. Shepherd, "Scholarly Restraints? ABA Accreditation and Legal Education," *Cardozo Law Review* 19 (1998): 2091–256; Andy Portinga, "Note: ABA

Accreditation of Law Schools: An Antitrust Analysis," *University of Michigan Journal of Law Reform* 29 (1996): 635–70; and Michael Ariens, "Law School Branding and the Future of Legal Education," *St. Mary's Law Journal* 34 (2003): 316–18.

154. Claude Solnik, "As State Raises Bar, Academics, Students Bristle," *Long Island Business News*, July 1, 2005; and Katherine S. Mangan, "Raising the Bar," *Chronicle of Higher Education*, September 10, 2004.

155. *Hoover v. Ronwin*, 466 U.S. 558 (1984).

156. See, for example, *Karlin v. Weinberg*, 77 N.J. 408 (1978); *Advanced Marine Enterprises, Inc. v. PRC Inc.*, 501 S.E.2d 148 (Va. 1998); and *Midwest Television, Inc. v. Oloffson*, 699 N.E.2d 230 (Ill. App. Ct. 1998).

157. Cal. Bus. & Prof. Code § 16600.

158. See *United States v. Addyston Pipe & Steel Co.*, 85 F. 271, 281–82 (6th Cir. 1898), *aff'd*, 175 U.S. 211 (1899).

159. See Linda Chavez and Daniel Gray, *Betrayal: How Union Bosses Shake Down Their Members and Corrupt American Politics* (New York: Crown Forum, 2004), pp. 139–58.

Chapter 4

1. U.S. Const. art. I, § 10.

2. Henry Maine, *Popular Government* (New York: Henry Holt & Co., 1886), p. 247.

3. *Allied Structural Steel Co. v. Spannaus*, 438 U.S. 234, 241 (1978).

4. For example, until Solon of Athens enacted the *seisachtheia*, debts were often secured by the personal labor of the debtor, meaning that defaulters were sometimes reduced to slavery. John V. A. Fine, *The Ancient Greeks: A Critical History* (Cambridge, MA: Belknap Press, 1983), pp. 198–99.

5. Samuel Eliot Morison, *The Oxford History of the American People* (New York: Mentor, 1972), vol. 1, pp. 390–94.

6. As Hadley Arkes writes, the laws canceling debts deprived every lender of "the rights he possessed under the original contract for the loan. It barred him, that is, from reclaiming money that was his; money that might have been invested in other ways, with more profit and less hazard. What was morally problematic in this arrangement was a point that could be obscured by the high-minded rhetoric. Cicero had crystal-lized the moral problem long ago. . . . What is the meaning, he asked, of an 'abolition of debts, except that you buy a farm with my money; that you have the farm, and I have not my money?'" Arkes, *The Return of George Sutherland* (Princeton, NJ: Princeton University Press, 1994), p. 244.

7. Clinton Rossiter, ed., *The Federalist Papers* (New York: New American Library, 1961), no. 10, p. 84; no. 44, p. 282.

8. *Federalist* no. 10, p. 79.

9. Ibid., pp. 79–80.

10. As the 19th-century lawyer Richard Henry Dana observed, "In all [nations] but ours, now existing or that have ever existed, the function of the judiciary is to inter-pret the acts of government. In ours, it is to decide upon their legality. . . . This is the result of a written Constitution, as a supreme law, under which there is no sovereign power, but only coordinate departments." Quoted in Brian McGinty, *Lincoln and the Court* (Cambridge, MA: Harvard University Press, 2008), pp. 136–37.

11. Douglas W. Kmiec and John O. McGinnis, "The Contract Clause: A Return to the Original Understanding," *Hastings Constitutional Law Quarterly* 14 (1987): 526.

12. *Fletcher v. Peck*, 10 U.S. (6 Cranch) 87 (1810).

13. Ibid. at 26.

14. Ibid.

15. *Dartmouth College v. Woodward*, 17 U.S. (4 Wheat.) 518 (1819).

16. Ibid. at 627.

17. Ibid. at 633.

18. Ibid. at 653.

19. Ibid. at 647.

20. *Charles River Bridge v. Warren Bridge*, 36 U.S. (11 Pet.) 420 (1837).

21. Ibid. at 547–48 (quotation marks omitted).

22. Ibid. at 590 (Story, J., dissenting).

23. Ibid. at 601 (Story, J., dissenting).

24. Ibid. at 608 (Story, J., dissenting).

25. Ibid. at 649 (Story, J., dissenting).

26. *Butcher's Union Slaughter-House & Live-Stock Landing Co. v. Crescent City Live-Stock Landing and Slaughter-House Company*, 111 U.S. 746 (1884).

27. Ibid. at 753 (quoting *Stone v. Mississippi*, 101 U.S. 814, 819 (1879)).

28. *Stone v. Mississippi*, 101 U.S. 814 (1879).

29. *Ogden v. Saunders*, 25 U.S. (12 Wheat.) 213 (1827).

30. *West River Bridge Co. v. Dix*, 47 U.S. (6 How.) 507 (1848).

31. Ibid. at 507, 532–33.

32. Ibid.

33. *Ogden v. Saunders*, 25 U.S. at 338–39 (Marshall, C.J., dissenting).

34. Samuel R. Olken, "Charles Evans Hughes and the *Blaisdell* Decision: A Historical Study of Contract Clause Jurisprudence," *Oregon Law Review* 72 (1993): 542.

35. Alexis de Tocqueville, *Democracy in America*, trans. George Lawrence and ed. J. P. Mayer (New York: Harper Perennial, 1969), p. 292.

36. Olken, "Charles Evans Hughes," 548.

37. *Marcus Brown Holding Co. v. Feldman*, 256 U.S. 170, 198 (1921). See also *Block v. Hirsh*, 256 U.S. 135 (1921) (upholding a Washington, D.C., rent-control ordinance).

38. William L. Prosser, "The Minnesota Mortgage Moratorium," *Southern California Law Review* 7 (1934): 353–55.

39. Ibid., p. 355.

40. Olken, "Charles Evans Hughes," 574.

41. Prosser, "Minnesota Mortgage Moratorium," 362.

42. Ibid., 357.

43. *Home Bldg. & Loan Ass'n v. Blaisdell*, 290 U.S. 398, 444 (1934).

44. See G. Edward White, *The Constitution and the New Deal* (Cambridge, MA: Harvard University Press, 2000), pp. 212–13.

45. *Blaisdell*, 290 U.S. at 442–43. As Lino Graglia has put it, Hughes's opinion "is not an argument for a method of interpretation not dependent on the Framers' (and ratifiers') intent—there is no such method—but an argument against constitutionalism." Graglia, "The Burger Court and Economic Rights," *Tulsa Law Journal* 33 (1997): 48.

46. *Blaisdell*, 290 U.S. at 448–49 (Sutherland, J., dissenting).

47. David P. Currie, *The Constitution in the Supreme Court: The Second Century, 1888–1986* (Chicago: University of Chicago Press, 1990), p. 213.

48. *Veix v. Sixth Ward Building & Loan Ass'n of Newark*, 310 U.S. 32, 39 (1940).

49. John Milton, *Paradise Lost*, bk. 4, lines 393–94.

50. See also Rebecca M. Kahan, "Constitutional Stretch, Snap-Back, and Sag: Why *Blaisdell* Was a Harsher Blow to Liberty than *Korematsu*," *Northwestern University Law Review* 99 (2005): 1279–313.

51. *U.S. Trust Co. v. New Jersey*, 431 U.S. 1 (1977).

52. *Allied Structural Steel Co. v. Spannaus*, 438 U.S. 234 (1978).

53. *U.S. Trust Co.*, 431 U.S. at 22–23.

54. Ibid.

55. Ibid. at 26.

56. Bernard Schwartz, "Old Wine in Old Bottles: The Renaissance of the Contract Clause," *Supreme Court Review* (1979): 110.

57. *Spannaus*, 438 U.S. at 247.

58. *Keystone Bituminous Coal Ass'n v. DeBenedictis*, 480 U.S. 470, 472 (1987).

59. Stephen A. Siegel, "Understanding the Nineteenth Century Contract Clause: The Role of the Property-Privilege Distinction and 'Takings' Clause Jurisprudence," *Southern California Law Review* 60 (1987): 26.

60. Kmiec and McGinnis, "Contract Clause," 547.

61. Thomas E. Mitchell, "Rewriting the Terms: The Contract Clause and Special-Interest Legislation in *RUI One Corp. v. City of Berkeley*," *Harvard Journal of Law and Public Policy* 28 (2005): 691–712.

62. A "living wage" differs from a "minimum wage" in that minimum wages apply to all contracts and all employers, as a general regulation; a living wage applies to businesses that work for the government, lease land from the government, or have some other relationship by which they can consent to the living wage requirement.

63. See Donald Deere, Kevin M. Murphy, and Finis Welch, "Sense and Nonsense on the Minimum Wage," *Regulation* (Winter 1995): 47–56; Craig Garthwaite, Testimony before the House Subcommittee on Workforce, Empowerment, and Government Programs, April 29, 2004; Simon Rottenberg, ed., *The Economics of Legal Minimum Wages* (Washington: American Enterprise Institute, 1981); *The Employment Impact of a Comprehensive Living Wage Law: Evidence from California* (Washington: Employment Policies Institute, 1999), pp. 4–5; David Neumark, *How Living Wage Laws Affect Low-Wage Workers and Low-Income Families* (San Francisco: Public Policy Institute of California, 2002); Richard H. Sander, E. Douglass Williams, and Joseph Doherty, *The Economic and Distributional Consequences of the Santa Monica Minimum Wage Ordinance*, (Washington: Employment Policies Institute, 2002); and Carl F. Horowitz, "Keeping the Poor Poor: The Dark Side of the Living Wage," Cato Institute Policy Analysis no. 493, October 21, 2003.

64. *RUI One Corp. v. City of Berkeley*, 371 F.3d 1137, 1143 (9th Cir. 2004), *cert. denied*, 543 U.S. 1081 (2005).

65. See *Munn v. Illinois*, 94 U.S. 113, 148–49 (1876) (Field, J., dissenting).

66. Mitchell, "Rewriting the Terms," 695.

67. *RUI One Corp.*, 371 F.3d at 1148.

68. Ibid. at 1150 (citations omitted).

69. Berkeley City Attorney Manuela Albuquerque, quoted in Mitchell, "Rewriting the Terms," 702.

Chapter 5

1. See G. Edward White, *The Constitution and the New Deal* (Cambridge, MA: Harvard University Press, 2000), pp. 241–68.

2. For example, Justice Stephen J. Field, widely reputed to be the founder of economic substantive due process theory, quoted Adam Smith in his dissent in the *Slaughterhouse Cases*, 83 U.S. (16 Wall.) 36, 110 n. 39 (1873). But he quoted the following language: "'The property which every man has in his own labor,' says Adam Smith, 'as it is the original foundation of all other property, so it is the most sacred and inviolable. The patrimony of the poor man lies in the strength and dexterity of his own hands; and to hinder him from employing this strength and dexterity in what manner he thinks proper, without injury to his neighbor, is a plain violation of this most sacred property. It is a manifest encroachment upon the just liberty both of the workman and of those who might be disposed to employ him. As it hinders the one from working at what he thinks proper, so it hinders the others from employing whom they think proper.'" (Quoting Adam Smith, *An Inquiry into the Nature and Causes of the Wealth of Nations* (Indianapolis: Liberty Fund, 1976), vol. 1, p. 138). This is a moral, not an economic, argument.

3. Robert Green McCloskey, *American Conservatism in the Age of Enterprise* (New York: Harper & Row, 1964), p. 75.

4. Akhil Reed Amar, *The Bill of Rights: Creation and Reconstruction* (New Haven, CT: Yale University Press, 1998), pp. 148–49.

5. *Barron v. Baltimore*, 32 U.S. (7 Pet.) 243, 251 (1833).

6. Akhil Reed Amar, *America's Constitution: A Biography* (New York: Random House, 2005), pp. 5–53.

7. See William Freehling, *Prelude to Civil War: The Nullification Controversy in South Carolina, 1816–1836* (New York: Oxford University Press, 1966), pp. 160–62. Blackstone did believe in natural rights, unlike some of his 19th-century followers. But his attitude toward them was ambiguous. He explicitly rejected Locke's belief that these rights were enforceable against the state and appears to have regarded them more as principles of political wisdom than as meaningful limitations on the state. See Herbert J. Storing, "William Blackstone," in *History of Political Philosophy*, 3rd ed., ed. Leo Strauss and Joseph Cropsey (Chicago: University of Chicago Press, 1987), pp. 622–33.

8. James Madison, "Sovereignty," in *Writings of James Madison*, ed. Gaillard Hunt, (New York: G. P. Putnam's Sons, 1910) vol. 9, pp. 570–71.

9. Harry V. Jaffa, *A New Birth of Freedom* (Lanham, MD: Rowman & Littlefield, 2000); and Daniel Farber, *Lincoln's Constitution* (Chicago: University of Chicago Press, 2003).

10. *Sharpless v. Mayor of Philadelphia*, 21 Pa. 147, 168 (1853).

11. Ibid. at 160

12. Ibid. at 161.

13. *Billings v. Hall*, 7 Cal. 1 (1857).

14. Ibid. at 10.

15. Ibid. at 13.

16. Ibid. at 14.

17. *Slaughterhouse*, 83 U.S. (16 Wall.) at 79.

18. Ibid. at 77.

19. Ibid. at 78.

20. Ibid. at 96 (Field, J., dissenting). A startling example of the effect of the *Slaughterhouse* precedent was *United States v. Cruikshank*, 92 U.S. 542 (1875), a case that arose out of the "Colfax Massacre," one of the bloodiest incidents during Reconstruction. The massacre occurred when a local sheriff led a white mob in murdering more than 100 black citizens—perhaps twice that many—who had assembled to protest election irregularities. When the sheriff was brought up on federal charges, he was freed when the U.S. Supreme Court found that the Civil Rights Enforcement Act did not apply. That act prohibited people from acting to deprive others of "any right or privilege granted or secured . . . by the constitution or laws of the United States," but, relying on *Slaughterhouse*'s restrictive interpretation of the rights guaranteed by federal citizenship, the Court found that none of the rights of which the victims had been deprived were federally protected rights. Ibid. at 549.

21. Steven Sheppard, ed., *Selected Writings of Sir Edward Coke* (Indianapolis: Liberty Press, 2003), p. 858.

22. See, for example, H. L. A. Hart, *The Concept of Law*, 2nd ed. (Oxford: Oxford University Press, 1994).

23. James Wilson, Speech in the Pennsylvania Ratifying Convention (December 1, 1787), in *The Debate on the Constitution*, ed. Bernard Bailyn (New York: Library of America, 1993), vol. 1, p. 823.

24. See Hart, *Concept of Law*, especially pp. 18–25, 155–59; and Friedrich Hayek, *Law, Legislation and Liberty, Vol. 1: Rules and Order* (Chicago: University of Chicago Press, 1973), pp. 85–86.

25. Hart, *Concept of Law*, pp. 20–23.

26. James Wilson, *Lectures on Law* (1791), reprinted in Kermit L. Hall and Mark David Hall, eds., *Collected Works of James Wilson* (Indianapolis: Liberty Press, 2007), vol. 1, p. 468.

27. Clinton Rossiter, ed., *The Federalist Papers* (New York: New American Library, 1961), no. 10, p. 78.

28. Ibid., no. 51, p. 324. Madison's explanation of this point fills the gap that John V. Orth locates in substantive due process theory in his book *Due Process of Law: A Brief History* (Lawrence: University Press of Kansas, 2003). Orth argues that 19th-century courts erroneously applied the common-law principle that "no man may be a judge in his own case"—which had grown into the principle that government may not "take from A to give to B"—to legislation that redistributed wealth and opportunity among large groups or classes. See pp. 49–63. Orth argues that when large groups are involved, and where the transfer is the product of formal legislation, these prohibitions on direct transfers lack their original force. But as Madison explains, the same principles do apply to large groups, since in a republic the majority is the judge in its own case, and might abuse its law-making power to redistribute wealth, oppress "the weaker party or an obnoxious individual," or engage in some other "improper or wicked project." *Federalist* no. 10, pp. 81, 84. A constitutional requirement of lawfulness, restraining the majority's power over individuals or larger minorities, therefore helps prevent large-scale, classwide exploitation by the legislative majority.

29. Aristotle, *Politics*, 1279a, in Richard McKeon, *The Basic Works of Aristotle* (New York: Random House, 1941), p. 1185. The word "despotic" here somewhat obscurely translates Aristotle's actual words, "τὸ δὲ δυνάμενον τῷ σώματι ταῦτα πονεῖν ἀρχόμενον καὶ φύσει δοῦλον," which might be better rendered, "like the rule of the master over the slave." (δοῦλος)

30. Ibid. (1292a), pp. 1212–13.

31. James Madison to James Monroe, October 5, 1786, in *The Complete Madison*, ed. Saul Padover (New York: Harper Brothers, 1953), p. 45.

32. *Federalist* no. 51, p. 324.

33. *Federalist* no. 10, p. 78.

34. Thomas Cooley, *A Treatise on the Constitutional Limitations* (Boston: Little, Brown, 1868), p. 356.

35. Robert E. Riggs, "Substantive Due Process in 1791," *Wisconsin Law Review*, (1990): 941–1005.

36. *Dartmouth College v. Woodward*, 17 U.S. (4 Wheat.) 518 (1819).

37. Ibid. at 581–82.

38. *Federalist* no. 10, p. 78.

39. Justice Robert Jackson wrote in *Railway Exp. Agency v. New York*, 336 U.S. 106, 112–14 (1949), that it is "a salutary doctrine that cities, states and the Federal Government must exercise their powers so as not to discriminate between their inhabitants except upon some reasonable differentiation fairly related to the object of regulation. This equality is not merely abstract justice. The framers of the Constitution knew, and we should not forget today, that there is no more effective practical guaranty against arbitrary and unreasonable government than to require that the principles of law which officials would impose upon a minority must be imposed generally. Conversely, nothing opens the door to arbitrary action so effectively as to allow those officials to pick and choose only a few to whom they will apply legislation and thus to escape the political retribution that might be visited upon them if larger numbers were affected. Courts can take no better measure to assure that laws will be just than to require that laws be equal in operation." This expresses the principle of generality well. But Jackson erred in his belief that the principle applied only through the equal protection clause and not the due process clause. In fact, requiring the state to treat classes of *persons* equally except where a distinction is "fairly related to the object of regulation" has the same effect and justification as requiring the state to treat classes of *citizens' activities* equally except where a distinction is fairly related to the object of regulation. In other words, the generality principle requires the government to act in ways that serve general purposes, or that genuinely advance the whole public good, and not to deprive them arbitrarily of their rights, *or* to arbitrarily treat groups of them by different rules.

40. Of course, Parliament has periodically issued various declarations of rights, such as the Petition of Right (1628) and the Bill of Rights (1689). These documents did not purport to create such rights or authorize their enforcement; they are simply declaratory of existing, unwritten rights.

41. See *Twining v. State of New Jersey*, 211 U.S. 78, 99–102 (1908): "Some of the personal rights safeguarded by the first eight Amendments against national action may also be safeguarded against state action . . . not because those rights are enumerated . . . but because they are of such a nature that they are included in the conception of due process of law. Few phrases of the law are so elusive of exact apprehension as this. . . . There are certain general principles, well settled, however, which narrow the field of discussion, and may serve as helps to correct conclusions. . . . First. What is due process of law may be ascertained by an examination of those settled usages and modes of proceedings existing in the common and statute law of England before the emigration of our ancestors, and shown not to have been unsuited to their civil

and political condition by having been acted on by them after the settlement of this country. . . . Second. It does not follow, however, that a procedure settled in English law at the time of the emigration, and brought to this country and practised by our ancestors, is an essential element of due process of law. If that were so, the procedure of the first half of the seventeenth century would be fastened upon the American jurisprudence like a straight jacket, only to be unloosed by constitutional amendment. . . . Third . . . consistently with the requirements of due process, no change in ancient procedure can be made which disregards those fundamental principles, to be ascertained from time to time by judicial action, which have relation to process of law, and protect the citizen in his private right, and guard him against the arbitrary action of government." My discussion of this point differs slightly from that of David N. Mayer, but his article "Substantive Due Process Rediscovered: The Rise and Fall of Liberty of Contract," *Mercer Law Review* 60 (2009): 563–658, is an excellent overview of both the legal doctrine and the history of its development.

42. Sheppard, *Selected Writings of Sir Edward Coke*, p. 860.

43. *Norman v. Heist*, 5 Watts & Serg. 171, 1843 WL 5009, *3 (Pa. 1843).

44. *Wynehamer v. People*, 13 N.Y. 378, 393 (1856) (Opinion of Comstock, J.)

45. *Murray's Lessee v. Hoboken Land & Improvement Co.*, 59 U.S. (18 How.) 272, 276 (1856).

46. Robert Bork, for example, has argued that the term "due process" is "simply a requirement that the substance of any law be applied to a person through fair procedures by any tribunal hearing the case." Bork, *The Tempting of America: The Political Seduction of the Law* (New York: Free Press, 1990), p. 31.

47. *Federalist* no. 51, p. 324.

48. *Federalist* no. 10, p. 78.

49. Frank R. Strong argued in his lively book *Substantive Due Process of Law: A Dichotomy of Sense and Nonsense* (Durham, NC: Carolina Academic Press, 1986), that while the due process clause prohibited the state from granting outright monopolies that blocked a person from pursuing a lawful occupation, the early 20th-century courts confused this with a freedom from all government oversight: "Elevation of laissez-faireism to constitutional status was possible by confusion of 'freedom of contract' as a right to engage in common callings free of monopoly with 'freedom of contract' as a right to carry on a common calling free of governmental restrictions." Ibid., p. 95. Strong errs, however, because he overlooks the substantive similarities between the fundamental evils that the substantive due process doctrine addressed—outright monopolies on the one hand and arbitrary restrictions to benefit politically influential groups on the other. What made monopolies unjust violations of the principle of lawfulness was the very fact that they were perversions of the law-making authority to restrict one's economic freedom to profit another. This is also what arbitrary maximum-hours laws, or arbitrary licensing restrictions, or arbitrary minimum-price requirements do, albeit in different forms. But it is the hallmark of substantive due process theory that courts should not be distracted by the form, but should address the substance of a challenged law. Any restriction on liberty that lacks a genuine public reason but merely transfers wealth or opportunities or liberties from a politically unsuccessful group to the politically successful group is an act of usurpation or "faction" and, therefore, not a law, whether that restriction is characterized as a monopoly or noneconomic "morals" legislation. This, at least, was the view of the *Lochner*-era Court, which contrary to

Strong's implication, never held that anyone had the right to carry on a trade "free of governmental restrictions."

50. *Loan Association v. Topeka*, 87 U.S. (20 Wall.) 655, 663 (1874).

51. Ibid.

52. Ibid. at 664 (emphasis added).

53. *Davidson v. City of New Orleans*, 96 U.S. 97, 102 (1877) ("Can a State make any thing due process of law which, by its own legislation, it chooses to declare such? To affirm this is to hold that the prohibition to the States is of no avail, or has no application where the invasion of private rights is effected under the forms of State legislation.").

54. See also Kermit Roosevelt III, *The Myth of Judicial Activism: Making Sense of Supreme Court Decisions* (New Haven, CT: Yale University Press, 2006), p. 120; and Cass R. Sunstein, "Naked Preferences and the Constitution," *Columbia Law Review* 84 (1984): 1692.

55. *Hurtado v. California*, 110 U.S. 516 (1884).

56. Ibid. at 535–36 (quoting Daniel Webster's *Dartmouth College* argument).

57. Ibid.

58. *Twining v. State of New Jersey*, 211 U.S. 78 (1908).

59. Ibid. at 100.

60. Ibid. at 101.

61. Sunstein, "Naked Preferences," 1689–732.

62. As Richard Epstein has written, "The Constitution is very much a natural law document" in that "[u]nlike many modern statutes, the Constitution does not contain a definition section, although there are many terms, including 'contract,' that cry out for some definition. To say that the Constitution is a 'natural law' document is to say that its terms are to be understood in accord with their use in the general legal culture. Because in general legal usage the term 'contract' has a fixed and definite meaning, viewing the Constitution as a natural law document prevents the legislature from nullifying private arrangements by its own redefinition of the critical terms of constitutional discourse." Epstein, "Toward a Revitalization of the Contracts Clause," *University of Chicago Law Review* 51 (1984): 728.

63. Lawrence M. Friedman, *A History of American Law*, 3rd ed. (New York: Simon & Schuster, 2001), pp. 340–46.

64. *Dent v. West Virginia*, 129 U.S. 114 (1889).

65. *Munn v. Illinois*, 94 U.S. 113 (1876).

66. *Lochner v. New York*, 198 U.S. 45 (1905).

67. *Nebbia v. New York*, 291 U.S. 502 (1934).

68. *United States v. Carolene Products*, 304 U.S. 144 (1938).

69. *Munn*, 94 U.S. at 126.

70. Ibid.

71. Ibid. at 126.

72. Ibid. at 138.

73. Ibid. at 140.

74. Ibid. at 142.

75. Ibid. at 146.

76. Ibid. at 148.

77. Ibid.

78. Robert C. Post, "Defending the Lifeworld: Substantive Due Process in the Taft Court Era," *Boston University Law Review* 78 (1998): 1507–8.

79. *Allgeyer v. Louisiana*, 165 U.S. 578, 589 (1897).

80. *Chicago, M. & St. P. Ry. Co. v. State of Minn. ex rel. R.R. & Warehouse Com'n*, 134 U.S. 418 (1890); and *Smyth v. Ames*, 171 U.S. 361 (1898).

81. *Lochner*, 198 U.S. at 45.

82. Roscoe Pound, "Liberty of Contract," *Yale Law Journal* 18 (1909): 454.

83. *Lochner*, 198 U.S. at 53.

84. Ibid.

85. Ibid. at 57.

86. Ibid.

87. Ibid.

88. Ibid. at 59.

89. Ibid. at 62.

90. Ibid. at 56.

91. Edward Keynes, *Liberty, Property, and Privacy: Toward a Jurisprudence of Substantive Due Process* (University Park: Pennsylvania State University Press, 1996), p. 120.

92. *Lochner*, 198 U.S. at 65.

93. Ibid. at 69.

94. Ibid. at 75.

95. Ibid. at 76.

96. Ibid. at 75–76 (emphasis added).

97. Virginia Declaration of Rights (1776) ¶ XV.

98. *Lochner*, 198 U.S. at 75 (Holmes, J., dissenting).

99. Ibid.

100. Pound, "Liberty of Contract," 454.

101. Ibid., 473.

102. Keynes, *Liberty, Property, and Privacy*, p. 120; and Stephen A. Siegel, "*Lochner* Era Jurisprudence and the American Constitutional Tradition," *North Carolina Law Review* 70 (1991): 19, n. 77. The U.S. Supreme Court refers directly to these statistics in *Lochner*, 198 U.S. at 59.

103. *Muller v. Oregon*, 208 U.S. 412, 419 (1908).

104. Robert G. McCloskey, "Economic Due Process and the Supreme Court: An Exhumation and Reburial," *Supreme Court Review*, 1962: 50.

105. As one contemporaneous observer of Progressivism noted in 1903, "[T]he idea that liberty is a natural right is abandoned, and the inseparable connection between political liberty and political capacity is strongly emphasized." Charles Edward Merriam, *A History of American Political Theories* (New York: Macmillan, 1903), p. 313.

106. Louis Menand, *The Metaphysical Club* (New York: Farrar, Strauss, and Giroux, 2001), p. 409.

107. White, *The Constitution and the New Deal*, p. 252 (quoting Felix Frankfurter, *Law and Politics*, ed. Archibald MacLeish and Edward S. Pritchard (New York: Capricorn Books, 1962), p. 4).

108. Quoted in Walter Berns, "The Supreme Court as Republican Schoolmaster," in *The Supreme Court and American Constitutionalism*, ed. Bradford Wilson and Ken Masugi (Lanham, MD: Rowman & Littlefield, 1998), p. 11.

109. *Lochner*, 198 U.S. at 75 (Holmes, J., dissenting).

110. Thomas Paine, *Common Sense*, in *Thomas Paine: Collected Writings*, ed. Eric Foner (New York: Library of America, 1995), p. 6.

111. Eric Foner, *The Story of American Freedom* (New York: W. W. Norton, 1998), pp. 115–61.

112. *Lochner*, 198 U.S. at 76 (Holmes, J., dissenting) ("I think that the word 'liberty' . . . is perverted when it is held to prevent the natural outcome of a dominant opinion.").

113. James W. Ely, "The Oxymoron Reconsidered: Myth and Reality in the Origins of Substantive Due Process," *Constitutional Commentary* 16 (1999): 344.

114. Bork, *Tempting of America*, pp. 28–49.

115. *Dred Scott v. Sandford*, 60 U.S. (19 How.) 393 (1857).

116. Bork, *Tempting of America*, pp. 28–34.

117. *Roe v. Wade*, 410 U.S. 113 (1973).

118. These include the fugitive slave clause and the three-fifths clause, among others. As Harry V. Jaffa notes, "The recognition of the right of slave ownership is massively present within the Constitution of 1787." "Jaffa v. Bork: An Exchange," *National Review*, March 21, 1994, p. 56 (1994 WLNR 3406787).

119. *Dred Scott*, 60 U.S. (19 How.) at 403.

120. Ibid. at 411.

121. Ibid. at 425–26 (emphasis added).

122. There were, of course, many other problems with the *Dred Scott* decision. See Don E. Fehrenbacher, *The Dred Scott Case* (Oxford: Oxford University Press, 1978); Harry V. Jaffa, *A New Birth of Freedom* (Lanham, MD: Rowman & Littlefield, 2000), pp. 285–303; and Mark Graber, *Dred Scott and the Problem of Constitutional Evil* (Cambridge: Cambridge University Press, 2006).

123. "Taney's assertion that the Constitution expressly affirms the right to slave property, and by this reason enjoins a duty to protect slave property, rests mainly on a construction of Section 2, Article IV, and does not depend upon the Fifth Amendment at all. And this assertion, combined with the supremacy clause, certainly does yield, as a logical necessity, the conclusion that no state may destroy the right of property in a slave." Harry V. Jaffa, *Crisis of the House Divided* (Chicago: University of Chicago Press, 1959), pp. 290–91.

124. *Dred Scott*, 60 U.S. (19 How.) at 450.

125. Graber, *Dred Scott*, p. 64.

126. Bork, *Tempting of America*, pp. 44–45.

127. Ibid., p. 124.

128. Ibid.

129. Robert Bork, *Slouching towards Gomorrah* (New York: HarperCollins, 1996), p. 63 (quoting Irving Kristol).

130. Bork, *Tempting of America*, p. 139. In another place, Bork has claimed that "only a legal-positivist judge can be an adherent of the Framers' original intent." Robert H. Bork, "Original Intent and the Framers of the Constitution: A Disputed Question," book review, *National Review*, February 7, 1994, p. 61 (1994 WLNR 3412460).

131. James Madison, "Sovereignty," in *Writings of James Madison*, ed. Gaillard Hunt (New York: Putnam, 1900–1910), vol. 9, pp. 570–71. To borrow a line from J. M. Balkin, Bork's proposition is "about as Madisonian as Madison, Wisconsin. It is a tribute to a great man and his achievements, but bears only a limited connection to his actual views. . . . Madison was more likely to believe that the state existed

to protect individual rights or natural rights than that such rights existed to serve the just interests of the state." Balkin, "Populism and Progressivism as Constitutional Categories," *Yale Law Journal* 104 (1995): 1956. Balkin was actually discussing Cass R. Sunstein, who abuses Madison's name in the same way as Bork. I owe this reference to Eugene Volokh.

132. James Madison, "Charters," in *Madison: Writings*, ed. Jack Rakove (New York: Library of America, 1999) p. 502.

133. Robert H. Bork, *Coercing Virtue* (Washington: American Enterprise Institute, 2003), pp. 11–12.

134. *Seminole Tribe of Florida v. Florida*, 517 U.S. 44 (1996) (Souter, Ginsburg, and Breyer, JJ., dissenting).

135. Ibid. at 166. See also *College Savings Bank v. Florida Prepaid Postsecondary Education Expense Board*, 527 U.S. 666, 701 (1999) (Breyer, Stevens, Souter, and Ginsburg, JJ., dissenting). Cass Sunstein, "*Lochner*'s Legacy," *Columbia Law Review* 87 (1987): 873–919; Laurence Tribe, "The Curvature of Constitutional Space: What Lawyers Can Learn from Modern Physics," *Harvard Law Review* 103 (1989): 1–39; and Laurence Tribe, *Constitutional Law*, 2nd ed. (Mineola, NY: Foundation Press, 1988), p. 578.

136. Cass R. Sunstein, "Free Speech Now," *University of Chicago Law Review* 59 (1992): 268.

137. Cass R. Sunstein, *Democracy and the Problem of Free Speech* (New York: Free Press, 1993), p. 30: "[A] major problem with the pre–New Deal framework was that it treated the existing distribution of resources and opportunities as prepolitical and presocial . . . when in fact it was not. . . . [The] private or voluntary private sphere . . . was actually itself a creation of law and hardly purely voluntary. When the law of trespass enabled an employer to exclude an employee from 'his' property unless the employee met certain conditions, the law was crucially involved. Without the law of trespass, and accompanying legal rules of contract and tort, the relationship between employers and employees would not be what it now is; indeed, it would be extremely difficult to figure out what that relationship might be, if it would exist in recognizable form at all."

138. Cass R. Sunstein, "A New Deal for Speech," *Hastings Communications and Entertainment Law Journal* 17 (1994): 140.

139. Tribe, "Curvature of Constitutional Space," 7.

140. Ibid., 7–8.

141. Tribe, *Constitutional Law*, p. 578.

142. Lewis Carroll, *Through the Looking Glass* (New York: Harper & Bros., 1902), p. 32.

143. David E. Bernstein, "*Lochner*'s Legacy's Legacy," *Texas Law Review* 82 (2003): 33–43; and Keynes, *Liberty, Property, and Privacy*, pp. 117, 127.

144. See Bernstein, "*Lochner*'s Legacy's Legacy," 44–48; Hadley Arkes, *The Return of George Sutherland* (Princeton, NJ: Princeton University Press, 1994); Tom G. Palmer, Book Review, *Cato Journal* 19 (1999): 331–36; and Timothy Sandefur, "Does the State Create the Market, and Should It Pursue Efficiency?" *Harvard Journal of Law & Public Policy* 33 (2010) (forthcoming).

145. See, for example, *Lawrence v. Texas*, 539 U.S. 558 (2003); and Randy E. Barnett, "Justice Kennedy's Libertarian Revolution: *Lawrence v. Texas*," *2002–2003 Cato Supreme Court Review* (Washington: Cato Institute, 2003), pp. 21–41.

146. Sunstein, "A New Deal for Speech."

147. Paul Kens, *Lochner v. New York: Economic Regulation on Trial* (Lawrence: University Press of Kansas, 1998).

148. David E. Bernstein, "*Lochner* Era Revisionism, Revised: *Lochner* and the Origins of Fundamental Rights Constitutionalism," *Georgetown Law Journal* 92 (2003): 8, n. 21.

149. Kens, *Lochner*, p. 95.

150. See Frederick Mark Gedicks, "An Originalist Defense of Substantive Due Process: Magna Carta, Higher-Law Constitutionalism, and the Fifth Amendment," *Emory Law Journal* 58 (2009): 627–33.

151. *Butler v. Craig*, 2 H. & McH. 214 (Md. 1787).

152. *Ham v. McClaws*, 1 S.C.L. (1 Bay) 91 (S.C. Ct. Com. Pl. 1789).

153. *Anonymous*, 2 N.C. 28, 30 (1794).

154. *Hoke v. Henderson*, 15 N.C. 1, 7–8 (1833).

155. Kens, *Lochner*, p. 98. Kens does at least admit in one sentence that "[i]t is true . . . that the idea of substantive due process existed in American law before the Civil War," but he goes on to insist that in the 1860s there were "only a few scattered state court opinions to support [the] extension of due process to the substance of legislation." Ibid., p. 100. This is hardly surprising since there was no Fourteenth Amendment before the 1860s, and government regulation was much less ubiquitous than today.

156. Paul Kens, *Justice Stephen J. Field: Shaping Liberty from the Gold Rush to the Gilded Age* (Lawrence: University Press of Kansas, 1997).

157. Kens, *Lochner*, p. 120.

158. 1 William Blackstone, *Commentaries* *427.

159. *Allen v. Tooley*, 80 Eng. Rep. 1055 (K.B. 1614).

160. *Case of the Tailors*, 77 Eng. Rep. 1218, 1219 (K.B. 1615).

161. Ibid.

162. Clinton Rossiter, ed., *The Federalist Papers* (New York: New American Library, 1961), no. 10, p. 78.

163. Kens, *Lochner*, pp. 104–5.

164. Virginia Declaration of Rights (1776) (emphasis added).

165. Quoted in Kens, *Lochner*, p. 151 (emphasis in original). In fact, I have been unable to locate this quotation. In his article "Liberty of Contract," Pound writes, "The sociological movement in jurisprudence . . . [is a] movement for the adjustment of principles and doctrines to the human conditions they are to govern rather than to assumed first principles [and] . . . for putting the human factor in the central place and relegating logic to its true position as an instrument" (p. 484). Be that as it may, the fact is clear that the position of *Lochner*'s critics, both then and now, is based on a rejection of the first principle that individual liberty is the foundation of the Constitution.

166. Kens, *Lochner*, p. 167. Kens is quoting here from *Ives v. South Buffalo R. Co.*, 200 N.Y. 271 (1911). Again, the quotation is not rendered quite accurately since it omits an unimportant phrase without an ellipsis. But much more importantly, *Ives* did not reject workers' compensation schemes entirely, just this particular one. Judge Werner went out of his way to note: "So far as the statute merely creates a new remedy, in addition to those which existed before, it is not invalid. The state has complete control over the remedies which it offers to suitors in its courts, even to the point of making them applicable to rights or equities already in existence. It may change the common law and the statutes, so as to create duties and liabilities which never existed

before. . . . The power of the state to make such changes in methods of procedure and in substantive law is clearly recognized." Ibid. at 299–300.

167. The same proposition underlay *Wynehamer*, 13 N.Y. at 393.

168. Kens, *Lochner*, p. 181 (emphasis added).

169. See ibid., pp. 125–27, 131.

170. Ibid., p. 176.

171. One historical detail deserves mention: Kens implies that Henry Weismann, who argued *Lochner* before the Supreme Court, was not an attorney, writing that he had "no formal education, and that there is no record of where he read the law." Ibid., p. 114. In fact, Weismann was a graduate of Brooklyn Law School, class of 1903. He was also a baker himself, who learned firsthand of the unfairness of the maximum hours law that he had advocated years earlier. "When I was a young man—a journeyman baker—and secretary of their national organization," he reflected, "I thought labor was right in all things. I was fiery and full of ideals. Later I became a master baker and, undergoing an intellectual revolution, saw where the law I had succeeded in having passed was unjust to the employers." "Henry Weismann, Lawyer, Is Dead," *New York Times*, April 18, 1935. I thank Weismann's granddaughter Ann W. Gehring for forwarding me copies of Weismann's law degree, class picture, and obituary.

172. Kens, *Lochner*, p. 159.

173. *Marbury v. Madison*, 5 U.S. (1 Cranch) 137 (1803).

174. Perhaps the most sophisticated analysis of the meaning and effect of this dissent is G. Edward White, "Revisiting Substantive Due Process and Holmes's *Lochner* Dissent," *Brooklyn Law Review* 63 (1997): 87–128.

175. *Truax v. Corrigan*, 257 U.S. 312, 376 (1921) (Brandeis, J., dissenting).

Chapter 6

1. John Dewey, "The Future of Liberalism," *Journal of Politics* 32, no. 9 (1935): 225–30.

2. John Dewey, *Liberalism and Social Action* (Amherst, MA: Prometheus Books, 2000), p. 58; and Thomas G. West, "Progressivism and the Transformation of American Government," in *The Progressive Revolution in Politics and Political Science*, ed. John Marini and Ken Masugi (Lanham, MD: Rowman & Littlefield, 2005), p. 15.

3. Robert Horwitz, "John Dewey," in *History of Political Philosophy*, ed. Leo Strauss and Joseph Cropsey (Chicago: Rand McNally, 1963), pp. 746–62.

4. Explanations of the Progressive movement and its relationship to the intellectual tradition of the American Constitution can be found in Marini and Masugi, *The Progressive Revolution*; Richard A. Epstein, *How Progressives Rewrote the Constitution* (Washington: Cato Institute, 2006); Michael McGerr, *A Fierce Discontent: The Rise and Fall of the Progressive Movement in America, 1870–1920* (New York: Simon & Schuster, 2003); Gabriel Kolko, *The Triumph of Conservatism* (Chicago: Quadrangle Books, 1963); and Charles Edward Merriam, *A History of American Political Theories* (New York: Macmillan, 1903). See also Timothy Sandefur, "Mine and Thine Distinct: What *Kelo* Says about Our Path," *Chapman Law Review* 10 (2006): 19–26.

5. *Truax v. Corrigan*, 257 U.S. 312, 376 (1921) (Brandeis, J., dissenting) (emphasis added).

6. Dorsey Richardson, *Constitutional Doctrines of Justice Oliver Wendell Holmes* (Baltimore: Johns Hopkins Press, 1924), p. 41.

7. *Nebbia v. New York*, 291 U.S. 502 (1934).

8. Ibid. at 537.

9. *United States v. Carolene Products*, 304 U.S. 144, 152 n. 3 (1938).

10. Joseph Schumpeter, *Capitalism, Socialism and Democracy* (New York: Harper, 1975), pp. 82–85.

11. Amity Schlaes, *The Forgotten Man: A New History of the Great Depression* (New York: HarperCollins, 2007); and Arthur A. Ekirch Jr., *Ideologies and Utopias: The Impact of the New Deal on American Thought* (Chicago: Quadrangle Books, 1969).

12. Arthur A. Ekirch Jr., *The Decline of American Liberalism* (New York: Atheneum, 1976), p. 276. See also Harold L. Cole and Lee E. Ohanian, "New Deal Policies and the Persistence of the Great Depression: A General Equilibrium Analysis," *Journal of Political Economy* 112, no. 4 (August 2004): 779–816; Gary Dean Best, *Pride, Prejudice, and Politics: Roosevelt versus Recovery, 1933–1938* (New York: Praeger, 1991); Michael Weinstein, *Recovery and Redistribution under the NIRA* (Amsterdam: North-Holland, 1980); Gene Smiley, *Rethinking the Great Depression: A New View of Its Causes and Consequences* (Chicago: Ivan R. Dee, 2002); and Jim Powell, *FDR's Folly: How Roosevelt and His New Deal Prolonged the Great Depression* (New York: Crown Forum, 2003).

13. *People v. Nebbia*, 262 N.Y. 259, 261–62 (1933).

14. *Nebbia*, 291 U.S. at 537.

15. Ibid. at 556 (McReynolds, J., dissenting) ("If a statute to prevent conflagrations should require householders to pour oil on their roofs as a means of curbing the spread of fire when discovered in the neighborhood, we could hardly uphold it.").

16. *FCC v. Beach Communications, Inc.*, 508 U.S. 307, 315 (1993).

17. In *Chevron USA, Inc. v. Bronster*, 363 F.3d 846, 855 (9th Cir. 2004), for example, the trial court heard evidence and found as a matter of fact that the regulation at issue would actually raise oil prices—thus accomplishing the exact opposite of the legislature's declared intent. On appeal, the state "[did] not challenge the district court's conclusion" that the law "fails to advance Hawaii's goal of lowering retail gas prices." Nevertheless, the U.S. Supreme Court reversed. *Lingle v. Chevron*, 544 U.S. 528 (2005). "We find the proceedings below remarkable, to say the least," said the Court, "given that we have long eschewed such heightened scrutiny when addressing substantive due process challenges to government regulation. . . . The reasons for deference to legislative judgments about the need for, and likely effectiveness of, regulatory actions are by now well established, and we think they are no less applicable here." Ibid., at 545.

18. Margaret O'Brien-Strain and Thomas MaCurdy, *Increasing the Minimum Wage: California's Winners and Losers* (San Francisco: Public Policy Institute of California, 2000), pp. 37–40. See also Joseph E. Stiglitz, *Economics* (New York: W. W. Norton, 1993), pp. 130–33; Milton and Rose Freidman, *Free to Choose: A Personal Statement* (San Diego: Harvest/HBJ, 1990), pp. 237–38; Richard H. Sander, E. Douglass Williams, and Joseph Doherty, *The Economic and Distributional Consequences of the Santa Monica Minimum Wage Ordinance* (Washington: Employment Policies Institute, 2002); Matthew B. Kibbe, "The Minimum Wage: Washington's Perennial Myth," Cato Institute Policy Analysis no. 106, May 23, 1988; Donald Deere, Kevin M. Murphy, and Finis Welch, "Sense and Nonsense on the Minimum Wage," *Regulation* (Winter 1995): 47–56; Craig Garthwaite, Testimony before the House Subcommittee on Workforce, Empowerment, and Government Programs, 108 Cong., 2d sess., April 29, 2004, pp. 28–29; Simon Rottenberg, ed., *The Economics of Legal Minimum Wages* (Washington: American Enterprise Institute, 1981); *The Employment Impact of a Comprehensive Living Wage Law: Evidence from California* (Washington: Employment Policies

Institute, 1999); David Neumark, *How Living Wage Laws Affect Low-Wage Workers and Low-Income Families* (San Francisco: Public Policy Institute of California, 2002); Carl F. Horowitz, "Keeping the Poor Poor: The Dark Side of the Living Wage," Cato Institute Policy Analysis no. 493, October 21, 2003; Mark Turner and Berna Demiralp, "Higher Minimum Wages Harm Minority and Inner-City Teens," Employment Policies Institute, Washington, 2000; and Richard K. Vedder and Lowell Gallaway, "Does the Minimum Wage Reduce Poverty?" Employment Policies Institute, Washington, 2001.

19. *Beach Communications,* 508 U.S. at 315.

20. Ibid.

21. See Simon Greenleaf, *A Treatise on the Law of Evidence,* 10th ed. (Boston: Little, Brown, 1860), vol. 1, p. 103. Greenleaf cites the Digest of Justinian for this point.

22. Anthony de Jasay, *Justice and Its Surroundings* (Indianapolis: Liberty Fund, 2002), pp. 150–51.

23. *Madden v. Commonwealth of Kentucky,* 309 U.S. 83, 88 (1940).

24. *Arceneaux v. Treen,* 671 F.2d 128, 136 (5th Cir. 1982) (Goldberg, J., concurring).

25. Clark Neily, "No Such Thing: Litigating under the Rational Basis Test," *New York University Journal of Law and Liberty* 1 (2005): 905–6

26. Ibid., 904.

27. *Nollan v. California Coastal Com'n,* 483 U.S. 825, 834 (1987).

28. *Lawrence v. Texas,* 539 U.S. 558 (2003).

29. Ibid. at 605 (Thomas, J., dissenting).

30. G. Edward White, *The Constitution and the New Deal* (Cambridge, MA: Harvard University Press, 2000), p. 4.

31. For example, in *United States v. Morrison,* 529 U.S. 598, 629 (2000), Justice Souter listed "the mountain of data assembled by Congress," showing that violence against women had an effect on interstate commerce, contending that the Court should defer to these congressional reports. The Court, however, found that Congress's mere say-so could not convert activities that are beyond congressional power into the sort of thing that Congress can regulate. Ibid. at 614–15. More to the point, in *Grutter v. Bollinger,* 539 U.S. 306, 328 (2003), the Court relied on statements by the University of Michigan "and their *amici*" to hold that "racial diversity" was a legitimate state interest.

32. Richard A. Epstein, *Takings: Private Property and the Power of Eminent Domain* (Cambridge, MA: Harvard University Press, 1987), p. 109.

33. See Scott Douglas Gerber, *To Secure These Rights* (New York: New York University Press, 1995); and Timothy Sandefur, "Liberal Originalism: A Past for the Future," *Harvard Journal of Law and Public Policy* 27 (2004): 489–541.

34. Timothy Sandefur, "The Wolves and the Sheep of Constitutional Law: A Review Essay on Kermit Roosevelt's *The Myth of Judicial Activism,*" *Journal of Law and Politics* 23 (2006): 1–40.

35. Indeed, there is an interesting parallel here with Leo Strauss's description of modern, value-free politics as "retail sanity and wholesale madness." Strauss, *Natural Right and History* (Chicago: University of Chicago Press, 1950), p. 4. The parallel is no coincidence: the concept of rational basis scrutiny was devised as part of the Progressive assault on the Founders' natural law political theory, which connected ethics and politics. Relying on Pragmatist doctrines that rejected Enlightenment natural law theories, the Progressives replaced the Constitution's higher-law background with a modernistic reading that held that, in Louis Menand's words, "if the legal process was adhered to, the outcome is just. Justice does not preexist the case at hand; justice

is whatever result just procedures have led to." Menand, *The Metaphysical Club* (New York: Farrar, Strauss, and Giroux, 2001), p. 432.

36. *Beach Communications*, 508 U.S. at 323 n. 3 (Stevens, J., concurring in judgment).

37. *S.S. Kresge Co. v. Couzens*, 290 Mich. 185, 192 (1939).

38. Ibid.

39. *Meadows v. Odom*, 360 F. Supp. 2d 811, 823–24 (M.D. La. 2005), *vacated as moot*, 198 Fed. Appx. 348 (5th Cir. 2006).

40. *United States v. Carolene Products Co.*, 304 U.S. 144, 152–53 (1938).

41. Victoria F. Nourse makes a powerful argument that this evolution began with *Skinner v. Oklahoma ex rel. Williamson*, 316 U.S. 535 (1942), a case invalidating an Oklahoma law that required the forced sterilization of prison inmates. Nourse, *In Reckless Hands:* Skinner v. Oklahoma *and the Near-Triumph of American Eugenics* (New York: W. W. Norton, 2008), especially chap. 9. No single case, however, indicates the Court's change in direction. Beginning in the World War II era, the Court shifted from the almost total deference of New Deal cases like *Nebbia* toward a higher scrutiny—not in cases involving class legislation, as with the pre–New Deal cases, but in cases involving what the justices considered to be important rights of personal dignity or democratic participation. Also indicative of this shift is *West Virginia Bd. of Ed. v. Barnette*, 319 U.S. 624 (1943), which abandoned the extreme deference of *Minersville School District v. Gobitis*, 310 U.S. 586 (1940). See Epstein, *Progressives*, pp. 100–16.

42. Edward Keynes, *Liberty, Property, and Privacy: Toward a Jurisprudence of Substantive Due Process* (University Park: Pennsylvania State University Press, 1996), pp. 156–57.

43. Laurence Tribe, *American Constitutional Law*, 2nd ed. (Mineola, NY: Foundation Press, 1988), p. 1374.

44. *Dolan v. City of Tigard*, 512 U.S. 374, 392 (1994).

45. Cf. Ludwig von Mises, *The Anticapitalistic Mentality* (Grove City, PA: Libertarian Press, 1972); and F. A. Hayek, "The Intellectuals and Socialism," *University of Chicago Law Review* 16 (1949): 417–33.

46. *United States v. Carlton*, 512 U.S. 26, 41–42 (1994) (Scalia and Thomas, JJ., concurring in judgment).

47. *Williams v. Morgan*, 478 F.3d 1316 (11th Cir. 2007); *Williams v. Attorney General of Ala.*, 378 F.3d 1232 (11th Cir. 2004); and *Pleasureland Museum, Inc. v. Beutter*, 288 F.3d 988 (7th Cir. 2002). See also *This That and the Other Gift and Tobacco, Inc. v. Cobb County, Ga.*, 439 F.3d 1275 (11th Cir. 2006) (challenging law against advertising adult novelties).

48. *Williams*, 478 F.3d at 1322.

49. *Lawrence*, 539 U.S. at 571.

50. *Kelo v. City of New London*, 545 U.S. 469, 518 (2005) (Thomas, J., dissenting).

51. *City of Cleburne, Tex. v. Cleburne Living Center*, 473 U.S. 432 (1985).

52. *Romer v. Evans*, 517 U.S. 620 (1996).

53. Ibid. at 632–33.

54. As one commentator puts it, these are "'true rational basis' cases because they involve a true search for rationality." Donald Marritz, "Making Equality Matter (Again): The Prohibition against Special Laws in the Pennsylvania Constitution," *Widener Journal of Public Law* 3 (1993): 176.

55. *Washington v. Seattle School Dist. No. 1*, 458 U.S. 457, 486 (1982) (quoting *San Antonio Independent School Dist. v. Rodriguez*, 411 U.S. 1, 28 (1973)).

56. Robert G. McCloskey, "Economic Due Process and the Supreme Court: An Exhumation and Reburial," *Supreme Court Review*, 1962: 34–62.

57. Ibid.

Chapter 7

1. Quoted in R. H. Coase, *The Firm, the Market and the Law* (Chicago: University of Chicago Press, 1990), p. 196.

2. *New State Ice Co. v. Liebmann*, 285 U.S. 262 (1932).

3. Ibid. at 278–79.

4. Ibid. at 278 (quoting *Burns Baking Co. v. Bryan*, 264 U. S. 504, 513 (1924)).

5. Ibid. at 311 (Brandeis, J., dissenting).

6. Ibid. at 279–80. Justice Jackson would make a similar point almost 20 years later in *Skinner v. State of Okl. ex rel. Williamson*, 316 U.S. 535, 546 (1942): "There are limits to the extent to which a legislatively represented majority may conduct biological experiments at the expense of the dignity and personality and natural powers of a minority."

7. *Liebmann*, 285 U.S. at 279–80.

8. *Jones v. Temmer*, 829 F. Supp. 1226 (D. Colo. 1993), *vacated as moot*, 57 F.3d 921 (10th Cir. 1995).

9. Hadley Arkes, *The Return of George Sutherland* (Princeton, NJ: Princeton University Press, 1994), p. 55.

10. *Dent v. West Virginia*, 129 U.S. 114 (1889).

11. Ibid. at 122.

12. Ibid.

13. *Schware v. Bd. of Bar Examiners of the State of N.M.*, 353 U.S. 232, 239 (1957).

14. Lawrence M. Friedman, *A History of American Law*, 3rd ed. (New York: Touchstone, 2005), pp. 340–46.

15. *Debates and Proceedings of the Constitutional Convention of the State of California* (Sacramento: State Printing Office, 1880), vol. 1, p. 633.

16. Quoted in Stephen A. Ambrose, *Nothing Like It in the World* (New York: Simon & Schuster, 2000), p. 153.

17. Jean Pfaelzer, *Driven Out: The Forgotten War against Chinese Americans* (New York: Random House, 2007), especially chap. 2.

18. G. B. Willis and P. K. Stockton, *Debates and Proceedings of the Constitutional Convention of the State of California* (Sacramento: State Printing Office, 1880), p. 727.

19. *Yick Wo v. Hopkins*, 118 U.S. 356 (1886).

20. Ibid. at 368.

21. Ibid. at 370.

22. Ibid. at 373–74.

23. Ibid. at 370.

24. David E. Bernstein, "*Lochner*, Parity, and the Chinese Laundry Cases," *William & Mary Law Review* 41 (1999): 244–50.

25. David E. Bernstein, *Only One Place of Redress: African-Americans, Labor Regulations and the Courts from Reconstruction to the New Deal* (Durham, NC: Duke University Press, 2001), especially chap. 2.

26. *Replogle v. City of Little Rock*, 267 S.W. 353, 357 (Ark. 1924) (quoting *Lochner v. New York*, 198 U.S. 45, 64 (1905)).

27. Ibid. at 356.

28. Bernstein, *Only One Place of Redress*, p. 35.

29. Thurgood Marshall, "The Supreme Court as Protector of Civil Rights: Equal Protection of the Laws," in *Thurgood Marshall: His Speeches, Writings, Arguments, Opinions, and Reminiscences*, ed. M. Tushnet (Chicago: Lawrence Hill Books, 2001), pp. 119–20.

30. *Cornwell v. Hamilton*, 80 F. Supp. 2d 1101, 1105 (S.D. Cal. 1999).

31. *Cornwell v. California Bd. of Barbering and Cosmetology*, 962 F. Supp. 1260, 1277 (S.D. Cal. 1997).

32. See further Clark Neily, "No Such Thing: Litigating under the Rational Basis Test," *New York University Journal of Law and Liberty* 1 (2005): 898–914.

33. Timothy Sandefur, "Is Economic Exclusion a Legitimate State Interest? Four Recent Cases Test the Boundaries," *William & Mary Bill of Rights Journal* 14 (2006): 1061.

34. Milton Friedman, *Capitalism and Freedom* (Chicago: University of Chicago Press, 1962), p. 148.

35. Morris M. Kleiner, *Licensing Occupations: Ensuring Quality or Restricting Competition?* (Kalamazoo, MI: Upjohn Institute, 2006); S. David Young, *The Rule of Experts* (Washington: Cato Institute, 1987); Mario Pagliero, "What Is the Objective of Professional Licensing? Evidence from the US Market for Lawyers," University of Turin working paper, January 2005, http://www.fep.up.pt/conferences/earie2005/cd_rom/Session%20II/II.G/Pagliero.pdf (accessed June 18, 2005); David E. Bernstein, *Only One Place of Redress*, chap. 2; David E. Bernstein, "Licensing Laws: A Historical Example of the Use of Government Regulatory Power against African-Americans," *San Diego Law Review* 31 (1994): 89–104; Jonathan Rose, "Occupational Licensing: A Framework for Analysis," *Arizona State Law Journal* (1979): 189–202; Lawrence Shepard, "Licensing Restrictions and the Cost of Dental Care," *Journal of Law and Economics* 21 (1978): 187–201; Kathleen Sowle Stolar, "Occupational Licensing: An Antitrust Analysis," *Missouri Law Review* 41 (1976): 66–79; Walter Gellhorn, "The Abuse of Occupational Licensing," *University of Chicago Law Review* 44 (1976): 6–27; Alex Maurizi, "Occupational Licensing and the Public Interest," *Journal of Political Economy* 82 (1974): 399–413; "Note: Due Process Limitations on Occupational Licensing," *Virginia Law Review* 59 (1973): 1097–129; Thomas G. Moore, "The Purpose of Licensing," *Journal of Law and Economics* 4 (1961): 93–117; J. A. C. Grant, "The Gild Returns to America," *Journal of Politics* 4 (1942): 303–36, 458–77; and David Fellman, "A Case Study in Administrative Law: The Regulation of Barbers," *Washington University Law Quarterly* 26 (1941): 213–42.

36. Morris M. Kleiner, "Occupational Licensing," *Journal of Economic Perspectives* 14 (2000): 196.

37. Chris Cassidy, "Salem Struggles to Sort Out Psychic 'Free-for-All,'" *Salem News*, May 24, 2007, http://www.associatedcontent.com/article/283540/the_future_looks_good_for_palm_readers.html; and Dina Cardin, "The Futures Market," *North Shore Online*, June 15, 2007, http://www.townonline.com/northshoresunday/homepage/x504545030.

38. It is ironic, therefore, that one of the most important law review articles on economic liberty in the post–New Deal era was Robert McCloskey's "Economic Due Process and the Supreme Court: An Exhumation and Reburial," *Supreme Court Review* (1962): 34–62.

39. Lawrence M. Friedman, *History of American Law*, p. 341.

40. Institute for Justice, "The Right to Urn an Honest Living: Challenging Tennessee's Casket Monopoly," http://www.ij.org/index.php?option=com_content&task=view&id=767&Itemid=165.

41. 59 *Fed. Reg.* 1592, 1593 (1994). This regulation prohibits funeral homes from charging "handling fees," which are simply surcharges meant to discourage customers from purchasing caskets outside of the fineral home. But the regulation is routinely flouted.

42. Tenn. Code Ann. § 62-5-101(3)(A)(ii).

43. Rules of the Tennessee Board of Funeral Directors and Embalmers, http://www.state.tn.us/sos/rules/0660/0660-03.pdf (accessed April 18, 2003).

44. *Craigmiles v. Giles*, 110 F. Supp. 2d 658 (E.D. Tenn. 2000).

45. Ibid. at 663.

46. *Craigmiles v. Giles*, 312 F.3d 220 (6th Cir. 2002).

47. Ibid. at 225 (quoting *United States v. Searan*, 259 F.3d 434, 447 (6th Cir. 2001)).

48. Ibid.

49. Ibid. at 224.

50. *Powers v. Harris*, 2002 WL 32026155 (W.D. Okla. December 12, 2002), *aff'd*, 379 F.3d 1208 (10th Cir. 2004), *cert. denied*, 125 S. Ct. 1638 (2005).

51. 59 O.S. §§ 396.2.2.d, 396.3a.

52. 59 O.S. § 396.6.b. Unlike Tennessee law, the Oklahoma law does not appear to allow any way around the apprenticeship requirement.

53. *Powers* therefore was decided in direct contradiction to *Craigmiles*. Although it typically grants certiorari in cases in which the federal courts of appeal are divided, the U.S. Supreme Court denied certiorari in *Powers*, 125 S. Ct. 1638 (2005), and the division remains unresolved.

54. *Powers*, 2002 WL 32026155 at *15.

55. Ibid. at *18.

56. Ibid.

57. *Powers v. Harris*, 379 F.3d 1208 (10th Cir. 2004).

58. Ibid. at 1218.

59. Ibid.

60. Ibid. at 1221.

61. *City of Philadelphia v. New Jersey*, 437 U.S. 617, 624 (1978).

62. *H.P. Hood & Sons, Inc. v. Du Mond*, 336 U.S. 525, 537–38 (1949).

63. *Energy Reserves Group, Inc. v. Kansas Power & Light*, 459 U.S. 400, 411 (1983).

64. *Powers*, 379 F.3d at 1219.

65. Cass R. Sunstein, "Naked Preferences and the Constitution," *Columbia Law Review* 84 (1984): 1689.

66. See Clinton Rossiter, ed., *The Federalist Papers* (New York: New American Library, 1961), no. 45, p. 288; and Clint Bolick, *Grassroots Tyranny* (Washington: Cato Institute, 1993), pp. 13–52.

67. *Powers*, 379 F.3d at 1222.

68. Ibid.

69. Peter M. Cicchino, "Reason and the Rule of Law: Should Bare Assertions of 'Public Morality' Qualify as Legitimate Government Interests for the Purposes of Equal Protection Review?" *Georgetown Law Journal* 87 (1998): 178.

70. During the debates over the ratification of the Constitution, "Brutus" made the point well when discussing the "general welfare" clause of the Constitution: "It is as absurd to say, that the power of Congress is limited by these general expressions, 'to provide for the common safety, and general welfare,' as it would be to say, that it would be limited, had the constitution said they should have power to lay taxes, &c. at will and pleasure. Were this authority given, it might be said, that under it the legislature could not do injustice, or pursue any measures, but such as were calculated to promote the public good, and happiness. For every man, rulers as well as others, are bound by the immutable laws of God and reason, always to will what is right. It is certainly right and fit, that the governors of every people should provide for the common defence and general welfare; every government, therefore, in the world, even the greatest despot, is limited in the exercise of his power. But however just this reasoning may be, it would be found, in practice, a most pitiful restriction. The government would always say, their measures were designed and calculated to promote the public good; and there being no judge between them and the people, the rulers themselves must, and would always, judge for themselves." Bernard Bailyn, *The Debate on the Constitution* (New York: Library of America, 1993), vol. 1, pp. 618–19.

71. Transcript of deposition of Eric Paulsen, *Merrifield, et al. v. Lockyer, et al.*, April 19, 2005, pp. 115–16 (on file with author).

72. Ibid., p. 45 (emphasis added).

73. Ibid., pp. 46–47.

74. Ibid., p. 149.

75. *Merrifield v. Lockyer*, 388 F. Supp. 2d 1051 (N.D. Cal. 2005).

76. Ibid. at 1058.

77. Ibid.

78. *Merrifield v. Lockyer*, 547 F.3d 978, 991 (9th Cir. 2008).

79. Ibid.

80. Ibid. at 991, n. 15.

81. "Wal-Mart 2007 Annual Report," Wal-Mart Stores, Inc., Bentonville, AR, http://walmartstores.com/Media/Investors/2007_annual_report.pdf.

82. Richard Vedder and Wendell Cox, *The Wal-Mart Revolution: How Big-Box Stores Benefit Consumers, Workers, and the Economy* (Washington: AEI Press, 2006).

83. Eric R. Claeys, "*Euclid* Lives? The Uneasy Legacy of Progressivism in Zoning," *Fordham Law Review* 73 (2004): 731–70.

84. Anthony B. Sanders, "The 'New Judicial Federalism' before Its Time: A Comprehensive Review of Economic Substantive Due Process under State Constitutional Law since 1940 and the Reasons for Its Recent Decline," *American University Law Review* 55 (2005): 457–540.

85. George Lefcoe, "The Regulation of Superstores: The Legality of Zoning Ordinances Emerging from the Skirmishes between Wal-Mart and the United Food and Commercial Workers Union," *Arkansas Law Review* 58 (2006): 842; Ted Balaker, "Ban Wal-Mart, Hurt Families," *Los Angeles Daily News*, January 26, 2004; Julian Sanchez, "The Wal-Mart Crusade: Big-Boxing a Mega-Retailer's Ears," *Reason*, March 2006; and RiShawn Biddle, "Sam's Curse: Will Wal-Mart Superstores Really Devastate the City of Angels?" *Reason.com*, March 18, 2004, http://reason.com/archives/2004/03/18/sams-curse.

86. *Wal-Mart Stores, Inc. v. City of Turlock*, 138 Cal. App. 4th 273, 283 (2006).

87. Ibid. at 301.

88. Ibid.

89. Ibid. at 303.

90. Minutes of Hanford City Council, March 4, 2003 (on file with author).

91. Minutes of Hanford City Council, April 15, 2003 (on file with author).

92. Letter from Rusty C. Robinson to Hanford City Council, March 4, 2003 (on file with author).

93. Minutes of Hanford City Council, March 4, 2003 (on file with author).

94. *Hernandez v. City of Hanford*, 41 Cal. 4th 279, 296 (2007).

95. Ibid. at 297 (emphasis in original).

96. Adrian Hernandez's case bears a striking resemblance to the notorious decision regarding eminent domain in *Kelo v. City of New London*, 545 U.S. 469 (2005). There, the U.S. Supreme Court declared that local officials may condemn private property and transfer it to developers to construct shopping centers or luxury condominiums for their own profit because doing so creates jobs, which is a public benefit rather than a private benefit. Yet the Court insisted that taking property for a purely private benefit was still unconstitutional. Ibid. at 477–78. While this sounds nice, it is meaningless because every *private* business will "create jobs" or provide *some* sort of public benefits. If anything that benefits the public in *some* way, no matter how attenuated, can qualify as a "public benefit," it will be impossible to declare any condemnation unconstitutional for serving "private" benefits. The *Hernandez* decision is *Kelo* for zoning laws: government may control or eliminate fair economic competition in whatever way it wants, so long as it claims that some sort of vague public benefit will result from its actions.

97. Amity Shlaes, *The Forgotten Man: A New History of the Great Depression* (New York: HarperCollins, 2007), pp. 153–54; and Ashley Sellers and Jesse E. Baskette Jr., "Agricultural Marketing Agreement and Order Programs, 1933–1944," *Georgetown Law Journal* 33 (1945): 123–52.

98. Henry Hazlitt, *Economics in One Lesson* (San Francisco: Laissez-Faire Books, 1996), pp. 79–80.

99. Dennis Pollock, "Raisin Case Awaits a Ruling: Kerman Couple Are Accused of Breaking Rules," *Fresno Bee*, February 12, 2005, p. D1 (2005 WLNR 2050449).

100. Agricultural Marketing Agreement Act, 7 U.S.C. §§ 601–74.

101. Tracy Correa, "USDA Accuses Growers: Kerman Couple Face Complaint over Raisin Marketing Order," *Fresno Bee*, April 3, 2004, p. D1 (2004 WLNR 20529366).

102. Leon Garoyan, "Marketing Orders," *UC Davis Law Review* 23 (1990): 705.

103. Lawrence Shepard, "Cartelization of the California-Arizona Orange Industry, 1934–1981," *Journal of Law & Economics* 29 (1986): 120. See also Dennis M. Gaab, "The California-Arizona Citrus Marketing Orders: Examples of Failed Attempts to Regulate Markets for Agricultural Commodities," *San Joaquin Agricultural Law Review* 5 (1995): 147.

104. Ron Paarlberg, "The Political Economy of American Agricultural Policy: Three Approaches," *American Journal of Agricultural Economics* 71 (1989): 1161.

105. Neil Brooks, "The Pricing of Milk under Federal Marketing Orders," *George Washington Law Review* 26 (1958): 181–213; Kevin McNew, "Milking the Sacred Cow: A Case for Eliminating the Federal Dairy Program," Cato Institute Policy Analysis no. 362, December 1, 1999; William N. Eskridge Jr., "Politics without Romance: Implications of Public Choice Theory for Statutory Interpretation," *Virginia Law Review*

74 (1988): 330–34; and Kenneth W. Bailey, "Congress' Dairy Dilemma," *Regulation* (Winter 2001): 32–40.

106. S. Rep. No. 1011, 74th Cong., 1st sess. p. 3 (1935), quoted in *Block v. Community Nutrition Institute*, 467 U.S. 340, 342 (1984).

107. Peter Helmberger and Yu-Hui Chen, "Economic Effects of U.S. Dairy Programs," *Journal of Agricultural and Resource Economics* 19 (1994): 225–38.

108. Kenneth W. Bailey, "Impact of the Northeast Interstate Dairy Compact on Consumer Prices for Fluid Milk," *Review of Agricultural Economics* 25 (2003): 108–22.

109. McNew, "Milking the Sacred Cow," p. 6.

110. Ibid., p. 4.

111. Dan Morgan, Sarah Cohen, and Gilbert M. Gaul, "Dairy Industry Crushed Innovator Who Bested Price-Control System," *Washington Post*, December 10, 2006, p. A1; and Scott Wong and Kelly Carr, "Maverick Dairyman Fights Lobbyists and Lawmakers," *Arizona Republic*, November 14, 2006, http://www.azcentral.com/arizonarepublic/news/articles/1114dairy1114.html (accessed July 6, 2007).

112. *Milk Regulatory Equity Act*, Public Law 109-215 (2006).

113. *Milk Regulatory Equity Act of 2005*, S. 2120, 109th Cong., 2nd sess., *Congressional Record* (April 4, 2006): E497.

114. 7 C.F.R. § 900.3(a) (2007) ("A marketing agreement or a marketing order may be proposed by the Secretary or any other person.").

115. Daniel Bensing, "The Promulgation and Implementation of Federal Marketing Orders Regulating Fruit and Vegetable Crops under the Agricultural Marketing Agreement Act of 1937," *San Joaquin Agricultural Law Review* 5 (1995): 13.

116. Gaab, "California-Arizona Citrus Marketing Orders," 133–34.

117. *Cecelia Packing Corp. v. USDA*, 10 F.3d 616, 624–25 (9th Cir. 1993).

118. *Block*, 467 U.S. at 342 ("Before any market order may become effective, it must be approved by the handlers of at least 50% of the volume of milk covered by the proposed order and at least two-thirds of the affected dairy producers in the region. . . . If the handlers withhold their consent, the Secretary may nevertheless impose the order . . . [if] at least two-thirds of the producers consent[] to its promulgation and . . . [if the Secretary decides that] the order is 'the only practical means of advancing the interests of the producers . . . .'").

119. Ibid. at 347.

120. Ibid. at 352.

121. *Evans v. United States*, 74 Fed. Cl. 554, 563–64 (2006).

122. *Evans v. United States*, 2007 WL 2908212 (Fed. Cir. October 4, 2007), *cert. denied*, 76 U.S.L.W. 3375 (February 19, 2008).

123. See *Hinkle Northwest, Inc. v. SEC*, 641 F.2d 1304, 1307 (9th Cir. 1981) ("Ownership is a collection of rights to use and enjoy property including the right to sell and transmit the same" (quoting *Energy Oils, Inc. v. Montana Power Co.*, 626 F.2d 731, 736 (9th Cir. 1980)).

124. 2 William Blackstone, *Commentaries* *447.

125. *Ex parte Garland*, 71 U.S. (4 Wall.) 333, 370 (1866) (argument of Mr. Johnson).

126. *Gonzales v. Raich*, 545 U.S. 1 (2005).

127. Ibid.

128. Jim Chen, "The American Ideology," *Vanderbilt Law Review* 48 (1995): 829–30.

129. Motor Vehicle Franchise Act, 815 Ill. Comp. Stat. 710/4(e)(8) *et seq.*

130. 815 Ill. Comp. Stat. 710/12(c).

131. 815 Ill. Comp. Stat. 710/12(c)(7) (emphasis added).

132. *Prior of Christchurch Canterbury v. Bendysshe*, 93 Selden Society 8, 9 (1503).

133. Richard L. Smith, "Franchise Regulation: An Economic Analysis of State Restrictions on Automobile Distribution," *Journal of Law and Economics* 25 (1982): 146.

134. Ibid., 149.

135. Ibid., 151.

136. Ibid., 150.

137. Stewart Macaulay, "Changing a Continuing Relationship between a Large Corporation and Those Who Deal with It: Automobile Manufacturers, Their Dealers, and the Legal System," pt. 1, *Wisconsin Law Review* 1965: 483–575; and Stewart Macaulay, "Changing a Continuing Relationship between a Large Corporation and Those Who Deal With It: Automobile Manufacturers, Their Dealers, and the Legal System," pt. 2, *Wisconsin Law Review* 1965: 740–858.

138. Macaulay, "Changing a Continuing Relationship," pt. 2, 836.

139. Macaulay, "Changing a Continuing Relationship," pt. 1, 516–22.

140. Gary Michael Brown, "Note: State Motor Vehicle Franchise Legislation: A Survey and Due Process Challenge to Board Composition," *Vanderbilt Law Review* 33 (1980): 408, n. 142.

141. Gary Lawson, "Efficiency and Individualism," *Duke Law Journal* 42 (1992): 81, 93–94.

142. *Yamaha Motor Corp., U.S.A. v. Jim's Motorcycle, Inc.*, 401 F.3d 560, 571–72 (4th Cir. 2005), *cert. denied sub nom. Smit v. Yamaha Motor Corp., U.S.A.*, 546 U.S. 936 (2005).

143. Many courts have addressed these problems in the field of franchise acts, particularly in relation to automobile franchises. See *McDonald Ford Sales, Inc. v. Ford Motor Co.*, 418 N.W.2d 716 (Mich. Ct. App. 1987); *In re Application of Gen. Motors Corp. v. O'Daniel Oldsmobile, Inc.*, 439 N.W.2d 453 (Neb. 1989); *Benson & Gold Chevrolet, Inc. v. Louisiana Motor Vehicle Commission*, 403 So. 2d 13 (La. 1981); *McLaughlin Ford, Inc. v. Ford Motor Co.*, 473 A.2d 1185 (Conn. 1984); and *Metro Communications Co. v. Ameritech Mobile Communications, Inc.*, 788 F. Supp. 1424 (E.D. Mich. 1992).

144. *General Motors Corp. v. State Motor Vehicle Review Bd.*, 862 N.E.2d 209 (Ill. 2007).

145. Ibid. at 231 (Karmeier, J., dissenting).

146. Ibid. at 229.

147. Bernard H. Siegan, *Economic Liberties and the Constitution* (Chicago: University of Chicago Press, 1980), p. 331.

Chapter 8

1. Arthur B. Mark III, "Currents in Commerce Clause Scholarship Since *Lopez*: A Survey," *Capital University Law Review* 32 (2004): 671–760; and Douglas W. Kmiec, "*Gonzales v. Raich: Wickard v. Filburn* Displaced," *2004–2005 Cato Supreme Court Review* (Washington: Cato Institute, 2005), pp. 71–100.

2. The leading works on the Founders' views of the commerce clause are Randy E. Barnett, "The Original Meaning of the Commerce Clause," *University of Chicago Law Review* 68 (2001): 101–47; and Randy E. Barnett, "New Evidence of the Original Meaning of the Commerce Clause," *Arkansas Law Review* 55 (2003): 847–68.

3. *H. P. Hood & Sons, Inc. v. Du Mond*, 336 U.S. 525, 539 (1949).

4. *American Trucking Associations, Inc. v. Scheiner*, 483 U.S. 266, 285 (1987).

5. Grant S. Nelson and Robert J. Pushaw Jr., "Rethinking the Commerce Clause: Applying First Principles to Uphold Federal Commercial Regulations but Preserve State Control over Social Issues," *Iowa Law Review* 85 (1999): 23–24.

6. Brannon P. Denning, "Confederation-Era Discrimination against Interstate Commerce and the Legitimacy of the Dormant Commerce Clause Doctrine," *Kentucky Law Journal* 94 (2006): 75.

7. Clinton Rossiter, ed., *The Federalist Papers* (New York: New American Library, 1961), no. 7, p. 62.

8. *Federalist* no. 42, p. 268.

9. Ibid.

10. Max Farrand, ed., *The Records of the Federal Convention of 1787* (London: Oxford University Press, 1911), vol. 2, p. 625.

11. *Gibbons v. Ogden*, 22 U.S. (9 Wheat.) 1 (1824). See also Norman R. Williams, "Gibbons," *New York University Law Review* 79 (2004): 1398–499.

12. *Gibbons*, 22 U.S. (9 Wheat.) at 199–200.

13. Ibid. at 210.

14. See, for example, Michael DeBow, "Codifying the Dormant Commerce Clause," *Public Interest Law Review* 1995: 69–86; Julian N. Eule, "Laying the Dormant Commerce Clause to Rest," *Yale Law Journal* 91 (1982): 425–85; Martin H. Redish and Shane V. Nugent, "The Dormant Commerce Clause and the Constitutional Balance of Federalism," *Duke Law Journal* 1987: 569–617; Robert A. Sedler, "The Negative Commerce Clause as a Restriction on State Regulation and Taxation: An Analysis in Terms of Constitutional Structure," *Wayne Law Review* 31 (1985): 885–1027; and Mark Tushnet, "Rethinking the Dormant Commerce Clause," *Wisconsin Law Review* 1979: 125–65.

15. *Camps Newfound/Owatonna, Inc. v. Town of Harrison*, 520 U.S. 564 (1997).

16. Ibid. at 575.

17. Ibid. at 580–81.

18. *New Energy Co. of Indiana v. Limbach*, 486 U.S. 269, 278 (1988) (emphasis in original).

19. *Camps Newfound*, 520 U.S. at 607 (Scalia, J., dissenting).

20. *DaimlerChrysler Corp. v. Cuno*, 126 S. Ct. 1854 (2006).

21. Peter D. Enrich, "Saving the States from Themselves: Commerce Clause Constraints on State Tax Incentives for Business," *Harvard Law Review* 110 (1996): 377–467.

22. Ibid., 398.

23. Ibid., 392.

24. Ibid., 394–95.

25. Timothy Bartik, *Who Benefits from State and Local Economic Development Policies?* (Kalamazoo, MI: Upjohn Institute, 1991); John Anderson and Robert Wassmer, *Bidding for Business: The Efficacy of Local Economic Development Incentives in a Metropolitan Area* (Kalamazoo, MI: Upjohn Institute, 2000); and David Ewald, "CEO Makes Case against Corporate Welfare: An Interview with Mark Baker," *Budget and Tax News*, July 1, 2006, http://www.heartland.org/Article.cfm?artId=19291.

26. Eckhard Janeba and Guttorm Schjelderup, "Why Europe Should Love Tax Competition—and the U.S. Even More So," National Bureau of Economic Research Working Paper no. 9334, November 2002; Richard Teather, *The Benefits of Tax Competition* (London: Institute of Economic Affairs, 2005); Daphne A. Kenyon and John Kinkaid, eds., *Competition among States and Local Governments: Efficiency and Equity in American Federalism* (Washington: Urban Institute, 1991); Timothy J. Goodspeed, "Tax

Competition, Benefit Taxes, and Fiscal Federalism," *National Tax Journal* 51 (1998): 579–81; and Marius Brulhart and Mario Jametti, "Does Tax Competition Tame the Leviathan?" June, 2007, http://www.hec.unil.ch/mbrulhar/papers/leviathan.pdf.

27. "Tax and Trade," *Wall Street Journal*, September 22, 1999.

28. Enrich, "Saving the States from Themselves," 400.

29. Ibid., 400–1 (citation omitted).

30. Ibid., 402.

31. Ibid.

32. *New Energy Co. of Indiana*, 486 U.S. at 278.

33. *Cuno v. DaimlerChrysler, Inc.*, 386 F.3d 738, 744 (6th Cir. 2004).

34. Michael W. McConnell, "Federalism: Evaluating the Founders' Design," *University of Chicago Law Review* 54 (1987): 1498–500.

35. Cf. Enrich, "Saving the States from Themselves," 467.

36. Ibid., 380.

37. *DaimlerChrysler Corp. v. Cuno*, 547 U.S. 332, 353–54 (2006).

38. See Mark V. Tushnet, "Scalia and the Dormant Commerce Clause: A Foolish Formalism?" *Cardozo Law Review* 12 (1991): 1717–43.

39. *Granholm v. Heald*, 544 U.S. 460, 475 (2005).

40. By the time the federal government decided to wage a "war on drugs," courts had expanded Congress's commerce clause power to the point that no constitutional amendment was considered necessary.

41. U.S. Const. Amend. XXI (emphasis added).

42. Asheesh Agarwal and Todd Zywicki, "The Original Meaning of the 21st Amendment," *Green Bag (Second Series)* 8 (2005): 137–43.

43. Todd Zywicki and Asheesh Agarwal, "Wine, Commerce, and the Constitution," *New York Journal of Law and Liberty* 1 (2005): 609–54.

44. *Heald*, 544 U.S. at 472–73 (citations omitted).

45. *Powers v. Harris*, 379 F.3d 1208, 1221 (10th Cir. 2004), *cert. denied*, 544 U.S. 920 (2005) (emphasis added).

46. *Metropolitan Life Insurance v. Ward*, 470 U.S. 869 (1985).

47. Ibid. at 881.

48. Ibid. at 878.

49. Ibid. at 879.

50. Ibid. at 882.

51. *Bacchus Imports v. Dias*, 468 U.S. 263 (1984).

52. Ibid. at 273.

53. RiShawn Biddle, "Sam's Curse: Will Wal-Mart Superstores Really Devastate the City of Angels?" *Reason.com*, March 18, 2004, http://reason.com/archives/2004/03/18/sams-curse; Orly Lobel, "Big-Box Benefits: The Targeting of Giants in a National Campaign to Raise Work Conditions," *Connecticut Law Review* 39 (2007): 1685–712; and Richard C. Schragger, "The Anti-Chain Store Movement, Localist Ideology, and the Remnants of the Progressive Constitution, 1920–1940," *Iowa Law Review* 90 (2005): 1011–94.

54. Timothy Sandefur, "Plunder Gets a Boost," *The Freeman* 50, no. 2 (February 2000): 25–26.

55. *Island Silver & Spice, Inc. v. Islamorada, Village of Islands*, 475 F. Supp. 2d 1281, 1284 (S.D. Fla. 2007), *aff'd*, 542 F.3d 844 (11th Cir. 2008).

56. Ibid. at 1281.

57. Ibid. at 1287.

58. Ibid.

59. Ibid. at 1293 (quoting *Hunt v. Washington State Apple Advertising Com'n*, 432 U.S. 333, 351–52 (1977)).

60. Ibid. at 1291.

61. Ibid. at 1292.

62. Ibid.

63. Ibid. at 1293.

64. Ibid.

65. The Eleventh Circuit Court of Appeals, which includes Florida, has on occasion sounded sympathetic to the view that mere protectionism is an illegitimate goal, but it has not said so explicitly. See *Executive Town & Country Services, Inc. v. City of Atlanta*, 789 F.2d 1523, 1528 (11th Cir. 1986) (finding that minimum price law for limousines "passed the 'rational basis' test, albeit with little room for comfort"). See also *Alamo Rent-A-Car, Inc. v. Sarasota-Manatee Airport*, 825 F.2d 367 (11th Cir. 1987); and *American V.I.P. Limousines, Inc. v. Dade County Bd. of County Com'rs*, 757 F. Supp. 1382, 1393 (S.D. Fla. 1991) (upholding similar laws).

66. As a consequence, businesses are confronted with a paradox similar to the one that the U.S. Supreme Court strongly rejected in the famous 1938 case of *Erie v. Thompkins*, 304 U.S. 64 (1938). There, the Court held that federal courts hearing cases between citizens of different states must apply the substantive law of the relevant states rather than an independent body of federal common law. The decision was designed to remedy the unfairness of treating litigants differently depending on whether they file a case in the federal courthouse or in the state courthouse across the street. In a case like *Saiger*, though, a similar paradox is evident: if the city enacts a law designed to prohibit competition and to benefit a favored group of merchants, that law is subjected to rational basis scrutiny only and would most likely be upheld under the Fourteenth Amendment—but if one of the excluded businesses is headquartered in another state, the case is subjected to heightened scrutiny and is likely to be found unconstitutional.

67. *Powers v. Harris*, 379 F.3d 1208, 1215 (10th Cir. 2004), *cert. denied*, 544 U.S. 920 (2005).

68. Michael Kent Curtis, *No State Shall Abridge: The Fourteenth Amendment and the Bill of Rights* (Durham, NC: Duke University Press, 1986), p. 216.

69. *Ward*, 470 U.S. at 869.

Chapter 9

1. *Valentine v. Chrestensen*, 316 U.S. 52, 54 (1942).

2. James Madison, "Property," in *Madison: Writings*, ed. Jack Rakove (New York: Library of America, 1999), p. 515.

3. *Abrams v. United States*, 250 U.S. 616, 630 (1919) (Holmes, J., dissenting).

4. Ibid.

5. Louis Menand, *The Metaphysical Club* (New York: Farrar, Strauss, and Giroux, 2001), p. 432.

6. Aaron S. Resnik, "Freedom of Speech and Commercial Solicitation," *California Law Review* 30 (1942): 655–62. See also Barbara M. Mack, "Commercial Speech: A Historical Overview of Its First Amendment Protections and an Analysis of Its Future

Constitutional Safeguards," *Drake Law Review* 38 (1988): 60–61; and *Chrestensen v. Valentine*, 122 F.2d 511, 524 (2d Cir. 1941) (Frank, J., dissenting).

7. See, for example, Cass R. Sunstein, *Democracy and the Problem of Free Speech* (New York: Free Press, 1993), p. 3. ("for most of the nation's history, no serious person thought that commercial speech deserved constitutional protection").

8. Daniel E. Troy, "Advertising: Not 'Low Value' Speech," *Yale Journal on Regulation* 16 (1999): 85–144.

9. Merrill Peterson, ed., *Jefferson: Writings* (New York: Library of America, 1984), p. 1334.

10. *Valentine*, 316 U.S. at 54.

11. Alex Kozinski and Stuart Banner, "The Anti-History and Pre-History of Commercial Speech," *Texas Law Review* 71 (1993): 758.

12. Ibid.

13. *Mutual Film Corp. v. Industrial Commission*, 236 U.S. 230, 244 (1915).

14. *Virginia State Bd. of Pharmacy v. Virginia Citizens Consumer Council, Inc.*, 425 U.S. 748 (1976).

15. Ibid. at 762.

16. Ibid. at 763.

17. Ibid. at 765.

18. *City of Cincinnati v. Discovery Network, Inc.*, 507 U.S. 410 (1993).

19. *Metromedia, Inc. v. City of San Diego*, 453 U.S. 490 (1981).

20. *City of Renton v. Playtime Theatres, Inc.*, 475 U.S. 41 (1986).

21. *City of Los Angeles v. Alameda Books, Inc.*, 535 U.S. 425 (2002); and *Wexler v. City of New Orleans*, 267 F. Supp. 2d 559 (E.D. La. 2003).

22. Deborah J. La Fetra, "Kick It Up a Notch: First Amendment Protection for Commercial Speech," *Case Western Reserve Law Review* 54 (2004): 1230–36.

23. *Montgomery v. Montgomery*, 60 S.W.3d 524, 529 (Ky. 2001).

24. Ibid.

25. Alan Howard, "The Mode in the Middle: Recognizing a New Category of Speech Regulations for Modes of Expression," *UCLA Entertainment Law Review* 14 (2007): 88.

26. *Central Hudson Gas & Electric Corp. v. Public Service Commission of New York*, 447 U.S. 557 (1980).

27. Ibid. at 563.

28. Ibid. at 564.

29. See, for example, *Edenfield v. Fane*, 507 U.S. 761, 765 (1993) ("ambiguities may exist at the margins of the category of commercial speech"); *Zauderer v. Office of Disciplinary Counsel of the Supreme Court of Ohio*, 471 U.S. 626, 637 (1985) ("the precise bounds of the category of . . . commercial speech" are "subject to doubt, perhaps"); *Greater New Orleans Broadcasting Ass'n, Inc. v. United States*, 527 U.S. 173, 184 (1999) ("judges, scholars, and amici curiae have advocated repudiation of the *Central Hudson* standard and implementation of a more straightforward and stringent test for assessing the validity of governmental restrictions on commercial speech"); *44 Liquormart v. Rhode Island*, 517 U.S. 484, 527 (1996) (Thomas, J., concurring) (noting that commercial speech cases are impossible to apply "with any uniformity"); *Lorillard Tobacco Co. v. Reilly*, 533 U.S. 525, 554 (2001) ("several Members of the Court have expressed doubts about the *Central Hudson* analysis"); *Nordyke v. Santa Clara County*, 110 F.3d 707, 712 (9th Cir. 1997) ("the *Central Hudson* test is not easy to apply"); *Commodity Trend Serv., Inc. v. Commodity Futures Trading Com'n*, 149 F.3d 679, 684 (7th Cir. 1998); *Kasky v.*

Nike, Inc., 27 Cal. 4th 939, 958 (2002) ("Since its decision in *Bolger* . . . the United States Supreme Court has acknowledged that 'ambiguities may exist at the margins of the category of commercial speech'"); and *American Future Sys., Inc. v. Pa. State Univ.*, 752 F.2d 854, 867 (3d Cir. 1984) (Adams, J., concurring) ("The commercial speech doctrine, which offers lesser protection for commercial than for non-commercial communications, has been criticized almost since its inception for its failure to develop a hard and fast definition for this type of speech").

30. *Rubin v. Coors Brewing Co.*, 514 U.S. 476, 492 (1995) (Stevens, J., concurring). See also *44 Liquormart*, 517 U.S. at 501 ("The mere fact that messages propose commercial transactions does not in and of itself dictate the constitutional analysis that should apply to decisions to suppress them.").

31. *Kasky*, 27 Cal. 4th at 939.

32. *Kasky v. Nike, Inc.*, 93 Cal. Rptr. 2d 854, 862 (2000) (quoting *Pacific Gas & Elec. Co. v. Public Util. Com'n*, 475 U.S. 1, 8 (1986)).

33. *Kasky*, 27 Cal. 4th at 964.

34. *Nike, Inc. v. Kasky*, 539 U.S. 654 (2003).

35. *United States v. United Foods, Inc.*, 533 U.S. 405, 409 (2001).

36. Thomas C. Goldstein, "*Nike v. Kasky* and the Definition of 'Commercial Speech,'" *2002–2003 Cato Supreme Court Review* (Washington: Cato Institute, 2003), p. 73.

37. *New York Times v. Sullivan*, 376 U.S. 254 (1964).

38. Ibid. at 273 (quoting *Pennekamp v. Florida*, 328 U.S. 331, 342, 343, n. 5 (1946)).

39. Daniel A. Farber, "Commercial Speech and First Amendment Theory," *Northwestern University Law Review* 74 (1980): 386.

40. La Fetra, "Kick It Up a Notch," p. 1228 (citing Roger Parloff, "Is Fat the Next Tobacco?" *Fortune*, January 21, 2003).

41. Jonathan A. Loeb and Jeffrey A. Sklar, "The California Supreme Court's New Test for Commercial Speech," *Los Angeles Lawyer*, November 25, 2002, p. 16.

42. Julia Fisher, "Note: Free Speech to Have Sweatshops? How *Kasky v. Nike* Might Provide a Useful Tool to Improve Sweatshop Conditions," *Boston College Third World Law Journal* 26 (2006): 306.

43. Jonathan W. Emord, "Contrived Distinctions: The Doctrine of Commercial Speech in First Amendment Jurisprudence," Cato Institute Policy Analysis no. 161, September 23, 1991.

44. *Kasky*, 27 Cal. 4th at 985 (Brown, J., dissenting).

45. Goldstein, "*Nike v. Kasky*," pp. 74–75.

46. Martin H. Redish and Howard M. Wasserman, "What's Good for General Motors: Corporate Speech and the Theory of Free Expression," *George Washington Law Review* 66 (1998): 236.

47. The California Supreme Court itself acknowledged this in a 1985 case when it held that "an advertisement that cherries can be purchased for a dollar a box at store X may be commercial speech, but an advertisement informing the public that the cherries for sale at store X were picked by union workers is more: it communicates a message beyond that related to the bare economic interests of the parties." *Spiritual Psychic Science Church v. City of Azusa*, 39 Cal. 3d 501, 511 (1985). But that decision was overruled in *Kasky*, 539 U.S. at 654.

48. Timothy Sandefur, "Plunder Gets a Boost," *The Freeman* 50, no. 2 (February 2000): 25–26.

49. Robert Scally, "Calif. Retailers Defeat Big Box Legislation," *Discount Store News*, October 4, 1999, p. 1, http://findarticles.com/p/articles/mi_m3092/is_19_38/ai_56229578; and James Burger, "Big-Box Stores Urge Veto of California Legislation," *Bakersfield Californian*, September 16, 1999.

50. Redish and Wasserman, "What's Good for General Motors," 296. See also Martin Redish, "First Amendment Theory and the Demise of the Commercial Speech Distinction: The Case of the Smoking Controversy," *Northern Kentucky Law Review* 24 (1997): 583. ("[N]o free speech scholar (at least those lacking an overriding ideologically based result orientation) would suggest that either the personal interest of the speaker or the biased and incomplete nature of expression somehow reduces the level of First Amendment protection given to traditional contributions to public debate. Nor would the market's possible failure to portray all viewpoints ever be allowed to justify suppression of popularly held positions. Fundamental precepts of free speech theory obviously preclude such governmental tinkering with the expressive marketplace. Yet when commercial advertising is involved, for some reason, factors that are routinely ignored in First Amendment analysis appear—inconsistently—to assume overriding theoretical importance.").

51. *Pagan v. Fruchey*, 2004 WL 5338455 (S.D. Ohio, September 30, 2004), *rev'd*, 2007 WL 1853692 (6th Cir. June 29, 2007).

52. *Fruchey*, 2007 WL 1853692, *5.

53. Ibid.

54. *Ballen v. City of Redmond*, 466 F.3d 736, 743 (9th Cir. 2006).

55. Ibid.

56. Ibid. at 744.

57. *The Florida Bar v. Pape*, 918 So. 2d 240, 249 (Fla. 2005).

58. *Hurley v. Irish-American Gay, Lesbian and Bisexual Group of Boston*, 515 U.S. 557, 569 (1995) (citations omitted). In *Cohen v. California*, 403 U.S. 15, 26 (1971), the U.S. Supreme Court declared that expression frequently "conveys not only ideas capable of relatively precise, detached explication, but otherwise inexpressible emotions as well. In fact, words are often chosen as much for their emotive as their cognitive force. We cannot sanction the view that the Constitution . . . has little or no regard for that emotive function which . . . may often be the more important element of the overall message."

59. *Sambo's Restaurants, Inc. v. City of Ann Arbor*, 663 F.2d 686, 694 (6th Cir. 1981).

60. See, for example, *Chalifoux v. New Caney Indep. Sch. Dist.*, 976 F. Supp. 659 (S.D. Tex. 1997).

61. See, for example, *City of Erie v. Pap's A.M.*, 529 U.S. 277 (2000).

62. *Alabama & Coushatta Tribes of Texas v. Trustees of the Big Sandy Indep. Sch. Dist.*, 817 F. Supp. 1319 (E.D. Tex. 1993).

63. *Jeglin v. San Jacinto Unified Sch. Dist.*, 827 F. Supp. 1459, 1461 (C.D. Cal. 1993).

64. *Tinker v. Des Moines Indep. Cmty. Sch. Dist.*, 393 U.S. 503 (1969).

65. *Clark v. Cmty. for Creative Nonviolence*, 468 U.S. 288, 306 (1984).

66. *Sons of Confederate Veterans, Inc. v. Commissioner of the Va. Dep't of Motor Vehicles*, 288 F.3d 610, 620–622 (4th Cir.), *reh'g en banc denied*, 305 F.3d 241 (4th Cir. 2002). In *Transportation Alternatives v. City of New York*, 340 F.3d 72 (2d Cir. 2003), a nonprofit environmental organization that urged people to walk or use bicycles sought to use a public park for a rally. The city applied different permit fees for park use by commercial and noncommercial enterprises and, in a letter, offered to give the group a discount if they removed the corporate sponsorships from their event. Ibid. at 76–77.

Transportation Alternatives sued, arguing that the parks commissioner had overly broad discretion to set park fees and that this violated its free speech rights. The court agreed. "The City contends that, because TA receives commercial support for its event and displays the logos of sponsors in some of its promotional literature . . . [the event] involves 'commercial speech,' and hence receives less robust First Amendment protection than purely political speech. This is no answer. The commercial elements of the Bike Tour are relatively trivial. By far the main thrust of the event is a political demonstration by thousands of people advocating in favor of bicycle-friendly regulation by the City. Notwithstanding the presence of minor commercial elements, such as display of corporate logos, this speech was a far distance from commercial speech undertaken to solicit a commercial transaction." Ibid. at 78.

67. *Bad Frog Brewery, Inc. v. New York State Liquor Auth.*, 134 F.3d 87 (2d Cir. 1998).

68. Ibid. at 94.

69. Ibid. at 96–97.

70. *Friedman v. Rogers*, 440 U.S. 1 (1979).

71. Ibid. at 11.

72. Ibid. at 12–13.

73. Jerre B. Swann Sr., David A. Aaker, and Matt Reback, "Trademarks and Marketing," *Trademark Reports* 91 (2001): 796–97.

74. Virginia Postrel, *The Substance of Style: How the Rise of Aesthetic Value Is Remaking Commerce, Culture, and Consciousness* (New York: HarperCollins, 2003), p. 103.

75. Rochelle Cooper Dreyfuss, "Expressive Genericity: Trademarks as Language in the Pepsi Generation," *Notre Dame Law Review* 65 (1990): 397.

76. Matt Haig, *Brand Royalty: How the World's Top 100 Brands Thrive and Survive* (London: Kogan Page, 2004), p. 168.

77. Rodney A. Smolla, "Information, Imagery, and the First Amendment: A Case for Expansive Protection of Commercial Speech," *Texas Law Review* 71 (1993): 800.

78. "In short, a cultural, ritualistic theory of communication values expressive activity for the kind of comment it makes about the relationships between culture and society, or between expressive forms. It values the ways in which 'experience is worked into understanding and then disseminated and celebrated.'" Randall P. Bezanson, "Speaking through Others' Voices: Authorship, Originality, and Free Speech," *Wake Forest Law Review* 38 (2003): 1010.

79. *Wine and Spirits Retailers, Inc. v. Rhode Island*, 481 F.3d 1, 6 (1st Cir. 2007).

80. Daniel E. Troy, "Do We Have a Beef with the Court? Compelled Commercial Speech Upheld, but It Could Have Been Worse," *2004–2005 Cato Supreme Court Review* (Washington: Cato Institute, 2005), pp. 139–40.

81. *Wooley v. Maynard*, 430 U.S. 705 (1977).

82. Ibid. at 714.

83. *West Va. Bd. of Ed. v. Barnette*, 319 U.S. 624 (1943).

84. *Miami Herald Publishing Co. v. Tornillo*, 418 U.S. 241 (1974).

85. *Hurley v. Irish-American Gay, Lesbian and Bisexual Group of Boston*, 515 U.S. at 557.

86. *Glickman v. Wileman Brothers & Elliott, Inc.*, 521 U.S. 457 (1997).

87. Ibid. at 469–70.

88. *Davenport v. Washington Education Ass'n*, 127 S. Ct. 2372 (2007); *Abood v. Detroit Bd. of Ed.*, 431 U.S. 209 (1977); *Teachers v. Hudson*, 475 U.S. 292 (1986); and *Keller v. State Bar of California*, 496 U.S. 1 (1990).

89. *United States v. United Foods*, 533 U.S. 405 (2001).

90. Ibid. at 411.

91. Ibid. at 411–12.

92. Gregory Klass, "The Very Idea of a First Amendment Right against Compelled Subsidization," *UC Davis Law Review* 38 (2005): 1108. The appeal to a law's "comprehensiveness" as a measure of its constitutionality seems typical of Justice Kennedy. In his concurring opinion in *Kelo v. New London*, 545 U.S. 469 (2005)—providing the "swing" vote in that case—Kennedy found the issue to turn on the fact that the condemnation of Suzette Kelo's house "occurred in the context of a comprehensive development plan." Ibid. at 493 (Kennedy, J., concurring). This, he held, distinguished the case from one involving "impermissible favoritism of private parties."

93. *Johanns v. Livestock Marketing Ass'n*, 544 U.S. 550 (2005).

94. Ibid. at 560.

95. Ibid. at 562.

96. *Davenport*, 127 S. Ct. at 2372; *Abood*, 431 U.S. at 209; *Hudson*, 475 U.S. at 292; and *Keller*, 496 U.S. at 1.

97. Troy, "Do We Have a Beef with the Court?" p. 151 (emphasis added).

98. Ibid., p. 154.

99. *Duplex Printing Press Co. v. Deering*, 254 U.S. 443, 488 (1921) (Brandeis, J., dissenting).

100. See Timothy Sandefur, "The Wolves and the Sheep of Constitutional Law: A Review Essay on Kermit Roosevelt's *The Myth of Judicial Activism*," *Journal of Law and Politics* 23 (2007): 1–40.

Chapter 10

1. *Baltimore & O. S. W. Ry. Co. v. Voigt*, 176 U.S. 498, 505–6 (1900) (quoting *Printing & Numerical Registering Co. v. Sampson*, 19 L.R.-Eq. 462, 465 (1875)).

2. A. J. Langguth, *A Noise of War* (New York: Simon & Schuster, 1994), p. 58.

3. John P. Dawson, "Economic Duress—An Essay in Perspective," *Michigan Law Review* 45 (1947): 267, n. 36 (quoting Edwin W. Patterson, "Compulsory Contracts in the Crystal Ball," *Columbia Law Review* 43 (1943): 741). See also Anthony R. Chase, "Race, Culture, and Contract Law: From the Cottonfield to the Courtroom," *Connecticut Law Review* 28 (1995): 10–11. ("[T]he law of contracts created the illusion that all men were free to enter or not enter into contracts as they chose. However, the reality was that the law of contracts during the Industrial Revolution enabled the industrialists to control the working class, who either accepted the wages offered and hours demanded or starved.").

4. M. P. Ellinghaus, "In Defense of Unconscionability," *Yale Law Journal* 78 (1969): 767.

5. Frances H. Miller, "Trusting Doctors: Tricky Business When It Comes to Clinical Research," *Boston University Law Review* 81 (2001): 423–43; and Charity Scott, "Why Law Pervades Medicine: An Essay on Ethics in Health Care," *Notre Dame Journal of Law, Ethics, and Public Policy* 14 (2000): 271–75.

6. *Hojnowski ex rel. Hojnowski v. Vans Skate Park*, 868 A.2d 1087, 1098 (N.J. Super. A.D. 2005), *aff'd*, 901 A.2d 381 (N.J. 2006).

7. Duncan Kennedy, "Distributive and Paternalist Motives in Contract and Tort Law, with Special Reference to Compulsory Terms and Unequal Bargaining Power," *Maryland Law Review* 41 (1982): 620.

8. Ibid., 635.

9. Ibid., 623.

10. Ibid.

11. Ibid., 648.

12. Ibid., 649.

13. Ibid., 647.

14. *McHugh v. United Service Automobile Ass'n*, 164 F.3d 451, 460–61 (9th Cir. 1999) (Graber, J., dissenting) (emphasis added).

15. Susan M. Popik and Carol D. Quackenbos, "Reasonable Expectations after Thirty Years: A Failed Doctrine," *Connecticut Insurance Law Journal* 5 (1998): 425–49; Barbara J. Tyler and Thomas S. Tyler, "*Holt v. Grange Mutual Casualty Co.*: Children Not 'Insureds' under Policy Are Entitled to Death Benefits," *Cleveland State Law Review* 45 (1997): 699–710; Mark C. Rahdert, "Reasonable Expectations Revisited," *Connecticut Insurance Law Journal* 5 (1998): 107–50; Robert E. Keeton, "Insurance Law Rights at Variance with Policy Provisions," *Harvard Law Review* 83 (1970): 961–85; and Stephen J. Ware, "A Critique of the Reasonable Expectations Doctrine," *University of Chicago Law Review* 56 (1989): 1461–93.

16. Simon Winchester, *A Crack in the Edge of the World* (New York: HarperCollins, 2005), pp. 328–30.

17. *E.M.M.I. v. Zurich-American Ins. Co.*, 32 Cal. 4th 465, 474 (2004).

18. Ibid. at 474.

19. Ibid. at 486 (Chin, J., dissenting).

20. Tyler and Tyler, "*Holt v. Grange Mutual Casualty Co.*," 708.

21. Popik and Quackenbos, "Reasonable Expectations," 431 (quoting Michael E. Bragg, "Concurrent Causation and the Art of Policy Drafting: New Perils for Property Insurers," *Forum* 20 (1985): 390).

22. *Prudential-LMI Com. Insurance v. Superior Court*, 51 Cal. 3d 674, 699 (1990) (quoting *Home Ins. Co. v. Landmark Ins. Co.*, 205 Cal. App. 3d 1388, 1395–96 (1988)).

23. *Richardson v. Mellish*, 130 Eng. Rep. 294, 303 (Com. Pl. 1824) (Burrough, J.)

24. *R. R. v. M. H.*, 426 Mass. 501 (1998).

25. Ibid. at 511.

26. *Matter of Baby M.*, 537 A.2d 1227 (N.J. 1988).

27. Ibid.

28. Ibid. at 505.

29. Jessica H. Munyon, "Note: Protectionism and Freedom of Contract: The Erosion of Female Autonomy in Surrogacy Decisions," *Suffolk University Law Review* 36 (2003): 717–44.

30. Lorraine Ali and Raina Kelley, "The Curious Lives of Surrogates," *Newsweek*, April 7, 2008.

31. *Baby M.*, 537 A.2d at 441–42.

32. See Margaret Jane Radin, *Contested Commodities: The Trouble with Trade in Sex, Children, Body Parts, and Other Things* (Cambridge, MA: Harvard University Press, 1996), p. 137 (describing the "gray market" in which would-be parents "compensate" surrogate mothers by paying for health care and similar costs). See also Melinda Lucas, "Adoption: Distinguishing between Gray Market and Black Market Activities," *Family Law Quarterly* 34 (2000): 553–64; and Iris Leibowitz-Dori, "Womb for Rent: The Future of International Trade in Surrogacy," *Minnesota Journal of Global Trade* 6 (1997): 335–38.

33. See Richard A. Posner, "The Ethics and Economics of Enforcing Contracts of Surrogate Motherhood," *Journal of Contemporary Health Law and Policy* 5 (1989): 21–32.

34. *Johnson v. Calvert*, 5 Cal. 4th 84 (1993).

35. Ibid. at 97.

36. Ibid.

37. Erich Vieth and James P. Lemonds, "Whence Public Policy?" *Journal of the Missouri Bar* 52 (1996): 239–46.

38. *Vidal v. Girard's Ex'rs*, 43 U.S. (2 How.) 127, 197–98 (1844).

39. "[C]lear and objective rules—such as treating one's signature as assent to a contract—promote economic growth since they encourage long-term decisions and investments by giving economic actors confidence that they can predict how the state will use its coercive powers." Ware, "A Critique," 1489.

40. Joseph R. Grodin, "Are Rules Really Better than Standards," *Hastings Law Journal* 45 (1994): 569–72; Paul E. Loving, "The Justice of Certainty," *Oregon Law Review* 73 (1994): 743–66; and O. Lee Reed, "Law, the Rule of Law, and Property: A Foundation for the Private Market and Business Study," *American Business Law Journal* 38 (2001): 441–73.

41. Robert Braucher, "The Unconscionable Contract or Term," *University of Pittsburgh Law Review* 31 (1970): 337. See also John E. Murray Jr., "Unconscionability: Unconscionability," *University of Pittsburgh Law Review* 31 (1969): 1–80.

42. Philip Bridwell, "The Philosophical Dimensions of the Doctrine of Unconscionability," *University of Chicago Law Review* 70 (2003): 1513–31.

43. *Williams v. Walker-Thomas Furniture Co.*, 350 F.2d 445 (D.C. Cir. 1965).

44. "The furniture company began to market and sell to individuals who could not obtain credit at the large department stores in downtown Washington, D.C. It, and stores like it, were the only source of credit for the residents of the neighborhood." Eben Colby, "Note: What Did the Doctrine of Unconscionability Do to the Walker-Thomas Furniture Company?" *Connecticut Law Review* 34 (2002): 649.

45. Ibid., 647.

46. Muriel Morisey Spence, "Teaching *Williams v. Walker-Thomas Furniture Co.*," *Temple Political and Civil Rights Law Review* 3 (1994): 94–95.

47. *Williams*, 350 F.2d at 449.

48. Ibid.

49. Ibid. at 451 (Danaher, J., dissenting).

50. Colby, "Note," 658.

51. Richard A. Epstein, "Unconscionability: A Critical Reappraisal," *Journal of Law and Economics* 18 (1975): 293–315.

52. Allen R. Kamp, "Downtown Code: A History of the Uniform Commercial Code 1949–1954," *Buffalo Law Review* 49 (2001): 425.

53. Anthony de Jasay, *Justice and Its Surroundings* (Indianapolis: Liberty Fund, 2002), pp. 142–69. See also Robert Nozick, *Anarchy, State and Utopia* (Cambridge, MA: Harvard University Press, 1974), pp. 160–63.

54. *Aerojet-General Corp. v. Transport Indem. Co.*, 17 Cal. 4th 38, 75 (1997) (A contract between two parties "establishe[s] what [is] 'fair' and 'just' inter se.").

55. "[T]he unconscionability doctrine is paternalistic, inflicting psychic damage upon those it seeks to protect precisely by granting them such protection. . . . A party who is able to get out of a contract by claiming unconscionability is appealing to the

benevolence of an individual judge." Nancy S. Kim, "Evolving Business and Social Norms and Interpretation Rules: The Need for a Dynamic Approach to Contract Disputes," *Nebraska Law Review* 84 (2005): 552–53.

56. See, for example, *Buchwald v. Paramount Pictures Corp.*, 1990 WL 357611 (Cal. Super. 1990). See also Harry G. Prince, "Unconscionability in California: A Need for Restraint and Consistency," *Hastings Law Journal* 46 (1995): 465–66.

57. *Gentry v. Superior Court*, 42 Cal. 4th 443 (2007), *cert. denied*, 76 U.S.L.W. 3417 (March 31, 2008).

58. Christopher R. Drahozal, "In Defense of *Southland*: Reexamining the Legislative History of the Federal Arbitration Act," *Notre Dame Law Review* 78 (2002): 101–70; Lan Q. Hang, "Online Dispute Resolution Systems: The Future of Cyberspace Law," *Santa Clara Law Review* 41 (2001): 837–66; and Stephen J. Ware, "Paying the Price of Process: Judicial Regulation of Consumer Arbitration Agreements," *Journal of Dispute Resolution* (2001): 89–100.

59. *Linder v. Thrifty Oil Co.*, 23 Cal. 4th 429, 446 (2000).

60. *Gentry*, 42 Cal. 4th at 471.

61. Ibid. at 472.

62. Ibid.

63. Ibid. at 454 (quoting *Discover Bank v. Superior Court*, 36 Cal. 4th 148, 163 (2005)).

64. Ibid.

65. As my Pacific Legal Foundation colleague Deborah La Fetra pointed out in an amicus brief in the *Gentry* case: "This is analogous to the proliferation of credit cards, many of which also require arbitration of disputes. In that context, the New York Supreme Court noted that 'in this day and age when credit cards are rather easily available from any of a number of issuers, the fact that the customer who elected not to accept the Arbitration Agreement would have to terminate his/her account, would not be grounds for concern.'" Brief Amicus Curiae of Pacific Legal Foundation, *Gentry v. Superior Court*, no. S141502 (quoting *Johnson v. Chase Manhattan Bank USA, N.A.*, 784 N.Y.S.2d 921 (2004)).

66. Richard A. Epstein, "In Defense of the Contract at Will," *University of Chicago Law Review* 51 (1984): 947–82.

67. *Darlington v. General Elec.*, 504 A.2d 306, 310 (Pa. Super. 1986) (emphasis added).

68. Bureau of Labor Statistics, "Employee Tenure in 2006," http://www.bls.gov/news.release/archives/tenure_09082006.pdf.

69. Andrew P. Morriss, "Bad Data, Bad Economics, and Bad Policy: Time to Fire Wrongful Discharge Law," *Texas Law Review* 74 (1996): 1904.

70. "[L]ower income individuals are the ones most likely to experience loss in job opportunities and income because risk-averse employers are less likely to offer employment to marginal applicants, who tend to be less educated, low income, and . . . minority." Katy Rand, "Employment at Will in Maine: R.I.P.?" *Maine Bar Journal* 22 (2007): 17–18.

71. Epstein, "In Defense of the Contract at Will," 979.

72. *Ryan v. Dan's Food Stores, Inc.*, 972 P.2d 395, 404 (Utah 1998).

73. Morriss, "Bad Data," 1902. See also Andrew P. Morriss, "Exploding Myths: An Empirical and Economic Reassessment of the Rise of Employment at-Will," *Missouri Law Review* 59 (1994): 760–61.

74. Morriss, "Bad Data," 1902, n. 7.

75. Bradley R. Schiller, *Essentials of Economics*, 3rd ed. (Boston: McGraw-Hill, 1999), p. 110.

76. Kurt H. Decker, "At-Will Employment in Pennsylvania—A Proposal for Its Abolition and Statutory Regulation," *Dickenson Law Review* 87 (1983): 492–93.

77. David Ibison, "Real Swedish Jobless Rate 15%," *Financial Times*, June 16, 2006.

78. Arngrim Hunnes, Jarle Møen, and Kjell G. Salvanes, "Wage Structure and Labor Mobility in Norway, 1980–1997," National Bureau of Economic Research Working Paper no. 12974, March 2007, pp. 7–10.

79. See, for example, Rolf van der Velden, Riccardo Welters, and Maarten Wolbers, *The Integration of Young People into the Labour Market within the European Union: The Role of Institutional Settings* (Maastricht, Neth.: Research Centre for Education and the Labour Market, 2001), p. 52 ("It is primarily the employment protection of the existing labour force that has a damaging effect on the integration process of youngsters. In countries with a less strict employment protection legislation, school-leavers find a (stable) labour market position more easily than in countries with a high strictness of employment protection.").

80. See Statistics Canada, *Unemployment Rates of People Aged 16 and Over, Canada and the United States*, http://www.statcan.gc.ca/pub/71-222-x/2008001/sectionp/p-unemployment-chomage-eng.htm.

81. "General Survey: People Find Themselves Unemployed for Increasingly Longer Periods," *Japan Labor Bulletin* 42 (2003): 1.

82. Rand, "Employment at Will in Maine," 18 ("Although France's rejection of employment at will means employees enjoy great protection and job security, 'French employers and the French economy as a whole pay the price'" (quoting Carole A. Scott, "Money Talks: The Influence of Economic Power on the Employment Laws and Policies in the United States and France," *San Diego International Law Journal* 7 (2006): 394)); and James J. Heckman and Carmen Pagés-Serra, "The Cost of Job Security Regulation: Evidence from Latin American Labor Markets," *Economia* 1 (2000): 110 ("job security regulations reduce employment and promote inequality across workers").

83. *New Jersey Turnpike Authority v. Local 196*, 920 A.2d 88 (N.J. 2007).

84. *In re Pepsi Cola Bottling Co.*, 76 Lab. Arb. Rep. (BNA) 54 (1980).

85. John P. Frantz, "Market Ordering versus Statutory Control of Termination Decisions: A Case for the Inefficiency of Just Cause Dismissal Requirements," *Harvard Journal of Law and Public Policy* 20 (1997): 567. See also Stewart J. Schwab, "Life-Cycle Justice: Accommodating Just Cause and Employment at Will," *Michigan Law Review* 92 (1993): 8–62; and Todd H. Girshon, "Wrongful Discharge Reform in the United States: International and Domestic Perspectives on the Model Employment Termination Act," *Emory International Law Review* 6 (1992): 704 (restricting at-will employment can "translate into an institutionalization of mediocre performance").

86. James N. Dertouzos and Lynn A. Karoly, *Labor-Market Responses to Employer Liability* (Santa Monica, CA: Rand Institute for Civil Justice, 1992) (finding a 2 to 5 percent decline in employment due to courts finding exceptions to the at-will rule); Richard Vedder and Lowell Gallaway, *Laws, Litigation and Labor Markets: Some New Evidence* (San Francisco: Pacific Research Institute, 1995) (between 1970 and 1990, wrongful termination doctrine cost Americans 1,325,000 jobs and $42 billion); and Thomas J. Miles, "Common Law Exceptions to Employment at Will and U.S. Labor Markets," *Journal of*

Law, Economics, and Organization 16 (2000): 74–101 (finding that restrictions on at-will employment lead companies to shift from at-will employees to temporary employees).

87. David Millon, "Default Rules, Wealth Distribution, and Corporate Law Reform: Employment at Will versus Job Security," *University of Pennsylvania Law Review* 146 (1998): 1003 ("[S]hirking and other misconduct will be harder to punish and, therefore, more likely to occur under a job-security contract term than under an at-will term. This extra increment represents a cost peculiar to a job-security regime, and it is a cost that employers will seek to pass on to the work force."); and Rand, "Employment at Will in Maine," p. 17 (eliminating at-will employment will cause "employers [to] raise prices and become less competitive or return less to their shareholders").

88. Mary Jean Navaretta, "The Model Employment Termination Act—META— More Aptly the Menace to Employment Tranquility Act: A Critique," *Stetson Law Review* 25 (1995): 1033–35; and Morriss, "Bad Data," 1915.

89. Morriss, "Bad Data," 1922.

90. *Adair v. United States*, 208 U.S. 161 (1908).

91. Ibid. at 174–75.

92. Ibid. at 176.

93. Deborah L. Markowitz, "The Demise of at-Will Employment and the Public Employee Conundrum," *Urban Lawyer* 27 (1995): 305–31.

94. *Petermann v. Teamsters Local 396*, 344 P.2d 25 (Cal. 1959).

95. Max Schanzenbach, "Exceptions to Employment at Will: Raising Firing Costs or Enforcing Life-Cycle Contracts?" *American Law and Economics Review* 5 (2003): 473.

96. Dertouzos and Karoly, *Labor-Market Responses*, p. 51.

97. Ibid., pp. 62–63.

98. David H. Autor, John J. Donohue III, and Stewart J. Schwab, "The Costs of Wrongful-Discharge Laws," MIT Department of Economics Working Paper no. 02–41, November 18, 2002, p. 29, http://papers.ssrn.com/sol3/papers.cfm?abstract_id= 355861.

99. Bradley T. Ewing, Charles M. North, and Beck A. Taylor, "The Employment Effects of a 'Good Cause' Discharge Standard in Montana," *Industrial and Labor Relations Review* 59 (2005): 32.

100. David H. Autor, "Outsourcing at Will: The Contribution of Unjust Dismissal Doctrine to the Growth of Employment Outsourcing," MIT Department of Economics Working Paper no. 01–32, August 2001, http://papers.ssrn.com/paper. taf?abstract_id=281418.

101. Sharon Rabin-Margalioth, "Cross-Employee Redistribution Effects of Mandated Employee Benefits," *Hofstra Labor and Employment Law Journal* 20 (2003): 335. See also Autor, Donohue, and Schwab, "The Costs of Wrongful-Discharge Laws," p. 21 ("employment protection does reduce employment of less protected worker groups— females, and younger and less-educated individuals—at least in the short run").

102. *Darlington*, 504 A.2d at 309.

103. *Vizcaino v. Microsoft Corp.*, 97 F.3d 1187 (9th Cir. 1996), *aff'd*, 120 F.3d 1006 (9th Cir. 1997) (en banc), *cert. denied*, 522 U.S. 1098 (1998).

104. Ibid. at 1190.

105. Ibid. at 1195.

106. Ibid. at 1200–1 (Trott, J., dissenting).

107. Franklin G. Snyder, "The Pernicious Effect of Employment Relationships on the Law of Contracts," *Texas Wesleyan Law Review* 10 (2003): 64.

108. *Vizcaino*, 97 F.3d at 1202 (Trott, J., dissenting).

109. Ibid. at 1203 (Trott, J., dissenting).

Chapter 11

1. Lawrence J. McQuillan and others, *Jackpot Justice: The True Cost of America's Tort System* (San Francisco: Pacific Research Institute, 2007). Another report calculated the cost at $261 billion in 2005. "2006 Update on U.S. Tort Cost Trends," Towers Perrin Tillinghast, St. Louis, MO, 2006, http://www.towersperrin.com/tp/getwebcachedoc?webc=TILL/USA/2006/200611/Tort_2006_FINAL.pdf.

2. Robert A. Levy, *Shakedown: How Corporations, Government, and Trial Lawyers Abuse the Judicial Process* (Washington: Cato Institute, 2004); and David Little, "Instrumentalism and the Disintegration of American Tort Law," *The Objective Standard* 2 (2008): 43–64.

3. Levy, *Shakedown*, pp. 109–14; Fredrick C. Schaefer and Christine Nykiel, "Lead Paint: Mass Tort Litigation and Public Nuisance Trends in America," *Defense Counsel Journal* 74 (2007): 153–71; and James A. Henderson Jr., "The Lawlessness of Aggregative Torts," *Hofstra Law Review* 34 (2005): 329–43.

4. Warren A. Seavey, "Nuisance: Contributory Negligence and Other Mysteries," *Harvard Law Review* 65 (1952): 984.

5. John E. Bryson and Angus MacBeth, "Public Nuisance, the Restatement (Second) of Torts, and Environmental Law," *Ecology Law Quarterly* 2 (1972): 241.

6. Horace Wood, *The Law of Nuisances* (Albany, NY: John D. Parsons Jr., 1881), p. v.

7. *Grove Press Inc. v. City of Philadelphia*, 418 F.2d 82, 88 (3d Cir. 1969).

8. William Prosser, "Nuisance without Fault," *Texas Law Review* 20 (1942): 410.

9. F. H. Newark, "The Boundaries of Nuisance," *Law Quarterly Review* 65 (1949): 480.

10. Louise A. Halper, "Untangling the Nuisance Knot," *Boston College Environmental Affairs Law Review* 26 (1998): 96.

11. Donald G. Gifford, "Public Nuisance as a Mass Products Liability Tort," *University of Cincinnati Law Review* 71 (2003): 748.

12. *City of San Diego v. U.S. Gypsum Co.*, 30 Cal. App. 4th 575, 585 (1994) (quoting W. Page Keeton, *Prosser and Keeton on the Law of Torts*, 5th ed. (St. Paul, MN: West Publishing, 1984), p. 616).

13. *Restatement (Second) of Torts* § 821B (1979).

14. *Lucas v. S.C. Coastal Council*, 505 U.S. 1003, 1055 (1992) (Blackmun, J., dissenting).

15. *Rubin v. City of Santa Monica*, 823 F. Supp. 709 (C.D. Cal. 1993); *Connick v. Lucky Pierre's*, 331 So. 2d 431 (La. 1976); *Grove Press, Inc. v. City of Philadelphia*, 418 F.2d 82 (3d Cir. 1969); and *Napro Dev. Corp. v. Town of Berlin*, 376 A.2d 342 (Vt. 1977).

16. *State v. Palendrano*, 293 A.2d 747, 751 (N.J. Super. Ct. Law Div. 1972).

17. *People of California ex rel. Lockyer v. General Motors, et al.*, No. C06-05755-MJJ (N.D. Cal. 2006) (pending); and *City of Newark, et al. v. Atlantic Richfield Co., et al.*, No. 58,531 (N.J. 2007) (pending).

18. *Restatement* § 821B, comment e.

19. Ibid.

20. *Restatement* § 821B(2).

21. Cf. *Junction 615, Inc. v. Ohio Liquor Control Com'n*, 732 N.E.2d 1025, 1032–33 (Ohio Ct. App. 1999) (finding legal prohibition of "improper conduct" unconstitutionally

vague); and *In re Davis*, 242 Cal. App. 2d 645, 647 (1966) (finding statute that prohibited "an act which 'openly outrages public decency' " unconstitutionally vague).

22. *Restatement* § 821B, comment g.

23. Ibid. ("[T]he pollution of a stream that merely deprives fifty or a hundred lower riparian owners of the use of the water for purposes connected with their land does not for that reason alone become a public nuisance."). See also *City of Chicago v. American Cyanamid Co.*, 823 N.E.2d 126, 131 (Ill. App. 2005) (Public right is not "an assortment of claimed private individual rights.").

24. *Restatement* § 821B, comment g (defining public right as "an indivisible resource shared by the public at large, like air, water, or public rights of way"); and Halper, 96 ("The public nuisance action stems from the injury a private use inflicts on public rights, which may occasionally mean harm to real property owned by the public, but is more often an injury to common pool resources, like silence, clean air or water, or species diversity").

25. Gifford, "Public Nuisance," 782.

26. *Restatement* § 821C.

27. *Diamond v. Gen. Motors Corp.*, 20 Cal. App. 3d 374 (1971).

28. Ibid. at 382–83.

29. *In re Firearm Cases*, 126 Cal. App. 4th 959, 988 (2005).

30. Ibid (quoting *Ileto v. Glock, Inc.*, 370 F.3d 860, 868 (9th Cir. 2004) (Kozinski, J., dissenting from denial of rehearing)).

31. *United States v. Harriss*, 347 U.S. 612, 617 (1954); *Hill v. Colorado*, 530 U.S. 703, 732 (2000); *United States v. Jae Gab Kim*, 449 F.3d 933, 942 (9th Cir. 2006); and *Connally v. Gen. Constr. Co.*, 269 U.S. 385, 391 (1926).

32. *Arthur Andersen LLP v. United States*, 544 U.S. 696, 703 (2005) (citations omitted).

33. *SEC v. Gemstar-TV Guide Int'l, Inc.*, 401 F.3d 1031, 1048 (9th Cir. 2005), *cert. denied sub nom. Yuen v. SEC*, 546 U.S. 933 (2005).

34. *BMW v. Gore*, 517 U.S. 559 (1996).

35. Ibid. at 574.

36. *State Farm v. Campbell*, 538 U.S. 408 (2003).

37. See also *Philip Morris USA v. Williams*, 127 S. Ct. 1057 (2007).

38. Victor E. Schwartz and Phil Goldberg, "The Law of Public Nuisance: Maintaining Rational Boundaries on a Rational Tort," *Washburn Law Journal* 45 (2005): 541–83.

39. Richard C. Ausness, "Tell Me What You Eat, and I Will Tell You Whom to Sue: Big Problems Ahead for 'Big Food'?" *Georgia Law Review* 39 (2005): 839–93 (describing the ongoing case of *Pelman, et al. v. McDonald's Corp., et al.*, No. 1:02-cv-07821-RWS (S.D.N.Y. filed September 30, 2002), in which plaintiffs allege that McDonald's should be liable for making children obese); Samuel J. Romero, "Comment: Obesity Liability: A Super-Sized Problem or a Small Fry in the Inevitable Development of Product Liability?" *Chapman Law Review* 7 (2004): 239–78, 277 ("Whether the fast-food industry has created a public nuisance by promoting unhealthy products and whether courts should ever interfere in this area of personal choice are difficult questions"); and Aricka Flowers, "Caffeine: The Next Big Bad Wolf?" *Legal Newsline*, August 24, 2008, http://www.legalnewsline.com/news/215124-caffeine-the-next-big-bad-wolf.

40. *City of Chicago v. American Cyanamid Co.*, 823 N.E.2d at 139.

41. *In re Lead Paint Litigation*, 191 N.J. 405 (2007).

42. Ibid. at 421 (quoting Gifford, "Public Nuisance," 774).

43. Ibid. at 434.

44. Ibid. at 440 (quotation marks omitted).

45. *State of Rhode Island v. Lead Industries Ass'n, Inc.*, No. PC 99-5226 (R.I. Super. February 26, 2007). The lead paint trial is thought to have been the longest civil trial in state history. Peter B. Lord, "Jurors in Lead-Paint Trial Say They're Proud of Verdict," *The Providence Journal*, March 12, 2006, p. B1.

46. Rob Luke, "St. Louis City Joins Rush to Sue Lead Paint Makers for Clean Up Costs," *Legal Newsline*, January 10, 2007, http://www.legalnewsline.com/news/contentview.asp?c=188880.

47. *State of Rhode Island v. Lead Industries Ass'n, Inc., et al.*, No. 2004-63-M.P. (R.I. July 1, 2008), p. 26.

48. *County of Santa Clara v. Atlantic Richfield Co.*, 137 Cal. App. 4th 292 (2006).

49. Luke, "St. Louis City Joins Rush."

50. Cal. Bus. & Prof. Code § 17200.

51. *Gregory v. Albertson's, Inc.*, 104 Cal. App. 4th 845, 852 (2002).

52. Michael S. Greve, "Consumer Law, Class Actions, and the Common Law," *Chapman Law Review* 7 (2004): 165.

53. Julia B. Strickland, Lisa M. Simonetti, and Andrew W. Moritz, "An Overview of California's Unfair Competition Law," Practising Law Institute, March–May 2003, pp. 15–18, http://www.stroock.com/SiteFiles/pub168.pdf; Joshua D. Taylor, "Note: Why the Increasing Role of Public Policy in California's Unfair Competition Law Is a Slippery Step in the Wrong Direction," *Hastings Law Journal* 52 (2001): 1131–32; and Eliot G. Disner and Noah E. Jussim, "So Unfair and Foul," *L.A. Lawyer*, November 2003, p. 42.

54. Robert C. Fellmeth, "Unfair Competition Act Enforcement by Agencies, Prosecutors, and Private Litigants: Who's on First?" *California Regulatory Law Reporter*, Winter 1995, pp. 1–11.

55. *Midpeninsula Citizens for Fair Hous. v. Westwood Investors*, 221 Cal. App. 3d 1377, 1392–93 (1990).

56. See, for example, *Center for Biological Diversity, Inc. v. FPL Group, Inc., et al.*, No. C-04-0312-CW (N.D. Cal., complaint filed January 12, 2004).

57. Fellmeth, "Unfair Competition Act Enforcement," p. 11.

58. *Tall Club of Silicon Valley v. Alaska Airlines*, No. A102863, 2004 WL 363529 (Cal. App. February 27, 2004).

59. *Michaelson v. Ritz-Carlton Hotel Co. LLC*, No. G032032, 2004 WL 553008 (Cal. App. March 22, 2004).

60. *Beloff v. Brita Products Co.*, No. A099442, 2004 WL 187569 (Cal. App. January 30, 2004).

61. *Rezec v. Sony Pictures Entm't, Inc.*, 116 Cal. App. 4th 135 (2004).

62. Ibid. at 145 (Ortega, J., dissenting).

63. *Hull v. Safeway, Inc.*, 2007 WL 1576372 at *1 (Cal. App. 4 Dist. 2007).

64. *Benson v. Kwikset Corp.*, 15 Cal. Rptr. 3d 407 (2004), *vacated*, 24 Cal. Rptr. 3d 683 (2005).

65. *Clancy v. Hot Network*, 2004 WL 171333 (Cal. App. 2nd Dist. 2004).

66. *Bernardo v. Planned Parenthood Federation of America*, 9 Cal. Rptr. 3d 197 (2004).

67. *Kasky v. Nike, Inc.*, 27 Cal. 4th 939 (2002), *aff'd*, 539 U.S. 654 (2003).

68. *Kunert v. Mission Fin. Services Corp.*, 110 Cal. App. 4th 242, 265 (2003).

69. Greve, "Consumer Law," 166 (quoting Gail E. Lees, "The Defense of Private and Governmental Unfair Competition Law Claims," *Practising Law Institute Litigation and Administrative Practice Course Handbook Series, Unfair Competition Claims*, 2003, p. 306).

70. *People ex rel. Lockyer v. Brar*, 115 Cal. App. 4th 1315, 1316–17 (2004).

71. See 16 C.C.R. § 988.

72. Eugene S. Suh, "Stealing from the Poor to Give to the Rich? California's Unfair Competition Law Requires Further Reform to Properly Restore Business Stability," *Southwestern University Law Review* 35 (2006): 230.

73. Indeed, it seems that Trevor's downfall resulted from its accidentally targeting a business owned by Bridgestone/Firestone, which mounted a full-scale legal defense culminating in Trevor's being disbarred. Chris Cziborr, "Going after the Wrong Defendant?" *Orange County Business Journal*, December 16, 2002, http://www.allbusiness.com/north-america/united-states-california-metro-areas/949930-1.html.

74. Cal. Bus. & Prof. Code § 17204.

75. See, for example, *Hull*, 2007 WL 1576372.

76. Cal. Health & Saf. Code §§ 25191.7, 25249.7(d).

77. Julie Ann Ross, "Citizen Suits: California's Proposition 65 and the Lawyer's Ethical Duty to the Public Interest," *University of San Francisco Law Review* 29 (1995): 814–15.

78. *Consumer Def. Group v. Rental Hous. Indus. Members*, 40 Cal. Rptr. 3d 832, 854 n. 21 (2006).

79. Ibid. at 835.

80. Ibid. at 834.

81. Ibid. at 854–55.

82. Ibid. at 850.

83. Ibid. at 850, n. 19.

84. Ross, "Citizen Suits," 815, n. 44; and Yuri Orlov, "Proposition 65 and Its Effect on California Businesses," April 14, 2005, Holland & Knight, http://www.hklaw.com/id24660/PublicationId2218/ReturnId31/contentid49485/.

85. Nobody knows for sure how much money is involved in Proposition 65 lawsuits. Since 1988, about 26,000 businesses have received warnings of possible lawsuits under the law. According to the *Proposition 65 Handbook* by Roger Carrick, 1,561 lawsuits were filed under the law between 1988 and 2005, but none were dismissed as frivolous, largely because so many simply settle out of court. Carrick estimates that businesses have paid $189 million in legal defense costs alone, not counting the more than $61 million in attorney's fees and costs, $18 million in civil penalties, or the $75 million in restitution paid to plaintiffs. Nor does this include the $1 billion businesses have spent to reformulate their products to eliminate tiny traces of chemicals that could qualify as pollutants under the law. Susan Brink, "You've Been Warned," *Los Angeles Times*, December 18, 2005, p. 1. See also Eric Berkowitz, "Businesses Saw Law on Chemicals Is Being Subverted," *Daily Breeze*, July 11, 2006, p. A6; and *Life and Times*, PBS, March 30, 2007, http://www.kcet.org/lifeandtimes/archives/200703/20070330.php. One lawyer collected more than $9 million in attorney's fees in just four years for bringing Proposition 65 cases, leading the state's attorney general to send a warning letter noting that his "unwarranted" lawsuits "do not appear to be in the public interest." Lisa L. Halko, "California's Attorney General Acknowledges Prop. 65 Abuse,"

Washington Legal Foundation Legal Backgrounder, vol. 22, no. 29, July 27, 2007, http://www.wlf.org/upload/07-27-07halko.pdf.

86. *Koire v. Metro Car Wash*, 40 Cal. 3d 24 (1985); and *Angelucci v. Century Supper Club*, 59 Cal. Rptr. 3d 142 (2007).

87. *Angelucci*, 59 Cal. Rptr. 3d at 154.

88. See, for example, *Consumer Cause, Inc. v. SmileCare*, 91 Cal. App. 4th 454, 484 n. 9 (2001) (Vogel, J., dissenting); *Yeroushalmi v. Miramar Sheraton*, 106 Cal. Rptr. 2d 332 (2001); Monte Morin, "Lawyer Looks to Fine Print to File Never-Ending String of Lawsuits," *Seattle Times*, November 3, 2002, p. A13; and Denise Levin, "Lifting the Smoke Screen: Lawyer's Proposition 65 Practice Has Adversaries Seeing Green," *L.A. Daily Journal*, August 3, 1999.

89. *People v. Consumer Cause, Inc., et al.*, Case No. BC 316912 (L.A. Super. Ct. January 19, 2006); and Amanda Bronstad, "Judge Declines to Reject Lawsuit by Tenant of Sterling," *L.A. Business Journal*, June 21, 2004, p. 10.

90. Bronstad, "Judge Declines," p. 7.

91. *Coal. of Free Men v. State*, No. B172883, 2005 WL 713816 (Cal. Ct. App. March 30, 2005).

92. *Consumer Cause, Inc. v. Grand Ave. Nightclub*, 2004 WL 33431 (Cal. App. 2nd Dist. 2004).

93. Ibid. at *3.

94. Robert Rodriguez, "Fresno Businesses Are Sued over Act: Owners Are Outraged over an L.A. Attorney's Aggressive Practice," *Fresno Bee*, July 4, 2004, p. A1; and Amanda Bronstad, "'Ladies Night' Litigants Rack Up Another Courthouse Loss," *L.A. Business Journal*, June 14, 2004, p. 10.

95. *Yeroushalmi*, 106 Cal. Rptr. 2d at 332.

96. Transcript of hearing, *Yeroushalmi v. Miramar Sheraton, Grille, and Four Points Hotel*, No. BC200421 (L.A. Super. Ct. January 8, 1999) (hearing on motion to demurrer), pp. 40–45 (on file with author).

97. Ibid., p. 41.

98. Ibid., pp. 44–45.

99. *Angelucci v. Century Supper Club*, 41 Cal. 4th 160 (2007).

100. Walter Olson, *The Excuse Factory: How Employment Law Is Paralyzing the American Workplace* (New York: Free Press, 1997), p. 100.

101. *PGA Tour, Inc. v. Martin*, 532 U.S. 661 (2001).

102. *Bartlett v. N.Y. State Bd. of Law Exam'rs*, 970 F. Supp. 1094 (S.D.N.Y. 1997), *aff'd*, 156 F.3d 321 (2d Cir. 1998), *vacated*, 527 U.S. 1031 (1999). See also *Bartlett v. New York State Bd. of Law Examiners*, 2001 WL 930792 (S.D.N.Y. August 15, 2001).

103. *United States v. Hoyts Cinemas Corp.*, 380 F.3d 558 (1st Cir. 2004); *United States v. Cinemark USA, Inc.*, 348 F.3d 569 (6th Cir. 2003), *cert. denied*, 542 U.S. 937 (2004); and *Oregon Paralyzed Veterans of America v. Regal*, 339 F.3d 1126 (9th Cir. 2003), *cert. denied sub nom. Regal Cinemas, Inc. v. Stewmon*, 542 U.S. 937 (2004).

104. Olson, *The Excuse Factory*, p. 130.

105. Ibid., p. 135.

106. Ibid., pp. 111–12.

107. *Ackerman v. Western Elec. Co., Inc.*, 643 F. Supp. 836 (N.D. Cal. 1986), *aff'd*, 860 F.2d 1514 (9th Cir. 1988).

108. Mike Jaccarino, "No Window Desk? That'll Cost You $33M, She Says in Suit," *New York Daily News*, May 26, 2007, p. 8.

109. Lawrence Friedman, *A History of American Law*, 3rd ed. (New York: Touchstone, 2001), p. 347.

110. Carri Becker, "Note: Private Enforcement of the Americans with Disabilities Act via Serial Litigation: Abusive or Commendable?" *Hastings Women's Law Journal* 17 (2006): 101.

111. *Molski v. Kahn Winery*, 405 F. Supp. 2d 1160, 1167 (C.D. Cal. 2005).

112. *Molski v. Mandarin Touch Restaurant*, 347 F. Supp. 2d 860, 866 (C.D. Cal. 2004).

113. Ibid.

114. Walter Olson, "Occupational Hazards," *Reason*, May 1997, p. 22.

115. Philip K. Howard, *The Death of Common Sense* (New York: Random House, 1994), p. 134.

116. Willy E. Rice, "Insurance Contracts and Judicial Decisions over Whether Insurers Must Defend Insureds That Violate Constitutional and Civil Rights," *Tort & Insurance Law Journal* 35 (2000): 997, n. 10.

117. Ibid., 1001–2.

118. Martin H. Redish, "Class Actions and the Democratic Difficulty: Rethinking the Intersection of Private Litigation and Public Goals," *University of Chicago Legal Forum* 2003: 77.

Chapter 12

1. *Kelo v. New London*, 545 U.S. 469 (2005).

2. Timothy Sandefur, *Cornerstone of Liberty: Property Rights in 21st Century America* (Washington: Cato Institute, 2006), pp. 90–106. See also Carla T. Main, *Bulldozed: "Kelo," Eminent Domain, and the American Lust for Land* (New York: Encounter Books, 2007); and Jeff Benedict, *Little Pink House* (New York: Grand Central Publishing, 2009).

3. Timothy Sandefur, "The 'Backlash' So Far: Will Americans Get Meaningful Eminent Domain Reform?" *Michigan State Law Review* 2006: 709–77; and Ilya Somin, "Controlling the Grasping Hand: Economic Development Takings after *Kelo*," *Supreme Court Economic Review* 15 (2007): 183–271.

4. *Pumpelly v. Green Bay Co.*, 80 U.S. (13 Wall.) 166 (1871).

5. Although *Pumpelly* was decided in 1871, three years after the Fourteenth Amendment was ratified, the injury to Pumpelly's land predated the Fourteenth Amendment. Thus, *Pumpelly* was not a Fourteenth Amendment case. See ibid. at 176–77 ("though the Constitution of the United States provides that private property shall not be taken for public use without just compensation, it is well settled that this is a limitation on the power of the Federal government, and not on the States").

6. Ibid. at 177–78.

7. *Grand Rapids Booming Co. v. Jarvis*, 30 Mich. 308, 320 (1874).

8. Ibid.

9. Ibid.

10. *Mugler v. Kansas*, 123 U.S. 623 (1887).

11. Ibid. at 668.

12. Ibid. at 668–69.

13. Ibid. at 669.

14. *Stone v. Mississippi*, 101 U.S. 814 (1879).

15. Ibid. at 669–70.

16. Ibid. at 669.

17. *Pennsylvania Coal v. Mahon*, 260 U.S. 393 (1922).

18. Ibid. at 415.

19. Richard A. Epstein, *Takings: Private Property and the Power of Eminent Domain* (Cambridge, MA: Harvard University Press, 1985), p. 111. See also Roger Pilon, "Property Rights, Takings, and a Free Society," *Harvard Journal of Law and Public Policy* 6 (1983): 185–89.

20. *Loretto v. Teleprompter Manhattan CATV Corp.*, 458 U.S. 419 (1982).

21. Ibid. at 436.

22. *Lucas v. South Carolina Coastal Council*, 505 U.S. 1003 (1992).

23. Ibid. at 1015.

24. *Loretto*, 458 U.S. at 426 (emphasis added).

25. The U.S. Supreme Court did declare in *First English Evangelical Lutheran Church of Glendale v. Los Angeles County*, 482 U.S. 304, 318 (1987), that "'temporary' takings which, as here, deny a landowner all use of his property, are not different in kind from permanent takings, for which the Constitution clearly requires compensation." But in *Tahoe-Sierra Preservation Council, Inc. v. Tahoe Regional Planning Agency*, 535 U.S. 302 (2002), the Court found that "a regulation temporarily denying an owner all use of her property might not constitute a taking" in the first place, and the fact that such a regulation is temporary is one of the factors in determining whether a restriction qualifies as a taking. Ibid. at 337. This means that although property owners are in theory entitled to compensation for temporary infringements of their property rights, they can receive that compensation only after a court decides that the interference with their property qualified as a taking—and most courts will find that a temporary deprivation of the right to use property is not really a taking, because it was only temporary!

26. *Yee v. Escondido*, 503 U.S. 519 (1992).

27. Ibid. at 527–28.

28. Ibid. at 528.

29. Ibid. at 532.

30. *Palazzolo v. Rhode Island*, 533 U.S. 606, 616 (2001).

31. Ibid. at 631.

32. *Penn Cent. Transp. Co. v. City of New York*, 438 U.S. 104 (1978).

33. Ibid. at 124.

34. R. S. Radford, "Regulatory Takings Law in the 1990's: The Death of Rent Control?" *Southwestern University Law Review* 21 (1992): 1022.

35. *Eastern Enterprises v. Apfel*, 524 U.S. 498, 537 (1998).

36. Ibid. at 544–45.

37. *Good v. United States*, 189 F.3d 1355, 1362 (Fed. Cir. 1999).

38. Steve J. Eagle, "The Regulatory Takings Notice Rule," *University of Hawaii Law Review* 24 (2002): 537–38.

39. William P. Barr, Henry Weissmann, and John P. Frantz, "The Gild That Is Killing the Lily: How Confusion over Regulatory Takings Doctrine Is Undermining the Core Protections of the Takings Clause," *George Washington Law Review* 73 (2005): 484.

40. *Armstrong v. United States*, 364 U.S. 40, 49 (1960). See also *VanHorne v. Dorrance*, 28 F. Cas. 1012, 1015 (C.C. Pa. 1795) (No. 16,857) ("Every person ought to contribute his proportion for public purposes and public exigencies; but no one can be called upon to surrender or sacrifice his whole property, real and personal, for the good of the community, without receiving a recompence in value. This would be laying a burden upon an individual, which ought to be sustained by the society at large.").

41. Douglas T. Kendall, "The Limits to Growth and the Limits to the Takings Clause," *Virginia Environmental Law Journal* 11 (1992): 549.

42. Glenn P. Sugameli, "Takings Bills Threaten Private Property, People, and the Environment," *Fordham Environmental Law Review* 8 (1997): 523.

43. *Tahoe-Sierra*, 535 U.S. at 335 (quoting *Pennsylvania Coal*, 260 U.S. at 413).

44. *Fred F. French Investing Co., Inc. v. City of New York*, 39 N.Y.2d 587, 596–97 (1976).

45. Sandefur, *Cornerstone of Liberty*, pp. 85–87.

46. *Owen v. City of Independence, Missouri*, 445 U.S. 622 (1980).

47. Ibid. at 651.

48. Ibid. at 656.

49. Ibid. at 651–52.

50. Ibid. at 655.

51. Justice Brennan wrote the *Penn Central* decision that virtually absolves government of the costs of its regulatory activities. Justice Stevens wrote the *Tahoe-Sierra* decision, refusing to compensate property owners because doing so would be "prohibitively expensive."

52. The doctrine of sovereign immunity sits uneasily with the concept of individual rights. See Epstein, *Takings*, p. 42. Indeed, the doctrine's most eloquent defender, Oliver Wendell Holmes, based his argument for sovereign immunity on the notion that all rights are privileges granted by the state and that one could not therefore have any right to challenge the government's actions in court except where the government allowed it. Suing the government, Holmes wrote, "[S]eems to me like shaking one's fist at the sky, when the sky furnishes the energy that enables one to raise the fist." Holmes to Harold Laski, January 29, 1926, in *The Essential Holmes*, ed. Richard Posner (Chicago: University of Chicago Press, 1992), p. 235.

53. This frame shifting is a common tactic in the law; we have already seen it used in defining the relevant market for antitrust cases in ways that create a monopoly. Likewise, in commerce clause cases, shifting the frame of reference can change a law that entirely destroys a trade into a law that merely "regulates" commerce as a whole.

54. Steven J. Eagle, *Regulatory Takings*, 3rd ed. (Newark, NJ: Lexis-Nexis, 2005), pp. 823–24.

55. *Ruckleshaus v. Monsanto*, 467 U.S. 986 (1984).

56. *Nollan v. California Coastal Com'n*, 483 U.S. 825 (1987).

57. Ibid. at 833, n. 2.

58. *Philip Morris v. Reilly*, 113 F. Supp. 2d 129, 144 (D. Mass. 2000) (quoting *Philip Morris, Inc. v. Harshbarger*, 159 F.3d 670, 679 (1st Cir. 1998)).

59. Ibid. at 145.

60. *Philip Morris v. Reilly*, 267 F.3d 45, 59 (1st Cir. 2001).

61. *Philip Morris v. Reilly*, 312 F.3d 24, 47 (1st Cir. 2002) (en banc).

62. Ibid. See also *Harshbarger*, 159 F.3d at 677–79.

63. *Palazzolo v. State ex rel. Tavares*, 746 A.2d 707 (R.I. 2000).

64. *Palazzolo v. Rhode Island*, 533 U.S. 606 (2001).

65. Ibid. at 632–36.

66. J. David Breemer and R. S. Radford, "The (Less?) Murky Doctrine of Investment-Backed Expectations after *Palazzolo*, and the Lower Courts' Disturbing Insistence on Wallowing in the Pre-*Palazzolo* Muck," *Southwestern University Law Review* 34 (2005): 351–426.

67. *Evans v. United States*, 74 Fed. Cl. 554, 563–64 (Fed. Cl. 2006), *aff'd*, 250 Fed. Appx. 321 (Fed. Cir. October 4, 2007).

68. *First English Evangelical Lutheran Church v. County of Los Angeles*, 482 U.S. 304 (1987).

69. *Tahoe-Sierra*, 535 U.S. at 306.

70. John F. Hart, "Colonial Land Use Law and Its Significance for Modern Takings Doctrine," *Harvard Law Review* 109 (1996): 1252–300; and William Michael Treanor, "The Original Understanding of the Takings Clause and the Political Process," *Columbia Law Review* 95 (1995): 782–887.

71. Kris W. Kobach, "The Origins of Regulatory Takings: Setting the Record Straight," *Utah Law Review* 1996: 1211–92; David A. Thomas, "Finding More Pieces for the Takings Puzzle: How Correcting History Can Clarify Doctrine," *University of Colorado Law Review* 75 (2004): 497–545; Andrew S. Gold, "Regulatory Takings and Original Intent: The Direct, Physical Takings Thesis 'Goes Too Far,'" *American University Law Review* 49 (1999): 181–242; and Eric R. Claeys, "Takings, Regulations, and Natural Property Rights," *Cornell Law Review* 88 (2003): 1549–1671.

72. *Kyllo v. United States*, 533 U.S. 27 (2001).

73. Kobach, "The Origins of Regulatory Takings," 1286–87 (citing *People v. Platt*, 17 Johns. 195 (N.Y. Sup. Ct. 1819); *Transylvania University v. Lexington*, 42 Ky. (3 B. Mon.) 25 (1842); and *Woodruff v. Neal*, 28 Conn. 165 (1859)).

74. See, for example, Abraham Bell and Gideon Parchomovsky, "Givings," *Yale Law Journal* 111 (2001): 547–619; and Reza Dibadj, "Regulatory Givings and the Anticommons," *Ohio State Law Journal* 64 (2003): 1041–124.

75. "Every time the government 'upzones,' or changes a zoning ordinance to the benefit of certain property owners, it has executed a giving," write givings theorists Abraham Bell and Gideon Parchomovsky. "Similarly, when the government relaxes environmental regulations, a giving occurs." Government ought therefore to charge landowners for the privilege of being allowed to use their property, so as to ensure that "the public at large receives adequate consideration in exchange for the giving." Bell and Parchomovsky, "Givings," 550, 617.

76. Dibadj, "Regulatory Givings," 1124.

77. Cass R. Sunstein, *Democracy and the Problem of Free Speech* (New York: Free Press, 1993), p. 30.

78. Richard Pipes, *Property and Freedom* (New York: Knopf, 1999); and Tom Bethell, *The Noblest Triumph* (New York: St. Martin's Press, 1998).

79. John Locke, *First Treatise of Civil Government* § 2, rev. ed., ed. Peter Laslett (Cambridge: Cambridge University Press, 1963), p. 176.

80. Sunstein, *Democracy*, p. 247.

81. Anthony de Jasay, *Justice and Its Surroundings* (Indianapolis: Liberty Press, 2000), p. 150.

82. See *Freeman v. Blount*, 55 So. 293, 295–96 (Ala. 1911); and *Walker v. Palmer*, 1854 WL 396 at *4 (Ala. 1854) ("To prove this description of negative averment, involves a moral impossibility, and is therefore not required, no matter from which party it comes.").

83. Jasay, *Justice and Its Surroundings*, p. 150.

84. *Nollan*, 483 U.S. at 837.

85. As Thomas Jefferson wrote, "What is true of every member of the society individually, is true of them all collectively, since the rights of the whole can be no more

than the sum of the rights of individuals." Jefferson to James Madison, September 6, 1789, in *Thomas Jefferson: Writings*, ed. Merrill Peterson (New York: Library of America, 1984), p. 959.

86. Kris Hudson, "Rising Use of 'Impact' Fees Rankles New-Home Buyers," *Wall Street Journal*, November 21, 2007, p. B1.

87. Duncan Associates, "National Impact Fee Survey 2007," August 2007, http://www.impactfees.com/publications%20pdf/2007survey.pdf.

88. According to California's Department of Housing and Community Development, the state "leads the nation in imposing fees on new residential development . . . which vary widely from jurisdiction to jurisdiction, often with no explicit rationale. They average $20,000 to $30,000 per unit and account for more than 15 percent of new home prices in jurisdictions providing substantial shares of affordable housing." State of California Little Hoover Commission, "Rebuilding the Dream: Solving California's Affordable Housing Crisis," Report no. 165, May 2002, p. 39, http://www.lhc.ca.gov/studies/165/report165.pdf.

89. Marla Dresch and Steven M. Sheffrin, *Who Pays for Development Fees and Exactions?* (Sacramento: Public Policy Institute of California, June 1997), p. v, http://www.ppic.org/content/pubs/report/R_697SSR.pdf.

90. Ibid., p. 51.

91. California Department of Housing and Community Development, "Pay to Play: Residential Development Fees in California Cities and Counties," Sacramento, August 2001, p. 2, http://www.hcd.ca.gov/hpd/pay2play/fee_rpt.pdf.

92. Edward L. Glaeser, Joseph Gyourko, and Raven E. Saks, "Why Have Housing Prices Gone UP?"*American Economic Review* 95 (2005): 329–33, http://papers.ssrn.com/soL3/papers.cfm?abstract_id=658324; and "Sheltered Market," *The Economist*, February 10, 2005, http://www.economist.com/finance/displayStory.cfm?story_id=E1_PGRVTSR.

93. J. David Breemer, "The Evolution of the 'Essential Nexus': How State and Federal Courts Have Applied *Nollan* and *Dolan* and Where They Should Go from Here," *Washington & Lee Law Review* 59 (2002): 378–79.

94. *Nollan*, 483 U.S. at 828–29.

95. Ibid. at 838–39.

96. Ibid. at 837 (quoting *J.E.D. Associates, Inc. v. Atkinson*, 432 A.2d 12, 14–15 (N.H. 1981)).

97. Ibid.

98. Carlos A. Ball and Laurie Reynolds, "Exactions and Burden Distribution in Takings Law," *William & Mary Law Review* 47 (2006): 1513–85.

99. *San Remo Hotel v. City and County of San Francisco*, 27 Cal. 4th 643 (2002); and Sandefur, *Cornerstone of Liberty*, pp. 88–89.

100. Warren Richey, "Next Big Test of Power to Seize Property?" *Christian Science Monitor*, January 2, 2007, http://www.csmonitor.com/2007/0102/p02s01-usju.html.

101. *Didden v. Village of Port Chester*, 322 F. Supp. 2d 385, 390 (S.D.N.Y. 2004), *aff'd*, 173 Fed. Appx. 931 (2d Cir. 2006), *cert. denied*, 127 S. Ct. 1127 (2007).

102. *Griswold v. City of Carlsbad*, 2007 WL 2853933 (S.D. Cal. 2007).

103. Michael Burge, "Property Rights at Issue," *San Diego Union-Tribune*, August 16, 2006, http://www.signonsandiego.com/news/northcounty/20060816-9999-1mc16fee.html.

104. *Lingle v. Chevron U.S.A., Inc.*, 544 U.S. 528 (2005).

105. *San Remo Hotel, L.P. v. City and County of San Francisco*, 545 U.S. 323 (2005).

106. Timothy Sandefur, "The Total Failure of William Rehnquist," *Liberty*, November 2005.

107. *Wilkie v. Robbins*, 127 S. Ct. 2588 (2007). See Laurence Tribe, "Death by a Thousand Cuts: Constitutional Wrongs without Remedies after *Wilkie v. Robbins*," *2006–2007 Cato Supreme Court Review* (Washington: Cato Institute, 2007), pp. 23–76.

108. *Rapanos v. United States*, 126 S. Ct. 2208 (2006).

109. John F. Basiak Jr., "The Roberts Court and the Future of Substantive Due Process: The Demise of 'Split the Difference' Jurisprudence?" *Whittier Law Review* 28 (2007): 861–903.

110. James S. Burling, "John Roberts: A Supreme Property Rights Disaster in the Making," August 15, 2005, http://www.enterstageright.com/archive/articles/0805/0805robertsproperty.htm.

Chapter 13

1. *Helvering v. Davis*, 301 U.S. 619 (1937).

2. *NLRB v. Jones & Laughlin Steel Corp.*, 301 U.S. 1 (1937).

3. *West Coast Hotel Co. v. Parrish*, 300 U.S. 379 (1937).

4. *United States v. Carolene Products Co.*, 304 U.S. 144 (1938).

5. See, for example, Roger Pilon, "Politics and Law," *2004–2005 Cato Supreme Court Review* (Washington: Cato Institute, 2005), p. vii.

6. *Nebbia v. New York*, 291 U.S. 502 (1934).

7. *Home Building & Loan Assoc. v. Blaisdell*, 290 U.S. 398 (1934).

8. *United States v. Butler*, 297 U.S. 1 (1936).

9. *A.L.A. Schechter Poultry Corp. v. United States*, 295 U.S. 495 (1935).

10. Cass R. Sunstein, "Constitutionalism after the New Deal," *Harvard Law Review* 101 (1987): 447–48.

11. See generally Amity Shlaes, *The Forgotten Man* (New York: HarperCollins, 2007); Arthur Ekirch, *Ideologies and Utopias: The Impact of the New Deal on American Thought* (New York: Quadrangle Books, 1969); and Jim Powell, *FDR's Folly: How Roosevelt and His New Deal Prolonged the Great Depression* (New York: Crown Forum, 2003).

12. Francis W. Coker, *Recent Political Thought* (New York: Appleton Century Crofts, 1934), p. 554.

13. Ibid., p. 556.

14. Ibid., p. 558.

15. Ibid., p. 559.

16. Gary Lawson, "The Rise and Rise of the Administrative State," *Harvard Law Review* 107 (1994): 1236.

17. P. S. Atiyah, *The Rise and Fall of Freedom of Contract* (Oxford: Oxford University Press, 1979), p. 590.

18. Ibid.

19. Ibid.

20. *Lawrence v. Texas*, 539 U.S. 558 (2003).

21. *Bowers v. Hardwick*, 478 U.S. 186, 204 (1986) (Blackmun, J., dissenting).

22. Carlton F. W. Larson, "The Declaration of Independence: A 225th Anniversary Reinterpretation," *Washington Law Review* 76 (2001): 711 ("Invoking 'natural rights' in a modern law school is about as persuasive as citing Cotton Mather's treatise on

witchcraft"); and *Supreme Court of New Hampshire v. Piper*, 470 U.S. 274, 281, n. 10 (1985) ("The 'natural rights' theory . . . was discarded long ago").

23. *Griswold v. Connecticut*, 381 U.S. 479 (1965).

24. Ibid. at 484.

25. Ibid.

26. Michael McGerr, *A Fierce Discontent: The Rise and Fall of the Progressive Movement in America, 1870–1920* (New York: Free Press, 2003), p. 317.

27. Irving Brant, *Storm over the Constitution* (Indianapolis: Bobbs-Merrill, 1936).

28. Dean Alfange, *The Supreme Court and the National Will* (Garden City, NY: Doubleday, 1937).

29. Alphaeus Thomas Mason, *Brandeis and the Modern State* (Washington: National Home Library Foundation, 1936).

30. Brant, *Storm over the Constitution*, p. 147.

31. Ibid., p. 24.

32. Ibid., p. 33.

33. Paul Kens, *Justice Stephen Field: Shaping Liberty from the Gold Rush to the Gilded Age* (Lawrence: University Press of Kansas, 1997), p. 117.

34. Indeed, Kens never mentions Sir Edward Coke, which is ironic, since he elsewhere notes that the decision in *Munn v. Illinois* was based on the "age-old legal authority" of Lord Hale, another 17th-century English chief justice. Ibid., p. 161.

35. *Washington v. Glucksberg*, 521 U.S. 702, 720–21 (1997).

36. William Letwin, "Economic Due Process in the American Constitution and the Rule of Law," in *Liberty and The Rule of Law*, ed. Robert L. Cunningham (College Station: Texas A&M University Press, 1979).

37. Bernard Siegan, *Economic Liberties and the Constitution* (Chicago: University of Chicago Press, 1980). See also David E. Bernstein, "*Lochner v. New York*: A Centennial Retrospective," *Washington University Law Quarterly* 83 (2005): 1524, n. 361.

38. Bernstein, "*Lochner*," 1524.

39. Steven M. Teles, *The Rise of the Conservative Legal Movement* (Princeton, NJ: Princeton University Press, 2008), especially chaps. 4 and 6. Law and economics sits somewhat uneasily alongside the traditional defenses of economic liberty in American law, and particularly economic substantive due process, given that many law and economics scholars embrace the morally neutral Progressive outlook pioneered by Oliver Wendell Holmes. Judge Richard A. Posner, for example, the most prominent law and economics scholar, has routinely expressed his admiration for Holmes and embraced Holmes's rejection of morality. Richard A. Epstein, *Skepticism and Freedom: A Modern Case for Classical Liberalism* (Chicago: University of Chicago Press, 2003), especially chap. 3. Given that the liberty of contract cases were based on moral and political philosophy, and not economic theory, this lack of fit is to be expected. Nevertheless, because law and economics theory focuses on "economic efficiency" as its central value, such scholars usually end up advocating economic liberty, because "efficiency" has no other meaning than the free decisions of the parties to a contract. Tom Bethell, *The Noblest Triumph: Property and Prosperity through the Ages* (New York: St. Martin's Griffin, 1998), pp. 319–24.

40. Michael J. Phillips, "The Slow Return of Economic Substantive Due Process," *Syracuse Law Review* 49 (1999): 968–69.

41. Laurence Tribe, *American Constitutional Law*, 2nd ed. (Mineola, NY: Foundation Press, 1988), p. 1374.

42. Walter Dellinger, "The Indivisibility of Economic Rights and Personal Liberty," *2004–2005 Cato Supreme Court Review* (Washington: Cato Institute, 2005), pp. 9–21.

43. Nadine Strossen, "*Michigan Department of State Police v. Sitz*: A Roadblock to Meaningful Judicial Enforcement of Constitutional Rights," *Hastings Law Journal* 42 (1991): 285–390, 288, n. 15.

44. See, for example, Richard A. Epstein, "The 'Necessary' History of Property and Liberty," *Chapman Law Review* 6 (2003): 1–28.

45. Randy E. Barnett, "What's So Wicked about *Lochner?*" *NYU Journal of Law & Liberty* 1 (2005): 325–33.

46. See, for example, Clint Bolick, *Leviathan: The Growth of Local Government and the Erosion of Liberty* (Stanford, CA: Hoover Institution Press, 2004).

47. The scholarly attacks on *Slaughterhouse* are many. See Kimberly Shankman and Roger Pilon, "Reviving the Privileges or Immunities Clause to Redress the Balance among States, Individuals, and the Federal Government," *Texas Review of Law and Politics* 3 (1998): 1–48; David R. Upham, "Note: *Corfield v. Coryell* and the Privileges and Immunities of American Citizenship," *Texas Law Review* 83 (2005): 1483–534; William J. Rich, "Taking 'Privileges or Immunities' Seriously: A Call to Expand the Constitutional Canon," *Minnesota Law Review* 87 (2002): 153–232; John Harrison, "Reconstructing the Privileges or Immunities Clause," *Yale Law Journal* 101 (1992): 1385–474; Michael Ken Curtis, *No State Shall Abridge: The Fourteenth Amendment and the Bill of Rights* (Durham, NC: Duke University Press, 1986), pp. 171–96; Siegan, *Economic Liberties and the Constitution*, pp. 47–54; and William H. Mellor, "The Tragic Legacy of the *Slaughterhouse Cases*," speech delivered at the Cato Institute Forum "Revisiting *Slaughterhouse*," Washington, April 13, 1998, http://www.ij.org/publications/other/slaughterhouse/legacy.html. The only volume ever dedicated entirely to *Slaughterhouse* is Ronald M. Labbé and Jonathan Lurie, *The Slaughterhouse Cases: Regulation, Reconstruction, and the Fourteenth Amendment* (Lawrence: University Press of Kansas, 2003), but Labbé and Lurie provide no serious discussion of the legal issues at the heart of the case. See Timothy Sandefur, "Slaughtering the Fourteenth Amendment," *Claremont Review of Books*, vol. 4, no. 3, Summer 2004.

48. Akhil Reed Amar, *The Bill of Rights: Creation and Reconstruction* (New Haven, CT: Yale University Press, 1998), p. 213.

49. John C. Eastman, "Re-Evaluating the Privileges or Immunities Clause," *Chapman Law Review* 6 (2003): 126. Dean Eastman's article was based in part on an article he coauthored with John C. Eastman, Timothy Sandefur, and me—"Stephen Field: Frontier Justice or Justice on the Natural Rights Frontier?" *Nexus: A Journal of Opinion* 6 (2001): 121–29.

50. *Saenz v. Roe*, 526 U.S. 489 (1999).

51. Actually, in *Colgate v. Harvey*, 296 U.S. 404 (1935), the Court invalidated a law for violating the privileges or immunities clause, but that case was overruled only five years later in *Madden v. Kentucky*, 309 U.S. 83 (1940).

52. *Saenz*, 526 U.S. at 522, n. 1 (Thomas, J., dissenting).

53. Ibid. at 503.

54. *Troxel v. Granville*, 530 U.S. 57, 80, n.* (2000) (Thomas, J., concurring).

55. Clarence Thomas, "The Higher Law Background of the Privileges or Immunities Clause of the Fourteenth Amendment," *Harvard Journal of Law and Public Policy* 12 (1989): 63–70. As this book went to press, the U.S. Supreme Court agreed to review a

case, *McDonald v. Chicago*, 567 F.3d 856 (7th Cir. 2009), *cert. granted*, 77 U.S.L.W. 3691 (September 30, 2009) (No. 08-1521), to consider, among other things, whether the right to keep and bear arms is incorporated to the states via the privileges or immunities clause. The Court may very well overrule *Slaughterhouse* in this case.

56. See, for example, Clint Bolick, "The Grassroots Legal Reform Movement," in *Champions of Freedom Vol. 25: Between Power and Liberty—Economics and the Law*, ed. Richard M. Ebeling (Hillsdale, MI: Hillsdale College Press, 1998), pp. 75–83.

57. See, for example, *Green v. McElroy*, 360 U.S. 474, 492 (1959); *Phillips v. Vandygriff*, 711 F.2d 1217, 1222 (5th Cir. 1983); *Sanderson v. Village of Greenhills*, 726 F.2d 284, 286–87 (6th Cir. 1984); and *Benigni v. City of Hemet*, 879 F.2d 473, 478 (9th Cir. 1988).

58. Bruce Ackerman, *We the People Volume 2: Transformations* (Cambridge, MA: Harvard University Press, 1998). See also Lawson, "The Rise and Rise of the Administrative State," 1250–52.

59. David Skillen Bogen, *Privileges and Immunities: A Reference Guide to the United States Constitution* (Westport, CT: Praeger, 2003), p. 140.

60. Michael Kent Curtis, "Resurrecting the Privileges or Immunities Clause and Revising the *Slaughter-House Cases* without Exhuming *Lochner*: Individual Rights and the Fourteenth Amendment," *Boston College Law Review* 38 (1996): 1–106.

61. Barnett, "What's So Wicked about *Lochner*?" 333.

62. Lawson, "The Rise and Rise of the Administrative State," 1232, 1249.

63. *Powers v. Harris*, 379 F.3d 1208 (10th Cir. 2004), *cert. denied*, 544 U.S. 920 (2005).

64. Ibid. at 1222.

65. *Lemmon v. People*, 20 N.Y. 562 (1860); *Commonwealth v. Jennison* (Mass. 1783, unpublished); *Hone v. Ammons*, 14 Ill. 28 (1852); *State v. Lasselle*, 1 Blackf. 60 (Ind. 1820); and *Stoutenborough v. Haviland*, 15 N.J.L. 266 (1836).

66. Bethell, *The Noblest Triumph*, p. 181.

67. Erwin Chemerinsky, "Under the Bridges of Paris: Economic Liberties Should Not Be Just for the Rich," *Chapman Law Review* 6 (2003): 31–41; Charles L. Black Jr., "Further Reflections on the Constitutional Justice of Livelihood," *Columbia Law Review* 86 (1986): 1103–17; Peter B. Edelman, "The Next Century of Our Constitution: Rethinking Our Duty to the Poor," *Hastings Law Journal* 39 (1987): 1–61; and Frank I. Michelman, "On Protecting the Poor through the Fourteenth Amendment," *Harvard Law Review* 83 (1969): 7–59.

68. David Kelley, *A Life of One's Own: Individual Rights and the Welfare State* (Washington: Cato Institute, 1998).

69. Robert Nozick, *Anarchy, State and Utopia* (New York: Basic Books, 1974), p. 172.

70. Lin Zinser and Paul Hsieh, "Moral Health Care vs. 'Universal Health Care,'" *The Objective Standard* 2 (2008): 9–41, 28.

71. Nozick, *Anarchy, State and Utopia*, pp. 168–74; Kelley, *A Life of One's Own*; Tom G. Palmer, "Saving Rights Theory from Its Friends," in *Individual Rights Reconsidered*, ed. Tibor Machan (Stanford, CA: Hoover Institution Press, 2001), pp. 35–85; Frank B. Cross, "The Error of Positive Rights," *UCLA Law Review* 48 (2001): 857–924; Amy L. Wax, "Rethinking Welfare Rights: Reciprocity Norms, Reactive Attitudes, and the Political Economy of Welfare Reform," *Law and Contemporary Problems* 63 (2000): 257–97; and Amy L. Wax, "Social Welfare, Human Dignity, and the Puzzle of What We Owe Each Other," *Harvard Journal of Law and Public Policy* 27 (2003):121–35.

72. Jefferson to Joseph Milligan, April 6, 1816, in *The Writings of Thomas Jefferson*, ed. A. E. Bergh (Washington: Thomas Jefferson Memorial Foundation, 1907), vol. 14, p. 466.

73. Zinser and Hsieh, "Moral Health Care vs. 'Universal Health Care,'" 27–29; and Fitzhugh Mullan, "The Metrics of the Physician Brain Drain," *New England Journal of Medicine* 353, no. 17 (October 27, 2005): 1810–18.

74. Articles of Confederation, Art. IV (1776).

75. Chemerinsky, "Under the Bridges of Paris," 40; see also Douglas G. Smith, "A Return to First Principles? *Saenz v. Roe* and the Privileges or Immunities Clause," *Utah Law Review* 2000: 305–58.

76. Eastman, "Re-Evaluating," 136.

77. *Goldberg v. Kelly*, 397 U.S. 254 (1970).

Index

Ackerman, Bruce, 288
Adair v. United States, 235
Adams, John Quincy, 84
Adkins v. Children's Hospital, 7–11, 12, 15
advertising
    commercial versus noncommercial
        expression, 194–96
    deceptive or false, 199–200
    deemed a form of expression, 193–94
    see also commercial free speech
Agricultural Adjustment Act, 280
agricultural adjustment programs,
    164–70, 174
agricultural checkoff programs, 207–12
Agricultural Marketing Agreement Act,
    164–65
Ahmad, Mohammed, 275
*A.L.A. Schechter Poultry Corp. v. United
    States*, 15
Alabama, *Metropolitan Life Insurance v.
    Ward*, 185–86, 189
ALCOA, 50–51, 64
Alfange, Dean, 283
Allen, Thomas, 18
Allied Structural Steel v. Spannaus, 78, 79
Amar, Akhil Reed, 84, 287
American Revolution, right to earn a
    living and, 23–25
Americans with Disabilities Act, tort
    law and, 251–54
Angelucci, Marc, 250–51
Anonymous, 118
anti-monopoly traditions, 17, 18–23, 27,
    49, 50, 64–65
antitrust laws, 49
    government immunity from, 56–61
    immunity for favored groups, 61–63
    present day, 50–55, 65
    see also specific acts, e.g., Sherman
        Antitrust Act; *specific cases*
apprenticeship agreements, 22–23
arbitrary power, 98–99
Areopagitica (John Milton), 192
argumentum ad ignoratium fallacy, 129

Aristotle, 91–92
Arkansas, occupational licensing,
    147–48
Arkes, Hadley, 7
Articles of Confederation, privileges
    and immunities exception, 291
at-will employment, manipulation of
    contracts and, 230–38
Atiyah, P. S., 281
automobile industry
    protectionist franchise acts, 171–73
    public nuisance lawsuit, 241–42

Baby M case, 221, 222, 223
Bacchus Imports v. Dias, 185–86
Bad Frog beer company, commercial
    free speech case, 204–5
Ballen, Dennis, 202–3
Banner, Stuart, 193
Banzon, Jonette, 275
Barnett, Randy E., 287, 288
Barr, William P., 264
Barron v. Baltimore, 84, 85
Baxter, Marvin, 229
Bellamy, Edward, 46
Ben & Jerry's, 207
Bernstein, David E., 116, 147, 148, 285
Biden, Joseph, 290
big business
    judicial bias in 19th-century capital-
        ism, 5–6
    judicial protection from, xiv
    politics and, 13, 15
    Progressivism's attack on, 44–50
    protection from competition, 286. *see
        also* Sherman Antitrust Act
Bill of Rights
    emanations and penumbras, 282
    fundamental and nonfundamental
        rights, 2–3, 10, 24–25, 39, 114, 137,
        280, 282, 283
    negative rights concept, 290–92
    purpose, xv

Billings v. Hall, 86–87
Bingham, John, 41
Black, Charles, 290
Black, Jeremiah, 86, 89
Blackmun, Harry, 240, 267, 282
Blackstone, William, 26, 84–85, 118, 168–69
Blaisdell. see Home Building & Loan Assoc. v. Blaisdell
Blodget, Samuel, 28
BMW v. Gore, 242–43
Bogen, David Skillen, 288
Bolick, Clint, 287
Bork, Robert, on *Lochner,* 110–14
Bowes, Ralph, 18
boycotts and similar agreements, 22
Bradwell, Myra, 43
brain drain, 291
Brandeis, Louis, 8, 12, 108, 121, 124, 142, 191
branding, commercial free speech, 203–7
Brant, Irving, 283–84
Brennan, William, 267
Brewer, David, 8–9
Bridges, Dennis, 152
   see also Powers v. Harris
Brooke Group v. Brown & Williamson Tobacco, 53
Brown, Janice Rogers, 276
Buchanan, James, 86
burden of proof
   givings theory and, 273–74
   rational basis test and, 128, 129–30
Burger, Warren, 59–60
Burke, Edmund, 245
business-owners rights, xvi–xvii
   compelled speech and, 207–12
   see also advertising; commercial free speech
business torts
   Consumer Defense Group example, 248–49
   judgments in light of fairness principles, 242–43
   vagueness arising in abuse, 245–49
businesses, regulatory takings and, 255–56
Butcher's Union Slaughter-House & Live-Stock Landing Co. v. Crescent City Live-Stock and Slaughter-House Company, 73, 74
Butler v. Craig, 118

California
   abuse of Chinese workers and businesses, 146–47
   antitrust case under Cartwright Act, 54–55
   case against auto makers contributing to global warming, 243
   child surrogacy contracts, 223
   contract manipulation, 227–30
   Cornwell licensing case, 147–48
   environmental public nuisance lawsuits, 241–42
   greenmail, 248
   Griswolds and, 276–77
   living wage laws, 80–81
   milk production and sales, 166–67
   Nike v. Kasky, 196–97, 198–99, 200
   Nollan and, 269, 274, 275–76, 277
   noncompetition clauses and agreements, 64
   Planned Commercial Zones, 161–62
   Proposition 64, 247–48
   Proposition 65, 248–49, 250
   raisin confiscation, 164–65, 167–69, 270–71
   Unfair Competition Law, 197, 245–47, 248
   Unruh Civil Rights Act abuses, 249–51
   vague business torts, 245–49
   zoning cases, 161–62
Camps Newfound/Owatonna, Inc. v. Town of Harrison, 177–79
Canada, socialized medicine, 291
cartels, 167–70
   Sherman Act prohibition, 63
Cartwright Act, 54–55
The Case of Monopolies. see Darcy v. Allen
The Case of the Bricklayers, 21
The Case of the Tailors of Ipswich, 18
censorship
   commercial transaction restrictions as, 192
   motion pictures, 193
   New York Times v. Sullivan, 197–200
   Nike v. Kasky, 196–97, 198–99, 200
   Valentine v. Christensen, 193
Central Hudson Gas & Electric Corp. v. Public Service Commission of New York (*Central Hudson* test), 195–96, 202–3, 205
charitable organizations, state tax prerogatives and, 178–79

Charles I (England), 21
Charles River Bridge v. Warren Bridge,
    29–31, 71–73, 79
Chemerinsky, Erwin, 290
child surrogacy agreements and con-
    tracts, 221–23
Chinese immigrants, early American
    restrictions on, 145–47
Circuit City, employment contract case,
    228–30
citrus growers, cartels and, 168
*City of Cleburne, Tex. v. Cleburne Living
    Center,* 138–39
City of Memphis v. Winfield, 1–2, 5, 6
City of Philadelphia v. New Jersey, 153–54
Civil Rights Act of 1866, 4, 40
civil rights laws, tort law abuse and,
    249–54
classical liberalism, 10, 39, 47–48, 83,
    84–88, 109, 280
Clayton Act of 1913, 63
Coke, Edward, 2, 6, 18–23, 90, 95, 118,
    142
Coker, Francis W., 280–81
Colgate v. Bacheler, 21
collective decisionmaking, 11–16, 121,
    191, 279–81, 292
collectivism and collectivist doctrine,
    44–45, 124, 280–81
Colorado
    Romer v. Evans, 138–39
    taxi industry protectionism, 143–44
Commentaries on the Laws of England
    (William Blackstone), 26
commerce clause, 94–95, 175–77
    Gibbons v. Ogden and, 176–77
    preemptive effect of, 177–82
    raisin confiscation and, 169
    see also dormant commerce clause
commercial free speech, xvi–xvii,
    191–96
    compelled speech and, 207–12
    as individual self-expression, 201–3,
        206–7
    labels, logos, and branding, 203–7
    New York Times v. Sullivan, 197–200
    Nike v. Kasky, 196–97, 198–99, 200
    political speech, 198
    see also advertising
common-law tradition of legal protec-
    tions for economic liberty, xvi, 2–3
    see also English common law
compelled speech, 207–12

competition, xvi, 286
    limiting, restricting, or prohibiting,
        xiii, 5, 23, 45, 286. *see also* anti-
        trust laws; protectionism
    predatory pricing and, 52–54, 179–82
    Progressives protections against, 13,
        45–46
    Smith on, 25
    subjectivity of motive and intent to
        "injure," 55
consent, contracts and, 216, 227
Constitution, U.S.
    economic or financial emergency
        exceptions and, 76, 78
    as living document, 12, 77, 78
constitutional protection of economic
    freedom, xiv, 1, 124–27, 279–80,
    283–84, 286–93
    see also specific cases
constitutionality of economic regula-
    tions. *see* rational basis test
Consumer Cause, Inc., 249–51
Consumer Defense Group, 248–49
consumer protection, 21, 23
    see also public interest or public
        welfare
consumers
    economic versus political decision-
        making and, 14
    individual's role in economic sphere,
        281
consumption, Smith on, 25
contracts
    manipulation of. *see* manipulation of
        contracts
    public policy and, 214, 215, 220–24
    in restraint of trade, 22–23
    substantive and procedural uncon-
        scionability, 214–15, 226–27,
        228–29
    unconscionability, 214–15, 224–30
    unequal bargaining power, 214,
        215–20
contracts clause, 67–69
    economic or financial emergency
        exceptions, 75–78
    "living Constitution" theory, 77, 78
    modern, 75–81
    private contracts, 78–81
    protectionism and, 154
    public contracts, 69–73
    public interest or public welfare and
        protection, 75–81

reasonable abridgments, 78
states' reserved powers to regulate
and, 73–75
unreasonable abridgments, 78
Cooley, Thomas, 92, 118
cooperation, ethic of, 46
Corfield v. Coryell, 40–41
Cornwell, Jo Ann, 147–48
corporation, evolution, xvi, 17
general incorporation laws, 28–29
monopolistic corporate charters,
27–29
17th and 18th century, 26–29
19th century, 27–31, 48–49
see also monopoly, evolution
corporations
archaic vision of, 31–37
benefits of, 36–37
corporate charters, 27–31, 70–75
corporate privileges, 33–35
as creatures of the state, 29, 32–33
definition changes, 26–29, 37
Friedman on corporate social responsibility, 35
marriage analogy, 29
as monopolies, 29–31
as "persons," 34–35
pooled resources, 35, 36
present-day antitrust laws, 50–55
protection from social legislation, 5–6
stakeholder theory and stakeholders,
35–36
see also monopolies
Court of Federal Claims, raisin case
and, 168–69
Craigmiles v. Giles, 151–53, 159
creative destruction, 126
creative faculty, aspect of humanity, 3
creative works, freedom of expression,
194–95
Crescent City Livestock Landing and
Slaughterhouse Company, 42, 73
criminal law maxim (innocent until
proven guilty), 130, 274
Curtis, Michael Kent, 288

DaimlerChrysler Corp. v. Cuno, 179–82
dairy industry regulation. *see* milk
production and sales
Danaher, John, 226
Danbury Hatters' Case. *see Loewe v.
Lawlor*
Darcy, Edward, 18

Darcy v. Allen, 6, 18, 20–21, 43, 284
Dartmouth College v. Woodward, 29,
70–71, 72, 79, 93, 113, 118
Darwin, Charles, 7
Day, William R., 106
debt-relief laws, 67–69, 75–77
Declaration of Independence
creation of the Union, 84
guarantee of liberty, 10
inherent rights, 24, 85
Dellinger, Walter, 287
democracy
Aristotlean, 91–92
economic, 284
intellectual shift, 110, 136, 280–83,
292
as public decisionmaking, 279–80
rights protection and, 12, 286–87
Democracy in America (Alexis de Tocqueville), 4
Denning, Brannon, 176
Dent v. West Virginia, 100, 145
DeSantis, Vincent, 48
destruction of property, regulatory takings and, 256
Dewey, John, 47, 123, 124
Dibadj, Reza, 272
Diden, Bart, 276
discrete and insular minorities, rational
basis test and laws affecting, 125,
135–40
discrimination lawsuits
number and frequency, 253
tort law abuse and, 249–54
distributive justice theory, 290–91
District of Columbia, *Alaska Railroad*
case, 56–57
dormant commerce clause, xvi, 153–54,
175–76, 182–86
local communities and, 186–89
tax incentives and, 179–82
see also commerce clause
Douglas, Stephen, 40
Douglas, William O., 5, 267, 282–83
Douglass, Frederick, 3–4, 213
Dred Scott v. Sandford, 7, 10, 110–13, 114
Dreyer's ice cream company, 54
due process clause, 79
applied to public nuisance cases,
242–43
fairness principles, 242–43
legal clarity requirement, 242–43
protection guarantee in, 88
welfare rights and, 292

due process of law, 5–6, 90–100
  arbitrary power, 98–99
  government violations of, 94–96
  procedural overlapping substantive
    aspects, 96
  protection of unenumerated rights,
    93–94
  ultra vires actions, 94–95
  see also substantive due process
duty to community, 12

Eagle, Steven, 263, 268
Easterbrook, Frank, 53
Eastman, John C., 287, 291–92
economic decisionmaking
  government interference, 7. *see also*
    rational basis test
  individual rights and freedom in, 7,
    11–12
  through political versus economic
    process, 13–15
economic democracy, 284
economic discrimination
  by states, xvi. *see also* dormant com-
    merce clause
  see also protectionism
economic duress, 215–20
economic efficiency
  contracts and, 238
  government-planned, 126. *see also*
    rational basis test
  state taxes and, 180
economic freedom and liberty, xvii, 279
  balance between consumer protec-
    tion and, 23
  constitutional protection of, xiv, 1,
    124–27, 279–80, 283–84, 286–93
  discovering rather than restoring, 285
  discovery of economic liberty, 285–86
  early judicial review and decisions,
    1–7
  economic freedom and opportunity,
    23, 286
  entrepreneurs and innovators, xiv
  essential to exercise of other rights,
    137
  freedom of economic choice, 286, 293
  historically inconsistent protection,
    285–86
  implementing constitutional protec-
    tions, 286–93
  myths about, 5–11
  need to educate citizens on, 292–93

New Deal revolution and, 279–85
  perversion of vocabulary, 64–65, 106,
    110
  Populist Era, 123
  Pound and, xiv–xv
  as a privilege, 6, 16
  Progressive assault on, 11–16, 123–27,
    279–81, 290, 292
  17th and 18th century, 17–29
  see also right to earn a living
Economic Liberties and the Constitution
  (Bernard Siegan), 173, 283
economic self-interest, 45–46
economic substantive due process, 6–7,
    83–84, 99
  "naked preferences" for interest
    groups, 99–100
  see also Lochner v. New York; Munn v.
    Illinois; Nebbia v. New York; United
    States v. Carolene Products Co.
Edelman, Peter, 290
Edgar, R. Allan, 151–52
efficiency, free society and, 7
Elizabeth I (England), 17, 18
emergency (economic or financial)
  exceptions, 75–78
eminent domain doctrine, 31–32,
    255–60, 267
  police powers and, 257–60, 263
*E.M.M.I. v. Zurich-American Insurance
  Co.,* 219–20
Emord, Jonathan, 199
employment contracts
  at-will employment and, 230–38
  Gentry, 228–30
  job security rules and, 232–34
  wrongful termination lawsuits, 235–36
employment of women, legal cases, 7–11
Encyclopedia Britannica, corporation
  definition, 26
*Energy Reserves Group, Inc. v. Kansas
  Power & Light,* 153, 154
English common law, xvi, 2–3, 18–23,
    41, 83, 93–94
  see also Coke, Edward; Magna Carta
Enrich, Peter D., 179–82
entrepreneurs and innovators
  economic freedom and opportunity,
    xiv, 23, 286
  effect of *Slaughterhouse* on, 44
  franchises and, 170–73
  interfering laws and regulations, xiii,
    xvii. *see also* protectionism
  rational basis test and, xvi, 126

enumerated powers, 94–95, 280
Epstein, Richard A., 63, 133, 226–27, 232, 287, 290
equal protection clause, 154, 185–86
Europe
    authoritarian and collective theories, 280
    charters of liberty, 10
exactions, as regulatory takings, 274–77
exceptional circumstances, abridging freedom of contract and, 10
extortion
    California greenmail, 248
    Molski lawsuits, 252–53
    Nollan and, 274

fairness
    due process clause, 242–43
    notions of, xvii, 49
    procedural, 96, 119
    within regulatory takings, 263
Farber, Daniel, 198
Federal Trade Commission
    taxicab monopoly cases, 60–61
    Whole Foods antitrust violation, 54
Fellmeth, Robert, 245, 246
Field, Stephen J.
    corporations as persons, 34
    economic substantive due process, 83–84
    occupational licensing, 145
    right to go into business, 4–5, 6
    Slaughterhouse, 43, 48, 88–89, 118
    substantive due process, 101–2
Fifth Amendment
    just compensation clause, 255, 271
    protection of liberty, 284
    protection of private property, 255, 264
    see also regulatory takings
Filmer, Robert, 273
First Amendment
    business-owners rights, 191–96
    precision requirement, 204
First English Evangelical Lutheran Church of Glendale v. Los Angeles County, 271
Fisherman's Wharf Bay Cruise Corp. v. Superior Court, 54–55
Fletcher v. Peck, 69–70, 72, 79
Florida
    commercial free speech case, 203
    formula retail ordinances, 186–89
    taxi industry, xi–xiii, xiv, xv, xvi, 60, 286

Foner, Eric, 48
footnote four theory of scrutiny, rational basis test and, 134–40
formalism
    Lochner and, 108
    rational basis test and, xv, 140
Founding Fathers
    contract clause and, 67–69
    free speech and, 191–92
    natural or fundamental rights of all humanity, 2–3, 10, 24–25, 39
    priority of individual rights, 11–12
    purpose of Bill of Rights, xv
    see also specific founders
Fourteenth Amendment
    citizenship detailed in, 88
    corporations as "persons," 34
    enactment, 39, 84
    equal protection clause, 154, 185–86
    equality in equal protection clause, 88
    foundation for Civil Rights Act of 1866, 40–41
    Powers and, 153–54, 185, 188
    protection in due process clause, 88
    protection of liberty, 101–2, 189, 284
    right to welfare argument, 291
    rights in privileges and immunities clause, 88
    see also due process clause; privileges and immunities clause; *specific cases*
franchises
    formula retail ordinances and, 186–89
    monopoly. *see* trade monopolies or patents
    protectionism and, 170–73, 174
Franklin, Benjamin, 192
free markets, 6
    anti-monopoly traditions and, 20
    versus government planning, 14
    understanding, 292
free society, justice and, 7
freedom and liberty of contract, xiv–xv, 1–5, 12, 213–14, 238
    decline of, 50, 281–82
    freedom of choice versus coercion, 215–20
    Kens on, 117–18
    noncompetition clauses and agreements, 64–65
    Progressives and, 11–16
    as "shibboleth," 48, 107
    women and, 7–11

freedom of economic choice, 286, 293
  government interference, 7
freedom of speech, 191–92
  lobbyists, 61
  Sunstein on, 117
  see also commercial free speech
freedom of the press, 192–93
Friedman, Lawrence, 28, 252
Friedman, Milton, 35, 149–50
Friedman v. Rogers, 205–6
funeral homes and merchandise, occupational licensing, 150–55

Gentry v. Superior Court, 228–30
Gibbons v. Ogden, 176–77
Gilded Age
  laissez faire in, 48–49
  substantive due process, 83
Ginsburg, Ruth Bader, 9
givings theory, regulatory takings and,
  272–74
*Glickman v. Wileman Brothers & Elliot,
  Inc.,* 208–9, 210
Goldstein, Thomas, 197
government
  due process violations, 94–96
  economic decisionmaking, 7, 14. *see
    also* rational basis test
  freedom to create monopolies, 56–61,
    64
  the individual and, 12–13
  legitimate government or state inter-
    est, 132–33
  Progressivism's pro-government pre-
    sumption, xiii–xiv, 11–13, 44–50
  redistributive programs, 283
  shaping of society, 12–13
  see also local government
government abuse of power, xvi–xvii, 49
  local governments, 61
  special interests and, 163
government authority
  rights of individuals and, 85
  as superior to individual freedom,
    11–12, 46, 85, 91–92, 114. *see also*
    Progressivism
  see also states; states' rights
government contracts with private
  companies, 78–81
government elites, judicial protection
  from, xiv
Graber, Mark, 112
Graber, Susan, 218

Granger Cases, 100–102
  see also Munn v. Illinois
Great Depression, 75–78
Great Society, 283
Green Bay Company. *see Pumpelly v.
  Green Bay Company*
greenmail, 248
Griswold, Craig and Robin, 276–77
Griswold v. Connecticut, 282–83
guild system, 23
gun manufacturers, public nuisance
  lawsuits, 242

Ham v. McClaws, 118
Hand, Learned, 50–51
Harlan, John Marshall, 106, 257–58
Helvering v. Davis, 279
Hernandez, Adrian, 162
Hessen, Robert, 32–33, 34
Hettinga, Hein, 167
Hofstadter, Richard, 7
Hoke v. Henderson, 118
Holmes, Oliver Wendell Jr.
  freedom of contract as "shibboleth,"
    48, 107
  Lochner and, 7, 106–7, 110, 113, 121
  Mahon and, 258
  majoritarianism, 109, 120
  on property values and changes in
    the law, 265
  Richardson on, 124
Home Building & Loan Assoc. v. Blaisdell,
  76–79, 80, 280
Horne, Marvin, 164–65, 168
H.P. Hood & Sons, Inc. v. Du Mond, 153–54
Hughes, Charles Evans, 77–78
Hurtado v. California, 98

Illinois
  Bradwell's case against, 43
  franchise acts, 171–73
  lead paint public nuisance case, 239,
    244
  local monopolies, 60–61
imbalance of bargaining power, 215–20
In Defense of the Corporation (Robert Hessen), 32–33
individual rights and freedom
  in economic decisionmaking, 7, 11–12
  government authority as superior to,
    11–12, 46, 85, 91–92, 114. *see also*
    Progressivism

moral case for, 3
presumption of liberty, 130, 273–74
regulatory takings and, 265–66
substantive limits on state action
    and, 94. *see also* substantive due
    process
individuals and individualism
government and, 12–13
government coercion to serve soci-
    ety's needs, 46
individual autonomy, 281
individual's role in political sphere,
    281
Populist Era, 44
Progressivism and, 45–46
sovereignty of the individual, 281
Institute for Justice, 201, 202, 285
The Institutes of the Laws of England
    (Edward Coke), 20, 90
insurance companies, contracts,
    218–20
intellectual property, regulatory tak-
    ings, 269–70
interstate commerce, 170
    see also commerce clause; dormant
        commerce clause
Interstate Commerce Commission, 47

James I (England), 18–19
Japanese internment, 266
Jasay, Anthony de, 130, 273–74
Jefferson, Thomas, 192
on Coke's writing, 21
on corporations, 27
on natural or fundamental rights,
    24
Jim Crow, 147, 289
job security rules, 232–34
Johanns v. Livestock Marketing Ass'n,
    210–12
Johnson, Andrew, 86
Johnson, Reverdy, 169
Johnson v. Calvert, 223
Jones, Leroy, 143–44
judicial bias
constitutional legerdemain, 6
economic theories and, 6–7
19th century, 5–6
judicial restraint, legislative freedom
    from, 11, 12–13, 109
just compensation clause, 255, 271
commodity confiscation and, 168–69,
    170

justice, 7
constitutional guarantee of, 93
debt-relief laws and, 68–69
individualist concept of, 12
Madison on, 97–98

Kasky v. Nike. see Nike v. Kasky
Keeton, W. Page, 240
Kelo v. New London, 31, 137, 255, 276,
    277, 283
Kendall, A. Douglas, 265
Kennedy, Anthony, 138, 209–10
Kennedy, Duncan, 216–17, 218
Kens, Paul, on *Lochner,* 117–20
Kent, James, 20, 61
Kentucky, Montgomery case, 194–95
Keynes, Edward, 105–6
King, James Lawrence, 187–88
Klein, Brett, 250
Kobach, Kris, 272
Kolko, Gabriel, 13
Kozinski, Alex, 193
Kutler, Stanley, 30, 31
Kyl, Jon, 167

La Fetra, Deborah J., 194
labels, product, commercial free speech,
    203–7
labor unions
anti-competitive conduct, 62–63, 64
at-will employment and, 232
immunity from antitrust laws, 62–63
job security rules and, 233–34
laissez-faire economics, 6
Gilded Age and, 48–49
law
meaning and qualification of, 90–91,
    92, 99
permanent and aggregate interests of
    the community and, 91, 93
procedural overlapping substantive
    aspects, 96
unqualified legislative acts under
    due process, 95–96
see also due process of law
lawfulness, themes of, 97–98
Lawrence v. Texas, 132, 282
Lawson, Gary, 281, 289
lead paint, public nuisance cases, 239,
    244–45
legislative freedom from judicial
    restraint, 11, 12–13, 109

Letwin, William, 20, 285
liberty, 273
    charters of power granted by, 10
    definition of, 7
    European charters of, 10
    Jasay on presumption of, 130, 273–74
    Locke's presumption of, 273
licensing, occupational, 23, 99–100
    barrier to entry, 63
    florists, 133–34, 155
    funeral homes and merchandise,
        150–55
    as protectionism, 145–59, 174
    racial bias, 145–49
    rational basis test and, 133–34,
        148–49, 151
    wildlfe control example, 156–59
*Liebmann. see New State Ice Co. v.
    Liebmann*
limited liability privilege, 33
Lincoln, Abraham, 4, 40, 84
living Constitution theory, 77, 78
Lloyd, Henry Demarest, 45, 46, 49
Loan Association v. Topeka, 97–98
local government
    abuse of power, 61
    contracts clause and, 80–81
    formula retail ordinances, 186–89
    monopolizing trade, 60–61
    Owen and, 267
    regulatory takings, 264–68
    viewshed ordinances, 264
Local Government Antitrust Act, 61
Lochner v. New York, xvi, 6, 7, 8–9, 100,
    121, 125, 284–85, 286, 288, 289
    Bakeshop Act and, 103–5
    Bork on, 110–14
    economic substantive due process
        and, 102–7
    Kens on, 117–20
    modern criticism, 110
    Progressives' criticism of and attack
        on, 107–10
    Souter on, 114–17
*Lochner v. New York: Economic Regulation
    on Trial* (Paul Kens), 117
Locke, John, 24
    reply to *Patriarcha,* 273
    see also classical liberalism
Loewe v. Lawlor, 63
logos and insignia, commercial free
    speech, 203–7
Looking Backward (Edward Bellamy), 46

*Loretto v. Teleprompter Manhattan CATV
    Corp.,* 260–62
Louisiana, occupational licensing of
    florists, 133–34, 155
Lucas v. South Carolina Coastal Council,
    260–61, 262, 264, 268, 271
Lyons, Willie, 8, 12, 108

Macaulay, Stewart, 172–73
Madison, James, 10
    commerce clause, 176
    corporations and monopolies, 27
    justice, 97–98
    laws abolishing debts, 68–69
    natural or fundamental rights, 24, 114
    property rights, 25
    sovereignty and individual rights,
        85, 114
    will of majority, 92, 113–14
Magna Carta, 2, 18
    due process of law, 83, 90
    law of the land clause, 20–21, 90, 93, 94
Mahon. see Pennsylvania Coal v. Mahon
Maine, Henry, 67
    *Camps Newfound/Owatonna, Inc. v.
        Town of Harrison,* 177–79
majority
    Aristotlean democracy, 91–92
    majoritarianism, 110, 120–21
    majority rule and majority power, 69,
        92, 110, 113–14, 117, 120, 121
    over individuality, 11, 44–45, 109, 110,
        279, 292
manipulation of contracts, xvii, 75–81,
    213–15
    at-will employment and, 230–38
    public policy and, 220–24
    rule of law and, 223–24
    unconscionable contracts, 214–15,
        224–30
    unequal bargaining power theory,
        215–20
Marbury v. Madison, 120
Marshall, John, 69–70, 71
Marshall, Thurgood, 267
Maryland, corporate charters, 31
Mason, Alphaeus Thomas, 283
Mason, George, 3
    on inherent rights, 24
    on monopolies, 27
Massachusetts
    child surrogacy agreements and
        contracts, 221–22, 223

corporate charters, 31
tobacco company disclosure case,
    269–70
*Matsushita Electric Industries v. Zenith
    Radio,* 53
McCloskey, Robert, 83, 139
McGerr, Michael, 44–45, 283
McReynolds, James Clark, 127–28
Menand, Louis, 7, 109
Merhban, Morse, 248–49
Merriam, Charles Edward, 12
Merrifield, Alan, 156
Merrifield v. Lockyer, 156–59
Metropolitan Life Insurance v. Ward,
    185–86, 189
Michelman, Frank, 290
Michigan
    occupational licensing of florists, 134
    Supreme Court on evolution of cor-
        poration, 28
    wine importation laws, 182–83
Microsoft Corp., 51–52, 64
    temporary workers lawsuit, 237–38
Midwest Oil Company, 52–53
milk production and sales
    agricultural adjustment programs,
        165–67
    agricultural check off programs, 208
    Nebbia and, 126–27
Milk Regulatory Equity Act, 167
Mill, John Stuart, 6
Miller, Samuel, 42–43, 88–89
Milton, John, 78, 192
minimum-wage laws, 8
Minnesota
    mortgage laws and debt-relief meas-
        ures, 75–77
    predatory pricing, 52–54
minority groups
    laws affecting discrete and insular
        minorities, 125, 135–40
    19th-century deprivations, 285
    racial bias in occupational licensing,
        145–49
Molski, Jarek, 252–53
monopolies
    constitutional protection against,
        39–44
    corporations as, 29–31, 37
    government creation of, 56–61, 64
    market definition and, 55
    natural, 101
    perversion of the term, 64–65
    present-day antitrust laws and, 50–55

state powers and privileges, 44, 72,
    73–74
    see also corporations
monopoly, evolution, xvi, 17, 39
    anti-monopoly traditions, 17, 18–23,
        27, 49, 50, 64–65
    common law and, 18–23
    monopolistic corporate charters,
        27–29
    Progressives changing definition of
        monopoly, 44–50
    right to earn a living as a natural
        right, 23–25, 39
    17th and 18th century, 17–29
    19th century, 27–29, 44–50
    trade monopolies or patents, 19, 22
    see also corporation, evolution
monopoly protections, regulation as, 13
Monsanto. see Ruckleshaus v. Monsanto
Montgomery, John Michael, 194–95
moral case for individual rights, 3
Morriss, Andrew, 231
Motor Vehicle Franchise Act, 171–73
Mugler v. Kansas, 257–58
Muller v. Oregon, 8–9
Munn v. Illinois (The Granger Cases),
    100–101, 124–25
    see also rational basis test
Murphy, Kevin, 52

Nader, Ralph, 32
National Industrial Recovery Act, 280
natural rights of all humanity, 2–3,
    10–11, 291–92
    liberty as, 12
    rejection of the notion of. *see*
        Progressivism
    see also Founding Fathers; freedom
        and liberty of contract; right to
        earn a living
Nebbia v. New York, 100, 124, 125, 126–28,
    280
negative rights concept of Bill of Rights,
    290–92
Neily, Clark, 131
Nestlé, 54
Nevada, *Tahoe-Sierra,* 265, 271, 277, 278
New Deal, xv–xvi
    cases invalidating certain programs,
        15, 280. *see also specific programs*
    ensuring prosperity, 283
    jurisprudential revolution, 279–85
    Roosevelt's court-packing plan, 279–80

New Deal Supreme Court, xiii, xvi
switch in time that saved nine, 83–84,
279, 280
New Jersey
Baby M case, 221, 222, 223
lead paint public nuisance case, 239,
244
skateboard park contract example,
216
New State Ice Co. v. Liebmann, 142
New York
Bakeshop Act. *see Lochner v. New York*
commercial free speech case, 204–5
general corporation law, 28
wine importation laws, 182–83
New York Times v. Sullivan, 197–200
Nike v. Kasky, 196–97, 198–99, 200
Nineteenth Amendment, 9
NLRB v. Jones & Laughlin Steel Corp., 279
Noerr-Pennington doctrine, 61
Nollan v. California Coastal Commission,
269, 274, 275–76, 277
noncompensable regulation, *Mahon*
and, 258
noncompetition agreements and
clauses, 17, 22–23, 64–65
Nozick, Robert, 290
nuisance. *see* public nuisance
Nunes, Devin, 167

O'Connor, Sandra Day, 261, 270
Ohio
Cuno, 179–82
motion picture censorship, 193
Pagan's free speech case, 201–2
Oklahoma, *Powers v. Harris,* 152–55, 159,
162, 188, 289
Olson, Floyd, 76
Olson, Walter, 252, 253
organized labor. *see* labor unions
O'Scannlain, Diarmuid F., 159
Owen v. City of Independence, Missouri, 267

Pacific Legal Foundation, xvi, 285
Pagan, Christopher, 201–2
Parker v. Brown, 56, 57
patents. *see* trade monopolies or patents
Patriarcha (Robert Filmer), 273
Peckham, Rufus, 6–7, 105
*Penn Central Transportation Company v.
City of New York,* 260, 262–64, 268
Pennsylvania Coal v. Mahon, 258–59
Pepsi company, job security rules, 233–34

permanent and aggregate interests of
the community, 91, 93
Perry, Arthur Latham, 118
Petition of Right, 21
Planned Commercial Zones, 161–62
Populist Era
corporations and monopolies during,
39–44
economic freedom argument, 123
Munn and, 102
Postal Reorganization Act of 1970, 57, 58
post–Civil War America. *see* Populist Era
Postrel, Virginia, 206
Pound, Roscoe, xiv–xv, 12, 104, 107–8,
118–19
Powell, Thomas Reed, 11
Powers, Kim, 152
Powers v. Harris, 152–55, 159, 162, 188,
289
predatory pricing schemes, 179–82
price stabilization schemes. *see* agricultural adjustment programs
privacy rights, 282
private agreements
monopoly-like, 22–23
see also contracts; *specific types of
agreements*
privileges, corporate, 28, 29, 31, 33–35
*Privileges and Immunities: A Reference
Guide to the United States Constitution* (David S. Bogen), 288
privileges and immunities clause, 4
Corfield and, 40–41
dormancy, 43–44
overruling, revival, reversal of, 287–92
right to make and enforce contracts,
288–89
Slaughterhouse and, 41–44
states' rights and, 40–41
productive work, 3
professions
barriers to entry, 63, 141
licensing, 23, 63, 99–100, 145–56
restricted entry, 22, 23
restricting or eliminating competition, 289–90
unskillfulness, 23
Progressive Era, xiv–xv, 44–50
eminent domain and, 32
misconceptions about, 47–49
regulation of business and economy,
13, 15, 123–27, 136–37
Supreme Court, 15, 279. *see also
specific justices*

Progressivism
    agenda, ideology, and philosophy, 11,
        12–13, 44–50, 279–81
    assault on economic liberty, 11–16,
        44–50, 279–81, 290, 292
    changing American political philoso-
        phy, 44–50
    criticism of and attack on *Lochner,*
        107–10, 121
    doctrines, 279–81
    economic freedom argument, 123–27
    free speech and, 191–92
    majority over individuality, 11, 44–45,
        109–10, 121, 279, 292. *see also* col-
        lective decisionmaking
    notion of individual freedom, 116–17
    pro-government presumption,
        xiii–xiv, 11–13, 44–50
    rational basis test and, 125–27
    rights as permissions, 95, 109, 116–17,
        279, 282–83
    socialist nature of, 46, 123–27
    visionary zeal to do gooders, 13, 46
Prohibition, legacy of, 183–84
property
    corporate, 34
    regulation as secondary to, 272–73
property redistribution
    government redistributive programs,
        283
    Progressivism and, 13
property rights, xvii, 24–25
    of criminals, 259
    givings theory and, 272–74
    land-use regulation, 160. *see also* zon-
        ing laws, protectionism and
    Locke on, 273
    ownership as separate from right to
        use, 257
    partial property rights in other peo-
        ple, 290–91
    Rehnquist and Roberts Courts,
        277–78
    right of use of property or land, 257,
        271
    see also regulatory takings
*Property Rights from Magna Carta to the
    Fourteenth Amendment* (Bernard
    Siegan), 283
Prosser, William, 76
protection of the public. *see* public inter-
    est or public welfare
protection of unenumerated rights,
    93–94

protectionism, xvi, 141–44, 173–74
    agricultural adjustment programs,
        164–70, 174
    barriers to entry, 141
    contracts clause and, 154
    dormant commerce clause and, 153–54
    franchise acts and, 170–73, 174
    as legitimate state interest, 289
    licensing laws, 145–59, 174
    necessity of new business and certifi-
        cates of necessity, 143–44
    public choice theory and, 289–90
    tariffs, 141
    taxi industry example, xi–xiii, xiv, xv,
        xvi, 143–44, 286
    zoning laws, 159–63, 174
public choice theory, 289–90
public contracts, 69–73
public interest or public welfare
    contracts clause, 75–81
    Liebmann and, 142–43
    Munn and *Nebbia* and, 101, 125–27.
        see also rational basis test
    Powers and, 152–55, 159, 162, 289
    seizure of property. *see* eminent
        domain doctrine; regulatory
        takings
public nuisance, xvii
    Blackmun on, 240
    common or public right definition,
        241
    reasonable and lawful conduct, 243–45
    reasonableness and unreasonable-
        ness, 240–41, 242
    regulatory takings and, 258
    tort law abuse, 239–45
public policy, manipulation of contracts
    and, 214, 215, 220–24
public use, synonymous with public
    benefit, 255
Pumpelly v. Green Bay Company, 256–57,
    258

Radford, R. S., 262
railroads
    antitrust case *Alaska Railroad,* 56–57
    corporation as person in *Santa Clara
        County,* 34
    eminent domain doctrine and, 31–32,
        48
raisin-confiscation case, 164–65, 167–69,
    270–71
Rand, Ayn, 285

Rand Corporation employment
research, 235–36
rational basis test, xv, xvi, 15, 273, 286,
289
argumentum ad ignoratium fallacy, 129
burden of proof and, 128, 129–30
constitutional double standard,
136–40
defining legitimate state interest, 129,
132–33
evolution, 123–27
laws related to legitimate government interest, 132–33
occupational licensing and, 133–34,
148–49, 151, 153, 156–59, 174
problems with, 127–34
varying standards and levels of scrutiny, 135–40
realist school of legal thought, 12
Redish, Martin, 200, 201
regulation, secondary to concept of
property, 272–73
regulation of business and economy, 11
constitutionality of, xv
Populist Era, 39–44
Progressive Era, 13, 15, 44–50, 123–27,
136–37
protecting business from competition. *see* protectionism
in public interest, 5, 125–27, 142–43
unfettered, 6
see also rational basis test
regulatory state, 286, 289
entrenched interests and lobbyists
and, xiv–xv
regulatory takings, xvii, 255–56
categorical (with compensation) takings, 260–62
character of government action and,
262–63
compensation-denial tactics, 268–74
compensation requirement and, 255,
264–68, 271
constructive consent rule, 269
controversies surrounding, 264–68
definition of "take," 256–60
development and, 265, 271, 275–76
eminent domain and, 255–60, 267
exactions as, 274–77
extortion in, 274
fairness within, 263
Fifth Amendment and, 255
future of takings law, 277–78
givings theory and, 272–74

noncompensable regulation as actual
confiscation, 258–59
notice rule theory, 269
Penn Central test, 260, 262–64, 268
police powers and, 257–60, 263
public good over individual rights
protection, 265–66
reasonableness of owner expectations, 263–64, 270
reasons for, 256–60
right of use of property or land, 257,
271
types of, 260–64
Rehnquist, William, 277
Reinhardt, Stephen, 237–38
rent-control, 75
residential development fees, 275–76
resource allocation and use, Progressives and, 13–14
Restatement of Torts, 240–41
The Return of George Sutherland (Hadley
Arkes), 7
Rhode Island
common insignia laws, 207
lead paint public nuisance case, 239,
244–45
regulatory taking examples, 262, 270
Richardson, Dorsey, 124
right to earn a living, xvi–xvii, 1–5, 12
as a natural right, 23–25, 39, 48,
169. *see also* natural rights of all
humanity
noncompetition clauses and, 64–65
present-day attitude toward and
consensus on, 5–6
see also economic freedom and liberty
rights
limits of, 7
as permissions, 95, 109, 279, 282–83
Roberts, John, 277–78
Robinson-Patman Act, 53
Rockefeller, Edwin, 54
Romer v. Evans, 138–39
Roosevelt, Franklin D., court-packing
plan, 279–80
royal charters, 27
see also corporation, evolution
R.R. v. M.H., 221
Ruckleshaus v. Monsanto, 269
RUI One, 81

Saenz v. Roe, 287
Saiger, Glenn and Virginia, 186–89

Santa Clara County v. Southern Pacific Railroad, 34
Scalia, Antonin, 136, 179, 182
Schechter Poultry. see *A.L.A. Schechter Poultry Corp. v. United States*
Schmitter, Aman, 104, 105, 108, 119
Schumpeter, Joseph, 126
Schwartzer, William, 158
Sea-Land Service, Inc. v. Alaska Railroad, 56–57
segregation, 289
self-ownership, 290–91
Seminole Tribe of Florida v. Florida, 114–15, 116
sexual devices, laws restricting sales, 137, 189
shaping of society, 12–13
Sharpless v. Mayor of Philadelphia, 86
Shays's Rebellion, 67–68, 76
Sherman, John, 41
Sherman Antitrust Act, 45, 47, 49–50
  anti-competitive behavior described in, 62
  government-created monopolies and, 56–61
  immunity for favored groups, 61–63
Shiras, George, 214
Siegan, Bernard, 173, 283, 284, 285
Sills, David, 248–49
Skates by the Bay, 81
Slaughterhouse Cases, 41–44, 48, 73, 287–90
  demise of privileges and immunities clause, 88–89
  overturning, 288, 290
  questioning viability of, 289
slavery, 4
  declared unconstitutional, 289
  Dred Scott, 7, 10, 110–13, 114
  Taney on, 110–12
slavery debate, 85–86
Smith, Adam, 6
  competition, 45
  corporations, 26
  monopolies, 19, 25
social Darwinism, 6–7, 48, 117
social legislation, 5–6
socialized medicine, 291
Souter, David, 7, 114–15, 116, 117
sovereign power, intellectual backdrop of Civil War, 85–88
sovereignty of the individual, 281
special interests and lobbyists, xiv–xv, 289–90

antitrust immunity, 61–63
  in economic decisionmaking, 15
  government abuse of power and, 163
  monopolies and, 24
  "naked preferences" for interest groups, 99
  protection of preferred groups, 154–59, 162–63
Spencer, Herbert, 6, 48
stakeholder theory and stakeholders, 35–36
Stamp Act, 192
Standard Oil, 45, 53, 64
State Farm v. Campbell, 243
state regulatory powers, 15, 73–75
states
  abridging privileges and immunities of U.S. citizenship, 42
  antitrust laws, 54–55
  conference of power from Parliament to, 86
  constitutional and legislative power, 40–44, 73–75
  economic discrimination, xvi. see also commerce clause; dormant commerce clause
  economic interference, 10
  general incorporation laws, 28–29
  monopoly powers and privileges, 44, 72, 73–74
  police powers, 257–60, 263
  power over corporate charters, 70–75
  reserved powers, 15, 73–75
  sovereignty, 85, 154
  state citizenship over national citizenship, 85, 88–89
  taxing powers and prerogatives, 178–82
  see also Fourteenth Amendment; specific clauses
states' rights
  Civil War and, 85–88
  privileges and immunities clause and, 40–41, 42
  see also specific cases
Statute of Monopolies, 20, 61
Stevens, John Paul, 58–59, 184, 267, 271
Stone v. Mississippi, 73, 74–75, 258
Storm over the Constitution (Irving Brant), 283–84
Story, Joseph, 72–73
Strossen, Nadine, 287
substantive due process, xvi, 83–84, 90, 93–100, 118–19

connection between procedure and substance, 118–19
economic substantive due process, 6–7, 83–84, 99–100
Granger Cases, 100–102. *see also Munn v. Illinois*
"naked preferences" for interest groups, 99–100
sovereignty and its limits, 84–89, 94–96, 114
varying standards and levels of judicial scrutiny, 135–40
Werner on, 118
see also due process of law
Sugameli, Glenn, 265
Sumner, Charles, 4, 84
Sunstein, Cass, 99, 115, 116, 117, 154, 272, 280
supremacy clause, 43
Supreme Court, U.S.
New Deal Supreme Court, xiii, xvi
Progressive Supreme Court, 15, 279
on purpose of Bill of Rights, xv
role, xv–xvi
Roosevelt's court-packing plan, 279–80
switch in time that saved nine, 83–84, 279, 280
see also specific cases and justices
Sutherland, George, 9–11, 15, 77, 142–43
Swedenburg, Juanita, 183, 184

Tahoe-Sierra v. Tahoe Regional Planning Agency, 265, 271, 277, 278
Takings: Private Property and the Power of Eminent Domain (Richard A. Epstein), 259, 290
Taney, Roger, 71–72, 110–12
taxes, as wealth transfer, 141–42
taxi industry
monopolies, 60–61
regulation, xi–xiii, xiv, xv, xvi, 143–44, 286
technological advances and innovations, Progressive Era, 45
temporary workers, at-will employment, 236–37
Tennessee, *Craigmiles*, 151–53, 159
Texas, *Friedman*, 205–7
Thomas, Clarence, 137, 182, 283, 287–88, 290
tiers of scrutiny notion, compared to rational basis standard, 125
Tocqueville, Alexis de, 4, 75

tort law, xvii, 267–68
opportunism in, 254
tort law abuse, xvii, 239
Americans with Disabilities Act and, 251–54
business torts, 245–49
civil rights laws and, 249–54
definition of injury, 247–48
frivolous lawsuits, 246–48, 253
judgments in light of fairness principles, 242–43
legal clarity requirement, 242–43
opportunism in, 254
Proposition 64 and, 247–48
Proposition 65 and, 248–49, 250
public nuisance cases, 239–45
trade groups and organizations
barriers to entry, 63, 141
labor unions, 62–63, 64, 232, 233–34
restricted entry to professions, 22, 23
see also professions
trade monopolies or patents, 19, 22
trade restraints or barriers to trade
agreements in restraint of trade, 22–23
eliminating, 180
in interstate commerce, 183–85
trade secrets, *Monsanto* rule, 269
trespass, law of, 262
Trevett v. Weeden, 118
Trevor Law Group, 247, 253, 254
Tribe, Laurence, 114, 115–16, 117, 136, 287
Trott, Stephen, 237, 238
Troy, Daniel, 211–12
Turley, William B., 1–2, 3, 6
Twenty-first Amendment, 183–84
Twining v. State of New Jersey, 98–99

unconscionable contracts, 214–15, 224–30
unequal bargaining power theory, 215–20
Unfair Competition Law (California), 197, 245–47, 248
United States Trust Co. v. New Jersey, 78–79
United States v. Carolene Products Co., 100, 125, 135, 279
United States v. Trans-Missouri Freight Ass'n, 58
United States v. United Foods, 209–11
Unruh Civil Rights Act abuses, 249–51
U.S. Postal Service v. Flamingo Industries, 57–59

Valentine v. Chrestensen, 191, 192
vested rights, 31
Vindicating the Founders (Thomas E. West), 25
Virginia
    noncommercial free speech case, 204
    wine importation laws, 183
Virginia Declaration of Rights, 118
Virginia State Bd. of Pharmacy v. Virginia Citizens Consumer Council, Inc., 193–94, 195
Vizcaino v. Microsoft Corp., 237–38

Wal-Mart, zoning and, 159–61
Washington, commercial free speech case, 202–3
Washington, Bushrod, 40
Wasserman, Howard, 200, 201
wealth
    creation of, 3
    redistribution of, 216, 290–92
wealthy elite, judicial protection, xiv, 83
Weaver of Newbury's Case, 21
Webster, Daniel, 93, 98, 113, 118
Weismann, Henry, 104
welfare, constitutional basis for or right to, 290–92
welfare state, distributive justice theory and, 290–91
West, Thomas, 25
West Coast Hotel Co. v. Parrish, 279
West River Bridge Company v. Dix, 74–75
Whigs, anti-monopoly traditions, 17, 18–23, 27, 49, 50, 64–65

White, Byron, 106, 267
White, G. Edward, 132
Whole Foods Market, 54
Wild Oats Supermarkets, 54
Wilkins, Herbert, 221
will of the majority. *see* majority
Williams v. Walker-Thomas Furniture Co., 224–26
Wilson, James, 90
Wilson, Woodrow, 47
Winfield. see City of Memphis v. Winfield
Wisconsin, Microsoft antitrust case, 51–52
women
    Bradwell's case against Illinois, 43
    child surrogacy agreements and contracts, 221–23
    employment and freedom of contract cases, 7–11
    Sutherland on women's rights, 9–11
Wood, Gordon, 27–28
work hours. *see Lochner v. New York; Muller v. Oregon*
Workingman's Party, 145–46
Wright, J. Skelly, 225, 226
wrongful termination lawsuits, 235–36

Yee v. Escondido, 261–62
Yick Wo v. Hopkins, 146–47
Young, Andrew, 196

zoning laws, protectionism and, 159–63, 174

About the Author

Timothy Sandefur is an adjunct scholar at the Cato Institute and an attorney at the Pacific Legal Foundation, a nonprofit organization in Sacramento, California, dedicated to defending economic liberty and private property rights. Sandefur is also the author of *Cornerstone of Liberty: Property Rights in 21st Century America.*

Cato Institute

Founded in 1977, the Cato Institute is a public policy research foundation dedicated to broadening the parameters of policy debate to allow consideration of more options that are consistent with the traditional American principles of limited government, individual liberty, and peace. To that end, the Institute strives to achieve greater involvement of the intelligent, concerned lay public in questions of policy and the proper role of government.

The Institute is named for *Cato's Letters,* libertarian pamphlets that were widely read in the American Colonies in the early 18th century and played a major role in laying the philosophical foundation for the American Revolution.

Despite the achievement of the nation's Founders, today virtually no aspect of life is free from government encroachment. A pervasive intolerance for individual rights is shown by government's arbitrary intrusions into private economic transactions and its disregard for civil liberties.

To counter that trend, the Cato Institute undertakes an extensive publications program that addresses the complete spectrum of policy issues. Books, monographs, and shorter studies are commissioned to examine federal budget, Social Security, regulation, military spending, international trade, and myriad other issues. Major policy conferences are held throughout the year, from which papers are published thrice yearly in the *Cato Journal.* The Institute also publishes the quarterly magazine *Regulation.*

In order to maintain its independence, the Cato Institute accepts no government funding. Contributions are received from foundations, corporations, and individuals, and other revenue is generated from the sale of publications. The Institute is a nonprofit, tax-exempt, educational foundation under Section 501(c)3 of the Internal Revenue Code.

CATO INSTITUTE
1000 Massachusetts Ave., N.W.
Washington, D.C. 20001
www.cato.org